The National Economies of Europe

The National Economies of Europe

Edited by
DAVID A DYKER

LONGMAN
LONDON and NEW YORK

Longman Group UK Limited,
Longman House, Burnt Mill,
Harlow, Essex CM20 2JE, England
and Associated Companies throughout the world.

*Published in the United States of America
by Longman Publishing, New York.*

First published 1992.

ISBN 0582–059186 csd
ISBN 0582–058813 ppr

British Library Cataloguing-in-Publication Data

A catalogue record for this book is
available from the British Library.

Library of Congress Cataloging in Publication Data

The national economies of Europe / David A. Dyker.
    p.   cm.
  ISBN 0–582–05918–6 (cased). — ISBN 0–582–05881–3 (pbk.)
  1. Europe – Economic conditions–1945–   2. Europe – Economic policy.
  I. Dyker, David A.
HC240.N29 1992   92–12829
338.94–dc20   CIP

Set by 8 in 10/12.5 Times
Produced by Longman Singapore Publishers (Pte) Ltd.
Printed in Singapore

Contents

Preface

The origins of this work, and its companion volume *The European Economy*, go back to 1988 and a series of discussions between myself and Christopher Harrison of Longman and Professor Michael Sumner of the University of Sussex. That the works have come to fruition is at least as much a tribute to their vision and encouragement as to any efforts on my own part. Much has changed in Europe since 1988, and while this has highlighted the interest and importance of the subject matter, it has created its own species of editorial difficulty, as conscientious authors have sought to keep abreast of developments. To the extent that, in the end, events have still managed to get the better of us, we ask merely to be judged by the degree to which we have succeeded in catching the essence, and the issues, of a uniquely exciting time in European economic (and political) history.

The collective of authors of *The European Economy* and *The National Economies of Europe* is drawn largely from the University of Sussex – not just from the teaching staff of the Economics Subject Group, but also from the Geography Subject Group and from associated institutions – the Science Policy Research Unit and the Institute of Development Studies. Beyond that we have called on old friends, former colleagues and former students to make their own unique contributions. On the basis of these two volumes, then, the reader can judge the role of the University of Sussex, and of the 'Sussex connection', in the development of contemporary European studies. Finally I must thank Leila Burrell-Davis of the University of Sussex Computing Service, without whose skill in translating computer files of all shapes and sizes into a common format the task of editing would have been simply impossible.

David A Dyker
School of European Studies, University of Sussex
February, 1992

Acknowledgements

The publishers are grateful to the following for permission to reproduce copyright material:

The National Institute of Economic and Social Research for figures 5.2 and 5.3; The Organisation for Economic Cooperation and Development for tables 2.1, 2.3, 2.4, 4.3, 4.9, 5.1, 6.1 and 6.3.

Whilst every effort has been made to trace the owners of copyright material, in a few cases this has proved impossible, and we take this opportunity to offer our apologies to any copyright holders whose rights we may have unwittingly infringed.

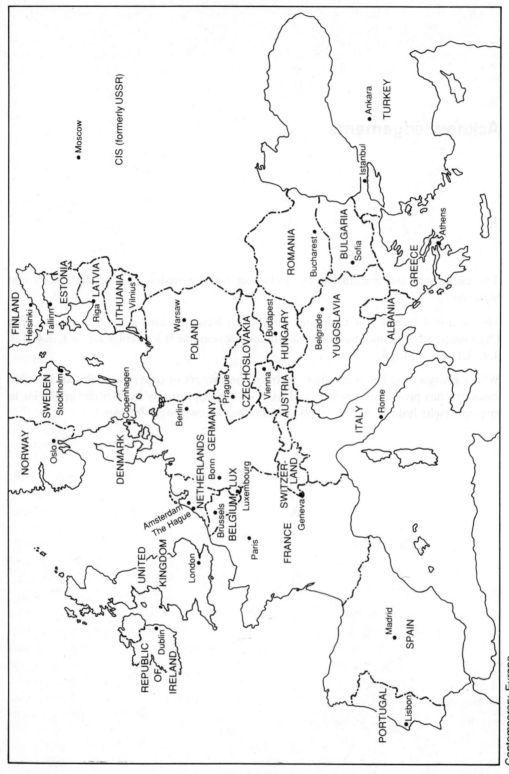

Contemporary Europe

CHAPTER 1

Introduction: the issues of European economic development

DAVID A DYKER*

Among all the high GNP per capita regions of the world, Europe is unique. In cultural and historical terms, it is extraordinarily heteregeneous, boasting some fifty major nationalities (not all of which enjoy separate statehood) and nearly as many major languages. European economic development has, therefore, proceeded in the face of, and as a constant challenge to, a whole range of cultural and linguistic barriers. It is a tribute to the strength of that developmental impetus, as well as to the small size of the typical European state and the comparative poverty of Europe in raw materials, that the economies of the continent characteristically trade a much higher proportion of their GNP than the countries of any comparable region. The contrast between all this and the richly endowed, super-state/melting-pot image of the United States is total. The point is still valid, if less comprehensively so, when we compare Europe with the countries of the Pacific Rim.

But Europe's heterogeneity does not stop there. For nearly half a century following the conclusion of the Second World War in 1945, Europe was cut in half by the bipolar politics of the East–West confrontation. While the term 'Iron Curtain' may seem now like a piece of quaint Cold War rhetoric, it is a fact that normal human and commercial intercourse between Western and Eastern Europe was for several decades severely hampered, if not totally excluded, by a bizarre collection of walls and barbed-wire fences. Behind the walls and barbed wire, East European countries, all under communist one-party rule and mostly under some degree of domination from Moscow, followed the model of the planned, socialist economy, which excluded large-scale private ownership of assets on principle, and excluded normal trading relations with other countries (including other socialist countries) in practice. Some of the socialist countries, notably Yugoslavia and Hungary, reintroduced substantial elements of the market into their socialist systems from an early date. But neither the centralised nor decentralised model of East European socialism was able to survive the economic and political challenges of the late 1980s and early 1990s; by 1992 there was hardly a state

* The author gratefully acknowledges the help of Peter Holmes and Michael Sumner in the writing of this introduction.

or proto-state in Eastern Europe that still referred to its (ideal) economic system as socialist.

But the East European revolution of 1989 and its aftermath, in removing many of the artificial barriers and politically imposed differences that had separated East and West, served only to bring into sharper relief the deep-seated underlying contrasts between the two major regions of the continent. In systemic terms, the East European countries continue, willy-nilly, to display a markedly 'state capitalist' profile, with the public sector totally dominant within industry, and likely to remain so at least for the next five or ten years. 'Shock therapy' has proved effective enough in re-establishing short-term macroeconomic stability, but has at best (the case of Poland) left fundamental restructuring problems unresolved, even exacerbated, thus building but a weak foundation for the extension of macroeconomic stability into the medium term. In the worst case (that of Yugoslavia) it has been torpedoed by the outbreak of regional conflict escalating into civil war. In more immediate terms, the priorities and circumstances of restructuring have produced sharp falls in levels of national income and real personal incomes everywhere in Eastern Europe, greatly reinforcing an East–West gap which was already substantial before the collapse of communism in the region.

Of course variations in economic system and level of economic performance are equally, if less dramatically, visible within 'rich' Western Europe. Two of the twelve full members of the European Community – Portugal and Greece – have levels of GNP per head of much less than half the EC average; another two – Spain and Ireland – report levels of GNP per head only a little above half of that average. Differences in levels of development between major regions have been a persistent problem in a number of West European states, notably Italy and Spain. But it is on the systemic dimension that intra-West European contrasts have been most clearly marked. While nearly all the West European economies have state sectors which are large by North American or Japanese standards, there are deep and abiding differences in style and approach to economic policy-making, whether for private or public sector, among the major West European countries. It has in the past often been the politically more conservative governments of France, Italy and Spain that have emphasised most strongly the role of the 'state as entrepreneur'. In archetypally social-democratic Sweden, by contrast, the role of the state in relation to everything that affects the citizen directly – wages, welfare, etc – has been as dominant as its role in relation to the *running* of industry has been low-key. We can talk of a degree of Europe-wide Keynesian consensus on macroeconomic policy-making in the period up to 1974, but even here West Germany stands out as a country which has consistently performed best of all on macroeconomic stability, on the basis of a conservative and very simple approach to monetary policy. On both macro- and micro-levels British economic policy in the 1960s and 1970s seemed to go some way towards institutionalising that most pernicious of East European characteristics – the 'soft budget constraint'.

Yet while the differences within Western Europe are plain for all to see, the *tendency* to convergence is just as obvious. The dominant policy themes of the 1980s – the fight against inflation, deregulation, privatisation, etc – have been equally the major preoccupations of nominally socialist governments in Paris as of Thatcherite ones in London. There has been a palpable tendency for all the EC countries to move towards the West German model of the social market economy and the West German style of macroeconomic management. Most important of all, the history of European integration, from the Treaty of Paris and the Treaty of Rome to the agreement in principle on the creation of the European Union in 1991, has, for all its hesitations and false steps, been a uniquely successful story of supranational economic policy co-ordination. The prospect that by the year 2000 the EC *may* encompass a single market, with a single currency and a single citizenship for some 400 million people, provides a counterpoint to the theme of heterogeneity, and a challenge to the great national economies of North America and the Far East, such as would have seemed quite inconceivable even a couple of decades ago.

While the theme of integration becomes ever more dominant in Western Europe, however, we find in the 'new' Eastern Europe an equally powerful theme of disintegration and fragmentation. In 1990 the CMEA (Council for Mutual Economic Assistance – Comecon) collapsed, ending a period of some thirty-five years of Soviet-dominated bilateralism in Eastern Europe. From now on settlements within the region would be on a hard-currency, multilateral basis. But while the principle of multilateralism seemed an irreproachable development, the practice that evolved through 1991 was full of disturbing features. A combination of lack of trust between the countries of Eastern Europe, fed partly by historical rivalries and conflicts, and an extreme shortage of hard currency intensified by debt service commitments to the West, was enough to send the volume of trade within the region plummeting at a time when the rigours of domestic restructuring were already having a big negative impact on production and welfare levels. The dramatic events of 1991 in Yugoslavia, culminating in the outbreak of a full-scale civil conflict, tended perhaps to divert attention from the underlying force of republic-level economic autarkism which had already taken deep root, particularly in Serbia. In the case of the Soviet Union, now a name of purely historical significance, the political drama of the break-up of the USSR was highlighted by the failure to achieve a workable agreement on economic union within Soviet economic space. In the meantime, against the background of the breakdown in the old union-level institutions and the collapse of the rouble, regional authorities, by late 1991 with the new status of 'independent states', were increasingly retreating into local fortress economies, mediated by a certain amount of crude barter.

Paradoxically, these themes of integration and disintegration had come by late 1991 to intertwine closely. As countries and republics freed themselves from the suffocating inheritance of Soviet communism, their integrationist aspirations, strong enough in themselves, focused sharply on the West, and in particular on the EC. Those aspirations were crowned in December 1991, for Poland, Czechoslovakia and Hungary, by the signing of a series of bilateral association agreements with the EC which laid out a path calculated to culminate in free trade within ten years. But these agreements highlighted the difficulties as well as the hopes engendered by this westwards integrationist orientation. In a Europe where countries have, in the post-war period, grown prosperous by trading with their neighbours, how will Poland, for example, fare if it trades only with Germany, and not with Lithuania, Byelorussia, Russia, the Ukraine and Czechoslovakia? The need for some kind of liquidity support mechanism to provide a minimal 'float' for intra-regional trade within Eastern Europe, in the context of an extreme shortage of hard currency throughout the region, seemed at least as urgent a consideration for the European Commission and West European governments at the end of 1991 as association *per se*. That urgency was not lessened by the knowledge that purely technical liquidity measures might in themselves be insufficient to break down the political and psychological barriers to the emergence of a new division of labour within Eastern Europe.

But the association agreements of December 1991 raised another complex of issues which take us well beyond the boundaries of Europe itself. The immediate value of the agreements to the three East-Central European countries was limited by the appending of special protocols covering the 'sensitive' areas of food, steel and textiles. Thus while the principle of free trade has been proclaimed, the governments in Warsaw, Prague and Budapest have been informed that that principle will not, at least for the time being, be put into practice in relation to precisely those sectors where the planned economies in transition (PETs) might be thought, on the basis of a consideration of the pattern of comparative advantage, to have a real chance of conquering hard-currency export markets. It is perhaps not surprising that West European governments, faced with chronic problems of long-term unemployment, should be anxious to protect employment in low-tech and traditional industries, especially when they are regionally highly concentrated, and should seek to do so through a complex of formal protectionist measures, 'voluntary' export restraints and murky customs procedures imposed, in some combination, on every region of the trading world. It is at the same time outrightly contradictory that a community dedicated to the development of free trade should take such an illiberal stance *vis-à-vis* the natural economic strengths of other regions.

The contradiction does, of course, go beyond the injury inflicted on non-EC trading partners or potential partners. Non-tariff barriers in particular are shown to be *particularly* injurious to the interests of the citizens *qua* consumers of the EC itself. Protection of essentially uncompetitive industries, whatever form it takes, deprives a country or region of the full benefit of its own economic strengths, distorting resource allocation and hindering the full exploitation of new technological possibilities. That is not to say that high-income countries are constrained to conform to a uniformly capital- and high-tech-intensive production profile if they are to maximise national income. On the contrary, as the examples of Italian textiles, leather goods, footwear and furniture demonstrate, there are plenty of opportunities for national economies to do well producing the 'wrong' things. The point is rather that free trade outside as well as inside the Community is the only sure way of ascertaining whether a particular sector is really as strong as it looks. The completion of the single market promises a narrowing of the scope for the imposition of non-tariff barriers. But it does not promise to get rid of them, and says very little at all about the Common Agricultural Policy (CAP). The issue of EC trade policy *vis-à-vis* the rest of Europe and the rest of the world will surely remain a burning one in the years after 1992.

The West European record on efficiency of resource allocation seems, then, to have been a mixed one. The EC has done perhaps surprising well on the internal market, but not so well in its global trading posture. Can we find further evidence from the detailed chapters of this volume and its companion volume to flesh out this provisional assessment of the efficiency record, and to extend it into the dimension of dynamic efficiency?

It is perhaps useful to start the inquiry beyond the boundaries of the EC, in Eastern Europe. Up to the 1960s most of the countries of that region seemed to present striking confirmation of the effectiveness of central planning as an engine of growth. For all the manifold and much publicised weaknesses of central planning in relation to short-term microeconomic efficiency, the system appeared to work very well as a vehicle for *extensive development*, producing a powerful industrialisation impetus, in the main through mobilisation of cheap labour and energy resources. Productivity trends were mediocre and wastefulness widespread, but the system was at least effective in implementing the goals of communist governments in terms of the growth of output, *as measured by criteria which admittedly often bore but a tenuous relationship to any concept of human welfare.*

It was against the background of the changes in resource availability in Eastern Europe, as the scope for rural–urban migration narrowed and the female participation rate reached its upper limit, and as energy became more expensive in terms of extraction costs in the Soviet Union and subsequently in terms of the world price of oil, that the debate about economic reform as an instrument for implementing a gear-change to *intensive development* came to dominate the agenda of the communist governments of the region, not excluding the more conservative ones. Behind this debate lay a plausible generalisation not inconsistent with much of standard Western development theory – that processes of industrialisation quite naturally have two stages – an early stage of extensive development, as fallow resources are mobilised, and a second stage of intensive development, as technological change in the broadest sense comes to be the dominant source of economic growth. Socialist planning on the Soviet model had been able to speed up the first stage. It stood to reason in terms of Marxist-Leninist ideology that the political commitment to continued progress towards 'full communism' would require – and deliver – thoroughgoing systemic change as that first stage come to its logical conclusion.

It is clear, with the benefit of hindsight, that for all its economic and ideological plausibility this line was little more than a convenient political rationalisation. The communist systems of Eastern Europe, including the market socialist ones of Yugoslavia and Hungary, showed themselves to be totally incapable of evolving new institutions and practices such as might have given productivity trends a fresh impetus. Indeed the period of the great debate about intensive development was marked by deterioration rather than improvement in productivity trends. It became clear that Soviet-style planning, even in much modified forms, could *only* generate growth on an extensive basis, whether the conditions were appropriate or not. It became equally clear that much of the reported growth of the extensive development period represented growth in sectors which were either of purely military significance, or were hopelessly hostile to the environment and/or obsolete in their technologies. By the time the debate about the future of socialism had turned into a debate about the restoration of capitalism, it was obvious that the 'triumphs' of extensive development would in the main be obstacles rather than bridges to any intensification of the economies in question.

It is not possible to make direct comparisons between Eastern and Western Europe in this regard, because most of Western Europe was in 1945 already much more developed economically than most of Eastern Europe. There is, certainly, a sense in which the post-war economic miracle in Western Europe was based on cheap labour, including female and immigrant labour, and cheap oil. It is equally striking that post-war economic development in France, one of the least industrialised of the West European countries with one the biggest shares of the working population still in agriculture in 1945, has been very largely based on productivity growth. Again, while the post-1974 period in the West has certainly been one of rapid technological and structural change, and of comparatively rapid productivity growth, it has also been marked by extremely high levels of unemployment. Thus the scope for extensive development in the West since the early 1970s has in fact been very considerable. The fact that that scope has not been fully exploited may to a degree be explicable in terms of policy errors on the part of governments. Beyond that, it seems to reflect, in particular, a pattern of technological change which makes few calls on unskilled labour. If the demand for labour comes through more and more in the form of demands for personnel with very specific skill and training profiles, then we may question how useful it is to seek to identify development patterns in terms of an aggregated L. If the answer to the question is negative, then the whole conceptual basis of the distinction between extensive and intensive sources of development is undermined.

What *is* clear from the West European record – and indeed from that of Eastern Europe as well in a negative sense – is that productivity trends are nearly always the best indicator of overall medium-to-long-term growth trends. To the extent that West Europe has done well since the Second World War it has done so through a sustained increase in total productivity. Countries like the UK which lagged behind systematically on growth in the period to 1975 also turn out to have poor productivity records over the same period. Equally significantly, the British revival in the 1980s was to a great extent based on a 'productivity miracle'. Patterns of productivity gain have in turn reflected a great diversity of factors, with technology in the narrow sense only one of the most important. Both British and Swedish cases testify, in their opposite ways, to the key role which socio-political factors can play in this regard. But if productivity is the key to sustained growth, then perhaps we should simply conclude that intensive development is the *only* kind of real development. We can make the point in a slightly different way if we observe that it was not the priority on industry *as such* that was wrong with the Soviet approach, it was rather the priority on the wrong kinds of industry. The Western experience demonstrates forcibly that, however much growth may have been concentrated in services sectors in recent decades, it is industry that remains the basis of international competitiveness, and of productivity dynamism, including in those services sectors. But the decisions that have formed the basis of that competitiveness, that productivity impetus, have been taken largely on the basis of an assessment of profitability, not obedience to some grand strategy of economic development imposed from above.

If the growth of the past has come largely from productivity gains, what about the growth of the future? We can read from the history of industrial front-runners, European and non-European alike, that strong productivity performance is nearly always reflected in a high level of competitiveness on international markets – indeed this is merely to reiterate, from a different angle, the point of the last paragraph. It is particularly noteworthy that of the three chapters of *The European Economy* that concentrate on key industrial sectors accounting for large proportions of European output, with good prospects for the future in terms of the pattern of demand and built on significant European technological leads from the past – chemicals, electronics and motor vehicles – the latter two highlight key competitive weaknesses, including technological weaknesses, while the first stresses the critical importance of facing up to the competitive challenges to the European industry that the world economy will undoubtedly present in the l990s. It is clear, to return to an earlier theme, that it will be difficult for Europe to concentrate on the reinforcement and development of comparative advantage if it continues to devote substantial resources and substantial attention to the preservation of declining sectors. Quite apart from matters of trade policy narrowly defined, the Commission of the European Communities will find itself after 1992 under increasing pressure to resolve highly sensitive issues – for example, should the EC extend the coverage of its technology-support initiatives, which feature particularly strongly in the electronics industry, to US and Japanese firms based within the EC? There must be many European policy-makers who scorn the notion of Fortress Europe, but who would nevertheless baulk at such a move.

To say that the European economy will still face serious problems after 1992 is, of course, simply to restate the implications of participation in a dynamic world system. The capacity of the EC to resolve these problems has, certainly, been enhanced by the refinement of its collective problem-solving apparatus, particularly in connection with the revival of the practice of majority voting on a range of important policy headings within the Council of Ministers. The developments of the 1980s have in particular highlighted the dimensions of *credibility* and *trust* within the dynamic of the integration process, and the increasing commitment to conduct calculated to consolidate rather than strain the system. To take one rather technical example, the essential rationale for membership of the ERM for any country apart from Germany must be understood in terms of the possibility thus afforded of drawing on the credibility of the Bundesbank, the German central bank, as a bulwark against inflation. But as Michael Sumner shows in his chapter in *The European Economy* on monetary integration, the accretion of credibility is a slow business, for the trust of others, and in particular of the money markets, does not come with the mere publication of a policy goal. The failure of early attempts to progress towards monetary union demonstrates, indeed, that the declaration of ambitious objectives, even in conjunction with the creation of new institutions like the Snake, can achieve nothing unless the participants behave consistently, that is in a way conducive to the development of mutual trust. The frequency of exchange rate realignments during the first few years of the ERM confirms how difficult it is to create a 'zone of monetary stability'. But from 1983, as exchange rate changes came increasingly to be viewed as a matter of *common* rather than national concern in the spirit of the Treaty of Rome, the ERM began to show results. What this meant in practice was that the frequency of significant realignments was substantially reduced. To take the case of The Netherlands, the country perhaps most heavily committed to the accretion of credibility, there has been no change in the bilateral guilder–deutschmark rate since 1983. In entering the ERM on the understanding that exchange rate adjustments are permissible, then, a given country bent on extracting maximum benefit from membership in fact puts itself under the obligation largely to eschew such adjustments.

A similar story can be told in relation to the wider drama of the implementation of the Single European Act. As Peter Holmes shows in his chapter in *The European Economy* on the political economy of European integration, the adoption of the Single European Act and implementation of the 1992 programme would have been inconceivable without a degree of something akin to self-hypnosis. Had the signatories of the Single European Act not in effect committed themselves implicitly to a good deal more than they were committing themselves to explicitly, it is doubtful whether the dynamic policy impetus which is the essence of 1992 would ever have got going. The fact that the UK government, in particular, is manifestly unhappy about all this must surely reflect some basic lack of trust of the Commission, and indeed of the whole EC structure, on the part of that government. The fact that the other EC governments take a much more positive view surely reflects a sense of mutually reinforcing accretion of credibility at Commission *and* national government level.

It is instructive to extend this mode of analysis to the very different conditions of Eastern Europe. One of the most striking aspects of the Yugoslav civil war of 1991 was the total ineffectuality of one cease-fire after another. The reasons for this certainly lay partly in the fragmented nature of the war itself, with no single line of command on either side which could be relied upon to have the capacity to 'deliver' a cease-fire. There was also manifestly an element of bad faith. Military leaders seemed content repeatedly to promise much *more* than they were in reality prepared to deliver.

But the Yugoslav civil war, the reader may say, has nothing to do with the articulation of economic policy. In fact, perusal of the chapter on Yugoslavia in *The National Economies of Europe* will confirm that this same element of bad faith, this same practice of signing cheques knowing that they would 'bounce', was a key element in the degeneration of the economic policy mechanism which presaged the violent break-up of the old Yugoslavia. To bring the issue into sharper focus, however, let us try the same approach in relation to a process which was outwardly very similar to the processes of the Single European Act – namely, the attempt by Mikhail Gorbachev, in his last months as Soviet president, to forge a new economic and political union out of the old Soviet Union. Many of the issues that were raised in the course of the negotiations on these matters in late 1991 were just the issues that were simultaneously exercising the Commission and the national governments of the EC in the West – the question of free movement of goods and people, the various monetary options open, the problem of fiscal balance. The difference between the two processes is that whereas in the West commitment was being built upon commitment, in the East successive deals or near-deals were being torpedoed by a volte-face, a crucial failure to sign a critical document, or a flat refusal to accept the implications of integration. (The reader may find it instructive to compare the pattern with the earlier stages of the development of the EC.) This process of *decretion of credibility*, to paraphrase Michael Sumner's telling phrase, reached its climax in December 1991 when the leaders of the three Slav republics of the old USSR – Russia, the Ukraine and Byelorussia – announced after a private meeting at which neither Mr Gorbachev nor any other republican leader was present, that they were abandoning the idea of a new confederation, the idea on which Mr Gorbachev had staked his political future. The meeting was held the day before a planned meeting between the three leaders and Mr Gorbachev to discuss precisely the issue of confederation.

All of this came a couple of months or so after the three Slav republics had initialled Gorbachev's Treaty of Economic Union. Does that mean that Presidents Yeltsin, Kravchuk and Shushkevich think that they can create a single market – in a region of the world where there has been no market at all for seventy years – while simultaneously abandoning the quest for political reintegration? Does it mean that they believe it will be possible to remove the colossal macroeconomic imbalances that plague all the regions of Soviet economic space, in a part of the world which knows nothing of fiscal and monetary policy as we define them in the West, without a large measure of political goodwill? In reality, it may mean simply that they see new economic union and new political union as equally infeasible under present circumstances. If those goals ever do come back on to the agenda in this most easterly part of Europe, possibly under the rubric of Yeltsin's, Kravchuk's and Shushkevich's 'Commonwealth of Independent States', the experience of the EC with the 1992 programme will surely provide many valuable lessons on the importance of credibility and trust in any programme of economic integration.

Returning to more technical matters, the notion of independent national monetary policies begins to look increasingly unreal in a European context. On a world level, as RK Eastwood shows in his chapter on macroeconomic co-ordination in *The European Economy*, it is not clear that national independence has much meaning in relation to *any* aspect of macroeconomic policy-making for countries with liberal regimes on trade and capital movements. By the same token it is not evident that we can meaningfully talk about national policies of capital transfer. The crisis in Eastern Europe has triggered an extensive discussion of the role that aid might play in the restructuring of the economies of the region, and there has been talk of a 'Marshall Plan' for Eastern Europe. The pros and cons of different proposed aid packages are discussed in the relevant chapters of *The National Economies of Europe*. The anxieties which the issue of capital transfer to Eastern Europe has understandably given rise to in the Third World are treated in Christopher Stevens' chapter in *The European Economy*. At this introductory stage we seek merely to emphasise that only countries with surpluses on balance of payments, current account, can be net exporters of capital. There is, of course, nothing in principle to stop Western Europe borrowing from the surplus countries (most of them in East Asia) in order to re-lend, or even grant, to Eastern Europe. But such an operation could put colossal strain on the West European economies unless it were done on a strictly commercial basis. Again, there is nothing to stop West European countries adopting policies (presumably deflationary) such as would tend to generate 'investible' surpluses on current account. But the likely impact of any such policies on the world economy hardly bear thinking about. It would be an oversimplification to say that as long as Japan and the other Pacific countries are the only major trading nations consistently running current account surpluses, they are the only countries that can really help Eastern Europe. It is nevertheless clear that the ongoing debate within the developed industrial world about the problem of structural surpluses and deficits on balance of payments may have an important bearing on the structural problems of Eastern Europe.

Both *The European Economy* and *The National Economies of Europe* may seem, at a first reading, to represent straightforward celebrations of the vigour of the market principle. The concept of the single market is lauded, the notion of Fortress Europe rejected, the collapse of the socialist 'alternatives' of communist Eastern Europe duly recorded. Yet the limitations of the price mechanism are as clearly highlighted as its strengths. Devaluation, for instance, is generally rejected as an instrument of international adjustment: it lays an economy open to inflationary pressures, and, more insidiously, it tends to weaken the essentially socio-political pressures for higher productivity which, as we have seen, may represent one of the most important sources of economic growth. And while the virtues of competition and the strength of private enterprise are plain for all to see, the chapters of both volumes pose many searching questions about the role of the *public sector*. One of the recurrent themes of the West European coverage of *The National Economies of Europe* is long-term unemployment. Once a man or a woman has been out of work for more than a year, it seems, he or she can be reabsorbed into the labour force only through a major effort of self-motivation and retraining. Some West European countries, notably Germany, have seriously addressed the problem. None has so far solved it. And this theme of the importance of the *structure of human capital* comes out again, in a much more dramatic form, when we turn to Eastern Europe. In a region where nearly everyone is highly literate, and a large proportion of the population is well trained in basic industrial skills, hardly anyone is trained to do the kinds of jobs that market economies demand. It is difficult to see how the economies of Eastern Europe can be transformed unless there is a massive, and inevitably costly, restructuring of the human capital stock, in addition to the more obviously necessary restructuring of the physical capital stock. But in a situation where budgetary stringency in the name of macroeconomic stabilisation has to be the watchword for East European governments, it is not easy to see how massive retraining programmes could be financed by those governments themselves. Once again, the ball comes back into the court of Western Europe, and of the advanced industrial world as a whole.

Finally, and continuing on the same theme, we return to Western Europe to review a policy area which will be critical for the implementation of the single market programme. With the amalgamation of the EC Regional Fund, Social Fund and Agricultural Guidance Fund under a new Structural Funds rubric, the prospects for a rationalised, integrated approach to the wider implications of Western Europe's own internal structural problems are brighter than they have been for some time. As the chapters of *The European Economy* devoted to agriculture and regional problems make clear, this development has not come before time. It is clear, furthermore, that the implications of a steadfastly liberal approach to the question of the EC's economic relations with Eastern Europe and the rest of the world (not something that can be taken for granted!) could greatly increase the intensity of Western Europe's regional and socio-structural problems. If East European foodstuffs, Hong Kong textiles and South Korean consumer electronics were to be freed from existing EC importing restrictions, whole new areas of the West European economy could be threatened with massive contraction, with the attendant danger of another large increase in the pool of long-term unemployed people. In bringing the full benefits of the market mechanism, and of the international division of labour, to the consumers of Western Europe, national governments and European Commission alike would have to face up to the fact that in the conditions of the late twentieth century liberal economic policies may increase, rather than reduce, demands on the public sector, in quantitative terms and in terms of the quality and efficacy of programmes. Deficit financing will not be a medium-to-long-term option for the funding of such programmes, as witness the difficulties which so many European countries already have with their public sector borrowing requirements, not to mention the implicit fiscal requirements of EMU, so that there will inevitably be demands for increased tax revenue, at both EC and national level. It would almost certainly be impossible to accommodate such demands without a movement towards 'fiscal federalism', under which the European Community was empowered to levy its own taxes. Even in the context of the ambitious optimism of '1992' that would be an enormous undertaking. It is clear that the implementation of the Single European Act is but one more stage in a process, the end of which can only be guessed at.

CHAPTER 2

France

PETER HOLMES

Introduction: today's issues

In this chapter we shall look at the French economy, and try to assess its role within Europe. To do this, we need to place the French experience in historical context, and to link the developments of the 1980s back to much earlier patterns in French economic development.

The French economy stagnated for the first half of the twentieth century. But from 1945 to 1973 it enjoyed virtually continuous uninterrupted economic growth, averaging about 5 per cent per year in terms of GDP, with the rate rising slightly towards the end of the period. The French speak of the *trente glorieuses* (the thirty glorious years). Unemployment was very low, and inflation, though perceptible, was tolerable. The 1973–4 Oil Shock hit France badly, but growth resumed in 1976–80. France in the 1980s, however, presents a wholly different picture (see Table 2.1). Growth virtually ceased for most of the decade, though it did resume about 1987. The economy entered a painful phase of restructuring, not unlike that experienced in the UK. The whole post-war model of French economic development has accordingly been called into question. Acceptance of the dictates of European market forces has increasingly been seen as the only way forward. But the French pattern has not been identical to the British. An important difference is that French industrial production fell only very slightly from peak to trough of the 1980s recession. For the UK the corresponding fall was around 10 per cent. In France, then, as old industrial activities have been pruned, new ones have replaced them, and the service sector has taken on a new dynamism.

The conversion to market economics has ironically taken place under a socialist government, and in a historical perspective the radicalism of the early Mitterrand period (1981–2) can be seen as a learning experience in which the French public became convinced that the old model of state-led growth could not be revived. Thus the political changes of the 1980s in France have led to the emergence of a certain centrist consensus on economic policy. We shall argue here, however, that the role of the state in France has been frequently misunderstood. Although it is undeniably true that France has a more complex bureaucratic regulatory system than the average West

Table 2.1 Main macro aggregates

	1960–8	1968–73	1973–9	1979–89	1960–89
Growth of real GNP (average annual growth rate)					
France	5.4	5.4	2.8	2.1	3.7
(per capita)					(3.0)
Germany	4.1	4.9	2.3	1.8	3.1
(per capita)					(2.7)
Consumer prices (average annual growth rate)					
France	3.6	6.1	10.7	7.3	6.7
Germany	2.7	4.6	4.7	2.9	3.5
Unemployment – percentage of labour force (average)					
	1960–7	1968–73	1974–9	1980–9	1990
France	1.0	–	3.1	6.9	9.0
Germany	0.9	0.8	2.9	6.0	5.1

Source: OECD *Economic Outlook; Historical Statistics*

European state for many aspects of economic and social life, this does not mean that the central government has actually been able to control and direct all the aspects of the economy over which it has *sought* to have an influence. Very often regulation has meant self-regulation rather than coherent planning by the authorities. The socialists tried to grasp the reins of effective power through nationalisation in the early 1980s, but quickly discovered that they could control state-owned firms no better than the average shareholder can discipline managers. This was the basis of the new consensus between left and right that market forces and cash limits were the appropriate instruments of regulation. The story of the 1980s fits in with the secular trend of French economic development if we reinterpret the role of the state in the early post-war years. That state was not, we contend, trying to build a planned economy; rather it was using public policy as a device for building a modern industrial market economy to replace the regulated and uncompetitive – but unplanned – pre-war regime. By the mid-1960s the job was more or less done, but the rate of evolution of the state apparatus did not catch up with the pace of new developments until the 1980s.

It was in the late 1950s that France made the historic choice to integrate itself inextricably into the European mainstream, with consequences for French industry that have been gradual but ineluctable. In the 1980s it took a further historic decision to abandon the aspects of national sovereignty that had been retained under de Gaulle. The socialist government embarked on a new course of micro- and macroeconomic austerity that led to severe macroeconomic and social pressures in the mid-1980s, followed by a resumption of economic growth. At time of writing (1991), this resumption of momentum appears to be faltering, though the pattern may well be cyclical. While many structural problems remain, many have been overcome, perhaps the most important of them focusing on attitudes and expectations about economic policy. The rigorous obligation to remove the inflation differential with Germany implicit in membership of the EMS was accepted. Even so, unemployment was reduced between 1988 and 1990. French industry has revealed itself as having many unexpected strengths, including computer software. There is now a good chance that the government will manage to use the imperatives implicit in the impetus towards European integration as a way of keeping its nerve economically, just as de Gaulle's mandate to resolve the Algerian crisis in an earlier period gave him a margin of manoeuvre economically.

Economic and financial structures in historical context

In the 1950s France had an economic system that was certainly somewhat different from that of its immediate neighbours. Today the French economy looks much more like that of its European partners in terms of openness to trade, sectoral shares, and even growth and inflation rates. Some have questioned the genuineness of this socio-economic convergence on grounds of the strength of past traditions. France, they argue, has been since before the Revolution, and always will be, more centralised and more protectionist, more *dirigiste* than its partners. We can, however, challenge this interpretation of French economic history. France had a relatively open economy for most of the nineteenth century. From about 1880 to 1945 the picture alters sharply. But what we see in that period is not so much central planning as protectionism and government accommodation of archaic business structures. The French economy, it should be underlined, grew very slowly for the first half of the twentieth century.

The relatively pronounced orientation of the economy towards agriculture before the post-war industrial modernisation campaign should be seen as the result of a peculiar protectionist policy towards agriculture adopted in the late nineteenth century, rather than as reflecting some inherent tendency of the economy towards self-sufficiency. Protection of any one sector of a given economy does, of course, raise the cost of living, and thus undermines the competitiveness of the rest of the economy. Of the immediate impact of the introduction of agricultural protection, François Caron observes that agricultural protection slowed industrial growth because it 'hindered any decline in food prices and weighed heavily on industrial costs' (Caron 1979: 111). French industrial production was at the same level in 1937 as it had been in 1913. In the course of post-war recovery it got back to 1937 (ie 1913) levels in 1948. There were some positive legacies from the early years of industrialisation, but they were unevenly distributed. France was essentially a dual economy. It had some quite remarkable points of strength, in aluminium smelting, cars, aviation (cf the achievements of Blériot), hydroelectricity, up-market clothing. But most such successes rested on advantages that were in place at the start of the century. They had not been built on, and the vast bulk of the fabric of French industry was not touched by these advances. Agriculture, strong enough in the aggregate, was sharply differentiated between regions.

After 1945 the state certainly began to play a more active and positive role. But the goal was to produce a break with the past, and to force the French economy back on to the path it had set out on in the mid-nineteenth century. Thus the role of the state from the late 1940s to the 1960s was more as a catalyst than as a determining element in economic development. The objective of government policy in the post-war period was, paradoxically, to create a modern capitalist economy, *not* a regulated planned economy. In my view, many people, even in France, have confused the aims and the means of French economic policy. There is, in fact, no deep-rooted contradiction in the vision of France in the 1990s as part of the European economic system with no more, if no less, structural idiosyncrasies than any other nation in the EC. An earlier analysis (Estrin and Holmes 1983) argued that one of the most important roles the French state played in the post-war period was simply in moulding the climate of macroeconomic expectations. The macro-aspect was more effective than any detailed micro-objectives. It must be added, however, that one element in the conditioning of macro-expectations appears to have been a psychological climate in which the French state was for a long period content to claim credit for far greater influence over the economy than it actually had. Jacques Rueff, a liberal economist and adviser to de Gaulle, claimed that the plan was the 'cock that crowed and thought it had brought the dawn'.

This is not the place to enter into an extended debate about the nature of the French Revolution. But there is considerable debate among historians about its significance in terms of the role of the state in the economic arena. Schama, in his controversial *Citizens* (1989), argues that the *Ancien Régime* was already on the eve of the Revolution in the throes of a major campaign of deregulation – and that this indeed was one of the sources of popular unrest! Moving on historically, the idea that the nineteenth century in France was characterised by more bureaucratic regulation of industry than was prevalent in Britain in the same period is highly questionable. Caron avers that France's 1867 company legislation 'was in fact more favourable to company development than was English legislation, and even more the German legislation, at the time. In France there was no institutional obstacle to growth, except that which exists in the minds of certain historians' (Caron 1979: 43). Patrick Messerlin argues that from about 1840 to around 1880 France had a regime of relatively free trade and a record of relatively fast growth. Estimates of the ratio of foreign trade to national income in France in the 1880s place it between 20 and 30 per cent (see Messerlin 1985; Daisaigues 1985; Jeanneney 1985). This is close to corresponding figures for the present day. Even Léon Walras, the great nineteenth-century French economist, was afraid that *laissez-faire* had gone too far in nineteenth-century France. In a paper arguing for state regulation of the railways, he denounce economists for whom

> political and social economy can be expressed in these four words: laissez faire, laissez passer. Whatever question you may put to them, be it about women and children working in factories, the colonial question, the wheat trade, or the transport industry, they only ever see one single possible solution: the full and free exercise of individual initiative.
>
> (Walras 1980: 81)

During this 'liberal' period of the mid-nineteenth century, French banks did invest heavily and speculatively in industry: and there were some notable banking crises. Accordingly in the 1880s there was a major restructuring of the banking system. Thereafter the *banques de dépot* (commercial banks) were restricted to taking in deposits and making short-term secured loans; a separate category of *banques d'affaires* (merchant banks) were licensed to offer risk capital to industry from their own somewhat limited funds (see Beltrain and Griset 1988: 145). The strict legal distinction remained in force until the 1960s. Even today French deposit banks provide loan rather than equity capital to industry. This division of function, combined with the absence of an active stock market, was, indeed, one of the reasons for the involvement of the French state in the provision of credit to industry after the Second World War. French analysts speak of France as a 'debt economy' rather than a 'financial markets' economy. In fact, since the 1950s, the bulk of industrial investment has been self-financed, with the ratio of corporate debt to GNP falling sharply from the late 1960s to the late 1980s, despite an upturn in the early 1980s (Frochen et al 1989: 305).

If we are to identify a role for the French state in the post-war period that reflects the inheritance of the past, then, we must specify it in relation to the systemic vacuum created by the very passive character of the stock market. This meant that firms had very little opportunity to raise external equity capital, which could have been critical in the first years after the war in the context of the limited scope for self-financing at that time. It was easy and obvious for the state to come in and fill the gap. We can add to this a crucial political role for the state in the immediate post-war period. The defeat of 1940 led to the discrediting not only of the pre-war political elite, but also of the old business leadership. Some industrialists, like Jules Renault, had collaborated with the Germans; his property could simply be expropriated by the state. In other industries, the atmosphere was such that the old top management could be unceremoniously booted out and replaced by younger, more dynamic entrepreneurs, even if the former managed to stay out of jail (Holcblat and Husson 1990). A combination of luck and the post-war ethos of social responsibility led to a dramatic improvement in the quality of management which went far beyond a mere settling of scores. It also contributed to a general sense of legitimacy for the aims of economic reconstruction, as espoused by the new political leadership.

But though the state improved the overall climate for investment, it had little direct control over the use of investment funds. The so-called *encadrement de credit* system of quantitative controls, in force from 1968 to 1973 and again from 1983 to 1986, had as its principal objective the control of the money supply. The scope for selectivity in the system did certainly permit the favouring of certain categories of investment. But the most favoured categories were 'public housing, energy or raw material saving investments, and export credits' (Frochen et al 1989: 287). Loans for industrial investment were neither especially favoured nor closely scrutinised by the Ministry of Finance.

The individual sectors of the economy in outline since 1945

Agriculture

In 1950 French agriculture accounted for 16.2 per cent of GDP, as against 6.2 per cent for the UK. By 1980 the figures had partially converged to 4.6 and 2.2 per cent respectively. The fall in French agriculture's share in total employment is equally dramatic – from 29.2 to 8.4 per cent over the same period. The largest part of the fall was in the period of very rapid growth between 1960 and 1974. In recent years the exodus from agriculture has levelled off, and in 1989 agriculture still accounted for 6.4 per cent of the French work-force. It is interesting to observe that, from about 1975, the shift out of agriculture is no longer identified as it once was with 'rural exodus'. The currents of population and economic activity which once seemed to be drawn inexorably towards Paris are increasingly being drawn now to medium-sized towns and rural areas; for example, Brittany (Flockton and Kofman 1989). The 1982 census showed for the first time in decades an increase from 1975 on what the statisticians define as rural population (Gueslin 1990: 95). The fate of the countryside in France is, it seems, no longer intimately tied in with the fate of agriculture.

There is still an important element of small-scale and often part-time farming in the South, especially in the wine-growing regions. But the bulk of French agricultural output is grown in efficient large-scale farms in the Paris Basin and newly modernised agricultural regions such as Brittany, which specialises in higher value items. Modernisation has been facilitated by the development of the distribution system. Producer co-operatives and supermarket chains bypass the inefficient traditional practice of transporting food first to Paris and then sending it back to the provinces. The small shopkeepers' lobby was politically powerful in the 1950s, to the extent of having its own right-wing political party to represent it. Even today, there are laws restricting the growth of hypermarket chains. Despite the legal restraints, however, the big stores are constantly increasing their share of the market. In 1989 51 per cent of food sales were registered in hypermarkets or supermarkets.

Despite its reduced share in total output, agriculture today continues to play an important part in French external trade. The agricultural surplus is still referred to as France's 'green oil'. Agriculture proper accounted for 7.8 per cent of exports in 1989, with the food industries adding another 9.4 per cent. Looking at the balance of payments for the same year, we see that these two sectors together generated a trade surplus of FF 44 billion against an overall trade deficit of FF 114 billion. While the energy trade deficit fluctuates with oil prices, the agricultural trade surplus has been growing steadily since 1980. Agriculture is in fact one of the few sectors in which France has a trade surplus with the rest of the EC. French agriculture has modernised dramatically in recent decades, with the number of farms halving between 1955 and 1985 (Flockton and Kofman 1989). Even so, there are still pockets of unmodernised farming and areas, especially in the South, where modern techniques coexist with medieval strip holdings. About 500,000 farms (half the total) generate two-thirds of total agricultural output. The rest is divided between uneconomic small farms and part-time holdings. The different groups of farmers have quite different requirements, which the government seeks to reconcile in its posture *vis-à-vis* European farm policy.

In the 1960s the EEC established a *Common Agricultural Policy* (CAP: see Howe, Chapter 16 in *The European Economy*, on agriculture) in essence following the lines of a French proposal. In the 1960s the price of cereals (generally taken to represent the 'bench-mark' price in European agriculture) was higher in Germany than anywhere else in Europe. The German foodstuffs market was, therefore, in a sense ripe for a take-over bid. The deal underlying the CAP was that the level of EEC-external protection should be set so as to allow the French to have the lion's share of the German market, while still permitting the survival of the South German farmers whose votes were so crucial to the government in Bonn. Soon after the CAP was established, the currency realignments of 1969 led to the emergence of green currencies and the levying of 'Monetary Compensatory Amounts' (MCAs). Because France did not want a devaluation of the franc to lead to even higher food prices at home, it had to accept, through the medium of MCAs, what amounted to taxes on its exports to Germany and additional subsidies to German farmers.

Thus French policy has always been torn between a number of conflicting aims. It wants to maximise the opportunities for the stronger exporting farmers, while keeping quiet the potentially disruptive peasants. At the same time, it wants to keep domestic food prices down to a 'reasonable' level. Since the time of de Gaulle, the French government has been exploring more 'socially' oriented alternatives to the blunderbuss approach of price support, which produces structural surpluses and does not benefit those most in need. The government's acceptance of milk quotas in the 1980s provoked an angry reaction in some quarters, but the present government (1991) seems to agree with the line of argument that France might do better on balance if its stronger farmers did not have to suffer the production restraints imposed on account of the surpluses generated by excessively high prices. There is certainly a growing awareness that agriculture can no longer totally escape the logic that has been applied to industry.

Industry

French industry has grown extremely fast since the Second World War. The peak growth period was 1960–73, with an average rate of about 7 per cent. But growth has been slowing down since then, to an average rate of under 1 per cent in the 1980s. The results are certainly generally impressive, but recent trends have tended to focus attention on surviving weaknesses (see Table 2.2).

Table 2.2 Industrial output and trade by broad sector 1988[a]

	% of total[b] ind. output	Index number of output 1988/74	Trade balance (FF billion)
Metallurgical industries	39	108	−4.3
Traditional goods (textiles, leather, etc)	14	92	−39.5
Chemical industries	17	137	18.2
Electronics	17	157	1.6
Paper/printing	10	142	−17.3
Total[b]/average	100	118	
Food industries		123	8.9
Building and construction materials		101	−1.2

Notes:
[a] Classification is by filière, as defined by French statisticians, not by traditional sector
[b] Excluding food and construction

Source: Holcblatt and Husson 1990, using INSEE data

A worrying trend for France is that while the agricultural trade surplus grew in the

1980s, the manufacturing sector moved from surplus to deficit. Following on the great achievement of the post-war years in creating a modern industrial structure, this has caused a *perception* of crisis in France. Giving particular cause for concern is the fact that France now normally runs an industrial deficit with its EC partners financed by a surplus in LDC markets, indicating a 'low-tech' export orientation.

The French share of world manufacturing production fell by about 10 per cent between 1967 and 1984. It is estimated that about 1 per cent of this was due to specialisation of French industry in inherently slow-growing sectors. The rest is mainly due to loss of competitiveness *within* sectors (Riches et al 1989). As we noted above, French industry is adapting, and there are signs that it has reoriented itself in the 1980s towards EC markets. What troubles some French analysts, however, is the fact that the strengths of French exporting have in many cases become isolated in a set of products that do not develop as 'poles of competitiveness' generating external economies. A counter-example is provided by the sports equipment industry, where a flourishing market at home has led to specialisation in ski and other leisure equipment of various kinds, heavily linked to a thriving domestic service sector. Although poles of competitiveness analysis was first developed by writers anxious to stress the need for government intervention to support non-market linkages between firms, its concerns are echoed in the recent work of anti-interventionist Michael Porter of Harvard (1990).

France is now in the throes of a 'second industrial revolution'. This is partly a consequence of the dynamics of the world trading system, as the first generation of industrial products like cars, electronics etc are threatened by waves of international competition. It is partly because in the 1970s, the government, fearful of this tendency, to some extent pushed French industry in the direction of specialising in a number of markets that could not be sustained, notably in public procurement and in capital goods exports to LDCs. In the 1970s private sector investment fell away. But the government sustained levels of economic activity through massive investment programmes in telecommunications, high-speed trains (TGVs), and nuclear power. Adding the incentive of hugely generous export credits, the state banked on these products (plus arms) offering boundless opportunities in OPEC and newly industrialising markets. Sadly, a combination of factors prevented this gamble from coming off, notably the debt crisis, increased competition (especially in telecommunications), and disillusionment with nuclear power.

The public investment and the export credits usually benefited the same firms. A mere handful of companies received the lion's share of industrial subsidies, according to the unpublished Hanoun report (see Estrin and Holmes 1983: 187–91). In addition to the support given to high-tech firms like the Compagnie Générale d'Electricité (CGE) and Thomson, further subsidies were granted to the increasingly loss-making steel firms (see Dunford, Chapter 9 in *The European Economy*, on regional policy). In fact, none of the big firms receiving state support was prospering. Encouraged by the state to borrow money for expansion, they acquired assets abroad rather than making new investments in France. State-owned Renault made a disastrous investment in US American Motors in the late 1970s. The government's uncritical faith in mergers on grounds of scale economies allowed the creation of a number of poorly integrated groups. They were often more akin to holding companies than multi-divisional multinational firms.

The macroeconomic crisis of the 1970s did not halt the desire of the large French industrial groups to expand, but it did force them to rethink. Firms that had diversified broadly began to 're-centre' their activities on their core businesses. A Finance Ministry study from the early 1980s suggested that in their quest for reorientation, big firms tended to ease up on their efforts to integrate with the European Community (*Direction de la Prévision* 1981). Perhaps they sensed saturation in European markets. They certainly failed to develop the logic of involvement with those markets as far as they might have. The share of French exports going to the EC stagnated after 1973. French firms did, it is true, increase their overseas investments in the 1970s. A rising share went to the USA and Southern Europe (and a falling share to LDCs). The share of the EC, however, remained fairly stable through the 1970s. The Finance Ministry report quoted above estimated that about 30 per cent of the total foreign investment in that period of the twenty leading French industrial firms studied went to the EC (*Direction de la Prévision* 1981: 29). Aggregate data based on balance of payments financial flows alone (ie excluding reinvested profits) show the EC's share of total French outward investment at about 35 per cent in 1976 (*Les Chiffres Clés de l'Industrie* 1990: 127). Some attempts at European industrial co-operation from this period failed, notably UNIDATA. The government was not keen to see foreign (even EC) control of French industry. This put firms in a strong bargaining position *vis-à-vis* the government, as they were able to set a price for retention of a French presence in given sectors.

Services

The service sector has provided a major independent impetus to the development of the economy in recent decades. Tourism has in particular been a major source of foreign currency and a key element of domestic activity. There have been big shifts in household spending patterns towards new forms of leisure activity. This is reflected in the structure of the housing stock. Since 1975 new construction has been predominantly of individual houses rather than flats. These are still often rented rather than bought outright, but the advance of the owner-occupier in France has generated new service activities, associated with both purchase and maintenance. In 1988 54 per cent of households were owner-occupiers, and 11 per cent of households had a second home.

The banking system has been modernised in recent years. Paradoxically, under nationalisation 1982–6, vigorous steps to deregulate were brought in, and the French now have a more active market that ever before in terms of financial services available to households. The take-off of credit cards, associated with the development of electronic money transfer rather than unlimited consumer credit, can be dated essentially from 1983. The credit market remains somewhat more regulated than in the UK. For example, the diversion of housing finance for general consumption purposes, widespread in Britain, is rare in France; conditions for subsidised mortgages are stricter, and directed particularly towards new construction or improvements.

France is, of course, famous for the development of new services in the area of *informatique*. The 1970s saw a massive upgrading of what had been a very primitive phone system. As with other state-sponsored programmes (high-speed trains, nuclear power), the manufacturing sectors scheduled to benefit from the boom in equipment orders found themselves in difficulty when the investment programmes reached completion, but the infrastructure is in place, and continues to affect the pattern of economic activity. The 'Minitel' system was originally intended to provide a boost to the hardware manufacturers, via export sales. In the event, equipment exports have been of modest benefit to the French electronics industry. But France has found itself with a unique electronic communications system, extending far beyond the basic idea of an electronic telephone directory. The Minitel system is widely used for such purposes as travel reservations; it has also proved to be a money-spinner as a channel for *messageries roses*, the French equivalent of 'adult' telephone chatlines.

Expenditure on traditional public services, health and education has also risen faster than GNP. The health service is state-financed, but like many other continental European systems, the state-controlled social security system of France reimburses expenses rather than directly managing the health service. The education system has been a major source of controversy in recent years; it has been subject to the economic pressures of a rising population and ambitions for more extended schooling. It continues to display marked social and regional inequalities, despite a long-term government commitment to raising overall standards. About 30 per cent of school leavers gain a *baccalauréat*, which entitles them to a university place. But a significant proportion of post-16 education is accounted for by students who have been forced to repeat years. Youth unemployment is very high among unqualified people.

The social inegalitarianism of the higher education system is exacerbated by the distinction between the universities and the *grandes écoles*. While the universities have till now had no entrance requirements beyond the *baccalauréat*, the *grandes écoles*, of which the most famous is the *Ecole Polytechnique*, are highly selective. Facilities to prepare for their entrance exams are not available everywhere in the country. A *grandes écoles* graduate can, however, count on the pick of the best jobs. These well-funded elite schools concentrate on technical and commercial courses, while the universities have in the past been more 'academic'. The distinction is, however, now breaking down. Among the most successful innovations of the 1970s in the higher education system are the *Instituts Universitaires de Technologies*, which provide two-year courses on technical subjects and create excellent career opportunities.

Sectoral interrelationships

Although growth of output has been most spectacular in the industrial sector, growth of employment since the war has been concentrated in the service sector (see Table 2.3). Industrial employment at its peak in the early 1970s was barely 5 per cent above the levels of the early 1950s (see Carré et al 1975). The output growth achieved in the industrial sector is thus all the more impressive in that the overwhelming part of it was achieved through productivity growth, rather than just growth in the volume of inputs (see Table 2.4). The flight of labour from the agricultural sector did of, course, facilitate this achievement in an indirect way. Spare labour meant that the service sector could grow without causing tensions in the labour market.

After 1973, the availability of spare labour led not to growth, but to unemployment. Between 1973 and 1979 the continuing tendency for service sector employment to increase kept total employment rising, though the modest secular upwards trend in employment in industry turned into a decline. Even so, unemployment rose from under

Table 2.3 Employment by sector as % of total civilian employment

	1960	1968	1980	1989
Industry	37.6	38.6	35.9	30.1
Services	29.9	45.8	55.4	63.5
Agriculture	22.5	15.6	8.7	6.4

Source: OECD *Ecomomic Outlook; Historical Statistics*

Table 2.4 Productivity growth 1960–89 (average annual growth rate)

Real GDP per employed person	3.3
Real value added in industry (purchasing power equivalent)	4.1
Real value added in agriculture (purchasing power equivalent)	5.5
Real value added in services	2.3

Source: OECD *Economic Outlook; Historical Statistics*

3 per cent in 1974 to 6 per cent in 1980, as the total work-force continued to grow. In the 1980s rising employment in services was no longer enough to offset declining industrial employment, and total employment began to fall slightly. Unemployment rose sharply, and peaked at 11 per cent in 1988.

Structural and macroeconomic factors in the slowdown of the 1970s and 1980s

Some argue (see Boltho 1982: 1) that the general slowdown in the French economy (as elsewhere) after the Oil Shock was caused by the gradual drying up of the sources of surplus labour. Combining this approach with an analysis of changes in social attitudes, again not confined to France, some French commentators have seen a reaction in the work-force against the whole nature of the modern industrial system, to which the unrest of May 1968 was a precursor. The children of peasants, the argument runs, were no longer willing to work on motor assembly lines and the like without substantial compensation in the form of higher wages, thereby rendering unviable the so-called Fordist system of industrial organisation (see Dunford, Chapter 9 in *The European Economy*, on regional problems). But the mechanical assembly line system, it goes on, is now outmoded, for technological as well as sociological reasons. It is suggested that new technology has actually rendered the old industrial structures obsolete, as information technology has made rigid assembly-line mass-production methods redundant, and required more flexible structures in terms of firms and workers' skills. These issues do not, of course, concern France alone. But the notion of post-Fordism is a particular French preoccupation. The American writers Piore and Sabel (1984) have noted the survival in France, far into the mass industrial era, of networks of small firms. They point to the 'industrial district' formed by the silk industry of Lyon as an example of a kind of industrial structure that, they say, would have been in some ways better adapted to the eventual needs of 'post-Fordist' industry. A number of question marks must be raised over this analysis. The overwhelming part of the French labour force was never in giant assembly-line factories. It is the service sector that has seen the bulk of growth in employment in the post-war period. Unionisation is relatively low in France and the trade unions are weak and divided, along political rather than skill-demarcation lines. The slowdown of the whole economy after 1973 simply cannot readily be explained in terms of organised unrest in big factories.

In the 1950s and 1960s French policy-makers and industrialists were, certainly, over-impressed by the benefits of scale economies, and allowed a number of unwieldy conglomerates to develop. Since the mid-1970s, in contrast, France has seen a big revival in the importance of small firms. Between 1974 and 1989 the share of firms with fewer than 500 workers in industrial employment rose from 41 to 51 per cent. This is in part a reflection of the fact that smaller firms are genuinely more adaptable to changing economic circumstances. On average, they report lower productivity than larger firms, but manage to compensate through lower wage costs. The continuing rise in the service sector has added to the growth of the small firm sector. But some of the growth in the number of small firms is, indeed, due to a shrinking of the bigger firms (see *Les Chiffres Clés de l'Industrie* 1990).

Some analysts argue that whatever was happening at the micro-level, the economic slow down in France was really caused by the evolution of the macroeconomic profit–wage relationship. In the period up to 1973, the story runs, France had very high and stable levels of private investment. From the late 1960s onwards, however, it underwent a period of high inflation in which real wages outstripped productivity growth, and so squeezed profits and consequently private investment. It is certainly true that little of the growth in total output before 1974 can be explained in terms of the increase in labour supply (Gueslin 1990; Carré et al 1975). Statistical studies suggest, further, that it is the very high rate of capital accumulation that explains most of the increase in output per worker in that period. Since 1974 the rate of capital accumulation has, indeed, slowed down in France, but not by as much as output. There has been an increasing degree of underutilisation of capital, and a fall in the measured productivity of capital and the rate of profit. This is associated with (*inter alia*) the oil price rises, and the upwards pressure on wage bills, as workers sought higher money wages to compensate for higher oil prices. The trend was exacerbated in the early 1980s by rising interest rates, which ate further into corporate profits. Ironically, profitability levels have been restored under the socialist government, which has kept wages under control. But the mechanism of that restoration has been a deflationary policy that may, arguably, have made it impossible to ensure two further conditions for fast growth, namely strong expectations and low real interest rates.

Henry et al (1989) conclude that the slowness of growth must be attributable to demand factors.

Since there has not been a marked slow-down in technical progress, the growth potential of the French economy should not be less than 5 per cent a year as long as there is substantial unemployment. It is therefore not on the supply side that one must look for the cause of slow growth: the high level of profits would easily permit a strong growth of investment in the range of 5–10 per cent pa if the long-term growth prospects became favourable again and if real interest rates fell.

(Henry et al 1989: 204)

Should we, therefore, put the blame on government macroeconomic policy?

In the golden years before 1973 France had a relatively high inflation rate and the government followed a policy of allowing the franc to depreciate to preserve competitiveness. In overall macro-policy France oscillated mildly between expansionary and deflationary policies, on a pattern not unlike the UK's 'stop-go' policy (Gueslin 1990: ch. 3). The critical year 1974 saw a deflation induced by panic over the Oil Crisis. From 1975 onwards there was an ambiguous mixture of anti-inflation measures, incomes policy, etc, and high public spending to slow the rise in unemployment. High levels of investment in telecommunications, high-speed trains and nuclear power sustained the economy in a Keynesian way for a while, but left it with a capital stock not well adapted to the demands of the 1980s.

The Mitterrand government introduced a general macroeconomic reflation in 1981–2, largely on the back of strengthened consumer demand. The extra spending went on imports, not on French goods. This led to a dramatic worsening of the balance of payments and only a modest internal expansion. Analysts concluded that the supply side of the economy could not take the strain of demand expansion. After the balance of payments crisis of 1982–3 the government abandoned the idea of Keynesian policies at a national level, and began to down-play the desirability of reflation even at the European level.

The policy goal was now to create jobs through greater competitiveness. This was to be achieved by lowering inflation, and devaluation was to be avoided if possible. Behind that policy stance lay the view that the devaluations of the past had generated only more inflation and not extra growth. In fact, econometric evidence from those devaluations (Muet 1985) indicates that a combination of devaluation and fiscal austerity in the early 1980s might have relaunched growth sustainably. But the desire to build credible counter-inflationary policies has dominated to the exclusion of all else in French thinking in recent years. Keeping the franc strong within the EMS, and in effect matching German monetary policy, has, since 1983, been the overwhelming economic policy orientation of the French government, an orientation to which they have been unwilling to admit any alternative, either politically or economically.

Thus European monetary co-operation has become for France a form of incomes policy; there has also been an explicit pay policy for the public sector. And inflation has certainly come down. Whether this represents a straightforward victory for government policy is a more difficult question to answer. The vertical Philips curve theory suggests that there can be no possible long-term loss in employment from reducing inflation, and this theory appeared to be supported by econometric work from the mid-1980s (eg Sachs and Wyplosz 1986). But has France really brought inflation down at no cost? Opinions differ. Some recent research work suggests that the exchange rate policy France chose as part of its austerity plan has generated 'a significant cost in terms of activity and employment' (Le Cacheux and Lecointe 1989). But was there a benefit to set against that cost in terms of moderating inflationary expectations? An econometric study by Ray Barrell (1990) found no sign of a structural break in the 1980s in the way people in a number of countries of Western Europe, including France, formed inflation expectations, which lends support to a more conventional Philips curve interpretation, and places Barrell in the ranks of the EMS-sceptics. Gavin Davies (1989) argues, however, that after a long hard slog the impact of EMS membership on expectations was beginning to be felt in France by the late 1980s.

Be that as it may, France certainly had the lowest rate of inflation in the OECD area after Japan in 1990. But unemployment remains high, and we just do not know for sure how much that is attributable to deflationary policies. One key question that poses itself is this: have inflationary expectations moderated so slowly because people do not pay enough attention to exchange rate policy, or because the EMS discipline imposed, strict though it has been, has been insufficiently strict? What is clear is that the French government's enthusiasm for European monetary union is partly attributable to the belief that if there were a single currency in Europe, everyone would know that France simply could not devalue. This, it is felt, would make it possible for interest rates to be cut sharply. As we have seen, there is a powerful argument to the effect that one of the sources of France's *microeconomic* problems in the 1980s flowed from the fact that although inflation was close to German rates, interest rates were consistently higher by more than the inflation margin. The reason for this is that markets were expecting a devaluation of the franc which never came. This inevitably imposed higher real interest rates in France than in Germany. There are signs in 1991 of a clear convergence of interest rates between France and Germany, though unfortunately largely through rises in German rates.

On balance, therefore, France pursued a successful policy of reducing inflation to the same rate as Germany (around 3 per cent in 1991) during the 1980s. But it looks as if a significant price may have had to be paid for this. Whether it was really worthwhile in long-run terms will become clearer in the 1990s. Coming back to the central issue of this section, it seems probable that government macroeconomic policy did have something to do with the medium-term slowdown of the 1980s.

Industrial planning and policy and integration with Europe

When the European Economic Community was established in 1957, the member states set out on a path to full economic union involving unprecedented transfers of sovereignty. Despite General de Gaulle's political reservations, France became an economy open to Europe in the 1960s. The share of GDP traded was around 10 per cent in 1960, as it had been in the 1930s, but by 1970 the proportion had risen again to about 20 per cent. In the late 1950s France's major trading partner was Algeria, but by 1970 it was Germany. Between 1959 and 1968 the share of the EEC-6 in total exports rose from 27 per cent (close to the 1913 figure) to 47 per cent. The increase in the German share of French exports from 6 per cent to 20 per cent over this period is quite remarkable. The loss of Algerian markets explains part of the reorientation. There was also an important psychological element: the commitment to open frontiers was perceived as irreversible. The importance of EC trade continued to rise after 1970, but at a slower rate. The 1970s did, indeed, see an attempt to increase exports to non-EC markets (see earlier section on industry, pp. 18–20). The share of the EC-12 in the total French export market was the same in 1987, at 60 per cent, as it had been in 1973, after falling several points in the late 1970s.

Economic policy from the 1960s onwards was directed very much at creating an industrial structure that could compete internationally. In that sense there was no contradiction between the planning theme and the integration theme, and there were, indeed, still elements of industrial *dirigisme* present in the 1960s. But the state was being rolled back. The Vth Plan for the period 1965–70 saw a formal commitment by the government not to use industrial policy to direct investment, and to assign the responsibility for investment choices to business. The state did, of course, continue to play an important role in this phase, especially in providing credits for investment. But even in the 1950s it was firms that had made the key decisions about how to use the money. The post-war government had wanted to use the planning system to produce a modern European capitalist industrial system for France capable of surviving internationally, not to create a planned economy (Kuisel 1981). The problem is that while this job had been accomplished by the 1960s, the government continued to lead people to believe that it had a bigger role to play in directing industry than it was actually capable of playing any more, right up to the early 1980s.

Economists from the Harvard Business School (McArthur and Scott 1969) were surprised to find how little influence the Plan had on firms' choices in the 1960s. Later research in France and at Sussex suggested that the chain of influence from government to industry was often reversed. High-flying civil servants on ministerial staffs would be sympathetic to the interests of the firms they were dealing with, and whose employment they were likely to join under the system of *pantouflage* (see Cawson et al 1990; Sharp and Holmes 1989).

Although the government did not have a vision of its own to impose on the private sector, it was very eager to support the strategies of concentration and growth by acquisition that were being pursued by large French industrial groups such as Thomson and St-Gobain. In firms and in the state the view was widely held that major economies of scale would result. The outcome was equivocal, however, as we saw earlier. The nature of French company structures did not lend itself to the integrated multi-divisional firms typical in the USA or the UK. Subsidiaries were (and often still are) owned less than 100 per cent, with separate boards and legal personalities.

Antoine Auqier (1984), in a study also written at Harvard, argued that much of the industrial concentration in the late 1960s was not aimed at securing economies of scale, as the government had hoped. The main motive, he suggests, was the creation of strategic alliances, which enabled firms better to co-operate to reduce the intensity of competition within the French market as new entrants came in from the rest of the EEC. There was little rationalisation of production even where acquisitions were in the same sector. The Thomson group in the early 1980s still had several hundred factories, including more than a dozen making television sets. Concentration increased quite markedly in France in terms of ownership. Between 1958 and 1968 the share of the top 500 firms in aggregate sales in France rose from 38 per cent to 68 per cent (Gilly and Morin 1981), with the pattern stabilising after that date. These trends were clearly anything but congenial to the cause of deepening integration within Europe. And they conspired with the errors of public investment policy discussed earlier to produce the industrial crisis of the late 1970s, which was in turn soon followed by a socialist victory at the polls.

The motives lying behind the Socialist Party's 1982 nationalisation campaign, which brought leading firms accounting for about 15 per cent of industrial production and virtually the whole of the banking system into the public sector, seem to have been ideological rather than pragmatic. But they actually proved to be a useful instrument for restoring the momentum of market-led, Europe-oriented growth by French firms. It has been argued that the nationalisation measures of 1982 would have been taken in another form if the conservative Raymond Barre had won the presidential election in 1981. The steel industry had already seen one major bail-out. With their dependence on state subsidies and contracts, the other big firms would almost certainly have required massive injections of cash by the state, and consequential replacement of their top management from within the usual closed circle of *pantouflage* graduates. These were precisely the initial effects of nationalisation. But they were soon followed by a realisation on the part of the government that the state had neither the financial nor the human resources to run businesses in hard times. For a brief time in the period 1981–3 there was a belief by the industry minister that he could control the firms. But it rapidly became clear that in terms of information and expertise, the firms always had the upper hand (see Cohen and Bauer 1985). Studies commissioned by the government showed that subsidies to industry had got completely out of control (Commissariat au Plan 1982). The Planning Commission estimated that a large part of industrial subsidy money was being paid *par abonnement* (on subscription, with no clear objectives or monitoring.)

A psychological turning point came in 1983. There had always been a certain symbiosis between state and industry in France: big French firms had had an implicit guarantee against bankruptcy as long as they pursued strategies that seemed to accord with those of the state. The crunch came for the socialists when it became clear that the state itself was not always in command of this process. The sea-change in government thinking was symbolised by the government's 1984 decision to allow the private nuclear engineering firm Creusot-Loire to go bankrupt, despite its close links with the state.

The Finance Ministry had, of course, never been enthusiastic about open-ended subsidies, and financial pressures quickly reinforced the seemingly inexorable political logic of the time. The economic crisis of 1983 led to a perceived need to retrench financially, and this led in turn to instructions going out to state firms demanding that they become profitable by 1985. The state-owned banks, meanwhile, were being reorganised, not to become instruments of state industrial policy, but rather to shoulder the responsiblity of competing with one another (Simon 1984).

It was against this background that the government became convinced of the impossibility of going it alone, and came increasingly to see European integration as the only chance. The reasons were of course political as much as economic. In the context of the evolution of the European system, it seemed vital to retain and even strengthen the ties with Germany on both planes (see Chapters 3–6 in *The European Economy*, on European integration). The 1992 Single Market plan was embraced by France once more ambitious aims had been shown to be, for the time being at least, unsustainable. That plan served a multiplicity of purposes. In the first instance, in the present context, it gave a very clear signal to firms that the market of the future should be Germany. Equally importantly, European technological co-operation was seen as a basis for building up a high-tech industry, the products of which could be sold against Japanese competition. Significantly, the share of the EC in total French foreign investment had increased to 52 per cent by 1987, some 50 per cent higher than it had been in the mid-1970s (*Les Chiffres Clés de l'Industrie* 1990: 127).

A new social market economy model

On both right and left, then, there has come a growing feeling that the model adopted late 1960s to early 1970s had gone wrong. Europeanisation has now come to mean imitating Germany! A propos the Xth plan, for 1988 to 1992 (Commissariat Général au Plan 1989), Premier Rocard spoke of a 'European model' of industry, in which market forces would determine production but the state would care for the welfare of the workers. Just as in the domain of monetary policy France has deliberately sought to emulate German policy – in order to impose even more binding constraints on itself – so in industrial policy it has sought to move towards the principle of *sozial-marktwirtschaft*.

In the sphere of industrial policy, the trend towards the social market economy is certainly somewhat erratic. But it seems to be there. The replacement in 1991 of Michel Rocard by Madame Edith Cresson in the premiership could well prove to be more of a change of style than a return to active interventionism or protectionism. The case of Renault is illuminating. It became apparent in the 1980s that Renault, long the showpiece of French state enterprise, could no longer serve as a model. The subordination of commercial to technical and social criteria was simply no longer acceptable. The highly conspicuous firing of the chief executive in 1985 was a signal that losses would not be allowed to increase. More recently, the Finance Ministry has shown tacit willingness to accept the EC Commission's restrictions on subsidies that the ministry would prefer, of course, not to have to pay. The same ministry has certainly encouraged state-owned enterprises to go to capital markets for funds, and is anxious not to be seen as a source of risk-capital for private firms. The fate of Renault is again highly symbolic. In the 1970s it was encouraged to invest public money in very ambitious ventures in the USA on less than wholly commercial criteria. In contrast, a recent exchange of shares between Volvo and Renault raises the spectre of the ultimate privatisation of Renault, something which even five years ago (1986) would have been unthinkable. The privatisation programme of the right-wing Chirac government, which held power 1986–8, did not prove popular. But President Mitterrand's 1988 election pledge of neither privatisation nor nationalisation has given way to approval of a pattern whereby state-owned firms raise money by selling shares on the stock exchange.

It is remarkable how small an impression the privatisations of 1986–8 had on the policies of firms. We can find some cases where it does seem to have had a significant strategic impact, for example in the case of the Alcatel telecommunications group (in which the state still has a small stake), which made important steps in a European direction in this period. But what really stands out is how little corporate strategies were affected by the privatisations, or indeed the return to office in 1988 of a Socialist government.

The state has now become a 'shareholder state', setting an example to other providers of capital in France. A striking example of this is the recent bid by the state-owned Crédit Lyonnais bank for a small, Irish-owned finance house operating in the UK. The UK government, traditionally suspicious of the state's role in industry in France, referred the bid to the UK Monopolies and Mergers Commission (MMC). Would French government control lead to Crédit Lyonnais engaging in non-commercial activities? The French submissions were emphatic that the state was interested only in profitability, and the overwhelming majority of British experts consulted agreed that this was so. The MMC reviewed the various submissions, and concluded that even in banking the French government did not seem to exercise any more operational control over its firms than other governments did, and recommended that the bid be allowed to proceed.

The pattern of French industry is likely to retain many individual characteristics. It seems probable that the state will retain a significant stake in the business sector in a purely financial sense, and social relations between government and business will no doubt remain close. But the French set-up will come to resemble the rest of Europe in many behavioural characteristics. Even today, there is no longer the same open-ended financial support for big private firms. They *can* be taken over by foreign firms if they fail. The French government has acknowledged the importance that strong competition policy has to play in the '1992' plan, and has begun to enforce its *own* laws, notably in public procurement. Moreover the rise of the state as an active shareholder means that the performance of state-owned firms is monitored on the basis of criteria that the Finance Ministry understands well. Partly for these reasons, partly because of changes in the attitudes of businessmen themselves, the need to be 'European' rather than French-oriented seems to have been firmly taken on board by French industry.

There are, of course, the counter-pressures referred to at the outset, as the appointment of Madame Cresson indicates. The Planning Commission (*Commissariat Général au Plan* 1991) has published a report calling for tough action against Japanese electronics manufacturers, but its influence is now limited. If '1992' means anything, it means a truly common external trade policy and rigorous competition policy. In accepting the guidelines on industrial policy (EC Commission 1990), France has implicitly accepted those general principles, which will make discrimination against foreign firms legally very difficult. In adopting common policies, the EC has had to make a choice between the 'Fortress Europe' approach and liberalisation. It looks as if the latter option has been chosen, and although France will probably continue to make some noises about the need for tighter restrictions against Japanese imports, it has now abandoned many of its earlier principles. Whether as a matter of conviction or necessity, France now knows that it is not possible to keep Japanese investment out of Europe in the way some imagined might be possible in the 1960s with American investment. The French government is fully aware that common EC trade barriers promote attempts to produce inside the EC, and France wants its share of any incoming Japanese investment. It is worth noting, in this context, that despite past hostility to inward investment the share of foreign-owned manufacturing production capacity in France in 1986 was estimated at 26 per cent: higher than in the UK, Germany or the USA (Julius 1990: 53–6).

Conclusion

France has declared itself willing to accept the restructuring that market forces will dictate. This means that the loud and clear message going from state to business sector is that the latter must learn how to compete on European markets, above all against German industry. There are already cries, reminiscent of 1958 and coming mainly from the automobile and electronics sectors, that French industry will not be able to compete. At time of writing, however, the social market economy line seemed still to be holding. The signs are that Madame Cresson's appointment represented a political manoeuvre rather than a change of economic strategy. Economic policy remained in the hands of the non-interventionist Finance Minister Pierre Bérégovoy. If the 1990–1 recession proves temporary, and France can pull itself out of that recession by capitalising on a united Germany's thirst for imports, then it may see a dividend from its act of faith in market forces. The analysis of this chapter suggests, however, that even if the problems of the 1980s continue, the 'French *perestroika*' is irreversible.

References

Auqier A (1984) *French Industry's Reaction to the European Common Market*. Garland
Barrell R (1990) Has the EMS changed wage and price behaviour in Europe? *National Institute Economic Review* November
Beltrain A, Griset P (1988) *La Croissance economique de la France 1815–1914*. Armand Colin
Boltho A (1982) *The European Economy*. Oxford University Press
Caron F (tr. Bray B) (1979) *An Economic History of Modern France*. Columbia University Press and Methuen
Carre D, Dubois P, Malinvaud E (1975) *French Economic Growth*. Oxford University Press
Cawson A, Morgan K, Holmes P, Stevens A, Webber D (1990) *Hostile Brothers*. Oxford University Press
Cohen E, Bauer M (1985) *Les Grandes manoeuvres industrielles*. Belfond
Commissariat au Plan (1982) Les aides à l'industrie. Mimeo
Commissariat Général au Plan (1989) *Xth Plan 1988–92* Documentation Française
Commissariat Général au Plan (1991) Un stratégie d'urgence pour l'électronique. Mimeo
Daisaigues B (1985) Efficacité des politiques protectionnistes à la fin du XIXe siècle. In Lassudrie-Duchêne and Reiffers (eds) (1985)
Davies G (1985) *Britain and the European Monetary Question*. Institute for Public Policy Research
Direction de la Prévision (1981) Vingt groupes industriels et le redéploiement. *Economie et Prévision* **51**
Direction de la Prévision (1983) Facteurs de production et résultats des groupes publics 1973–1981. *Economie et Prévision* **60**
EC Commission (1990) *Industrial Policy in an Open and Competitive Environment* Communication to Council, October
Estrin S, Holmes P (1983) *French Planning in Theory and Practice*. Allen & Unwin
Flockton C, Kofman E (1989) *France*. Chapman

Frochen P, Sternyniak H, Topol R (1989) La politique monétaire. In Jeanneney (ed) (1989)

Gilly J P, Morin F (1981) *Les Groupes industriels en France*. Documentation Française

Gueslin A (1990) *Nouvelle Histoire Economique de la France Contemporaine. L'Economie Ouverte 1948–1990* La Découverte

Henry J, Leroux V, Muet P-A et al (1989) Capital, travail et progrès technique. In Jeanneney (ed) (1989)

Holcblat N, Husson M (1990) *L'Industrie Française*. La Découverte

Holmes P (1989) Economies of scale, expectations and Europe 1992. *World Economy* **12** (4): 525–37

INSEE (1990) *Tableau Economique de la France*. Documentation Française

Jeanneney J-M (1985) Allocution d'ouverture. In Lassudrie-Duchêne and Reiffers (ed) (1985)

Jeanneney J-M (ed) (1989) *L'Economie Française depuis 1967*. Seuil

Julius D (1990) *Global Companies and Public Policy*. Pinter/RIIA

Kuisel R (1981) *Capitalism and the State in Modern France*. Cambridge University Press

Lassudrie-Duchêne B, Reiffers J-L (eds) (1985) *Le Protectionnisme*. Economica

Le Cacheux J, Lecointe F (1989) La Politique de change. In Jeanneney (ed) (1989)

Les Chiffres Clés de l'Industrie (1990) *Documentation Française*. Paris

McArthur J B, Scott B R (1969) *Industrial Planning in France*. Harvard University Press

Messerlin P (1985) Les politiques commerciales et leurs effets sur longues périodes. In Lassudrie-Duchêne and Reiffers (eds) (1985)

Muet P-A (1985) Economic management and the international environment. In Machin H, Wright V (eds) (1985) *Economic Policy-Making Under the Mitterrand Presidency*. Pinter

OECD (1990) *Annual Survey of France*. Paris

OECD (1991) *Economic Outlook*. June

Piore M J, Sabel C F (1984) *The Second Industrial Divide*. Basic Books

Porter M (1990) *The Competitive Advantage of Nations*. Macmillan

Prate A (1978) *Les Batailles economiques du Général de Gaulle*. Plon

Riches V, Sigogne P, Guillaumat-Taillet F (1989) La France comparée à ses partenaires. In Jeanneney (ed) (1989)

Sachs J, Wyplosz C (1986) The economic consequences of President Mitterrand. *Economic Policy* **2**: 261–305

Schama S (1989) *Citizens*. Penguin

Sharp M, Holmes P (eds) (1989) *Strategies for New Technology*. Philip Allen

Simon C (1984) *Les Banques*. La Découverte

Stoffaes C (1978) *La Grande menace industrielle*. Calmann-Lévy

Stoléru L (1969) *L'Impératif industriel*. Seuil

Walras L (tr. Holmes P) (1980) The state and the railways. *Journal of Public Economics* **13**: 81–100

CHAPTER 3

Federal Republic of Germany

CHRIS FLOCKTON

Difficulties of adjustment: from the Oil Shocks to unification

The 1980s have seen fundamental shifts in West Germany's economic performance and prospects. The opening of the Berlin Wall in November 1989, which led to the economic and monetary union of the two Germanies in the following July and subsequently the political union in October 1990, have, of course, represented a series of events without historical parallel: they change Germany's relative political and economic weight in Europe, and alter quite fundamentally both short-term and longer-term growth prospects. In the light of the Federal Republic's strong growth performance and the record external surpluses achieved towards the end of the 1980s, few doubt its ability to assume the burdens of the moribund Eastern economy. With just under 30 per cent of the European Community's GDP and one-quarter of its population, a united Germany will wield greater influence but not dominate, as some have feared.

Yet this is a far cry from the traditional complaints heard earlier in the decade, when the 'snail-like' growth of West Germany was seen to constrain that of its European trading partners, and to constitute a major obstacle to international adjustment, in particular to the alleviation of the US twin deficits. If relatively price-stable West Germany did not quite suffer from the stagflationary disease rampant elsewhere, it did exhibit, it was claimed, symptoms of 'eurosclerosis' – rigidities in labour and product markets, rigidities in the form of tight regulation and, finally, the burden of high social expenditure commitments. All of these, the argument went, slowed its response to changed international conditions. Of course such criticism may well have been overdone, as witness the excellent output, investment and trade performance towards the end of the 1980s.

In an international perspective, relatively slow growth in West Germany over the period 1971–87 (when growth exceeded the OECD average in only three years), a situation accepted by the federal government as the price of beating inflation, did have major consequences in terms of international exchange rate policy and trade balances. The significance of the German export sector and the role of the deutschmark as the third international reserve and investment currency could not be ignored. Germany's annual current account surpluses with the USA and the EC over the years 1986–9 averaged DM 38 billion and DM 42 billion respectively, which clearly constrained the macroeconomic policy options of these trading partners (see Eastwood, Chapter 7 in *The European Economy*, on co-ordinating macroeconomic policy).

From a domestic West German point of view, the argument that slow growth reflected a growing inflexibility in the economy suggested problems in the 'German model' of economic management. Critics laid much stress on the fact that the practice of the social market economy was limited primarily to the manufacturing sector, and that, even here, distortions had begun to creep in as intervention grew over the 1970s. They not only saw oligopolistic behaviour and growing subsidisation in the manufacturing sector, but also emphasised the traits of corporatism, of consensus-building, and the close regulation both of services and of sectors in decline – all of which may serve to slow adjustment and to weaken economic performance. It is not surprising, then, that in line with the international current towards deregulation and the strengthening of market forces, authorities such as the OECD consistently stressed the need for such reforms in West Germany, if growth was to be speeded up, especially in the sheltered sectors, so making a contribution to the redressing of international trade imbalances.

The evolution of the West German economy and of the economic policy of the federal government after the 1973–4 Oil Shock followed a similar pattern to that experienced in other major industrial countries. The experience of stagflation led to a loss of faith in demand management, and 'supply-side' policies were given increasing prominence after the Second Oil Shock of 1979. For an economy as open, and as oil-dependent, as that of West Germany, the two Oil Crises represented a formidable challenge. By the same token, the 'counter-shock' of late 1985, when the dollar oil price collapsed, brought great gains in terms of price stability, interest rate levels and the external account, easing the policy constraints on the Kohl government.

Standard economic analysis suggests that an external supply shock such as an oil shock represents a fourfold challenge. In the particular case in hand, the 'tax' imposed on oil-consuming countries by OPEC would have a world-wide deflationary effect if the petrodollars were not recycled to sustain world demand. The disequilibrating effect on the balance of payments of oil consumers must be met by (1) energy-saving and (2) an increased export effort, in the short term by reducing domestic absorption to free resources for export. This can be achieved in part by an appropriate cut in the real incomes of the final consumers of the oil, which implies that they must not seek to recover the initial inflationary impact in higher wages, otherwise a wage-price spiral will ensue. Finally, an enhanced investment effort is needed to pursue energy-saving initiatives, and to replace plant rendered obsolete by changed relative input prices. As we know, the actual experience in many industrial countries was otherwise: the downwards rigidity of real wages produced an inflationary spiral. With the ensuing switch to deflationary macroeconomic policies, unemployment soared, the profit rate slumped and investment activity fell to a low level. In the German case, the pattern was less stark than in several other West European countries, but its features remain discernible in spite of a relatively positive response – to the First Oil Shock at least.

To highlight the main features of the evolution over the last two decades, we look

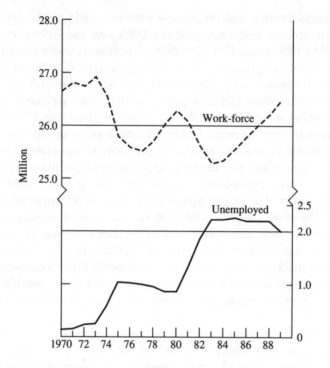

Figure 3.1 Labour market
Source: Council of Economic Advisers 1989

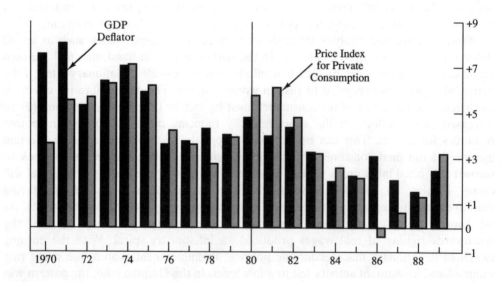

Figure 3.2 Inflation
Source: Council of Economic Advisers 1989

first at the major economic trends. Table 3.1 and Figures 3.1 to 3.5 give an indication of the unevenness of West German performance. This comes through in terms of both Germany's historical evolution and international comparisons. The dramatic evolution of real GDP during the *Wirtschaftswunder* of the reconstruction period, and the sustained though slower growth of the 1960s, is clear from Table 3.1. Equally apparent, however, is the fact that the Federal Republic grew relatively slowly compared with major industrial countries in the 1970s and 1980s. Associated with this is the marked slowdown in real investment in plant and machinery. As would be expected, therefore, the recent unemployment record of the Federal Republic appears to be poor (Figure 3.1) – unemployment grew rapidly in the 1974–5 recession to over 1 million, and had only been reduced to 876,000 when the Second Oil Shock occurred. The rapid rise in unemployment to 2.25 million or over 9 per cent of the employed work-force fast on the heels of the 1981–2 recession was put in reverse only from mid-1988, after five years of unprecedentedly high unemployment. There were, admittedly, demographic factors which seriously hampered the attack on unemployment, but even the creation of 1.5 million jobs since 1983 has not offered significant alleviation.

Table 3.1 The Federal Republic of Germany in international comparisons

	USA	Japan	FRG	France	UK	Italy
Real GNP % change, yearly average						
1950–60	3.3	4.2	8.8	5.0	2.8	6.3
1960–70	3.8	11.7	4.5	5.6	2.9	5.7
1970–80	2.8	4.7	2.7	3.6	1.9	3.1
1980–87	2.6	3.8	1.5	1.7	2.3	2.1
1982–87	3.8	4.0	2.3	1.6	3.2	2.6
Real investment in plant and equipment % change, yearly average						
1960–70	6.4	—	6.7	8.7	3.7	—
1970–80	4.8	3.0	2.2	5.1	2.2	2.4
1980–87	4.2	6.9	1.5	1.0	1.9	2.8
1982–87	7.7	8.2	4.5	1.8	4.7	5.7
Export share of GNP						
1960	5.7	5.6	15.2	10.8	18.3	9.3
1970	6.6	8.6	20.4	14.3	22.0	15.3
1980	10.2	13.7	26.5	21.5	27.7	21.8
1986	8.7	15.9	31.0	22.5	29.2	24.0

Sources: IMF; OECD; Hinze 1988

Figure 3.2 shows the excellent price stability record of the Federal Republic. The rising trend in consumer prices prior to the 1973–4 Oil Shock was in fact subsequently reversed, under the impact of a continuing rise in the deutschmark exchange rate and tight monetary policies. The relaxation of macroeconomic policy following the June 1978 Bonn Economic Summit, when Germany agreed to take on the 'locomotive' role of pulling the international economy out of recession, can be detected in a renewed tendency for the rate of inflation to rise, which was very much compounded by the Second Oil Shock. From the depths of the 1981–2 recession onwards, and under the influence of tight Bundesbank policy, the inflation rate fell consistently to a low of minus 0.5 per cent in 1986, powerfully assisted by the collapse in the dollar oil price.

Finally, Figures 3.3 and 3.4 present trends in the current external balance and the real external value of the deutschmark. The record current account surplus in 1989 of DM 104 billion represents the culmination of a series of large surpluses through the second half of the 1980s of an average of over DM 80 billion per year. During the period as a whole, sluggish domestic demand and the oil price collapse were the main explanatory factors, but in 1989 and 1990 strong world demand for West German capital goods boosted the trade balance. Figure 3.3 also demonstrates not only how successfully the German economy weathered the First Oil Shock but also the contrasting experience of the Second Oil Shock, when large external deficits were incurred. Figure 3.4 shows the evolution in the real external value of the deutschmark. The real downward trend in the deutschmark to early 1984 (from a 1980 base year) in fact continues a pattern of deutschmark weakness which began in 1979. Prior to that, from the collapse of the Bretton Woods system in 1973, the real external value of the deutschmark had risen by as much as 39 per cent.

What is the story behind those economic statistics? As a first approximation, they confirm the picture (until mid-1988) of a relatively slow-growing Germany over a period of two decades, with an unsatisfactory employment record, this having in part been the price paid for generally commendable achievements in the realm of control of inflation. The 'growth weakness' is related to an 'investment weakness', with the excess of domestic savings over investment finding its counterpart in the large external surpluses.

This sketch of economic trends helps illuminate changes in the perception of the underlying problems and the accompanying shifts in economic policy. It was the level of performance in the later 1970s and especially, in West German eyes, the traumatic effects of the Second Oil Shock, which led to a loss of faith in Keynesian prescriptions, so ushering in the supply-side policies of Chancellor Kohl's government. From the depths of the post-Oil Shock recession in 1975, the SPD–FDP government of Chancellor Schmidt introduced no fewer than twelve budgetary programmes to sustain demand, whether through improved investment allowances, job creation measures or, later, tax reductions. A combination of these measures was a major feature in the expansionary package introduced after the 1978 Bonn Economic Summit. Critics, among whom were numbered the Council of Economic Advisers, stressed at this point the limits to demand management when, in their view, the problems were primarily structural in nature. The weakening of the growth rate, the failure to reduce unemployment significantly below 900,000, and the beginnings of an upturn in the inflation rate, were all interpreted as so much evidence of the onset of stagflationary conditions. *Investitionsschwäche* – the failure to invest adequately in new capacity, in energy-efficient plant, in high-technology sectors – formed the focus of critical attention, as did weaknesses in the German labour market.

The subsequent pattern of events provided strong ammunition for such critics. The assumption of the 'locomotive role' in the second half of 1978 proved a major policy error to the extent that it was immediately followed by the Second Oil Shock. The

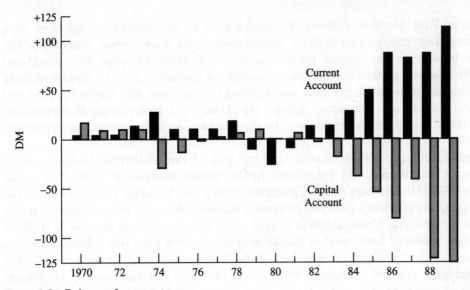

Figure 3.3 Balance of payments
Source: Council of Economic Advisers 1989

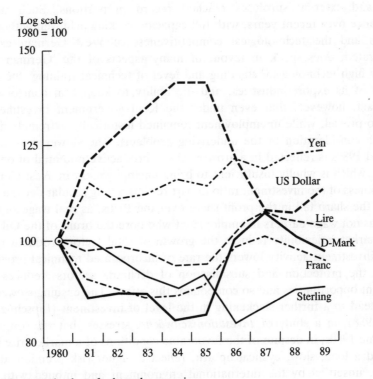

Figure 3.4 Real external value of selected currencies
Source: Council of Economic Advisers 1989
Note: Exchange rate-adjusted relative change in average export values against the 16 principal Western industrial countries weighted by their share in world exports.

boost to West German domestic demand led to an acceleration of inflation, to a yawning trade gap, and to the first depreciation of the deutschmark since 1951. The extra burden on the public purse breached the limits of what was considered supportable, and evoked fears of unsustainability in public finances. In the face of these stagflationary conditions the view that demand management had reached a dead-end became increasingly prevalent: and so the 'U-turn' in policy towards supply-side, 'monetarist' remedies was announced by the incoming Kohl government in September 1982.

Before turning to a necessarily brief analysis of the *underlying* problems, short reference may be made in parenthesis to the specific experience of the 1980s. The CDU–CSU/FDP coalition under Chancellor Kohl came to power in the depths of the recession, and pursued a policy of budgetary austerity alongside the tight money policy of the Bundesbank. Unemployment peaked at the end of 1983, but the slow haul out of recession produced little relief in the labour market. Only the price inflation indicator proved satisfactory. Export demand and home demand alternated in their contribution to aggregate demand (reflecting fluctuations in the DM/$ rate), while investment remained weak; the shift to rapid rates of growth of GDP of approximately 4 per cent per year from mid-1988 can be explained by the concurrent rise in domestic investment and foreign demand for German investment goods, reflecting partly the '1992' effect on business sentiment (SBGE 1989). In this last period, unemployment fell below 2 million and external surpluses reached record proportions. Such strong output performance over recent years, with full capacity working achieved without rising cost pressures and the technological competitiveness of West German exports amply demonstrated, does speak in favour of many aspects of the 'German model' – its generally high technological standing and level of technical training, the international presence of its export industries, and the ability to keep firm control over costs.

The fact, however, that even under the Kohl government investment weakness tended to prevail, while unemployment remained historically extremely high, leads us back to a consideration of the underlying problems. The slower growth path of the 1970s and 1980s is reflected in a growth rate of productive potential of only 2 per cent per year, which is wholly insufficient to bring unemployment in West Germany down. The weakness of the investment ratio in part reflects a long secular decline, but is also a result of the sharp fall in the profit share over the 1970s, as real wage rigidity ensured that it was not wage-earners in employment who bore the brunt of the Oil Shock. Such labour market inflexibility reduces the growth of total factor productivity, and more sluggish investment activity lowers the rate of incorporated technical progress. A third element, the protection and subsidisation of declining sectors, reduces growth and investment opportunities and so compounds this effect. The ensuing slower growth will of itself lead to a further slackening in the level of investment (Lipschitz et al 1989). Hinze (1988), in a study of *Investitionsschwäche*, stresses that the lower investment rates of the 1980s, in despite of the favourable conditions of a marked rise in the profits share and a long, slow, cyclical upturn, reflect a higher risk premium demanded by investors, unsettled by the international environment and imbued with the 'growth pessimism' which has prevailed in Germany.

In the labour market, the emergence of a high and sustained level of unemployment poses the question of whether the weaknesses of that market are due primarily to a deficiency in demand or to structural factors. The reorientation of policy away from Keynesian to supply-side remedies suggests that many see unemployment as primarily structural in origin. A range of studies, including that by Burda and Sachs (1987), have found, for example, the NAIRU (non-accelerating inflation rate of unemployment), in other words the hypothetical rate of unemployment compatible with a stable rate of inflation, to have risen broadly in line with the observed rate of unemployment. While this tendency may have frictional causes, studies have stressed the primary role of real wage rigidity, which has restricted the recruitment of unemployed people on any significant scale (see Barrow and Newell, Chapter 5 in this volume, on the UK, pp. 116–18). Real wage gaps, which measure the gap between the prevailing real wage level and that which would produce a desired level of employment, became substantial over the 1970s. There is disagreement as to whether substantial gaps of this nature still exist. It is a matter of record that wage moderation in the late 1970s led to real income falls in the trough of the recession, and to almost stationary unit wage costs throughout the 1980s, allowing the profit rate to recover.

Lastly, brief mention must be made of a recurring West German anxiety: whether the unsatisfactory investment rate, combined with certain institutional features, may have led to a growing technological backwardness of the export sector, in the face of strong US and Far Eastern competition. These concerns seem to come to the forefront of public debate in periods when the deutschmark has in fact been appreciating, as in the later 1970s and later 1980s. Studies by the Economics Ministry (BMWi 1984) and the Council of Economic Advisers (SBGE 1988) stress the difficulties surrounding any attempt at assessment, but point to the position of West Germany as the world's largest exporter, and to the breadth of its export range. In the very high technology sectors the technological competitiveness of West German industry is, certainly, low, and even in investment goods and chemicals its comparative advantage over the 1980s has receded somewhat. However, the record trade balances of recent years are in need of no improvement.

The next section in this chapter is devoted to the macroeconomic and structural policies and reforms pursued by the Kohl government, including Bundesbank policy. Subsections within it treat the conflicts over the thirty-five-hour week and between environmentalists and energy interests in the nuclear field. We finish with a discussion of the economic role of the Federal Republic in the EC and the economic prospects offered by German unification. There are in fact several links between the last two themes, of which the strategy over economic and monetary union is the most important. In an EC setting, the Federal Republic has argued over twenty years for a slow, parallel advance in the economic and monetary fields: in an all-German setting it has made the mistake, under an overwhelming political imperative, of proceeding at breakneck speed, with the resultant damage for all to see.

The supply-side policies of the Kohl government

The CDU–CSU/FDP coalition government of Chancellor Kohl came to power in September 1982 when the small liberal party broke with its SPD partner in government. The key issue in contention concerned the degree of budgetary tightness at a time when the economy was moving into deep recession. The FDP had pressed for a cut in public expenditure, and a restructuring of the budget to promote private investment. Public opinion seemed traumatised in 1981–2 by the deterioration in public finances, by the falling deutschmark and the external deficit. Influential commentators (Giersch 1983; Fels 1983; SBGE 1981) pointed to the need for reforms to overcome the structural impediments to growth and employment creation. Chancellor Kohl's programme of September 1982 embraced this diagnosis, and the U-turn (*Die Wende*) away from the demand management emphasis of the SPD shared much with the conservative revolutions in the USA and UK. Although vulgarly called 'monetarist', the approach must be understood against the background of the independence of the Deutsche Bundesbank in monetary policy: the Kohl programme rested on a medium-term framework for budgetary consolidation and tax reform, and on structural policy measures to strengthen market forces, especially in the labour market. Key elements are therefore to be found in the budget laws of 1983 and 1984, the tax reforms of the second half of the decade, the privatisation programme announced in 1983, and the Employment Promotion Law of 1985. More recently, the health and pension reforms of 1989 should be seen as continuing attempts to rein back social expenditure.

Overall, we can say that macroeconomic policy has contributed to supply-side improvements through its price stability successes, its re-establishment of a healthy profit rate, and the marked improvement of the financial position of the corporate sector. Many elements of the programme remain to be completed, however, especially in the domains of taxation, subsidies and structural policy. After eight years of the Kohl government in power, this testifies to the difficulties of reaching a consensus in a federation in which responsibility for *Strukturpolitik* rests primarily with the *Länder*.

Budgetary consolidation, subsidies and social security reform

It was held by many that the misconceived use of budgetary stimuli (namely the failure to achieve balance over the cycle) had harmed private business investment and so led to poor growth prospects. 'Expectations-induced crowding-out', as the Council of Economic Advisers formulated it, meant that the net stimulus to aggregate demand of a public budget deficit might be negative, because increased uncertainty, fears of tax increases and a weakening currency, in addition to the interest rate effect of public borrowing, harmed investment and consumption. The beneficial 'crowding-in' effect on private business investment would arise if, by contrast, budget deficits and public borrowing were cut (so reducing long-term interest rates) and real wage moderation contributed to a rise in the real return to capital. This expansion of private investment would, it was held, more than compensate for the short-term deflation of demand arising from budgetary stringency.

The objectives of budgetary consolidation were, then, to reduce the ratios of public expenditure, taxation and public debt to GNP. This was broadly the task of 'quantitative' consolidation, while the later phase of 'qualitative' consolidation would reduce and restructure taxation to improve incentives, and would shift the balance of public expenditure towards investment at the expense of public consumption. No official targets were published, but attention focused on the need for the eradication of the 'structural' deficit (those fiscal imbalances that would have prevailed if the economy had grown along its 'normal' trend, rather than experiencing cyclical fluctuations) (Lipschitz et al 1989).

The containment of expenditure package focused on reductions in state benefits and holding down rises in public sector salaries. In terms of benefits, the 1983 and 1984 budgets delayed increases in state pensions, reduced early retirement pensions and cut maternity pay. Contributions to the unemployment insurance fund were raised, and workers had to fulfil a longer qualifying period in order to claim unemployment benefit. There were also cuts in contributions to the pension fund schemes of the unemployed by the Federal Labour Office. Further cuts in social assistance for unemployed people, and the transfer of the long-term unemployed to the social security system from the unemployment insurance scheme, ensured that for the first time in a number of years the Federal Labour Office budget moved into surplus (Owen Smith 1989). At the same time, investment allowances were increased, a housebuilding programme instituted, youth training expanded, and in 1984 a law on the promotion of venture capital was passed.

Looking back, the Kohl government does seem to have been successful in budgetary consolidation. The structural budget deficit on general government account had been eradicated by 1985 (going from −2.5 per cent of GNP to +0.1 per cent in 1985) and the public expenditure ratio (general government expenditure/nominal GDP) fell from a 1982 peak of 49.8 to 46.4 per cent in 1988; in 1989 a public sector surplus of 0.2 per cent of GNP was achieved. But within this general evolution there does appear to be a marked change from 1986, when a shift from quantitative to qualitative consolidation occurred (OECD 1989). In mid-decade, international pressure on West Germany to relax its budgetary stance was intense, as the US dual deficits built up, and the 1987 stock exchange crash fuelled fears of international recession. Domestically, there were persuasive arguments for a change of course: first, spending pressures for infrastructure and health and education investments were building up at *Land* levels; second, partly because public investment had been squeezed, the deficit reduction had not elicited the 'crowding-in' of private investment as forecast. The emphasis shifted to tax reform, as a way of inducing higher growth rates through improved work incentives. The implementation of a three-stage reform, involving net tax reliefs of DM 11 billion in 1986, DM 14 billion in 1988 (including DM 5 billion brought forward as part of the 1987 Louvre Accord – see p. 44) and DM 24 billion in 1990, substantially reduced state revenues.

Although there have been fluctuations in both revenue and expenditure components in the period since 1982, the broad pattern can be clearly detected. Within general government expenditure, the previously rapid growth of social transfers and government consumption has been reined back, while public investment has been cut drastically. In contrast, the share of subsidies had grown to 4.8 per cent in 1988 from 3.7 per cent in 1982. The share of debt-service costs has also risen sharply, reflecting deficits and high real interest rates. On the revenue side, slow but steady economic growth has made a contribution, while the marked fluctuations in the Bundesbank profits transferred to the government account have had a substantial impact on the final balance. The successive stages of tax reform have, of course, cut revenues substantially. The budget surplus for 1989 was, therefore, the result of a favourable but temporary set of circumstances, and does not alter the broad conclusion that there has been a shift away from quantitative consolidation. OECD (1989) seeks to compare the outcome with the implicit assumption in 1982 government financial plans of a growth of nominal general government expenditure of 3 per cent per year and the achievement of a budget surplus by 1988. Allowing for intervening tax changes and fluctuating Bundesbank profits, it would appear that the budget was broadly in balance by 1988, rather than in surplus as the plans intended.

If we stand back from the financial detail, however, it is apparent that in two interrelated ways the policy has been less than successful. The failure to cut subsidies has weighed heavily on public investments in economic and social overhead capital, which has depressed growth prospects. In turn, the rate of 'crowding-in' of private business investment has disappointed, principally because long-term real interest rates have scarcely fallen, while investors have raised their risk premia. The claim by Fels and Fröhlich (1987) that the sustained upturn since the end of 1982 is evidence of the correctness of Kohl's policy is not well founded: private business investment and consumption were major components in the rise in aggregate demand in 1983, but were superseded in 1984 and 1985 primarily by export demand from the USA.

Subsidies, and the Kohl government's failure to cut them back, have been a principal target for criticism. Business subsidies increased steadily in nominal terms (to DM 31.4 billion in 1989), though not as a share of GNP. Comparing subsidy: GNP ratios within the EC, the German level of 2.1 per cent turns out to be among the lowest. Most subsidisation takes place outside the manufacturing sector – in agriculture, coal-mining, the railways and housing. The 20 per cent which does flow to manufacturing is directed either to structurally weak branches (iron and steel, shipbuilding) or to 'sunrise' industries (OECD 1989). For example in 1986 the Federal Research and Technology Ministry spent DM 7.6 billion in aid, while slightly more was spent by the Economics Ministry (subsidies for coal and nuclear energy, shipbuilding, aerospace and export guarantees). It is readily apparent that such subsidies are anything but temporary, in contradiction of the 'Schiller guidelines' issued on aid to industry in 1968.

Through the 1970s the scope of financial intervention grew rapidly as Japanese and NIC competition came to be felt keenly, and as Bonn lost trade policy decision-making prerogatives to Brussels. Regional aid and R&D support (nuclear technologies, aerospace, computing) rose steadily. The seemingly intractable problems of declining industry apart, the R&D programme attracted heavy criticism, since it was very narrowly focused and benefited a clutch of dominant enterprises. Calculations of the scale of financial assistance vary for definitional reasons. The figure quoted above (2.1 per cent of GNP) covers only 'general government subsidies', while the wider national accounts definition (3.7 per cent) includes capital transfers. The government *Subsidy Report* also includes tax reliefs, to give a total of 4 per cent. Widest of all in its catchment is an approach which includes the *Kohlepfennig* support to coal, CAP support and transfers to the federal post and railways. This brings the figure up to over 6 per cent of GNP (Jüttemeier 1987). Given the degree of decentralisation of decision-making in this area – there are over 10,000 budget headings for the grant of business aid – reform is a wearisome business, and meets the resistance of the *Länder*, which, as we saw, are primarily responsible for *Strukturpolitik*.

The tax and social security reforms form an intrinsic part of the programme for the consolidation of public finances, with the tax reform at least designed to offer incentives to improved resource allocation. While the bulk of the effort has so far focused on changes to the personal taxation regime, reforms are pending on corporation tax and the regional redistribution of tax revenues (*Länderfinanzausgleich*). The tax reform of 1986–90 offered net tax reliefs amounting to DM 48.5 billion in three stages. It was designed to address the very high marginal rate of taxation for middle-income earners, to simplify the regime and eliminate its distortions. In the process, cuts in the thicket of allowances, together with some promised subsidy cuts, were calculated to save the fisc DM 19.4 billion per year. The effect by 1990 has been to introduce a linear progressive tax scale which reduces marginal rates over the whole income range. The entry rate of taxation has been reduced from 22 to 19 per cent and basic personal and child allowances have been raised. As to the incentive effects of such changes, these remain hotly disputed, with the distribution of the benefits obviously depending on occupational and family status.

Within the social security system, the major reforms have concerned the pensions system and health insurance. While pensions reform takes a medium-term view, urgent changes in the health sector were imperative to rein back escalating costs. Social security contributions have risen steadily and now amount to 17.25 per cent of GNP, and the burden of these is felt keenly by wage-earners and employers alike. The Pension Reform of 1989 introduced fundamental changes to a 100-year-old system grounded in the principle of self-financing. In recent years, federal contributions to cover deficits, along with rising pension contribution rates, have signalled the growing difficulties of maintaining a high benefit system among an ageing population. Demographic forecasts have simply confirmed fears that by the end of the century the burden of the old on the working population would impose insupportable contribution rates if the present structure of benefits were to be maintained. The reform therefore links benefits more closely to the evolution of effective wages (ie that pensions will be adjusted to net wages) and it raises the retirement age gradually to a uniform 65 years for men and women, though early retirement provisions will remain. The federal government hopes to stabilise its contribution at a more or less fixed proportion: after 1992, its payments will be linked to general income trends and to the evolution of contribution rates (OECD 1989).

The 1989 Law on the Structural Reform of the Public Health System is the culmination of a series of attempts to reform the sector stretching back to 1977. As much as 6 per cent of GNP is spent on the social security-financed part of the health sector, through an insurance-based system which has met directly almost all of the costs incurred by the insured. Escalation in the costs of health provision is a common problem throughout the West, arising from a lack of cost consciousness on the part of consumers and insufficient cost discipline on suppliers. The technology intensity of modern medicine has been a further factor driving costs upwards. In West Germany the dual-financing of the hospital system, whereby capital costs are borne by the Federation and running costs by the insurance funds, was modified by the 1985 Hospital Financing Reform. However, the system continues to come under heavy fire for its bias towards oversupply, through poor planning at *Land* level (Aufderheide 1990). The 1989 reform has sought cost savings by cutting some benefits and increasing cost-sharing on the part of consumers, while at the same time balancing this with cuts in contribution rates. Measures to raise cost efficiency include fixed price contracts, audits of hospital accounts, and increased reliance on home-based care.

The monetary and exchange rate policies of the Deutsche Bundesbank

The exceptional West German achievements in price stability during the 1980s owe much to the cautious and relatively steady policy of the Bundesbank, which gives signals to wage negotiators and affects expectations of all economic agents. Another factor has been the favourable shift in the terms of trade arising from the fall in dollar oil prices. The independence of the Bundesbank does not mean, however, that its decisions have been free from political dispute. Both at the beginning and in the second half of the decade its stance was criticised as being by turns too lax and then too severe. In this section, we shall focus on monetary targeting, the target aggregates and the *post hoc* nature of Bundesbank controls. We finish by looking at the deutschmark within the European Monetary System (EMS), and at German objectives in the moves towards EC monetary union. However, a short history of Bundesbank policy is first required to provide the necessary context.

The decade opened with a long period of monetary tightness, beginning at the end of 1979, when the central bank lowered its monetary growth targets and raised its leading interest rates, following a dear money policy in spite of the gathering recession. This decidedly procyclical action was taken after the Second Oil Shock, but should be seen as an atonement for a period of monetary laxness through the later 1970s, when monetary targets were consistently overshot. That occurred especially in 1978, in the context of the 'locomotive role' policy, which was also calculated to have the desired effect of moderating the rate of appreciation of the deutschmark. (This policy was repeated in 1987 in far more restrained form as a consequence of the Louvre Accord, which sought concerted action by the leading industrialised countries to stabilise the dollar, and of the international stock exchange crash of that year.) The errors of the locomotive role period ushered in a period of policy tightness to 1983. That cooled inflationary pressures at the expense of a serious exacerbation of the recession. It did, however, establish the bases for relative price stability throughout the decade.

Through the 1980s money stock growth targets were only one-half those of the 1970s and, with the exceptions of 1986 and 1987, were clearly met. In the years 1984 and 1985 targets were oriented to the underlying growth rate of production potential, whereas in 1986 and 1987 monetary relaxation, with a view to moderating the rise in the deutschmark and offering the dollar support, prevailed (see Figure 3.5). In this clear subordination of domestic price stability to an exchange rate objective, the Bundesbank was going beyond mere fulfilment of its Louvre Accord responsibilities: it was responding to the heavy pressure exerted by its EMS partners to counter excessive dollar depreciation, which was placing the EMS cross-rates under great strain. The fear by 1988 was that excess deutschmark liquidity had been allowed to build up, considerably in excess of nominal GDP. With the strengthening of the dollar in mid-1988, policy was tightened markedly.

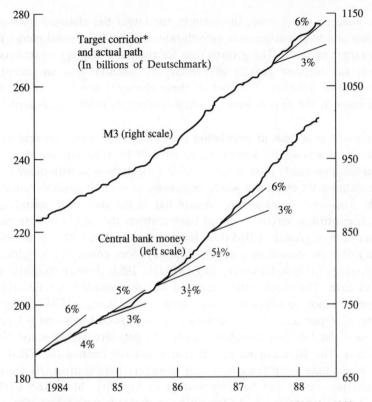

Note: *The target corridor applied to central bank money up to 1987; for 1988, the corridor applies to M3

Figure 3.5   Central Bank money and broad money (M3)
    Source: Deutsche Bundesbank, *Monthly Report, Supplement 4*, various issues, quoted in Lipschitz et al 1989: 9

A target for money stock growth was first set by the Bundesbank in December 1974. Prior to this, under the earlier Bretton Woods system of fixed exchange rates, the German target variable in monetary control had been the free liquid reserves of the domestic banks (unused rediscount quotas, reserves in excess of minimum reserve requirements, foreign currency holdings, and holdings of domestic money market paper), which constituted 'potential' credit creation. The main instruments for influencing this variable had been liquidity policy instruments, principally changes in the minimum reserve requirement. The active use of interest rates had been shown by bitter experience to increase the scale of destabilising flows of speculative money across the exchanges. This had had the self-defeating effect of expanding the West German money supply, unless sterilisation took place. The collapse of the Bretton Woods agreement freed Germany from policy constraints of this nature.

Persuaded that the earlier relationship between free liquid reserves and credit creation had broken down, the Bundesbank instituted the targeting of the central bank money stock (CBM). It hoped, in the first place, that this would have an important announcement and confidence-building effect. At the time, accelerating inflation arising from the oil price rise, and aggravated by domestic wage settlements, was giving rise to grave concern. Over time, the form of the target has changed from an annual average growth rate to a year-on-year growth rate. In 1988 M3 (broad money) replaced CBM as the target variable. The growth rate for the monetary aggregate incorporates two elements: the forecast growth of production potential and an acceptable and unavoidable level of inflation. The first of these elements acts to exert an automatic stabilising linkage to the real economy, when it diverges from the 'potential' growth path.

CBM comprises total cash in circulation plus the banks' minimum reserves held at the Bundesbank. It was adopted as target variable in 1974 because its income velocity of circulation had previously proved fairly stable (in comparison with other aggregates) and because data on its evolution were, of course, also more readily available to the central bank. This form of monetary control has in the past been misinterpreted as monetary base control, whereby a central bank restricts the supply of base money to a predetermined rate of growth. CBM does have close affinities with the monetary base, but it should rather be viewed as a weighted money stock concept: a weighted average of the components of broad money, M3 (MRDB 1985; 1988a) comprising a large component of cash. The other components of M3 are included in CBM through the minimum reserve ratios, to which they were subjected in January 1974 (16.6 per cent of sight deposits, 12.4 per cent of time deposits and borrowed funds and 8.1 per cent of savings deposits: the last two categories limited to deposits having maturities of less than four years). The Bundesbank line is that it did not control the CBM supply in advance, as would have been the case under monetary base control. As lender of last resort it could not starve the banking system of liquidity. Since the CBM it was targeting in any given period had already been created, its control was essentially retrospective, or *post hoc*.

Under the CBM system, therefore, the Bundesbank acted to influence the demand for money through interest rates, and to influence banks' willingness to offer credit by affecting the profitability of credit business. Using instruments available to most central banks, it intervened in the money market through the medium of open-market operations, primarily by securities repurchase agreements, so as to influence bank liquidity and therefore the CBM needs of the banking system. The minimum reserve requirement instrument of credit control tended to lose its independent importance and to become increasingly simply an adjunct to interest rate policy, since the minimum reserves deposited with the central bank did not attract interest and so affected bank profitability directly.

It will be apparent that the adoption of M3 as the target variable in 1988 represented no fundamental change, since M3 and CBM move in parallel over the longer term. Because M3 encompasses portfolio shifts, it fluctuates less with short-term interest rate changes. Most important, it is better known internationally.

It is sometimes suggested that the Bundesbank has pursued domestic monetary policy objectives with little regard for its international obligations. Such assertions ignore the fact that the deutschmark is the world's third investment and reserve currency, and that Germany is highly export-dependent. We have already alluded to the fact that exchange rate considerations have at times seemed paramount – to the extent that policy under the later years of the Bretton Woods era was acknowledged to be externally constrained (Emminger 1977). Likewise, the wide fluctuations of the deutschmark against the dollar under floating exchange rates have forced the Bundesbank into painful choices to avoid serious deutschmark misalignment, even where this has conflicted with domestic price stability objectives. The debate in the counsels of the European Monetary System about the 'asymmetry' of its operation (see Sumner, Chapter 8 in *The European Economy*, on European monetary integration) encapsulates this conflict.

The EMS is said to operate asymmetrically, in that the burden of adjustment falls on countries with weaker currencies rather on those with stronger: this imparts a deflationary bias to the system, with priority given to price stability over economic growth. The asymmetry is not intrinsic to the system, but arises from the way in which the Bundesbank has interpreted the currency intervention rules. At the inception of the EMS in 1979, many Germans feared being drawn into an 'inflation community' whereby they would once again lose firm control of domestic monetary policy by having to buy up weak currencies. In practice, no such threat has been manifest, as the EMS has operated as a deutschmark-dominated bloc. Until the French policy U-turn in March 1983 (when 'Keynesianism in one country' was abandoned), tensions in the system were accommodated through realignments, and there has since been a progressive convergence in performance towards the low German inflation rate (as well as towards the relatively low German growth rate).

The deutschmark has acted as anchor to the system, with its rate of issue reflecting primarily domestic German price stability objectives. The Bundesbank has been reluctant to intervene to support weaker currencies (and so validate inflationary pressures originating in other member countries), leaving intra-marginal intervention to other central banks. Likewise, it has refused to change its policy on the composition of its reserves in the direction of holding more of the weaker Community currencies. Through the earlier years, other member states were willing to subordinate their domestic monetary autonomy by linking to the deutschmark anchor, because this visible commitment eased the real economic costs of disinflation. There were, of course, benefits for the Federal Republic: the system forbade competitive devaluations by its main EC trading partners, thereby stabilising German competitiveness. The EMS also reduced the deutschmark exposure to dollar fluctuations. Finally, it gave Bonn and Frankfurt substantial influence over the macroeconomic priorities of the EC member states.

Once disinflation had been largely achieved (with the aid of the oil price collapse of the mid-1980s), attention turned to the need to restart growth, and the slow growth of Germany, the principal trading partner of the rest of the Community, now appeared as a major constraint. To induce a more expansionary credit policy by the Bundesbank, France and Italy directed heavy criticism at its failure to intervene in the form of intra-marginal currency support, and to hold weaker currencies in its reserves. This hostility was lessened by the September 1987 Basle–Nyborg agreement, which extended the very short-term financing facility of the European Monetary Cooperation Fund to cover intra-marginal interventions. Indeed, the Bundesbank undertook concerted action with other EC central banks twice at the end of 1987. However, such concessions were diplomatic, for the German central bank continues to insist that its discretion remains absolute, since its approval is still needed for interventions against a rising deutschmark, which would involve an expansion of the supply of deutschmark, with possible liquidity effects within Germany. The French resumed their criticisms in 1988 and early 1989 in the Franco-German Finance Council, an organ which the Bundesbank sees as part of an explicit French design to dislodge it from its dominant role (Kloten 1988).

The contention over 'asymmetry' is instructive, since it helps us to understand German fears and German objectives in the movement towards European monetary union. Bundesbank representatives (Kloten 1988; Pöhl 1988) have laid great stress on the autonomous status of a future European central bank and on its commitment above all else to price stability: in fact, a system which promised less would not be passed by the Bundestag, which would have to repeal the 1957 Bundesbank Law. There are tensions in Germany over the strategy to be adopted in this connection, as indeed there are over German economic and monetary union. Foreign Minister Genscher (1989), for example, puts more stress on the political desirability of EC monetary union and its role as an essential accompaniment to the Single Market programme. EMU would also, of course, anchor a newly unified Germany in the West. Subsequent German assessments of the Delors Report proposals of April 1989 on Economic and Monetary Union in the Community support the Report's underlying principles and final objectives, but question the soundness of the intervening stages proposed. Both Hasse (1989) and the Council of Economic Advisers (SBGE 1989) focus on three inadequacies. There are only weak provisions for achieving independence of central banks at a sufficiently early stage; there is a risk that co-ordination will lead to currency stability at the expense of price stability; and there are insufficient controls over budget deficit financing, which could raise the common inflation rate in the EC. These fundamental German points of principle are asserted in forthright manner by the Bundesbank in its review of the commencement of stage I of the Delors Plan (MRDB 1990).

The deregulation and privatisation strategies of the federal government

The contribution of microeconomic reforms to improvements in supply-side conditions has been slow and inadequate, and is widely regarded as the major failure among the Kohl government's policies. Without surviving impediments to efficient resource allocation, growth and employment would have been higher, and this would have contributed to external adjustment, by raising domestic absorption. As if in acknowledgement of these policy failures, the federal government appointed in 1988 an expert 'Deregulation Commission' to assess the cost of regulations and to propose steps to minimise them. For those who naively equate the German practice of the 'social market economy' with market liberalism tempered by a social commitment, the degree of regulation and corporatism which actually exists may well be a cause for surprise. Only the traded goods sector has been relatively free from intervention (exceptions are classic declining branches and aerospace), while services have been closely regulated without interruption since the Weimar Republic. Wider social goals such as consumer protection (in the case of finance), protection of the railways (justifying controls on road haulage), and uniformity of service (telecommunications) have provided the grounds for intervention. Until very recently finance, utilities and transport were exempt from the *Kartellgesetz* anti-trust provisions.

Nationalisation as a tool of industrial policy has been abjured during the post-war period, and every effort was made to avoid anything more than a quasi-nationalisation during the coal crisis of 1967, when Ruhrkohle AG was formed. Most public industrial holdings are inherited from the pre-war period. Public enterprises are found in a narrow range of branches, reflecting, for example, employment objectives in structurally weak regions, the control of natural monopoly in the utilities, housing policy, or technological objectives in the nuclear industry. Privatisation policies were first introduced in the late 1950s (Owen Smith 1983). The Kohl government resurrected this policy line in 1983, with a list of proposed sales of public assets which covered 100 state-owned companies with 900 subsidiaries. After hard bargaining at federal and *Land* levels, this was pared down to twelve candidates. Three principles underlie this programme: first, publicly owned enterprises should complement private activities rather than substitute for them; second, the sale of public assets should be gradual; third, public companies should be made profitable before sale.

The federal government has now divested itself of its major industrial holdings (in terms of turnover and employment), though the municipalities and *Länder* retain sizeable interests. Proceeds of privatisation for the period 1984–9 amounted to DM 9.7 billion and many companies were fully privatised, of which the largest were VIAG (electricity, chemicals, aluminium), VEGA (energy and chemicals), and the Salzgitter AG steel company. The federal government sold its stake in Volkswagen and reduced its stake in Lufthansa, although state participation in this latter case remains important. The Bavarian *Land* government did, indeed, strongly resist the sale of Lufthansa, for fear that it would damage the market outlets of Deutsche Airbus AG, which is based in the southern state. This serves to exemplify the widespread conflicts of interest which can come to the fore in a federation, and which may result in a slowing of structural change.

Turning to the deregulation of protected services, the pressures for liberalisation have originated to a good degree from the process of globalisation, as well as from the EC Single Market programme. It will come as no surprise to the reader that those service activities in which the greatest changes have occurred (telecommunications, transport, finance), are those for which decisions and directives have been issued by Brussels. At the same time the multinationalisation of firms has also been an important force. Subsequent reports by OECD and the Council of Economic Advisers have analysed these issues in detail. In outline, the main changes within Germany have been in transport, telecommunications and finance.

Transport

In transport both passenger and goods carriage have in the past been subject to detailed regulation. Long-distance road haulage has been subject to licensing, and to the setting of price brackets. Sub-optimal-sized firms and inefficiencies arising from empty return journeys have typically been the result (SBGE 1988). The economic costs are manifest both in freight rates, which are estimated to be 30–40 per cent higher than they would be under decontrolled conditions, and in monopoly rents accruing to licensed operators, since licences change hands at a high premium. Cross-border trucking has been subject to licensing, and so-called 'cabotage' (plying for trade within

Germany by foreign hauliers) has been forbidden. The cost to German industry is estimated at DM 12 million. Following wearisome negotiations in Brussels, these controls on prices, licences and cross-border movements will be abolished progressively, with full liberalisation by 1993. However, the German government is insisting on a harmonisation of road taxation and of legislation governing working conditions in parallel with this opening up of the market.

Telecommunications

In telecommunications the Bundespost held until very recently the legal monopoly for telecommunications services, including the market for related equipment. Through its uniform technology (*Einheitstechnik*) agreements with German suppliers, it effectively excluded foreign equipment manufacturers, to the extent that Siemens alone supplied three-quarters of the German telecoms equipment market. Prices for users were consequently high, especially for international calls, and it was commonly asserted that the Bundespost could not keep pace with the rapidity of changes in technology and demand. The EC Commission's Green Paper of June 1987 called for the liberalisation of the market, especially in equipment, but also for a limiting of monopoly to voice transmission. The Witte Commission, which reported to the federal government in the autumn of 1987, offered a compromise which reflected the strength of SPD and postal union feelings on the relaxation of the Bundespost monopoly. Subsequent deliberations led to major changes in the Bundespost statutes, brought into effect by the Post Office and Telecommunication Reform Act 1989. Not only is Deutsche Telekom now an autonomous, wholly owned subsidiary of the Bundespost, but also it has lost its monopoly over supply of terminal equipment and value-added services. It retains the voice telephony monopoly and the accompanying obligation to provide a telephone service throughout the Republic under a uniform price structure. Other services such as satellite and mobile radio communication will be opened up to the private sector. Private companies may now bid to supply services which by statute must be offered throughout the territory, namely teletext and data transmission. In comparison with the reforms in the USA, UK and Japan, this package is, of course, more modest in scale (Aufderheide 1990; SBGE 1987, 1988; von Weizsäcker and Wieland 1988).

Finance

In finance regulatory changes affect the German regional stock exchanges, the insurance industry and domestic banking. The last has been subject to two major EC banking directives in the context of the Single Market programme. The small role played by the stock exchanges in financing the capital needs of the corporate sector reflects in part the long, secular tradition of universal banking, whereby the Big Three (Deutsche, Dresdner, Commerzbank) conduct relationship banking with their industrial clients, acting as house banks and often having holdings in the client firm. The fact that comparatively few companies have a stock exchange listing also reflects the high underwriting costs and reporting requirements entailed. With the buoyant stock markets of the 1980s, however, the regional stock markets (dominated in turnover by

Frankfurt, with Düsseldorf far behind) came to embrace reform in an attempt to rival Paris as the main continental centre. As a first step, a new regulated market was created in 1987, which was less demanding in its reporting requirements and involved substantially lower commission charges. The Deutsche Terminbörse, or futures market, began operation in January 1990, and financial instruments such as swaps and CDs (certificates of deposit) were introduced for the first time in the late 1980s. Major costs in the form of the stock exchange turnover tax (to be abolished in 1991–2) and the penalty on the early resale of government securities remain the focus of debate; the ill-fated withholding tax on interest income survived briefly, and was a major cause of capital flight until its abolition in July 1989. Finally, the insurance market, which has been very heavily regulated, and from which non-German suppliers have been effectively excluded, will be subjected to great upheavals as a result of European Court cases and Brussels directives. Until recently, each insurance business area was separately regulated and no insurance company could supply more than one market. Hence an oligopolistic structure developed in each, and conglomerates formed to cover several markets. As a result, German insurance premia are very high by EC standards. Foreign insurers could offer a service only if they had a German subsidiary, a situation which clearly offended against the Treaty of Rome provisions for the free supply of services. Following a European Court decision in the early 1980s, British insurers were able to compete in the business of large commercial risks, but the supply of life assurance remains closely regulated (Lipschitz et al 1989).

In other areas of commercial life tight regulations abound, notably on shop opening hours and the supply of professional services, but it is in the regulation of the labour market that the principal remaining rigidities are to be found.

Inflexibilities in the labour market and employment strategies

As we have already seen, unemployment rose rapidly after the two Oil Shocks and it stayed, through most of the 1980s, at the 9 per cent level, falling below 2 million only in 1989. As the federal government sees this problem to be primarily structural in origin, it has directed its efforts towards the alleviation of labour market rigidity, and towards retraining and a reduction in the size of the work-force by early retirement. In stark contrast, the trade unions have pushed, with considerable negotiating success, for a reduction in the working week towards the goal of thirty-five hours. This they have done on the basis of the argument that cutting supply per head, for a given volume of work, will substantially increase recruitment from the army of unemployed.

Labour market rigidity in West Germany is often ascribed to the centralised nature of collective bargaining and to labour laws. Unlike in the case of the UK, unions are organised on an industrial basis, with the DGB (*Deutscher Gewerkschaftsbund*) union confederation comprising seventeen members. The approach to wage determination is legalistic, and contracts are legally enforceable. Collective bargaining over wage rates and conditions of employment takes place at a relatively high level between the employers' association for the given industry and the industry union. At local level, negotiations between management and the works council cover, for example, the organisation of working time, and therefore encompass actual earnings paid. Workers' co-determination in the works council and on the supervisory board are essential elements of this substantially consensual system (Koch 1989).

It is not, however, institutions alone which promote 'responsible' trade unionism and the remarkable wage moderation which one finds in West Germany. There is relatively broad agreement (although this broke down from the end of the 1960s to the mid-1970s) on the need for productivity improvements to finance wage rises, if inflation and unemployment are to be kept at bay. The 'cost-neutral' wage settlement is far better understood than in Britain. This is not, however, to deny that a real wage rigidity problem still exists in spite of pronounced real wage moderation over the last decade. The OECD (1987) and IMF (Lipschitz et al 1989) stressed through the 1980s the downwards rigidity of real wages in the face of labour market disequilibria, and pointed to legal and institutional features which obstruct flexibility.

In the Federal Republic of Germany, centrally negotiated wage agreements apply to union and non-union members alike, and are binding on all employers who are association members. There have also been significant extensions of the wage contract system within the services sector, which has a much lower union density. The general effect has been to introduce a wage floor, so that the labour made redundant from manufacturing has not been absorbed by the services sector. Rather, the response in services has been to raise capital intensity. Other impediments to an adequate supply-side response include the narrowness of inter-industry and regional wage differentials, the high replacement ratio (of unemployment benefit to net of tax pay), the legal obstructions to and costs of redundancy, high non-wage costs, and housing market difficulties.

Since the federal government has direct influence only over the wage levels of public employees, its policy has had a threefold focus. It has made legislative changes to the conditions of employment; it has sought to reduce the supply of labour by early retirement; and it has sought to raise the training level of the unemployed. Key changes were introduced by the Employment Promotion Act 1985:

1 The unrestricted opportunity (until 1990) for employers to recruit staff on fixed-term contracts of up to eighteen months' duration.
2 An easing of the redundancy provisions which specify obligatory payments in the form of a 'social plan'. Firms of fewer than twenty employees were now exempted from the 'social plan' requirement, and if appropriate alternative employment had been offered to the potentially redundant employee, no severance payment had to be paid.
3 Part-time workers and job-sharers were henceforth to be offered the same working conditions as full-timers.

Legislative changes were also made in 1986 to the Work Promotion Act 1969. These focused on the problems of the older unemployed worker, and on the need for a 'training offensive'. For older unemployed people, the period of unemployment benefit was extended, while at the same time two-year wage subsidies were made available to firms recruiting such workers. The training offensive was directed at younger unemployed people, and sought to promote both occupational and regional mobility.

Measures such as these had the effect of reducing the number of registered unemployed people by over 440,000 by 1987. The Early Retirement Act 1984 introduced the '58 rule', which extended pension payments to those of 58 years of age and over whose job could be filled by an unemployed person. As much as 35 per cent of the early retirement pension costs borne by the employer would be reimbursed by the state. This provision remained valid until 1988 (Owen Smith 1989).

Paragraph 116 of the Work Promotion Act 1986 raised great passions among union militants by its modification of the legislation governing strikes. Its effect was to withhold lay-off pay from union members temporarily laid-off as a result of a strike elsewhere conducted by their own union. This legal change was stimulated primarily by the fact that during the seven-week-old strike pursued by I G Metall and I G Druck und Papier in 1984 in favour of a thirty-five-hour week, union members in non-striking regions were able to claim lay-off pay and so prolong the conflict.

Coming now to the issue of the thirty-five-hour week, it is quite apparent that the goal is in sight for the engineering and print unions, after a first attempt by steelworkers in 1978. Wage agreements in 1990 in Baden-Württemberg provide for a phased move to thirty-five hours by 1995, but contain provision for up to 18 per cent of the work-force to work extra hours up to a forty-hour week if they desire. Having achieved agreement in 1984 to a cut to thirty-eight and a half hours and then to thirty-seven hours for 1988, I G Metall (closely followed by the print union) has set the negotiating agenda for other unions. In 1984 I G Metall argued that a reduction in the working week from forty to thirty-five hours would create (on the most favourable assumptions) 2.8 million jobs, and so absorb most of the unemployed people; it argued that the cut to thirty-seven hours had already created or secured almost 200,000 jobs in metal-working alone. These optimistic calculations seem to rest on a simple association between the total demand for labour, the working week and work-force size. In reality, the variables at work are complex and difficult to estimate (Pätzhold 1989; Franz 1984). Even were output to remain constant, a full assessment would have to take account of the effects on unit labour costs of shorter working time, the relative influence of autonomous productivity changes and those induced by more flexible working, as well as induced effects on labour supply potential because of possibly higher hourly wage rates.

In negotiations, German unions have insisted on 'full wage compensation' – that is, nominal weekly pay should remain unaffected by the cut in hours. In practice, to offset adverse effects on labour costs, cuts in hours have been 'productivity-oriented', meaning that the shorter working time is supposed to be offset by annual productivity gains. If, in this context, wage increases fail to keep pace with inflation (as measured by the GDP deflator), then a shift in income shares in favour of profits will be the result. For part of the 1980s this did, indeed, occur, and real wages rose modestly, supported by terms of trade changes (principally falling world oil prices). German employers, for their part, have insisted in the course of these negotiations on greater flexibility in working practices, in particular over the use of part-time workers, and on Saturday working. The effect, even by 1986, was to increase machine-running time by about 10 per cent, with marked beneficial effects on unit capital costs and profits. These multi-year wages and hours agreements have in practice, then, been conducive to notable wage moderation and stable unit costs. Whether large numbers of workers are recruited as a result remains doubtful, since productivity improvements have, in the event, matched cuts in hours.

Policies for energy and the environment

The interrelatedness of these two fields extends further than conflicts in objectives, for similar questions of policy orientation arise in both: how much scope to leave to market-based adjustment, and how much regulation to impose and in what form? The two-decades-long battle in West Germany between environmentalists and the consortium of energy interests has resulted in an undeclared victory for the former, since the nuclear energy programme has been brought to an extremely costly halt, and a 'green' awareness now suffuses all public debate. After other successful battles over power station and car emissions to cut acid rain, the focus of 'green' demands has switched to energy-saving, and to the use of non-carbon dioxide producing, non-nuclear, fuels (Michelsen 1988; Müschen and Romberg 1986). Official discourse on energy policy never ceases to stress its market orientation: no price controls or quotas for petroleum imports, minimal regulation of the domestic petroleum supply industry, dependence on price and financial inducements for energy efficiency. In practice, support for coal distorts the policy fundamentally, and the accumulated public financial commitments to the nuclear industry have prolonged government support for the nuclear option, in spite of widespread hostility among the electorate.

Protection for domestically produced coal in the form of import quotas and subsidies has been a feature of most of the post-war period. A marked strengthening of domestic preference was introduced after the coal crisis of 1966–7, just at the time when the SPD came to power in Bonn. In 1967 legislation was passed limiting coal imports from non-EC countries to 6 million tonnes annually; concurrently, legal provisions were introduced to ensure that the electricity utilities relied for one-half of their primary energy needs on domestic coal. The subsidy which bridged the price differential with imported fuel was, after 1974, met through a tax on electricity prices to the consumer – the so-called *Kohlepfennig*, which now represents 8.5 per cent of consumers' bills. Utilities are committed to taking 47.5 million tonnes of domestic coal to 1995, under the so-called *Jahrhundertvertrag*. And the steel industry has likewise been constrained to burn domestic coking coal. The *Hüttenvertrag*, which dates from 1968, provides a coking coal subsidy. The current agreement, which expires in the year 2000, sets an upper limit to subsidised coking supplies to the steel industry. Clearly, these subsidies are highly sensitive to world dollar energy prices, and lead to significantly higher domestic electricity costs: rates to industrial users are 30 per cent higher than in France. The system is now threatened both on grounds of budgetary cost and because the EC Commission is eager to scale back such domestic protection in its desire to set in place an open energy market, based on a 'common carrier' system (Pick and von Weizsäcker 1989).

An ambitious *nuclear power programme* was already envisaged by the First Federal Energy Programme of 1973, published before the First Oil Crisis, but its role was substantially enhanced thereafter. From a minimal nuclear output in 1973, the forecast output for 1985 was 45–50 GW, fed by a network of pressure water reactors (PWR). Further decisions were taken in the mid-1970s to engage in experimental fast breeder and high temperature reactor (HTR) technologies. In addition, it was considered essential that West Germany master the uranium cycle by constructing a reprocessing plant for spent reactor fuel, which would also serve to supply plutonium for the fast breeder reactor. At the time, Kraftwerkunion (owned by Siemens and AEG) was the largest European nuclear engineering group, with an annual building capacity of seven nuclear power sets. The reality has turned out to be totally different from the plans: only two dozen PWR reactors have been built in Germany, with an installed capacity of only 18.5 GW; the fast breeder and high temperature reactors have never supplied electricity to the grid, and the reprocessing plant at Wackersdorf, halted in a costly state of half-completion, has been taken over by Siemens to produce solar cells.

A quasi-moratorium on new nuclear construction was imposed in 1979 when, after continuous protest demonstrations, the SPD–FDP coalition decided to link future approvals to the availability of facilities for the safe disposal of fissile waste. This principle found legal expression in the *Atomgesetz*, and so forced the decision to proceed with the building of the reprocessing plant at Wackersdorf and of deep storage facilities at Gorleben. The 1981 Energy Programme placed clear priority on energy-saving and expressed great hesitancy over the future of the nuclear option, in spite of the findings of a 1980 parliamentary inquiry which linked future approvals to the safe disposal of waste, but had at the same time insisted that Germany could not forgo the nuclear option completely. Though the incoming Kohl government continued to proclaim its faith in nuclear energy, no new contracts have been issued since 1983.

Demonstrations and court cases led to construction lead-times of eleven years for a PWR (compared with six years in France), while violent opposition to the Gorleben and Wackersdorf projects ensured that the condition of safe waste disposal remained unmet. However, the weakness of the economics of nuclear power has also ensured that, in spite of expenditures of DM 7 billion on the fast breeder, and DM 2.6 billion on reprocessing facilities (out of a total estimated public expenditure of DM 30 billion on reprocessing technology), such capacities will now make no contribution to energy supply (*Der Spiegel* 1990 (16)). Very high capital costs have arisen as a result of high real interest rates, construction delays, safety modifications and the non-materialisation of economies of scale. The fast breeder programme has been rendered uneconomic by the fact that its fuel, plutonium, a possible factor of atomic weapons proliferation, has become rare and expensive. (The plunge in world uranium prices makes the alternative PWR system now relatively more attractive.) Reprocessing, to which Germany has committed so much money, remains far more expensive than either long-term storage of waste or contracts with the French reprocessing authority, COGEMA. In addition, there is the small matter of the price of oil, which for much of the 1980s lay below its real level prior to the 1973 Oil Crisis. Of course, there are those who claim a future for nuclear power in Germany by the year 2000, within a context of rising real oil prices and difficulties in the cutting of CO_2 emissions to an internationally agreed level.

The third main thrust of energy policy, that of energy efficiency, has gained in importance as parties such as the SPD and FDP have come to favour a progressive *Ausstieg* out of nuclear power. The energy intensity of economic activity in West Germany has been much reduced, to such a degree that, for example, for the period 1973–86 primary energy consumption rose by 0.14 per cent annually, while GDP rose by 1.9 per cent per year. The period of greatest public financial support came in the period 1981–3, when a total budget of DM 7 billion was allocated for subsidies to energy-saving, and to the creation of energy-efficient products (automobiles, household appliances). This included the so-called '4.35 billion Mark Programme' for household energy-saving.

The environmental debate in the Federal Republic is conducted at a sophisticated level, and broad agreement exists across the parties on using market signals for environmental ends. These would buttress the present impressive array of legal norms on emissions. While public investment in environmental improvement has stagnated in the 1980s as special investment programmes have ended, so private sector expenditure has soared. In the period 1977–87, a total of DM 212 billion was invested for environmental protection, and nominal expenditure at the end of the period was double that at the outset. Private industrial expenditure on the environment quadrupled (IFO-Institut, quoted in *Der Spiegel* 1989 (16)). The federal government has recently offered tax inducements for the fitting of catalytic converters and has imposed disincentives on use of plastic packaging.

It is the tax instrument, however, which is now gaining most attention. The SPD 1990 election programme proposed an 'eco-tax' for an ecological restructuring of the economy. The centrepiece would be a shifting of the motorist's tax burden to a tax on petrol consumption, while the proceeds would be redistributed through the income tax system. In a report of August 1989 to the federal environment minister by the chairmen of the Council of Economic Advisers and of the Advisory Committee on the Environment, proposals for ways of strengthening the present legal norms by market-based instruments were detailed. Examples include the selling of emission licences, emission fees and compensatory arrangements between firms. It has to be admitted that a major weakness of the existing system lies in the poor local supervision of legal norms. Improvement in administrative arrangements would be equally important for the development of market-based instruments. The view of industry is, unsurprisingly, that only a common European system could ensure that such instruments would be effective. This would maintain German competitiveness and address the very sizeable problem of pollution 'imported' from neighbouring countries.

Germany as the 'dominant economy' in the European Community?

The trade and GNP shares of the Federal Republic in the respective West European totals testify to the central importance of Germany in the European Community. With one-quarter of EC GNP, and accounting for one-quarter of EC external and intra-Community trade alike, the economic weight of West Germany, and its influence on the level of activity in other member states, has been readily apparent. Domestically, the EC has long been considered an extension of the home market, accounting for one-half of West German exports and imports in the late 1980s. The scale of German direct investment in the Twelve, together with the decisive importance of foreign investors in German capital markets, underline the growing multinationalisation of economic activity.

This emphasis on material interests tends, however, to divert attention from the

Federal Republic's longstanding and fundamental interest in political union in Europe. At the end of the 1980s, the spotlight was focusing once again on the common Franco-German stance in favour of both economic and political union. This Franco-German axis has lain at the inner core of the Community, and had provided the impetus behind moves to political union from the 1950s until de Gaulle's open conflict with supranationalism in the mid-1960s. Adenauer, the first Federal Chancellor, anchored the new, immature Republic in the West, and achieved through his enthusiastic support for European integration and NATO membership both international acceptance and sovereignty (Bulmer and Paterson 1987). That this policy blocked any chance for German reunification as a neutralised, central European state was accepted by him, on the grounds that the Soviet zone of East Germany would have to accede to a liberal, democratic West. Of course, the opening to the East at the beginning of the 1970s, in the form of the *Ostpolitik*, was counter-balanced by an even more secure anchoring of Germany in the Community.

No attempt will be made here to conduct a cost-benefit analysis of Germany's Community membership, given the complexity of such a calculation: rather, the impact of key policy areas will be discussed in relatively simple terms. First, on the customs union for manufactures, it is clear that here lies West Germany's fundamental economic interest. The zone of free trade gives free play to its comparative advantage and the liberal economic principles of free competition and a minimum of external trade restrictions, enshrined in the Treaty of Rome, accord with German principles, even if the frequency of derogations arouses irritation in Bonn. Germany's trade surplus with the Community of DM 85 billion in 1988 represented two-thirds of its total surplus, though only in recent years has its current balance been positive overall with the Community (MRDB 1987). Of considerable policy interest is the conflict between the Republic's role of paymaster to the Community and its stout defence of the Common Agricultural Policy (CAP), with all its distortions. For connoisseurs of delicious irony, let it be said that the FDP has traditionally supplied the economics minister in Bonn, who has always attacked the illiberalism of the CAP, while, until recently, the FDP has also supplied the agriculture minister. Support for the small farmer is also strong in the CDU and CSU conservative parties, and it is not by chance that the last three agriculture ministers (incumbent for twenty-five years) have been Bavarian.

The paymaster role which has fallen to Bonn has naturally led to considerable public disenchantment with the Community. In the period 1971–84 Bonn's net nominal payments to the EC budget rose fourteenfold, and almost three-quarters of the net financial transfers made among member states were made from 'German' resources. In net per capita terms and as a proportion of GDP, Bonn's contribution is by far the largest (May 1985). In recent years, this pattern has continued, though the growing sums involved (DM 10 billion net payment in 1987) have imposed a heavier burden on general government expenditure, at a time when deficit reduction has been a key objective (MRDB 1988b). Net transfers to Brussels have risen at twice the rate of other general government expenditure, and, to meet the rise in contributions following the February 1988 Community budget settlement, several indirect tax rates were increased. It is, of course, the structure of the Community budget which creates this problem: richer countries which trade more with the rest of the world pay more in VAT and import duties to Brussels, while the dominant weight of the CAP among Community expenditures ensures that those countries with a large surplus production of CAP-supported crops and livestock products are the main recipients.

In direct conflict with its budgetary interest, Germany has consistently opposed any fundamental reform of the CAP. Although the farm sector contributes less than 2 per cent of GDP and farm employment just 5.3 per cent of total civilian employment (1986), one-half of the former territory of West Germany and 250,000 farms from that area are classed as 'naturally-disfavoured'. Of course, a high proportion of these are worked part-time, and the German structural surpluses of wheat, sugar and milk products are produced in the commercial farming sector. The touchstone of a farm minister's commitment to his constituents has always been the maintenance of the wheat price, and so there is intense sensitivity in Germany to any cut in the price support level for that crop (Hendriks 1989). In the mid-1960s German farmers were granted a transition period, so as to adjust to a cut in the wheat price from that of DM 475 per tonne then prevailing in Germany to the new common price level of DM 425. The latter initially rose to DM 473 by 1983, but by September 1989 it had fallen back to DM 345. Over the 1980s farmers suffered falling real incomes, caught as they were between falling real product prices and constantly rising input costs. There seems no solution to the problem which does not include a large cut in production capacity. Much of the structural adjustment cost is borne by the Bonn and *Land* agriculture ministries, and their total expenditure within Germany is broadly equal to that spent by Brussels on price support in that country.

The CAP has, admittedly, provided a relatively stable framework for rapid productivity advances and output expansion. In particular, the Federal Republic has become a major food exporter, in contradiction to its comparative disadvantage. Instrumental has been the system of monetary compensatory amounts (MCAs) made necessary by the use of 'green' currencies, which stop the common CAP prices in DM to the German farmer from falling *pari passu* with the appreciation of the DM against the ECU. These 'positive' MCAs act as a tax on food imports and a subsidy on exports. The system benefits the farmer to the extent that he receives the old DM price (pre-revaluation) for his produce, but finds the cost of imported inputs reduced. French farmers in particular have been seriously aggrieved by this damage to their own export prospects, and so, on French insistence, realignments within the EMS have been accompanied by a German commitment to phase out 'positive' MCAs.

At the same time, the German government won agreement on financial compensation to its farmers to balance the fall in the DM support price as the 'green' exchange rate is abolished. In 1984 VAT concessions for farmers were introduced; in 1985 a 'milk compensation subsidy' for those giving up dairying was instituted, and in 1986 lower-income farmers were granted relief on their social security contributions. More generally, the February 1988 reforms to the CAP (in the context of which Chancellor Kohl performed a difficult balancing act as president of the EC Council) have brought only a brief respite from the problems of oversupply of foodstuffs. The land set-aside scheme will cost DM 5 billion over five years in West Germany (borne primarily by the Federal and *Land* governments), and an enhanced early retirement scheme introduced in 1989 is expected to cost DM 615 million per year by 1992.

Towards the end of the 1980s, economic integration gained a new impetus with proposals for economic and monetary union (see Sumner, Chapter 8 in *The European Economy*, on European monetary integration). As we have already seen, there is considerable political support in Bonn for the three-stage progression toward a common currency and a European Central Bank, as proposed by the Delors Report, though the Bundesbank has sought to ensure that its successor will be a 'super-Bundesbank'. But one concomitant of irrevocably fixed exchange rates, namely, financial transfers to less competitive regions, has met with the chilly response from Bonn which it previously reserved for appeals for an expansion of the regional and social funds. Economic union, in the guise of the Single Market Programme, clearly offers the powerful German export sector even further opportunities for EC market penetration. At the same time, the deregulatory thrust of the 1992 programme presents many challenges to the sheltered sectors, and to Germany's corporatist features.

The Single Market Programme (see Holmes, Chapter 3 in *The European Economy*, on general integration trends) aims to abolish the multiplicity of non-tariff barriers which fragment the Common Market. These include product norms and standards, exclusionary public procurement practices and the tight national regulation of services, not to mention border posts, which alone impose significant form-filling and waiting-time costs. The completion of the Common Market therefore rests primarily on frontier-post abolition, the mutual recognition of norms and standards, open tendering for public contracts and deregulation (or re-regulation at a European level) in services such as transport, telecommunications and finance. Of course, the enhanced competition could lead to a lowering of product standards, a relaxation of employment legislation and of non-wage benefits, and downwards pressure on tax rates. As would be expected, debate among the public at large in Germany has focused on fears for public health and the environment, fear of 'social dumping' (an erosion of social protection and workers' co-determination in Germany): the converse is heard from the employers' side, which stresses the high cost of a production location in Germany – the *Standortfrage*. One should perhaps not forget that three important European Court cases (two of which established the principle of mutual recognition of the norms and standards applied in member countries) – the cases relating to 'Cassis de Dijon', the German beer *Reinheitsgebot*, and the supply of insurance services into Germany – were pursued expressly so as further to open up the German market. It is certainly true that German industry does use the most advanced system of product standards in Europe in the shape of the 20,000 DIN standards to exclusionary effect, nowhere more so than under the system of *Einheitstechnik* developed by the Bundespost for its telecommunications services.

That German manufacturing will benefit from market opening is in little doubt, given its trade surpluses, its 6,300 subsidiaries within the EC, and its revealed comparative advantage in those branches which have up to now been the most protected in Europe. Surveys by the Economics Ministry (BMWi 1989) and the IFO-Institut (Gürtler and Nerb 1988) support the view that the broad range of German manufacturing expects to benefit from further market integration. Business spokesmen, however, never cease to stress the *Standortfrage*, averring that Germany's high direct and indirect wage costs, corporation tax and local taxation all burden its competitiveness. Closer study does present a more nuanced picture. Expressed in constant exchange rates, German unit labour costs are not out of line with those of its competitors; on the question of corporation tax, if favourable depreciation and additions to reserves provisions are included, then German profits taxation is not unduly heavy (*DIW-Wochenbericht* 1988b). The corporation tax rate of 52 per cent is in any case scheduled to be reduced to 50 per cent. The local business tax, the *Gewerbesteuer*, will be replaced, as it is seen as a heavy impost on physical investment by firms. The question of deregulation in the services sector was discussed earlier, and sweeping changes are being felt in the transport, finance and telecommunications spheres.

The 1992 programme has far-reaching consequences for public finances in several countries arising from the need to implement some harmonisation of VAT (into two broad bands, perhaps), and to set bands for excise duties. In Germany the effect in aggregate is minor, since present VAT rates in that country fall around the mid-points of the bands proposed by the EC Commission; revenue losses arising from the different product coverage of these rates would be more than compensated by higher revenues from excise duty (*DIW-Wochenbericht*, 1988a). Finally, the federal government has expressed the firm intention of saving Germany's social protection and workers' co-determination system from the depredations of 'social dumping'. At the first *Europa Konferenz* in December 1988, Chancellor Kohl warmly embraced the Social Charter concept. Market liberals in Germany, however, as elsewhere, not only oppose this attempt to harmonise upwards social legislation in a hasty manner, but also point out that the free movement of workers into Germany, who could then qualify for the high level of social benefit, would impose intolerable strains (SBGE 1989).

The economics of German unity

The entry into force of the treaty on economic, currency and social union between the two Germanies on 1 July 1990 exposed the uncompetitiveness of the economy of the German Democratic Republic (GDR) in the most brutal way. After four decades of protection behind the wall of an inconvertible currency, and of undemanding bilateral trade contracts within Comecon, the GDR suddenly had to price its goods in deutschmarks, in a unified economic zone with its Western sister. Union also brought with it the adoption of West German economic law, social security and tax systems, and subordination to the monetary policies of the Bundesbank. The abolition of central planning, the system of administered prices and the prevailing regime of social ownership of the means of production (replaced by the constitutional rights of free disposition over property) were a death-knell to authoritarian, highly centralist, Leninist socialism. One must presume that the incorporation of the GDR into the Federal Republic was the intention of the majority who voted for the right-wing coalition in the GDR elections of 18 March 1990. For many others, emigration to the West was the chosen alternative: this flood of immigrants into the Federal Republic, and the threat of complete breakdown in the East, left Chancellor Kohl's government with little option over timing, even when a long time-scale for economic and monetary union was arguably a prime necessity.

If East Germans mistakenly believed that the adoption of the deutschmark would make them all wealthier in the short term, they were soon cruelly disabused. Economic and monetary union immediately exposed whole branches of the old GDR economy as totally uncompetitive, in addition to causing huge short-term dislocations as market pricing and Western banking and tax systems were introduced and the all-pervasive system of subsidisation dismantled. The slow freeing-up of controls over property rights and the myriad of legal claims to property titles which have surfaced will hamper the workings of the market for years. The statistics give some measure of the impact of forced-draft reunification: output and employment in the East have collapsed and the trough may be reached only in mid–late 1991. In 1990 GNP in the East fell by 20 per cent (with a halving of industrial output) and forecasts for 1991 foresee a further GNP fall of 5–10 per cent. At the end of March 1991, unemployment in 'the new *Länder'* totalled 808,400 workers, or 9.2 per cent of the work-force, while more than 2 million workers were on short-time working (many with no actual work to do). The federal government's annual economic report, presented to Parliament on 7 March 1991, forecast that unemployment would reach something under 2 million, or a quarter of the work-force, by the end of 1991. Severe output losses have been experienced in all branches: in metals, chemicals, vehicles, food, textiles and light engineering. Thus the dislocation of reunification in practice bears no relation to the confident public statements of politicians of the Bonn ruling coalition in the heady days of 1990. Belatedly, and under the pressure of street demonstrations, a change of policy course for the East was introduced in February–March 1991. But the financial and political impact of the course of events after unification continues to reverberate widely and deeply.

The cost of unity to public finances in Bonn has ballooned out of all recognition, and has brought the Bundesbank once more into conflict with the federal government. After early tensions over the proposed terms of the currency union, public differences arose in March 1991 when the Bundesbank president referred to economic union as a 'disaster'. There are, in fact, five public sector funds for financing reunification, but if we focus on the federal budget alone, the deterioration is fully apparent. From a position of budget balance for West Germany in 1989, the predicted all-German federal deficit for 1991 is DM 140 billion, taking into account receipts from tax increases agreed in Februrary 1991. Among further commitments may be listed the DM 13 billion funding of the removal of Soviet troops from the territory of the former GDR, and there are also debt write-offs in Eastern Europe (DM 4.5 billion in relation to Poland alone).

The transitional arrangements for economic union included among others the establishment of a DM 115 billion German Unity Fund as a 'shadow' budget alongside the federal public budget, the *Kreditabwicklungsfond* for the assumption of the East German state debt, investment funding borne by the federal post and railways budgets, the *Treuhand* or *Treuhandanstalt* (trustee institution) to hold and dispose of East German state assets and, finally, special arrangements for paying those on short-time working intended to facilitate the retraining of displaced workers (see p. 62). On 2 July 1990 those *Kombinate* (conglomerates into which publicly owned enterprises were organised in the GDR) which had still not been broken up, together with all other state enterprises, were required to prepare an asset inventory and deutschmark valuation, and to draw up a short-term business plan for transmission to the *Treuhand*. This had to specify their short-term financing needs in this new world without subsidies and state investment credits. In the event, their liquidity needs were three times the DM 7 billion (DM 10 billion for 1991) allocated to the *Treuhand*, and allegations abounded that efficient enterprises were sinking with the rest. In cases where enterprises in difficulty were forced to cut back on employment, the union treaty provided for those on short-time working to be paid (primarily be the state) 65 per cent of their previous earnings, and to have a retraining entitlement at this benefit level for up to two years.

In the first months of economic union, enterprises and farm co-operatives in the new *Länder* suffered extreme dislocation in the process of adjustment to the market economy, and saw their markets simply melt away. Uncompetitive, debt-burdened, and with markets in the CMEA collapsing, East German producers also had to cope with a complete shift in domestic consumer preferences towards West German produce. The monopolistic regional retail chains simply abandoned East German suppliers. By late 1990 the *Treuhand* was in a position to decide which firms it would force to close. Spokesmen reported that at least 1,000 of the 8,000 larger companies under *Treuhand* control would have to cease trading. Those already closed at time of writing include the state airline Interflug, the Trabant and Wartburg car production lines, and the Pentacon camera works. Elsewhere, in the shipyards, in optics, in chemicals, rationalisation will require work-force cuts of at least one-half. Inward investment has been meagre (due to disputes over legal title, rationalisation and environmental clean-up costs) and *Treuhand* privatisation receipts for 1990 were a mere DM 4 billion. The relatively non-interventionist stance of Bonn was reversed in February and March 1991 as a result of street demonstrations, and finally by the assassination of the head of the *Treuhand* by terrorists.

The policy changes now promulgated reflected a very tardy public acknowledgement of the economic costs of reunification, which if known were not admitted during the successive phases of elections in 1990. First, increases in tax and social security charges were announced, with effect from July 1991, implying a reduction in purchasing power of DM 48 billion over two years. In order to alleviate the pressure of unemployment, the short-time working provisions were extended to cover the second half of 1991. Major changes in policy direction came, however, in three other areas:

1 The *Treuhandanstalt* was enjoined in March 1991 to consult closely with the new *Länder* east of the Elbe on the unemployment impact of its closure decisions. Effectively, this implies a moratorium on large plant closures without *Land* agreement, which is fully consistent with a shift towards an interventionist stance based on restructuring and financial reorganisation rather than privatisation and closure. The Finance Ministry has estimated the gross financial needs of the *Treuhand* at DM 400 billion over the years 1991–2000.

2 The tax increase was accompanied by a new *Aufschwung Ost* recovery programme for the East, whereby an additional DM 24 billion would be available for infrastructural projects and local authority investment. Enhanced assistance for private investors was also included in the package, such that tax breaks, grants and interest rebates now account for more than one-half of the initial allocation to the programme.

3 The original principle of restitution of property expropriated under the Nazi regime

or by the East German state, which effectively blocked many direct investment and privatisation proposals in the early days after unification (there are 1.2 million claims, of which 10,000 relate to companies) was modified by a law passed by the Bundestag on 16 March 1991. The effect of the new law is to give preference up to the end of 1992 to investors promising to invest more than the legal owner, in which case financial compensation to the owner is made.

What were the key economic issues underlying this course of events? To explain the poor competitiveness of the East German economy we need to consider the terms of the currency union, the structural weaknesses of East German industry, pressures for nominal wage equalisation, and the collapse of CMEA markets. The impact on West Germany can be analysed in terms of a 'demand shock' and of financial variables such as the price level, and interest and exchange rates.

It has often been said with the benefit of hindsight that the terms of the monetary union of 1 July 1990 imposed a heavily overvalued exchange rate on East Germany. At the time, however, the position was by no means so clear cut, and many commentators did not consider the terms too burdensome. Simply put, the Bundesbank had proposed a conversion rate of Ost Mark to deutschmark of 2:1, though this was on the assumption of very substantial wage inflation. Under strong political pressures, the final terms were of conversion at parity for all current payments, for net foreign debt and for savings and cash holdings up to DM 2,000, DM 4,000 and DM 6,000 for children, adults and pensioners respectively. Money holdings in excess of those limits and net enterprise debt were to be converted at 2:1. This differential treatment of the assets and liabilities of the GDR Staatsbank involved a financing gap of about DM 28 billion, the burden of which the Bundesbank had to assume. As a first observation, it may be said that exchange at 2:1 would have imposed relative poverty on wage-earners, unemployed people and pensioners, in the absence of any uprating of wages and transfers, given the fact that average wages in Ost Mark were 31 per cent of their Western equivalent, and that transfers were linked to this level. This would have served only to speed migration. Low wages would, though, have secured employment and attracted inward investment.

Various commentaries (*DIW-Wochenbericht* 1990c; MRDB 1990) considered the terms of the currency union to be bearable, and based this on a comparison of physical productivities between the two countries. Since, under West German tax and social security rules, average wages in the East would be only 37 per cent of their Western equivalent (assuming no wage mark-up for price changes and income tax), then this would not be out of line with relative productivities. Studies of physical productivities placed Eastern at 40–50 per cent of Western, with the margin of error largely reflecting differences in assumptions concerning the services sector (*DIW-Wochenbericht* 1990a). Of course, most East German products were not of world market standard, and so price reductions were clearly *de rigueur*. Scope for price reductions of up to 30 per cent was offered to producers by the shift from the heavy production-related taxes of the command economy to the VAT system of the Western system. Other production cost savings, it was argued, would be found in far more realistic plant valuation and depreciation rates and in cheaper raw material costs under the unified currency (*DIW-Wochenbericht* 1990b).

Ideally, the chosen conversion rate should, to maintain competitiveness of the real economy, have reflected purchasing power parity. In a system of administered prices and currency inconvertibility, such a yardstick could not be calculated. However, data did become available towards the end of 1989 on the Ost Mark resource cost of East German exports for every deutschmark earned. These calculations revealed a substantial devaluation of the Ost Mark over the 1980s, to a rate of 4.4:1 in 1989, which implies that one Ost Mark would equal DM 0.23 (DIW 1990). In terms of East German tradeables output, therefore, conversion at parity represented a very significant overvaluation. This approach did, of course, automatically take into account the lower quality levels of GDR products, a fact substantiated by the consumers of the East, who have now completely rejected regional produce in favour of Western (three-quarters of foodstuffs in the shops are now of West German origin).

The currency union had further consequences in terms of enterprise debt and wage inflation. The enterprises of the old GDR carried a total of DM 115 billion of inherited debt in their balance sheets, though this, of course, in no way reflected their underlying financial position. Rather such debt had been accumulated as a result of the interplay of central allocation of investment funds, compulsory profit levies and inflated investment goods prices under the command economy. With the asset write-downs under the new opening balance sheet regime, rates of inherited debt to revised equity may now amount to as much as 37 per cent (*DIW-Wochenbericht* 1990e), representing an unacceptably high gearing level in German conditions. The federal government has continued to insist on interest payments on this debt, but it is now generally accepted that the *Treuhand*, in its new restructuring function, may undertake write-offs, case-by-case.

It is in the wage inflation subsequent to the currency union that many commentators see the root cause of a significant loss of competitiveness. Since the enlarged Federal Republic has rapidly become one labour market, the pressures towards wage equalisation are great, and immensely damaging, given the low levels of productivity in the new *Länder*. In 1989 and 1990 2 million East Germans and ethnic Germans, mainly from the Soviet Union, migrated to West Germany. It is estimated that during 1991 Easterners were migrating at the rate of 20,000 per month. In addition, 200,000–300,000 now commute. In that context it is perhaps not surprising that in the summer and autumn of 1990 wage-earners in the East secured wage rises averaging one-third to compensate for the levying of income tax and the rise in prices of basic foodstuffs (though the aggregate price level barely changed – it was retired and unemployed people who faced substantial price rises). Wage agreements for municipal workers, for example, now offer rates 60 per cent of those in the West, and provide for equalisation by the mid-1990s. Only a policy of wage subsidies, or of subsidies for living costs (rents, energy, transport) can now prevent the emergence of a highly damaging differential between real wages and productivity in the East.

It was always recognised that, almost regardless of the terms of currency union, certain branches of the old GDR economy would come under severe rationalisation pressure, because they were grossly polluting or grossly inefficient. Of industrial capacity, between one-third and two-fifths was thought at the time of reunification to face closure in part or in full (*DIW-Wochenbericht* 1990e), and much of this would be in continuous process industries using obsolete technology or lignite fuel. Even the oil-feedstock-based chemicals industry faces heavy rationalisation, given the change to dollar prices in oil supplies from the Soviet Union. In the farm sector, a cut in employment by one-half, or 500,000 workers, together with production cuts of 20 per cent is in prospect. Eastern farm labour productivity was only 40 per cent of that of the West, in spite of the much-vaunted scale economies achieved on the 4,700 hectare-sized co-operative farms. The guaranteed producer price level in 1988 was also 2.5 times the West German level (converted at parity). The adoption of the CAP brings with it not only lower prices but also production controls and quality norms: the new *Länder* have been afforded an eighteen-month transition during which farm produce exempt from these norms may be sold locally or exported to CMEA countries.

A final, and weighty, contribution to the collapse of East German output has come from the break-up of the CMEA (see Alan Smith, Chapter 6 in *The European Economy*). The old official statistics for CMEA trade gave a very misleading impression of overall trading trends, since they were calculated in (inconvertible) transferable roubles. They showed that up to 75 per cent of East Germany's total trade was with Comecon. This is almost certainly an exaggeration. Nevertheless the East German economy was closely tied in to a fairly crude division of labour (machinery for raw materials), particularly with the Soviet Union. As many as 15 per cent of East German industrial employees were said to be engaged in producing for export to the USSR, and 31 per cent of GDR primary energy was supplied by Moscow (*DIW-Wochenbericht* 1990d). Although trade values began to decline from the mid-1980s, the extrication of East Germany from these trade, production specialisation and co-operation agreements was bound to be profoundly disruptive: the adoption of the deutschmark also rendered traditional exports to the USSR very price-uncompetitive. Article 13 of the State Treaty between the two Germanies provided for heavy subsidisation of existing supply contracts with Eastern Europe. At the same time Moscow has insisted on dollar pricing for its oil supplies. Meanwhile, amidst all the administrative chaos in the Soviet Union (see Dyker, Chapter 12 in this volume), Soviet orders for exports from the old GDR amounted to only DM 1.4 billion in the first quarter of 1991.

We come, finally, to an assessment of the effects of German economic and monetary union on what was West Germany. These may be analysed under the headings of, first, the initial consequences for the price level of monetary union; second, the 'demand shock' for West German capital goods (and consumer goods) producers; and finally, the consequences for interest and exchange rates of this 'shock' and of the explosion in state debt to finance consumption in the East.

In mid-1990, just before monetary union, much of the concern expressed focused on the scale of the monetary expansion arising from the issue of deutschmark in East Germany. Conversion at parity meant a very substantial monetary expansion placed in the hands of East German consumers charged with pent-up demand. If this now effective demand were addressed in full to Western producers, overheating and inflation would result. The currency union involved an expansion in the CBM money supply, assuming a comparable pattern of demand for money in the East to that in the West, of 9 per cent. This, it was said, did indeed reflect the ratio of the two countries in marketed goods and services. In the event, savings balances in the East have been maintained for precautionary motives and because real interest rates are now positive.

Beyond that, the openness of the Federal economy, and the elasticity of world supply, ensure that excess demand can be met by imports. Thus there has been no extreme pressure on production capacity in the former West Germany.

The 'unity bonus' to the former West Germany was thought to have raised GDP growth by 1.5 percentage points in 1990 and to be likely to do so by 1 point in 1991. In the very short term, consumer goods producers have benefited, but as investment in infrastructure and plant in the East proceeds, so the demand for capital goods will rise rapidly. (As indeed it will if growth in 'liberalised' Eastern Europe takes off.) A central estimate of these investment needs is DM 100 billion annually over ten years, of which one-half may be in economic and social overhead infrastructure. Given the excess of planned investment over savings and the consequent need to attract world savings, interest rates are bound to rise. The counterpart to this savings investment imbalance will be excess demand, especially for German capital goods. In this situation a real deutschmark appreciation (involving an ERM realignment), fuelled by optimism over the expansion of investment and of the investment goods industries, would help transfer resources from the external account to domestic use, and would help counter overheating. It would also contribute to a rundown of Germany's record current account surpluses. Signs of such pressures on interest and real exchange rates, and in the external account, did, indeed, become apparent at the turn of 1990/91.

In practice, such a 'virtuous circle' is unlikely to be maintained. The full magnitude of the task of integrating the old East German economy is now apparent, with the budgetary cost (notably of transfers to unemployed people, short-time workers, etc) occupying an increasingly dominant position in public attention. State sector transfers to the East are expected to reach DM 100 billion in 1991. In spite of the buoyancy of tax revenues in the West, consumption in the East by those not working has been borne to an increasing extent by public borrowing (now running at 5 per cent of GDP). Thus the excess of total domestic demand over output, and the consequent deterioration in the trade balance (by the spring of 1991 the current account was already in deficit), have been much more a function of *consumption* than of *investment* trends. Were this situation to continue, foreign assets would have to be run down to finance imports, and external income from those assets would be reduced. With worries about the budget deficit denting confidence, there is a real possibility of a consequent cumulative downwards trend in the value of the deutschmark (CEPR 1990). This would in turn, of course, tend to cut off capital import into Germany, whether for consumption or investment purposes, producing a pattern of 'vicious' rather than 'virtuous' circle.

The experience of economic unification has been one of profound upheaval in the East, and of discomfiture in the West attendant on the financial, labour market and housing consequences. However, having proclaimed the goal of unity for so many decades, the West Germans surely cannot baulk at the transitional costs. While one cannot predict with certainty the ultimate ramifications of these momentous events, it is possible to pinpoint certain general economic implications. The Federal Republic will wish to approach European monetary union more gingerly after experiencing in spectacular fashion the consequences of a rapid currency union between countries of widely differing performance and structure. It is equally clear, however, that the reconstruction of the Eastern economy will absorb real product and capital from the former West Germany for many years and so assist the international adjustment of trade balances. Western Germany has already experienced the 'unification bonus' to growth, but the heavy resource costs of the absorption of the East are taking their toll on interest and exchange rates, and will continue to do so. Finally, the representation of East Germans in the federal institutions – the government, Bundesbank and the Upper House (Bundesrat) – can serve only to dilute the resolute policy orientations of the previous era. Of one thing we can be absolutely certain. The united Federal Republic will be qualitatively different from its predecessor.

References

Aufderheide D (ed) (1990) *Deregulierung und Liberalisierung*. Kohlhammer, Stuttgart

Bulmer S, Paterson W (1987) *The Federal Republic of Germany and the European Community*. Allen & Unwin

BMWi (*Bundesministerium für Wirtschaft*) (1984) Hochtechnologien und internationale Wettbewerbsfähigkeit der deutschen Wirtschaft. *Dokumentation* **263**

BMWi (1989) Die deutsche Industrie befürwortet die Schaffung eines europäischen Binnenmarktes. *Mitteilung der Pressestelle* 4 August

Burda M C, Sachs J D (1987) *Institutional Aspects of High Unemployment in the Federal Republic of Germany* NBER Working Paper **2241**, Cambridge, Mass., National Bureau of Economic Research, May

CEPR (Centre for Economic Policy Research) (1990) *Monitoring European Integration: the Impact of Eastern Europe*, CEPR, London

DIW (1990) *DDR Wirtschaft im Umbruch: Bestandsaufnahme und Reformansätze*. Berlin, January

DIW-Wochenbericht (1988a) EG-Steuerharmonisierung:geringe fiskalische Wirkungen fur die BRD. 7: 91–101

DIW-Wochenbericht (1988b) Die Besteuerung der Unternehmensgewinne im internationalen Vergleich. 29: 329–43

DIW-Wochenbericht (1990a) Zum Produktivitätsvergleich BRD-DDR. **14**: 172–5

DIW-Wochenbericht (1990b) Quantitative Aspekte einer Reform von Wirtschaft und Finanzen in der DDR 17: 221–5

DIW-Wochenbericht (1990c) Gesamtwirtschaftliche Auswirkungen der deutschen Währungs-, Wirtschafts- und Sozialunion auf die BRD 20: 269–77

DIW-Wochenbericht (1990d) Aussenwirtschaftliche Verflechtung zwischen DDR und UdSSR 21: 285–94

DIW-Wochenbericht (1990e) Alt-Schulden: Streichung unumgänglich. 36: 563–70

Emminger O (1977) The DM in the conflict between internal and external equilibrium. *Essays in International Finance* **122**: Princeton University

Fels G (1983) Die Konsequenzen der Staatsverschuldung. In Siebert H (ed) *Perspektiven der Deutschen Wirtschaftspolitik*. Kohlhammer, Stuttgart

Fels G, Fröhlich H-P (1987) Germany and the world economy: a round table discussion. *Economic Policy: a European Forum* **4**: 177–95

Franz W (1984) Is less more? The current discussion about reduced working time in Western Germany: a survey of the debate. *Zeitschrift für die Gesamte Staatswissenschaft* **140**(4): 626–54.

Genscher H-D (1989) Die Rolle der BRD bei der Vollendung des EWS. In Gaddum J W et al *Die Vollendung des EWS: Ergebnisse einer Fachtagung*. Verlag Bertelsmann Stiftung, Gütersloh

Giersch H (ed) (1983) *Wie es zu Schaffen ist, Agenda für die Deutsche Wirtschaftspolitik*. DVA, Stuttgart

Gürtler J, Nerb G (1988) *Erwartete Auswirkungen des Europäischen Binnenmarktes auf die Industrie der BRD und der Partnerländer. IFO-Studien zur Industriewirtschaft* **33**, Munchen

Hasse R H (1989) *Die Europäische Zentralbank: Perspektiven für eine Weiterentwicklung des EWS*. Verlag Bertelsmann Stiftung, Gütersloh

Hendriks G (1989) Germany and the CAP: national interests and the EC. *International Affairs* **65**(11): 75–88

Hinze J (1988) Die Gründe der Investitions- und Wachtumsschwäche. *Wirtschaftsdienst* **9**: 457–62

Jüttemeier K H (1987) Subsidizing the Federal German economy – facts and figures, 1973–84. *Kiel Working Paper* **279**, Institut für Weltwirtschaft, Kiel, January

Kloten N (1988) Wege zu einem Europäischen Zentralbanksystem. *Europa Archiv* **43**(11): 285–98

Koch K (1989) West German Industrial Relations. In Koch K (ed) *West Germanv Today*. Routledge

Lipschitz L, Kremers J, Mayer T, McDonald D (1989) The Federal Republic of Germany: adjustment in a surplus country. *IMF Occasional Paper* **64**, Washington

May B (1985) *Kosten und Nutzen der deutschen EG-Mitgliedschaft*. Europa Union Verlag, Bonn

Michelsen G (ed) (1988) *Die Zukunft der BRD: Szenarien und Prognosen*. öko-Institut, Rasch und Rohring, Hamburg

MRDB (*Monthly Report of the Deutsche Bundesbank***)** (1985) The longer-term trend and control of the money stock. January: 13–25

MRDB (1987) The balance of payments of the FRG with the other countries of the EC. July: 13–20

MRDB (1988a) Methodological notes on the monetary target variable M3. March: 18–21

MRDB (1988b) Recent developments in the financial relations of the FRG with the European Communities. November: 36–41

MRDB (1990) The first stage of European economic and monetary union. July: 29–37

Müschen K, Romberg E (1985) *Strom ohne Atom*. Öko-Institut, Fischer, Frankfurt

OECD (1987, 1989, 1990) *Economic Survey of Germany*. Paris

Owen Smith E (1983) *The West German Economy*. Croom Helm

Owen Smith E (1989) A survey of economic policy. In Koch K (ed) *West Germany Today*. Routledge

Pätzhold J (1989) *Stabilisierungspolitik*. UTB Haupt, Stuttgart

Pick H, von Weizsäcker C (1989) Energiewirtschaft: vierzig Jahre staatlich protegiert. *Orientierungen zur Wirtschafts- und Gesellschaftspolitik* **39**(1): 31–5

Pöhl K-O (1988) Pressekonferenz: Anschliessend an der Sitzung des Zentralbankrats, 5 Mai 1988. *Auszüge aus Presseartikeln* DBB, 7 May 1988

SBGE (*Sachverständigenrat zur Begutachtung der gesamtwirtschaftlichen Entwicklung* – Council of Economic Advisers) (1987, 1988, 1989) *Jahresgutachten* Metzler-Pöschel, Stuttgart

Weizsäcker von C, Wieland B (1988) Current telecommunications policy in West Germany. *Oxford Review of Economic Policy* **4**(2): 20–39

CHAPTER 4

Italy

PIERELLA PACI

Introduction: the Jekyll and Hyde economy

> To those accustomed to thinking of Italy as the home of a happy-go-lucky, at times irresponsible life-style, with shabby workshops and an electoral system incapable of producing stable government, the figures on industrial production may appear surprising.
>
> (Goodman 1989: 1)

When, at the end of the Second World War, the process of rebuilding the Italian economy (*la ricostruzione*) began, agriculture was the main source of the nation's income, and the level of industrialisation was among the lowest in Europe. Despite substantial fluctuations, the next forty years saw Italy become one of the seven major industrial powers. As late as 1970 the level of GDP per head in Italy was less than 80 per cent of that of the UK. By 1986, according to OECD figures, what became known as *il sorpasso* had occurred, with Italy 'overtaking' the UK as the fifth richest country.[1] The beginning of the 1990s have, however, seen the wild euphoria of Italy's latest economic boom of the early 1980s rapidly fading away.

The achievements since the early 1950s have been won under conditions typical of a small open economy: Italy has been dependent on international trade, because poor in natural resources and raw materials, and therefore forced to develop the increasing flow of exports required to balance its need for imports. Lacking an adequate level of technological autonomy, Italian exports initially gained ground thanks to low prices. In the first stage of development this price advantage was simply the result of comparatively low labour costs. However, since the 'Hot Autumn' (*Autunno Caldo*) of 1969, when wage costs begun to increase relatively faster than in other countries, a combination of steady increases in productivity and incremental but recurrent devaluations of the Italian lira against the currencies of its major European partners was required in order to avoid complete erosion of the price advantage.

Map 4.1

More recently – partly as a response to the reduced scope for exchange rate adjustments resulting from Italy's entrance into the European Community's Exchange Rate Mechanism (ERM) – the emphasis has shifted on to quality improvement as the driving force behind the success of Italian exports. Since 1989, however, export growth has slowed, with Italian goods losing more than 3 percentage points in the international competitive index in 1989. As a result, the beginning of the 1990s saw the bright optimism of Italian business leaders gradually giving way to a wait-and-see attitude, even before the full effects of the Gulf Crisis were perceived, against the background of the 1987 decision, by referendum, to forgo the use of nuclear energy in the production of electricity.

Within the framework of this rather gloomy picture, anxieties focus most strongly on the country's failure to master, on the eve of '1992' and of full implementation of the ERM, the Jekyll-and-Hyde nature of its economy, characterised by, first, a widening gap between the efficient dynamism of private industry and the negligent rhetoric of the politically dominated and deficit-generating public sector; and second, the everlasting division of the country between a rich and efficient North and a poor and inefficient South. It is the view of many that the time has come when Dr Jekyll and Mr Hyde can no longer cohabit. Italy's economic future depends crucially upon its ability to fill the efficiency gap currently yawning between the 'public' and the 'private', and between the regions.[2]

The purpose of this chapter is to provide an overview of the extent of the gap, and of the problems involved in bridging the existing disparities. It begins by outlining those major post-war developments which have provided the contemporary Italian economy with its very distinctive features. It then moves on to analyse the crucial peculiarities of the economy. On the Jekyll side, the growth of small business is presented as the single major source of Italian success. On the Hyde side, the extent of the two main Italian evils – the relative underdevelopment of the South and the inefficiency of the public sector – are assessed, and the prospects for their excision evaluated.

From the *Italia contadina* to the *Terza Italia*[3]

By the late 1960s Italy seemed well set on the way to becoming a successful industrial mixed economy. The aftermath of the war and post-war recession had left little permanent damage. In the wave of optimism and enthusiasm that marked the return to democracy, wartime industries had been converted into peacetime enterprises under both private and public-sector management.[4] Private as well as public capital had been systematically channelled into the development of heavy industry in what has since become known as the *Northern industrial triangle* – the area bounded by the cities of Turin, Milan and Genoa. Following improvements in the infrastructure of many neighbouring areas, light industry – mostly engineering – also began to develop in many towns in Northern and Central Italy. As the standard of living improved, the need for secondary industry also increased, leading to further industrial growth and (as Figure 4.1 shows) a continuous increase in industrial employment at the expense of the agricultural sector.

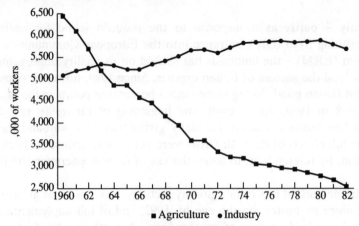

Figure 4.1 Employment levels in agriculture and industry
Source: Bank of Italy data

The agricultural sector as reserve of entrepreneurial skill

The role played by the agricultural sector as a reserve of labour has been crucial to the development of the industrial sector in Italy.[5] In 1960 6.5 million people (31 per cent of the labour force) were employed in this sector. By the end of the 1960s these figures had fallen to 3.6 million and 18.4 per cent respectively. The decline continued throughout the 1970s – albeit at a slower rate – and by 1982 employment in agriculture had fallen to 2.5 million (12.1 per cent of the work-force). The size of the exodus appears even more striking if regional figures are considered. Agriculture in the Centre-North employed 34 per cent of the labour force in 1955 but only 8 per cent in 1984, while the corresponding figures for the South are 53 and 22 per cent respectively. At a time of rapid expansion, the availability of such an extensive reserve of labour was crucial in alleviating any potential supply constraint on the development of the industrial sector (M. Paci 1974).

The flow of newcomers was initially made up of young farmers from Northern and Central Italy, brought up in an agricultural system (known as the *mezzadria*) which closely resembles that of a small industrial complex, being characterised by small production units worked by extended families, but all forming part of a single estate with a common landowner, and physically housed in close proximity to one another. The head of the family was experienced in organising the various operations, in negotiating with the estate manager, and in selling the products of the *mezzadria* in the local market. The women were trained in the making and selling of home-produced goods, from linen to perfume and tanned leather. The younger men were knowledgeable not only in land-related skills, but also in the skill of mending equipment and vehicles, and in several other subsidiary trades – namely woodcraft, shoemaking, building, etc – plied in winter to earn additional income (Beccatini 1989). On leaving the countryside, some adapted their skills to the newly articulated needs of heavy industry. Others preferred to apply them in the more directly related areas of traditional industry and services. All took with them the basic entrepreneurial ability and sound business experience gained by running their small production units and selling their agricultural and handicraft products in local markets.

The process of industrialisation, however, brought a wave of radical changes in both the production techniques used in agriculture and the way the production process was conceived. As the traditional family-based units were replaced in the North by modern medium-sized farms, agriculture came to lose the role of reserve of labour (Sylos Labini 1987).[6] The flow of *contadini* from the Northern countryside was replaced initially by a stream of migration from the South and later by migration from abroad.[7] However, as supply constraints in the industrial sector become more binding, labour relations grew more turbulent.

The *Autunno Caldo* and its impact on the labour market

As Table 4.1 shows, the Italian unionisation rate was by the 1960s the second highest (at over 50 per cent) in Europe. Moreover, by the late 1960s what had previously been a weak and deeply divided Italian labour movement had grown into a robust, militant and united front. This phenomenon was partly the result of the considerable shift of employment away from agriculture – a sector characterised by very low union militancy – into heavy industry and public sector employment, with their high density of unionised labour. But equally important was the militancy of the migrant workers, who saw union loyalty as a way of showing their acceptance of the values of the Northern working class, and the union movement as the most promising way of improving their working conditions, living standards and social status.

Table 4.1 Union membership (percentage of employees)

Country	1960	1965	1970	1975	1980
Belgium	62	62	66	75	76
France	24	23	22	23	28
Germany	37	36	36	39	40
Italy	55	55	50	50	60
Netherlands	42	40	39	44	44
UK	45	45	50	53	57

Source: Eurostat, Industrial Relations

Conscious that long-lasting divisions had proved in the past to be a major weakness, the three main union confederations joined forces in what became known as the CGIL–CISL–UIL Federation.[8] Militant grass-roots factory committees were set up locally and, in response to criticisms from the leaders of those committees (the *delegati*) the Federation become actively involved at plant level. The power of the reunited labour movement grew steadily, thanks to a combination of economic and political factors. The rapidly increasing demand for labour resulted in a considerable shortage of labour in the North and, thanks to active intra-regional emigration policies, in a country-wide reduction in unemployment. Political factors were also important, notably the presence of the small centre-left parties in the coalition government, which meant that both CISL and UIL could, via their strong party links, successfully impose direct pressure on the government (Sassoon 1986) to pursue policies to their advantage.

The climax in this process of unionisation of the Italian economy came with the *Autunno Caldo* of 1969. Its impact on the union movement were considerable. The aftermath for industry was disastrous in terms both of reduced flexibility and increased labour costs.

The impact of the Autunno Caldo *on labour market flexibility*

The Italian labour market has always suffered from serious rigidities. The *Autunno Caldo* reinforced this historical tendency by providing workers with 'almost cast-iron security of employment' (Goodman 1989) and considerable protection against real wage fluctuations.

Regulations covering individual dismissals and collective redundancies, long-established and extensive, were reinforced by the 1970 *Statuto dei Lavoratori* – the 'Workers' Statute' – one of the major achievements of the reunited labour movement. Trade unions' opposition to any significant alteration of the statutory procedure for employment of new workers (the *collocamento*)[9] meant that the system, although by the mid-1960s widely perceived as obsolete, remained basically unchanged until 1984, when employers were finally given the option of recruiting up to 50 per cent of new employees on a 'calling-by-name' or 'head-hunting' basis (*chiamata nominativa*) rather than by the 'calling-by-number' procedure, based on position in the 'queue' of unemployment (*chiamata numerica*), imposed by the *collocamento*. Finally, the early 1970s saw the extension of the sphere of implementation of *Cassa Integrazione Guadagni* (CIG) compensation,[10] beyond that of short-term lay-offs due to temporary difficulties ('ordinary intervention') into the area of collective redundancies arising from sectoral/local crisis and restructuring ('extraordinary intervention'). Firms coming under the umbrella of the CIG are required, during the period of CIG coverage, to fill any vacancy from the list of lay-offs. The extension of CIG coverage imposed this constraint on an increasing number of firms.

Flexibility in the wage settlement mechanism had long been limited by the existence of the *Scala Mobile*, the system of automatic indexation of wage increases to price inflation otherwise known as the 'Escalator'. Prior to 1975 the *Scala Mobile* provided for adjustments in wage rates which were proportional to the contractual wage for each category of worker. The *Scala Mobile* component of a worker's wage increase was accordingly equal to the product of the contractual wage for his category and the percentage increase in retail prices. Wage differentials were therefore basically unaffected by the mechanism. However, the system was later amended, in response to union pressure, so as to link the adjustments to a *common* indexation factor defined as 1 per cent of the average nominal wage in 1959 – the so-called 'indexation point'. Thus the increase in wages in each quarter became an *absolute* amount for all workers, wage differentials were progressively squeezed, and the automatic component of wage increases rose sharply (Figure 4.2).

The discontent among skilled workers which followed the revision of the indexation formula explains much of the pressure for more extensive use of local negotiations and a general increase in the non-automatic component of employees' earnings. The result

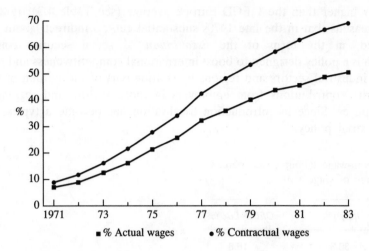

Figure 4.2 Indexed elements as percentage of total wages
Source: Bank of Italy data

was a worsening of the price-wage spiral and a generalised sharp increase in the cost of labour.

The impact of the Autunno Caldo *on the cost of labour*

Table 4.2 presents the average rate of growth of nominal and real wages in the private sector by five-year periods. Given the pattern of the *Scala Mobile*, it is not surprising to find that in the years of high inflation of the 1960s and 1970s, nominal wages increased sharply. It is perhaps more interesting to note that *real wages* also show considerable increases. In the 1970s, for example, despite an average rate of price inflation of over 12 per cent, nominal wages in the private sector increased enough to guarantee an average real wage increase of around 7 per cent, a rate of growth well above the average of the major OECD countries.

Table 4.2 Wage increases (private sector)

Years	Nominal (%)	Real (%)
1960–4	13.2	7.7
1965–9	7.2	4.3
1970–4	16.6	6.9
1975–9	21.1	4.5
1980–4	19.7	0.5

Source: ISTAT, Statistiche del Lavoro

While wages were increasing, *non-wage labour costs* remained proportionately basically unchanged until the late 1970s. Their absolute level was, however, considerably higher than the OECD-Europe average (see Table 4.3). It was for this and other reasons that in the late 1970s substantial cuts to indirect labour costs were implemented, in the form of the *fiscalisation* of social security contributions. Fiscalisation is a policy designed to boost international competitiveness and profitability in targeted industrial sectors and regions by shifting part of the burden of the related social security contributions from employers in those sectors and regions onto the general taxpayer. Since its introduction fiscalisation has become a typical feature of Italian industrial policy.

Table 4.3   Non-wage labour costs (percentage of wages)

Years	Italy (%)	OECD–Eur (%)
1970	38.5	16.6
1975	39.9	20.8
1980	35.3	24.0
1982	35.5	24.1
1983	38.0	24.5
1984	39.0	19.5

Source: OECD, Labour Costs Statistics

The impact of the Autunno Caldo on industrial action

As Table 4.4 shows, Italy had, in the decade 1970–80, the second highest number of work stoppages among the countries considered (after France), and the stoppages, although relatively short (average length only 1.9 days, compared to a European average of 2.9), involved a large number of workers. They resulted in a number of lost working days over four times the European average and higher than that experienced by the other 'conflict-based regimes', such as Britain and France.

The impact of the Autunno Caldo on small firms

The combination of labour market rigidities, high labour costs, and a high level of industrial militancy, brought about by the wave of discontent of the late 1960s, forced the industrial sector to operate under labour market conditions which were considerably less favourable than those experienced in previous decades. However, there was considerable variation in the way that firms were affected by these changes.

During the period leading up to the changes, associations of small businesses had used their political influence to lobby political parties into accepting the need for special concessions in their favour. Small firms – initially defined as having fifteen employees or fewer[11] – were exempted from the principal provisions of the *Statuto dei Lavoratori* and the *Collocamento*. They were given exemption from payment of VAT and of some forms of social security contributions and, assessed for local taxes at a special, low rate. On top of that, they experienced relatively lower levels of industrial

Table 4.4 International strike statistics (average 1970–80)

Country	Days lost (000s)	Workers involved (000s)	Average length	Number of strikes
Belgium	771	80	9.6	201
Denmark	478	92	5.2	201
France	3,087	1,266	2.4	4,035
Germany	1,185	195	6.1	569
Ireland	532	33	16.3	141
Italy	17,609	9,511	1.9	3,618
Netherlands	155	25	6.2	135
UK	12,788	1,545	8.3	2,514
EEC (Aver)	4,622	1,618	2.9	1,436

Source: Eurostat, Industrial Disputes

action and union militancy. It is therefore not surprising that they should have performed better than their larger counterparts in the years to follow.

The *ristrutturazione* of the industrial sector and the birth of the *Terza Italia*

The changes in the structure of the industrial sector brought about by the *Autunno Caldo*, in terms of both the industrial relations system and the potential for profitability, led to a phase of profound 'restructuring'. Generally this took the form of first, substantial technological changes, intended to boost productivity, and second, decentralisation of production, designed to take advantage of the preferential treatment granted to small firms (Barca and Magnani 1989).

The strategy of accelerated modernisation adopted by large-scale industry – often referred to as 'internal restructuring' (Graziani 1989: 85) – was not an entirely new phenomenon. It followed the same path to international competitiveness as taken in the early 1960s, which had already borne fruit in rapid productivity growth (see Table 4.5).

The strategy of decentralisation developed along two main lines (Piore and Sabel 1984). In the Northern areas – particularly in the Turin area, dominated by Fiat – it assumed its most typical form, with entire sections of the productive process being transferred from large-scale firms to smaller producers, which soon grew highly dependent on local large firms in terms of the pattern of output produced, the technology adopted, and the conditions of the market – the typical 'dependent sector' of 'dualist theory' (Berger and Piore 1980). In the regions of Veneto, Emilia-Romagna and other central regions, by contrast, decentralisation resulted in the birth of a myriad of little firms, spread uniformly across the area, and independent of any larger producers in all aspects of the production process (New Technology-Based Small Firms) (Rothwell and Zegveld 1982).[12]

In the long run, this second type of production structure prevailed, and, under the collective name of *Terza Italia*, has been seen by many as the single major factor behind Italy's most recent 'economic miracle' – the ace up Italy's sleeve in the aftermath of the Second Oil Crisis.[13]

Table 4.5   Trends in labour productivity

Years	Annual average rate of growth (%)
1960–4	6.3
1965–9	6.1
1970–4	4.3
1975–9	2.4
1980–4	1.4

Source: ISTAT, Statistiche del Lavoro

The Dr Jekyll side: the success of small firms

The dramatic change in the role of the small firm, from one of subordination to the large establishment to that of leader in the process of industrial development, was officially recognised when a comparatively small producer of household appliances from the Marche region, Giovanni Merloni, succeeded Gianni Agnelli to the presidency of the *Confindustria* (Confederation of Italian Industry) (Graziani 1989).

In little more than a decade, what had previously been a 'crown of satellite producers' (Graziani 1989) had replaced the large establishments they were originally producing for, and had given birth to a numerous and varied set of new producers, ranging from medium and small firms to self-employed workers. Often firms working in the same sector showed a tendency to crowd into the same area, generating the phenomenon commonly referred to as 'industrial district' (Beccatini 1987).

The extent of the success

Comparison of data from the 1971 and 1981 industrial censuses conducted by the Central Statistical Office (Istituto Centrale di Statistica, ISTAT) shows a significant change in the size structure of Italian industry. The number of small and medium firms – with a maximum of 99 employees – increased by 21 per cent, compared to an increase of only 5.8 per cent in the number of firms of 100 employees or more. The increase in the relative importance of small-to-medium-sized firms was even more noticeable in terms of employment. Their share of total employment rose from 48.5 per cent in 1971 to 55.5 per cent in 1981, and by 1984 reached levels comparable only to those of Japan

(Table 4.6). In absolute terms, employment increased by 28.5 per cent 1971–81, while the average size of firm fell, with the average number of employees in firms of 100 employees or more being reduced from 438 to 402.

Table 4.6 The structure of total
manufacturing employment
(firms with < 100
employees, %)

Country	1971	1984
France	15.5	27.7
Germany[a]	12.5	16.0
Japan[b]	23.6	66.5
USA[c]	15.0	16.5
UK	53.7	22.0
Italy	53.1	59.0

Notes:
[a] Firms with more than twenty employees
[b] Data for the second period refer to 1981
[c] Data refer to 1976 and 1982 respectively

Source: Vercelli *et al* 1989

Among small-to-medium-sized firms, the highest growth rate, in terms of both the number of firms and the employment level, was experienced by firms of between ten and nineteen employees. The very smallest size category (up to nine employees), however, remained the most numerous. In 1985 it was estimated that firms employing fewer than ten workers still made up 80 per cent of all Italian manufacturing units.

Analysis of the distribution of gross profits across firms also confirms the vitality of small and medium-sized firms. Figures from the 1983–5 ISTAT surveys on gross product indicate a stable inverse relationship between profitability and the size of the firm, a relationship which is still evident even after the data have been corrected to reflect the different percentages of self-employed workers in the two categories of firm (+12 per cent in small firms).[14] Although the advantage of small firms was to a degree eroded during the period 1983–5 – with profit levels of large firms growing considerably in some sectors – in 1985 the highest ratio of profit to value added was recorded among the firms with fifteen to nineteen employees for over half the total number of industrial branches (Rey 1989).

Small and medium-sized firms have typically been found in the traditional industries. However, a work-force of around thirty has also been typical in sub-branches like 'instrument engineering' and 'manufacture of metal goods not elsewhere specified'. Moreover, the most dynamic branch in terms of increases in employment in smaller firms 1983–5 was 'metal goods, engineering and vehicles', with 'instrument engineering' recording a rise of as much as 12 per cent.

The interpretation of the developments

The different interpretations put on the increased importance of the small firms arise from their highly diversified characteristics as well as from different theoretical standpoints.

The traditional view

The traditional models of oligopoly and dualism explain the expansion of *dependent* small firms as a transitory development, designed to overcome increased rigidities in the labour market and reduce union influence over the production process. Once these difficulties have been overcome, average size might be expected to increase again in order to take full advantage of economies of scale.

This interpretation appears to be confirmed by the data on labour cost differentials between different categories of firms. According to the ISTAT survey, labour costs in 1983 were on average 40 per cent higher in large firms than in smaller firms, despite the mitigating effect of the operation of the *Cassa Integrazione Guadagni* on labour costs in the former (Rey 1989). Moreover, the major differences were found in the actual wage levels, rather than in relation to the payment of social security contributions. This pattern has been reinforced by the recent trend towards payment of higher compulsory contributions by small businesses and higher rates of remuneration in large firms following the restructuring.

The model of flexible specialisation

The main alternative interpretation addresses itself to the *New Technology-Based Small Firms*, and sees their growth as a more permanent feature of the industrial sector resulting from recent radical changes in production techniques (Brusco and Sabel 1981). The 'model of flexible specialisation', which lies at the heart of this view, emphasises the tendency of small firms to employ a skilled labour force, and to take a central role in innovative processes by specialising in a limited number of phases of production essential in the manufacturing of many different goods. Radical changes in the production process are seen as the cause of this development. Technological innovation, no longer to be found mainly in large firms, has, it is argued, led to a progressive decrease in the importance of economies of scale, and to a considerable reduction of the minimum efficient scale (Birch 1984). Moreover, the dynamic pattern of international specialisation has tended to shift mass production towards developing countries, thereby reducing the scope for economies of scale in technologically advanced countries.

In this context, smaller size enables firms to master the uncertainty of a market that is increasingly oriented to personalised production, by reacting more quickly to changes in product demand via a more efficient and flexible use of new technology. Reduced labour market rigidities allow a more systematic substitution of machinery for labour and a closer match between the skills of the labour force and market demand. The final outcome, it is argued, is the success story of the small business in Italy.

Why is the phenomenon so much more sharply delineated in Italy?

While obviously important in explaining current international trends in the relative importance of small firms in industry, the interpretations outlined above shed little light on why the trend has been so much more pronounced in Italy than in most other countries. The previous section of this chapter points to two possible causes: first, the availability of a reserve of labour with sound business experience and basic entrepreneurial ability; second, the particularly severe rigidities operating in the labour market. Italian social and economic history suggests two additional factors: third, the crucial role traditionally played by self-employment in the Italian economy; fourth, the strength of the tradition of political decentralisation inherited from the medieval *Comuni*.[15]

It is certainly true that self-employment has long been of great importance in the Italian economy. In 1960 over 40 per cent of those in employment were self-employed, and, despite a sharp decline in the mid-1960s, the proportion of the labour force in self-employment was still as high as 28 per cent in 1982 (P. Paci 1988), three times higher than in Britain (Britton et al 1986). Moreover, the importance of self-employment has steadily increased in industry, where the 'ideology of self-employment', as the ideal occupation for the risk-loving Italian free-thinker, has gained considerable ground (Graziani 1989: 144).

Historically, self-employment in Italian industry has been identified with the master craftsman, the *artigiano*. For centuries he has been the man of skill, sensitivity and inventiveness, with a passion for detail, his work and his independence, and with a flair for design. Given the small scale of its activity, the *artigiano firm* has always felt the need to please customers and economise on costs. This has given him the incentive to constantly improve his skill, explore new techniques and improvise.

There is obviously much common ground between the *artigiano firm* and the new high-technology-based small business. The latter builds on the craftsman's time-honoured characteristics of independence and inventiveness. In the world of high technology, the *artigiano*'s natural capacity to innovate has led to that revival of traditional industries – by means of the extensive application of new technology – which is one of the most promising features of the *Terza Italia*, and to the successful development of a new high-technology sector as such. The old objective of providing bespoke production for individual customers has been reflected in the concept of 'customised production'. It is the passion for detail and the natural flair for design that have created the up-market image of the 'Made in Italy' logo.[16]

Last in the list of factors behind the success of the *Terza Italia* phenomenon is the policy of intervention actively pursued by the local governments of the regions involved. Over the years the rather rhetorical motto 'in defence of local society' has found practical implementation in, first, the development of co-operative movements; second, the creation of a strong local banking system, based on institutions often called 'savings banks' or '*artigiane* banks', designed to channel *local* savings into *local* firms; third, the provision of high-quality adult education – especially of a technical and professional nature; and (later) fourth, the creation of trading and industrial estates – where small factories could be built or let at advantageous terms – and fifth, the provision of financial incentives for small businesses setting up in 'depressed areas' within the boundaries of the region.

A critical assessment of the success story

Given the differences in wage levels between large and small firms, the change in the structure of employment away from the former and into the latter has inevitably resulted in a reduction in average wages. According to some, the trend has also led to a worsening of working conditions: longer working hours, more overtime, more intense working patterns and less job security (see Becattini 1987). Moreover, the growth of small business has resulted in the extensive use of *irregular* work, not only in its traditional forms of moonlighting and 'hidden employment', but also in that of the more recent phenomenon of illegal immigration from developing countries (Dell'Aringa and Neri 1987).

It was for these reasons that the unions and the political parties of the left adopted in the first instance a rather hostile attitude towards the new industrial structure. Only when it became clear that that structure had the potential, by boosting employment considerably to increase family incomes, despite its negative effect on wage levels, did the unions and political left come round to approving the change.

The reality of the small firm is, however, complex. Within the category, innovative firms operate alongside technically backward ones. Thus, for example, the ISTAT-CNR (National Research Council) study on innovation in firms of twenty employees and more reveals that technological advances were introduced by only 63.3 per cent of the respondents, compared to 88.9 per cent of firms with 500 employees or more.[17] These figures would suggest that traditional, less innovative firms still account for a significant proportion of the small firm category. However, the highest percentage of innovative firms are in 'manufacture of office machinery and data-processing equipment' (95.2 per cent) with 'mechanical engineering' (82.5 per cent) in third place.[18] Both are sectors where the proportion of small firms has increased rapidly.

Mr Hyde 1: the persistent problem of the South

Successful though it may be, the area of the *Terza Italia* is but a small part of Italy. While recent years have seen prosperity expanding from the traditionally rich regions of the North-East into a growing area of the country, Italy's regional problem is still one of the most severe in Europe, with relative poverty remaining the prevailing feature of the area commonly referred to as the *South*. According to the traditional definition, this area includes the eight regions of the *Mezzogiorno* (the land of the midday sun),[19] containing about 40 per cent of the land, 35 per cent of the population and 24 per cent of Italy's GDP. In absolute terms the population of the South in 1990 was 20.5 million, more than that of Greece and Portugal together.

The long history of government intervention

The establishment of the *Cassa per il Mezzogiorno* in 1950 signified the political victory of the *nuovi meridionalisti* who – contrary to previously dominant liberal tradition – believed that, given the special features of the area, the development of the

Mezzogiorno required direct government intervention. After a decade in which the activity of the *Cassa* was largely limited to the provision of civil infrastructures (such as roads, schools and hospitals), the focus was diverted to the industrial sector, and the creation of employment became the main objective. A system of financial incentives for firms settling in the South was introduced, with the emphasis on those small firms that, using less capital-intensive technology, were expected to have a more significant employment effect.

Soon, however, the fear that focusing on small businesses would prevent the development of a large and modern industrial sector led to the progressive extension of the incentives to larger firms. The unexpectedly powerful wave of investment which followed came from the private and the public sector alike. While private firms were increasingly more attracted by the lower degree of union militancy still prevailing in the Southern regions,[20] the growth of public investment in the area was a direct reflection of the increasing importance of public holdings in the Italian industrial sector as a whole.

One major result of this flow of capital was a shift of emphasis away from small enterprises and towards sectors in which large firms prevailed. It was, in fact, in just these sectors that 'public holdings' dominated and industrial relations problems were most common. The trend was further reinforced by the structure of the regional incentives, designed to reduce production costs, with little attention being devoted to the marketability of the products. They therefore appealed mainly either to large firms with well-established distributional channels, or, to a lesser extent, to small firms selling exclusively on the local market. Thus the industrial development of the *Mezzogiorno* came progressively to be identified with the establishment of heavy industry, such as steel and chemicals – the building of the infamous 'cathedrals in the desert'.

For a while this process of accelerated industrialisation helped to narrow the gap between the South and the rest of the country. However, when in the 1970s the world demand for the products featured in *Cassa* development programmes dropped, and the South remained impervious to the technological revolution which the North had undertaken, the 'cathedrals' were progressively abandoned as monuments to past mistakes ('museums in the desert'), and the gap between the two parts of the country grew larger again. In recognition of the failure of the *Cassa per il Mezzogiorno* successfully to handle the problem of underdevelopment of the South, a new mechanism was sought.

In 1986, after years of negotiations – and a policy vacuum which did not help the economic development of the South – a radical reform of the system of intervention was implemented. Two newly established bodies – the *Agenzia per la promozione dello sviluppo del Mezzogiorno* and the *Dipartimento per il Mezzogiorno* – share the responsibilities previously assigned to the *Cassa*: the *Agenzia* having mainly a financial role and the *Dipartimento* one of control and general administration. The new 'programme of intervention' focuses on regional and local responsibility, and, in recognition of the errors of the past, the emphasis is now again on small private enterprise, while the coverage of the incentive system has been extended to include the service sector.[21]

The benefits offered to firms setting up in the *Mezzogiorno* are substantial: grants of up to 40 per cent of capital costs, up to two-thirds interest-rate relief, tax exemptions, social security concessions and special assistance for the development of business services and R&D. However, to date this plethora of incentives has shown little sign of achieving its target. 'Investors remain stubbornly unattracted by the South' (*Economist* 1990: 22), and the *Mezzogiorno* remains substantially worse off than the rest of the country.

The current extent of the North–South divide

A few figures are sufficient to illustrate the extent of the Italian regional problem. In 1989 the average level of GDP per head in the *Mezzogiorno* was almost 30 per cent below the European average. The corresponding figure for Northern Italy was 24 per cent higher than the European average, 10 per cent higher than in the Federal Republic and 15 per cent higher than in France (Wolleb 1990). To take a different angle, the country contains four of Europe's richest twenty-five regions but it also has seven of Europe's poorest.

It is more difficult to find a precise measure of the gap. Traditionally the ratios between, first, average consumption per head in the South and that in the rest of the country, and second, gross regional product per head in the two areas, have been used. The conclusions reached depend crucially on the indicator adopted.

Recent trends in the former ratio lead to the optimistic conclusion that 'the problem of the *Mezzogiorno* is no longer one of poverty and underconsumption' (Wolleb 1990): in 1987 average consumption per head in the South was as much as 83 per cent the national average, a considerable improvement on the post-war figure. However, comparisons of GDP per head across different regions present a very different picture. Table 4.7 presents index numbers of regional product per head in 1987, with the Italian average equal to 100. The extent of the regional differences is striking: the highest level of GDP per head (that of Lombardia) was almost two and a half times the lowest (that of Calabria). On average, GNP per head in the *Mezzogiorno* was only 67 per cent of the Italian average.

Underlying the differences in the results obtained with the alternative indicators is the widely acknowledged fact that in the South consumption is consistently higher than gross regional product. This phenomenon highlights the problem of the artificial boosting of Southern standards of living which derives from the huge scale of government transfer payments. The extent of that boosting, often expressed in terms of the so-called 'indicator of dependency' (*indicatore della dipendenza*), increased over the 1980s, when investment levels in the South began to fall, following the contraction in heavy industry, and the traditional flow of Southern surplus labour to the North went into reverse, due to the 'restructuring' of Northern industry.

Similarly bleak conclusions are reached if differences in unemployment rates are considered. The official unemployment rate was 7.7 per cent in the Central-Northern regions in 1988, while it was 21.1 per cent in the South (ISTAT 1989). Moreover, in the Central-Northern regions unemployment is of an essentially 'selective' character: it is found mainly among women (12.8 per cent) and the young, and is basically absent in the market for mature male workers, with an average unemployment rate for males of 4.7 per cent in 1988. In the South, by contrast, not only is female unemployment particularly high (32.8 per cent), but also the average unemployment rate for males is as high as 14.5 per cent. Even if forms of irregular employment are considered, therefore, unemployment in the South remains a mass phenomenon with characteristics of deep structural imbalance.[22]

Table 4.7 Gross GDP per head 1987

Region	Index number Italy = 100
Piemonte	117.7
Valle d'Aosta	122.5
Lombardia	133.1
Trentino-Alto A.	117.0
Veneto	114.8
Friuli-V.G.	112.6
Liguria	113.3
Emilia-Romagna	124.5
Toscana	109.7
Umbria	90.2
Marche	102.7
Lazio	113.1
Abruzzi	83.8
Molise	71.0
Campania	65.6
Puglia	70.5
Basilicata	56.2
Calabria	55.2
Sicilia	66.5
Sardegna	73.7
North-Centre	118.8
South	67.3

Source: ISTAT Le Regioni in Cifre

Even more striking differences between the two parts of the country are found in the level of socio-economic infrastructure. Despite a level of public investment per head of population in the South which greatly exceeds that in the North (43.5 per cent of the Italian total in 1978), a recent European Community report found that the South is about half as well served as the North in terms of energy, water, transport, telecommunications and other elements of economic infrastructure (Di Palma 1986). The same pattern is evident from Table 4.8, which also shows the poor housing conditions of the South compared with the rest of the country. Differentials in the same range have also been found with respect to the availability of both private and public services – such as schools, transport and health service – and in the degree of efficiency with which they are provided (Graziani 1989; Gattei 1982).

To add to the problem, many fear that the extent of the inter-regional gap may be set to increase as full European integration approaches and as, following the upward revision of estimates for Italian GDP, the EC contests some regions' eligibility for money from the Community's Regional and Social Fund (*Economist* 1988; 1990).

Table 4.8 Comparisons of civil infrastructure (1987) and housing conditions (1981) in the North and the South

	Measurement unit	South	North	Italy
Civil infrastructure				
Railways	(km/100 km^2)	6.5	6.6	6.6
Roads	(km/100 km^2)	86.1	110.3	100.4
Telephones				
connections	(no/100 inhab)	25.1	38.0	33.3
working sets	(no/100 inhab)	33.9	57.4	48.9
Housing conditions				
Unfit accommodation	(no/100 accom)			
urban areas		28.3	13.6	
others		32.0	13.3	

Sources: ISTAT Le Regioni in Cifre; Padoa Schioppa 1990

Prospects for the future

So is the *Mezzogiorno* set to become the victim of Italy's economic success? Essential for the evaluation of the economic prospects of the South is an assessment of the factors which have kept investment away from the area, despite the considerable financial incentives involved. Among those firms which have shied away from the *Mezzogiorno*, some have continued to prefer the more advanced Northern regions, while others have settled in areas at a comparable stage of development, such as Spain or Portugal.

Crucial to the decisions of both groups have, undoubtedly, been the comparatively high labour costs per unit of output that production in the South entails. While nation-wide negotiations guarantee equal wage levels across the whole of Italy, productivity levels in the *Mezzogiorno* are still considerably lower than in the North – by 20 per cent in 1990 (Wolleb 1990). Labour costs per unit of output are therefore significantly higher than in the North. They are also considerably higher than those prevailing in countries at a comparable stage of development. However, labour cost differentials are not the only factor channelling capital away from the South.

The decision of those who prefer the North is also heavily influenced by the comparative lack of socio-economic infrastructure in the South (see pp. 85–6), by the relative difficulty of recruiting suitably qualified workers, by inefficient local administrations, and by the relative scarcity of local suppliers of business services and complementary products. In contrast, the preference shown by some foreign investors to countries such as Spain or Portugal seems to reflect mainly consideration of socio-economic factors, such as the presence in the *Mezzogiorno* of powerful elements of organised crime and political corruption, and the climate of uncertainty surrounding law enforcement, which imposes considerable pressure on newcomers to acquire the protection of local politicians and criminal gangs.

The reluctance to take advantage of the abundance of financial incentives evinced by both local and external capital suggests that, large though it may be, the 'carrot' offered is not enough to compensate for the relative disadvantages under which the South labours. Grants and loans are not enough to compensate for the lack of economic infrastructure and the uncongenial social structure of the area, and the social security concessions extended do not fully compensate for higher labour costs per unit of output.

This line of argument lends support to the view of those who believe that the constraints on the development of Southern Italy can no longer be interpreted in purely economic terms (Graziani 1989). Rather, they spring from serious shortcomings in the socio-economic infrastructure (Saraceno 1983; Salvati 1989), and from deeply rooted historical and cultural factors (Sylos Labini 1985). Any policy of intervention needs therefore to go beyond purely financial incentives and address itself to a radical reform of the socio-economic structure of the area. Indeed, in pursuit of the curbing of the power of organised crime and the problem of political corruption, a growing school of thought advocates the abolition of any type of financial incentive involving administrative discretion and the replacement of the existing government transfers – such as salaries for non-existent jobs, bogus disability pensions, financial support to unproductive firms, etc, with 'unemployment benefits paid by right rather than as a personal favour' (Wolleb 1990).

Moreover, many stress the importance of implementing policies designed to boost local supply so as to reduce the level of the 'indicator of dependency' of the region (Padoa Schioppa 1990). Others go further, in arguing against any further external attempts at *industrializazione forzata* (forced industrialisation) of the *Mezzogiorno* by means of external subsidies, and in favour of an increased stress on local entrepreneurship. In support of the latter argument, commentators point to recent developments in the Adriatic regions – and, to a lesser extent, in Sardinia – where some prosperity has been achieved with the extension southwards of that 'Adriatic line of development' (*linea adriatica di sviluppo*) which has proved so successful in the north-eastern regions of the *Terza Italia*, and which, as seen earlier, is primarily based on the success of private small business. Hence the rediscovered interest in the theory of 'internal diversity' (*divari interni*), which stresses the economic heterogeneity of the South.

Mr Hyde 2: the public deficit and the inefficiency of the public sector

Directly related to the problem of the South is the other chronic illness of the Italian economy – the huge public debt. The roots of this problem are to be found in the recession of the 1970s, when government intervention in industry increased considerably, and generous social legislation was passed without an adequate counter-balance in the form of increased taxes. Although the rising trend of the 1970s was reversed in the 1980s, the public deficit has remained a constant feature of the Italian economy, with levels still as high as 11 per cent of GDP in 1990 – about five times, in relative terms, that of the USA.

For a while inflation helped to disguise the costs of supporting this deficit, by generating negative real interest rates from 1971 to 1981. When, however, interest rates shot up, the negative effects on the public deficit were soon evident; by 1987 the *public debt ratio* – the ratio of public debt to GDP – had reached 100 per cent, and was, according to OECD forecasts, set to rise to 200 per cent by the early years of the twenty-first century.

For years economists have warned of the dire implications of running a debt of this magnitude, claiming that Italy would soon enter the 'debt trap' unless first, it stopped running a primary deficit;[23] and second, it could maintain a rate of growth higher than the interest rate, so as to prevent the public debt ratio rising. Neither of these conditions has been met. The government was planning to run a balanced budget in 1991 for the first time in decades, but observers were sceptical of the chances of success. At the same time growth rates, high in the past, are slowing down; in real terms gross domestic product grew by just 3 per cent in 1990.

Nevertheless the Italian economy has continued to thrive, with one of the fastest growth rates in Europe and a level of business investment which, far from being 'crowded out' by government borrowing, accounts for a bigger share of GDP than in most countries. The magic formula behind this result is to be found in the way the public deficit is financed. Contrary to what happens in other countries, barely 3 per cent of borrowing comes from abroad. The rest is met out of the high savings of Italian families, who are the thriftiest in the industrialised world (see Table 4.9) and who, given the tight controls operating until recently on both the domestic financial system and capital movement abroad, have been offered little choice of financial assets.

Table 4.9   Budget deficits and household savings (standardised definitions, % GDP) 1987

Country	Budget deficit	Household savings
Belgium	−7.3	13[a]
UK	−2.1	9
Canada	−4.4	10
France	−2.8	14
Netherlands	−6.3	3[b]
Japan	−1.2	18
USA	−2.4	4
FRG	−1.7	13
Italy	−10.3	23

Notes:
[a] Data refer to 1985
[b] Data refer to 1986

Source: OECD

However, this magic formula cannot be relied upon forever. Some have perceived a tendency for the propensity to save of the Italians to fall in response to pressures from financial intermediaries (*Economist* 1988). Others see the 1991 lifting of the last remaining restrictions on capital movements as an opportunity for Italian savers to desert government bonds in favour of more challenging capital investments abroad. Although the first stage of capital movement liberation – between the end of 1988 and 14 May 1990 – has seen a net inflow rather than an outflow of capital,[24] many relish the prospect of Italian savings being wooed away by foreign financial intermediaries (at a time when about 60 per cent of public sector debt falls due for renewal), as the external shock necessary to force the government to get its finances under control.

With pressure on the government to reduce its deficit increasing, the focus of the debate has shifted towards the question of how best to achieve this target. The options to choose from are the obvious ones: 'raise more, spend less or privatise' (*Economist* 1990). Let us now look at these options in turn.

Why raising taxes is not a viable option

Total tax revenue in 1988 was equivalent to 39 per cent of Italy's GDP, well below the EC average of 46 per cent. However, it would be wrong to conclude from this that tax rates could easily be raised. Income tax and VAT are already relatively high. The source of the apparent contradiction is the leaky system of tax collection. While the burden of direct taxation on dependent workers has progressively increased as a result of 'fiscal drag',[25] evasion has remained the norm among self-employed people and in the *underground economy*. Recent estimates from the Ministry of Finance suggest that in 1991, even after considerable attempts to reduce evasion, one-quarter of income tax and one-third of VAT would still go uncollected. Many fear, therefore, that, quite apart from further increasing the inequity of the system, higher taxes would merely encourage more tax evasion. Thus the temptation – if any – is to cut rates.[26]

Curbing evasion is, accordingly, the only feasible way of increasing revenue. The prospects of succeeding in this mammoth task, however, are not bright. Over the years, every such attempt has served only to bring unpopularity to the government of the day. The two major difficulties encountered have been the very fragmented character of the Italian production and retail system, and the fact that the scale of evasion is so huge that almost everyone is involved in it and has an interest in maintaining the status quo. Italian politicians are therefore fully aware that there is no political dividend to be drawn from trying to change the situation.

The political opposition to privatisation

Given the limited scope for increasing tax revenue, and the renewed vigour with which the 'ideology of the private' was spreading in the country, it is not surprising that in the mid-1980s Italians should turn to privatisation as an obvious solution to the problem of public deficit. Selling off public enterprises could impact on both the revenue and the expenditure sides of the budget by bringing in some cash and, in most cases, saving the government the money required to cover losses. Accordingly IRI,[27] under its then president Romano Prodi, began in the early 1980s a policy of privatisation which led, over the years 1983–9, to the selling off of seventeen firms – with a total labour force of nearly 64,000 people – including Alfa Romeo and Montedison, and to a considerable inflow of private capital into publicly owned banks.

However, the recent struggle for the control of Enimont has shown that the majority of politicians are deeply suspicious of privatisation.[28] Although some of them may see it as a useful device to reduce the public deficit, for most of them, whatever their political ideology, it presents a threat to the patronage system (see p. 92) which has long been the basis of their votes and their power. Recent experience, such as the profound changes affecting the labour force at the newly privatised Alfa Romeo (there were no lay-offs, but productivity has shot up and union membership dropped as a result of the breakdown of the patronage system) have reinforced their fears. Outside the world of professional economists, privatisation is seen as desirable by relatively few people. It was tolerated during the 1980s as a way of resurrecting the major state holdings, IRI and ENI, from incipient bankruptcy. However, support for it, always lukewarm, seems to be dying away, and the chances of it being extensively used in the future as an additional source of revenue are slim.

The strategy of scaling down public spending and restructuring the public sector

Quite apart from the practical difficulties likely to be met in any attempt at increasing revenues, a general consensus is emerging among economists that the roots of the Italian budget problem lie in excessive spending rather than in insufficient revenue. The argument emphasises that, having risen from 37 to 51 per cent of GDP in the period 1980–90, the level of public spending in Italy is now one of the highest in the Western world. The services provided remain, however, considerably inferior to those offered in other countries. A considerable slimming down and restructuring of the government's *longa manus* is therefore advocated (see for example Padoa Schioppa 1990).

Potential areas of intervention

Some see the artificially high levels of transfer to the private sector, the abuse of provisions for financial benefits to firms, and the frequent and expensive take-overs of firms in financial difficulties, as obvious areas where economies should be introduced (Censis 1987). Others point to the flagrant tendency to overspend on the part of some departments and the high level of inefficiency of others as additional potential sources of savings (Padoa Schioppa 1990).

The most striking case of overspending is found in the area of pensions. The level of both old-age and disability pensions is currently less than 40 per cent the average wage: nothing very extravagant! Nevertheless the *Istituto Nazionale della Previdenza Sociale* (INPS) – which administers the state pension system – is fast heading for bankruptcy.[29] Since the 1960s expenditure on pensions has increased about ten times in real terms, and is expected to rise equally fast in the years to come (Grasso 1991). This trend has been the result of the operation of two main factors: a considerable increase in the average size of the pension and a sharp rise in their number. Currently, out of a population of 57 million, nearly 19 million people receive pensions, over half of them being disability pensions.[30] The high proportion of the latter does not reflect any particular health weakness of the Italian race: it simply results from the fact that disability pensions act as social shock-absorbers. They are often paid to able-bodied workers, particularly Southerners, as a way of concealing unemployment and poverty, in a welfare system where unemployment and social security benefits as such are insufficient for some and non-existent for most.

More controversial is the question of overspending in another important area of the Welfare State – health care. Notwithstanding claims to the contrary, international comparisons show that Italy neither overspends nor underperforms in this area. In terms of proportion of GNP spent on health care in 1987, Italy recorded the third lowest figure among the OECD countries – a position that it occupied more or less throughout the period 1977–87 – though the growth in the proportion 1977–87 was relatively impressive (19 per cent compared to a OECD average of 18 per cent) (Office of Health Economics 1989). Similarly, only three OECD countries spent less per person on health care in 1987 than Italy. Though many sources acknowledge the presence of widespread dissatisfaction among the public, the only relevant survey suggests that 73 per cent of those who used the public care system in 1985 found the service received more than satisfactory (Centro Europa Ricerche 1988).[31] There is, furthermore, no obvious evidence that the Italian health care system is inefficient. Indeed, given its low level of expenditure, Italy scores relatively well in terms of crude outcome measures, such as infant mortality and life expectancy.

However, the same cannot be said for other public sector departments. Although it is always difficult to measure efficiency in public utilities, the clear efficiency gap between anything private and anything public in Italy is in general so overwhelming that even the casual observer finds it impossible not to notice it.

> Give an order to one of Italy's countless entrepreneurs for the shoes or gaskets or machine-tools you require and he will meet your requirements more efficiently than his competitor anywhere in the world. Go to the post office, pick up the telephone, despatch your goods by train, and pray for serenity lest in your frustration you explode like Vesuvius.
>
> (*Economist* 1990: 4).

The postal service, the telecommunications system and the railways are indeed the areas of particularly acute inefficiency, according to the few general studies available on the subject (Nomisma 1987). More specific data confirm this overall picture.

A recent survey by the Confindustria found that an ordinary letter took an average of ten days to get from Treviso, in the North, to Rome, and eighteen days to get to Naples (*Economist* 1990). Information from the Post Office itself suggests that the average delivery time for a letter to Rome is eight days if sent from a city, and nine and one-third days otherwise (Padoa Schioppa 1990). These figures not only compare very badly internationally – in Germany and the UK, for example, three-quarters of correspondence reaches its destination by the next day – but also reveal a worsening in the trend over time. Whilst institutional factors[32] may go some of the way to explaining such poor performance, it is difficult to imagine why delivering mail in Italy should take eight times as long as in other countries, and should become a more time-consuming exercise as time goes by.

According to official figures, the telephone system does not perform any better (STET 1988, in Padoa Schioppa 1990). The quality of the service not only is inferior to that of any other EC country, except Spain and Greece, but also has been declining over the 1970s and 1980s. So, for example, the average waiting time for a telephone connection, which was three months in 1968, had increased to five months by 1986, having reached over ten months in the period 1980–2. In 1986 the average waiting time was three months in The Netherlands, two weeks in Belgium, France, Germany and Switzerland and only a few days in the UK.

A very similar story emerges from an analysis of the railways. Whatever indicator of efficiency and quality of the service is used, the conclusions are very gloomy. In 1987 the average speed was below 100 km/h, less than in 1972. The average delay was seven minutes for local trains and twelve minutes for others. Moreover, international comparisons highlight poor Italian performance in terms of both the number of employees per kilometre of track and the productivity of labour. In 1986, for every 100 workers employed on one kilometre of Italian railways, there were 77 in the UK, 74 in Germany and 50 in France. Moreover, if we take productivity of labour on the Italian railways in 1986 as 100, the comparable figures were 146 for the UK, 176 for Germany and 193 for France.

The major source of inefficiency and overspending

Contrary to the situation in other countries,[33] the causes of inefficiency in the Italian public sector go far beyond the isolation of the sector from market forces. It derives above all from the system of *lottizzazione*, a patronage system which parcels out jobs in the public sector to political appointees in rough accordance with the electoral strength of the parties, and which permeates the entire public sector.

Patronage results in public utilities being run by managers and employees who have the correct political qualification rather than the appropriate skills and abilities, and public administration being controlled by bureaucrats whose loyalty lies with the party rather than with the government or the public, and whose prime ambition is a position with life tenure and with the possibility of a second job. Returning to an earlier theme, patronage means, for example, that invalidity pensions are allocated, not on the basis of entitlement, but on that of *raccomandazioni*, so that many of those receiving them would probably not qualify for equivalent transfers under an objective social security system. More generally, it means that the entire area of transfers to the private sector is dominated by clientism, and the large size of this category of expenditure bears testimony to the appetite of political parties for the acquisition of power and votes via the patronage system.

Is there light at the end of the tunnel?

Any attempt to reduce the size of the public sector and any radical reform of that sector must therefore encompass a dramatic reduction in the power of patronage. But that requires a degree of political commitment that none of Italy's forty-nine governments since 1945 have been able, or willing, to provide. The crucial question, then, is whether the present government – or any future one – would be significantly more willing than past ones have been to undertake the necessary steps.

Few believe in any increased willingness. The major feature of the Italian political system is its volatile stability, from which only limited and non-abrasive changes result. Although the average life-span of governments has been less than one year, Italy is alone among West European democracies in having had no real alteration of government for the duration of the post-war period: each of the forty-nine governments have been dominated by one single party (the Christian Democrats), and by the same men. The current (1991) prime minister, Giulio Andreotti, has been in the same position seven times before and has held senior positions in twenty-eight Cabinets: a sudden and radical change in his position seems most unlikely.

There are those who put their trust in some external shock forcing the government to act. This could take the form of an old-fashioned financial crisis, induced perhaps by refinancing difficulties, or of increased pressure from the EC, following Italy's entrance into the 2.5 per cent band of the ERM and the full implementation of the Single European Act. Neither of these things, however, is likely to happen in the short run. Things are still going too well, and, as long the economy continues to thrive, politicians will feel no need to change anything.

Conclusions

Although widely recognised as excelling in many areas of civilisation, Italy was, at the end of the Second World War, lagging somewhat behind its European partners in two very important areas – the degree of economic development and the socio-political infrastructure.

The last few decades have seen Italy confound its critics and engineer an economic miracle that has transformed it into one of the major industrialised countries. The secrets of this success are rooted in Italian culture and history, and are symbolised by the phenomenon *Terza Italia*. Many issues, however, remain unresolved. Prominent among these are the relative underdevelopment of the South, and the chronic public sector deficit. Underlying both evils is the system of patronage which impregnates Italy's socio-economic structure, and on which much of its political structure is based.

The story of the 1990s will therefore be one of a battle for political reform. Although an unreformed Italy might still remain a formidable power, thanks to the Italians' natural knack for ingeniously circumventing government inefficiency, it would nevertheless be less successful than an Italy which had mastered its Mr Hyde side. In assessing the economic prospects of the country the crucial question to be addressed is whether Italy will be able to find the political strength to implement the radical reforms that are necessary to resolve the contradictions under which it presently labours. Will Dr Jekyll finally prevail over Mr Hyde? Only time will tell.

Notes

1   These figures were later revised downwards by the Italian Institute of Statistics, leaving the UK GDP in excess of the Italian for the year in question. The difference, however, was minimal. Since the Italian population is marginally larger than the British one, GDP per

head remained in any case slightly higher in the UK (14,265 purchasing power parity units compared to 14,250 in Italy in 1986).

2   For a somewhat different interpretation of the interrelation between the Dr Jekyll and the Mr Hyde sides of the Italian economy, see Brunetta (1991).

3   Literally translates as the *Third Italy*. The term *Terza Italia* was first used by Bagnasco to distinguish the area of Central and North-East Italy from the two areas on which attention had been mainly concentrated in the past: the heavily industrialised North-West and the more agricultural South. It includes the regions of Trentino-Alto Adige, Friuli-Venezia Giulia, Veneto, Emilia-Romagna, Tuscany, Marche and Umbria.

4   The conversion of starting motors of wartime airplanes into engines for the widely popular Vespa scooters is a well-known example of this process.

5   The role of the agricultural sector as a labour reserve at that time is verified by the strong, inverse correlation between the rate of change in agricultural employment and the business cycle.

6   This is confirmed by the observation that by the 1970s the marked correlation between the rate of change in agricultural employment and the business cycle characteristic of the previous period had largely disappeared (Sylos Labini 1987).

7   It is thought that around 1 million to 1.5 million immigrants now live in Italy, most of them of African origin.

8   From the names of the three major union confederations it represented: the Communist-Socialist CGIL (*Confederazione Generale Italiana del Lavoro*), the Socialist/Republican/Social Democratic UIL (*Unione Italiana del Lavoro*) and the Christian Democratic CISL (*Confederazione Italiana dei Sindacati dei Lavoratori*). The debate over the reform of the *Scala Mobile* in 1984 highlighted once again the basic differences between the individual confederations, and this led to the *de facto* dissolution of the Federation and the opening up of a clear split between the Communist and the Socialist wings of the CGIL.

9   The *Collocamento* hiring procedure, introduced in the 1940s, was designed to meet the needs of a mainly agricultural economy with large pockets of unskilled unemployment. It required that new workers be employed in numerical order from a list of job-seekers based on age, family circumstances and length of unemployment, with little consideration given to matching the skills of the potential worker with those sought by the firm.

10 The CIG is a (primarily) government-financed compensation fund which currently pays up to 90 per cent of the wages of industrial and construction workers who have been temporarily laid off (ie without official termination of employment) because of cyclical fluctuations (up to three months) or industrial restructuring (up to two years). For more details see P Paci (1988).

11 The number was later increased to twenty.

12 The founding of larger establishments – eg television or household appliance producers in Veneto – did also occur, but this development has proved to be comparatively less important in the long run.

13 For details of the evolution of the structure of the Italian industrial sector see Barca and Magnani (1989).

14 Differences in the proportion of self-employed workers in the different categories introduce a distortion into the crude data because the remuneration of self-employed workers is included, for accounting purposes, in gross profit. Profit levels therefore appear artificially high in those categories of firms in which the incidence of self-employment is highest.

15 In medieval Italy the *Comuni* were the city-states which emerged, after the break-up of the Roman empire, as self-contained, self-governing towns.

16 For an extensive treatment of this point see Goodman (1989).

17 The firms were asked whether they had implemented innovations in 1987 in any of the following three areas: products manufactured, the production process, and organisation. There are no striking regional differences in the figures, with 65.5 per cent of small firms in

the North introducing some form of innovation, compared to 58.5 per cent in the South (Rey 1989).

18   The second most innovative sector was artificial fibres (94.1 per cent).

19   These regions are Abruzzi, Molise and Apulia along the Adriatic coast; Campania, Basilicata and Calabria on the west coast; and the two islands, Sicily and Sardinia.

20   See for example the Fiat decision to decentralise the production process by opening up new production facilities at Vasto, Cassino and Termini Imerese.

21   The new 'programme of intervention' is intended to run for nine years (from 1985 to 1993) and is broken down into three *programmi triennali di sviluppo* (three-year programmes of development) and nine *piani annuali di attuazione* (annual implementation plans).

22   For details of the extent and composition of unemployment in different regions, see Accornero and Carmignani (1986: ch 2) and Bodo and Sestito (1989).

23   'Primary deficit' is defined as an excess of expenditure, excluding interest payments, over revenue.

24   The main reasons for these trends are first, the renewed stability given to the lira by its entrance into the narrow band of the exchange-rate mechanism of the European Monetary System, second, Italy's high interest rates, and third, the strong tendency for Italian firms to raise loans abroad.

25   The term 'fiscal drag' describes the phenomenon whereby in periods of inflation tax-payers are pushed up into increasingly higher tax brackets by the growth in nominal incomes, even where real incomes are constant.

26   This was, for example, the rationale behind last year's decision to index tax brackets to inflation in order to reduce the rate of fiscal drag.

27   The *Istituto per la Ricostruzione Industriale* (IRI) is a huge state holding company. It owns shares in 140 companies, employing a total of around 500,000 workers.

28   Enimont is a joint venture involving the state-owned energy group ENI and the now private chemical company Montedison.

29   For details of the crisis of the system and proposals for reform, see Vitaletti (1988).

30   The trend in the relative share of disability pensions does, however, appear to be downwards (Grasso 1991).

31   The survey was conducted in 1986, based on a sample of 3,000 people.

32   Such as the fact that, following devolution of responsibilities for public transport by road to regions, the latter refused to carry items for the Post Office.

33   A notable exception is Japan, whose public sector is characterised by degrees of inefficiency and levels of corruption very similar to that experienced in Italy. The similarities between the two countries extend much further, as many have emphasised.

References

Accornero A, Carmignani F (1986) *I Paradossi della Disoccupazione*. Il Mulino, Bologna

Barca F, Magnani M (1989) *L'Industria tra Capitale e Lavoro*. Il Mulino, Bologna

Beccatini G (1987) *Mercato e Forze Locali: Il Distretto Industriale*. Il Mulino, Bologna

Berger S, Piore M J (1980) *Dualism and Discontinuity in Industrial Society*. Cambridge University Press

Birch D (1984) The contribution of small enterprise to growth and employment. In Giersch H (ed) *New Opportunities for Entrepreneurship*. Mohr, Tubingen

Bodo G, Sestito P (1989) Disoccupazione e dualismo territoriale. *Temi di Discussione della Banca d'Italia* **123**

Britton A, Eastwood F, Major R (1986) Macroeconomic policy in Britain and Italy. *National Institute Economic Review* **4**: 38–53

Brunetta R (1991) *Il Modello Italia*. Marsilio, Venice

Brusco S, Sabel C F (1981) Artisan production and economic growth. In Wilkinson F (ed) *The Dynamics of Labour Market Segmentation*. Academy Press

Censis (1987) I trasferimenti publici alle imprese. *Note e Commenti* **5**

Centro Europa Ricerche (1986) Indagine sui consumi sanitari delle famiglie italiane: Primi risultati. *Rapporto* **1**

Centro Europa Ricerche (1988) La spesa sanitaria. *Rapporto* **2**: 84–95

Dell'Aringa C, Neri F (1987) Illegal immigrants and the informal economy. *Labour* **1**: 107–26

Di Palma M (1986) Summary of the Italian Report. In Biehl D (ed) *The Contribution of Infrastructures to Regional Development*. Commission of the European Communities, Brussels

Economist (1988) A survey of the Italian economy. 27 February

Economist (1990) Italy. 26 May

Gattei S (1982) Il divario nelle condizioni ambientali e civili del Mezzogiorno e del Centro-Nord. *Studi Svimez* **8–9**

Goodman E (1989) Introduction: the political economy of the small firm in Italy. In Goodman and Bamford (eds) (1989)

Goodman E, Bamford J (eds) (1989) *Small Firms and Industrial Districts in Italy*. Routledge

Grasso F (1991) L'evoluzione degli squilibri del sistema pensionistico: uno studio previsionale per il fondo pensioni dei lavoratori dipendenti. In Brunetta R, Tronti L (eds) *Welfare State and Redistribuzione*. Franco Angeli, Milan

Graziani A (1989) *L'Economia Italiana dal 1945 a Oggi* 3rd edn. Il Mulino, Bologna

ISTAT (Istituto Centrale di Statistica) (1989) *Le Regioni in Cifre*. Rome

Istituto Centrale di Statistica/CNR (1987) Indagine sulla diffusione della innovazione tecnologica nell'industria manifatturiera italiana. *Collana d'Informazione* **19**

Nomisma (1987) *La Produttività nell'Economia Italiana*. Edizioni Il Sole 24 Ore, Milan

Office of Health Economics (1989) *Compendium of Health Statistics*, London

Paci M (1974) *Mercato del Lavoro e Classi Sociali in Italia*. Il Mulino, Bologna

Paci P (1988) A profile of the Italian labour market since 1960. International Economics Research Centre, University of Sussex, *Discussion Paper* **88/51**

Padoa Schioppa F (1990) *L'Economia sotto Tutela*. Il Mulino, Bologna

Piore M J, Sabel C F (1984) *The Second Industrial Divide*. Basic Books

Rey G (1989) Small firms: profile and analysis. In Goodman and Bamford (eds) (1989)

Rothwell R, Zegveld W (1982) *Innovation and Small and Medium-Sized Firms*. Pinter

Salvati M (1989) Offerta e domanda di lavoro, offerta e domanda di prodotti: la disoccupazione nel Mezzogiorno. *Politica e Economia* **5**: 13–15

Saraceno P (1983) *L'Intervento Straordinario nel Mezzogiorno nella Nuova Fase Aperta dalla Crisi Industriale*. Svimez, Rome

Sassoon D (1986) *Contemporary Italy*. Longman

STET (1988) Tempi medi di evasione della domanda telefonica in Italia e nei principali paesi europei. Mimeo

Sylos Labini P (1985) L'evoluzione economica del Mezzogiorno negli ultimi trent'anni. *Temi di Discussione della Banca d'Italia* **46**

Sylos Labini P (1987) Occupazione e disoccupazione: tendenze di fonde e variazioni di breve periodo. *Temi di Discussione della Banca d'Italia* **97**

Vercelli A, Belvisi P L, Carnazza P (1989) Piccole imprese innovative in Italia: flessibilità tecnologica, contributo all'innovazione e fragilità finanziaria. *Economia e Politica Industriale* **63**: 47–81

Vitaletti G (1988) *Le Pensioni degli Italiani*. Marsilio, Venice

Wolleb E (1990) Growth is inhibited. *Financial Times* 23 October

CHAPTER 5

United Kingdom

MICHAEL BARROW and ANDREW NEWELL

Introduction

In this chapter we look at the British economy first from a microeconomic, then from a macroeconomic viewpoint. This is not meant to imply that these are two different, unrelated dimensions, for microeconomic policy (changing tax rates, for example) can, of course, have macroeconomic effects (eg on the rate of growth of output). However, the categorisation is a convenient one for our purposes.

The British economy has in recent years been the subject of much interest, not only to British economists. The 'Thatcher experiment' of the 1980s – aimed in part at arresting and reversing the relative decline of the British economy in comparison with many of its European neighbours – has been closely followed, and sometimes imitated, abroad. That this experiment had a strong ideological foundation makes it even more interesting to economic commentators.

The microeconomy

At the microeconomic level, economic policy since the early 1980s has been guided by the general principle of reducing state involvement in the economy, and letting private markets work. As we shall see, policy has not always been consistent in this regard, and other objectives have sometimes supervened. However, the general principle is a useful bench-mark against which to measure policy and performance.

We pursue our examination of policy in three broad sections. First, we look at how taxation has changed since 1980 and how it is likely to change in the future. This covers local as well as central government finances, including the poll tax. Second, we examine privatisation, which, broadly defined, encompasses issues of competition policy and regulation, as well as the sale of public assets. These two areas are important components in the process of reducing state involvement in the economy. Finally, we look at an area – that of environmental policy, for which the problem of externalities is an important issue – where competitive markets are known not to work well, to see if government has recognised their limitations, and the implications of those limitations for its own role.

Taxation policy

Background

The Conservative government came to power in 1979 with a commitment to cut taxation. The rationale for this was that heavy taxation was stifling both initiative and effort, and preventing healthy growth in the economy. Part of the rationale for tight control of public expenditure was that it would make room for reductions in tax rates, and thus encourage enterprise. Tax cuts were to be applied to both individuals and to firms, where high rates of corporation tax were seen as hindering investment and growth.

For all the rhetoric, Britain was not, by international standards, a particularly heavily taxed nation in 1979, nor has the overall burden of taxation changed very much during the 1980s. Figure 5.1 shows general government revenue from all sources as a percentage of GDP, for the twelve members of the European Community, in 1980 and 1990. Although not all revenue is from taxation (some may be in the form of direct charges for services, for example), these data do provide an idea of the 'burden' of government upon the economy.

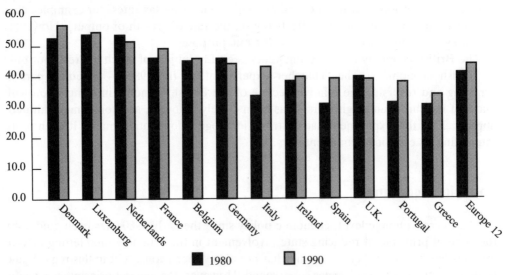

Figure 5.1   General government revenue as a percentage of GDP
Source: *European Economy*, December 1990, Table 54

In 1980 Britain's position lay in between the high-taxing Northern European states such as Denmark, and the low-taxing Southern states such as Portugal and Greece. In comparison with countries with similar levels of GDP, such as France and Belgium, Britain was relatively lightly taxed.

By 1990 Britain had slipped down the ranking, mainly because of tax increases by countries such as Italy and Spain, which had previously had particularly low levels of taxation. In general, it was countries with relatively low levels of GDP per head which had low rates of taxation in 1980, so we might interpret the evidence for 1990 in terms of some kind of catching up. It is true to say that Britain was one of only two countries (Germany being the other) to have reduced its ratio of government revenue to GDP by 1990. The change is, however, relatively small – from 39.7 per cent of GDP to 38.8 per cent.

A further insight into the tax burden may be gained by looking more closely at personal taxation over roughly the same period. Here we measure the average direct tax ratio as follows:

$$\text{tax ratio} = 1 - \frac{\text{personal disposable income}}{\text{total personal income}}$$

This provides a yardstick for the average burden of direct taxation which is particularly interesting because of the special priority government has given to reducing direct taxation. As it turns out, the direct tax ratio actually *rose* from 20.1 per cent of personal incomes in 1979 to 20.4 per cent in 1989. Figure 5.2 shows the time path of this ratio. The ratio reached a peak of 21.1 per cent in 1983 and has since fallen more or less consistently.

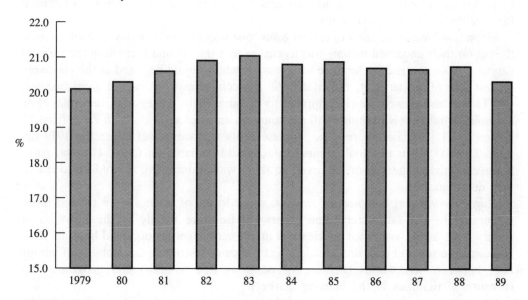

Figure 5.2   The average direct tax ratio in the UK 1979–89
Source: National Institute Economic Review, February 1991, Statistical Annex, Table 8.

The empirical evidence therefore appears to be at odds with the tax-cutting rhetoric of the Thatcher era. How can we explain this paradox? Is it possible to tie down the true targets and outcomes of tax policy during the 1980s?

The tax system: restructuring and rationalisation

Although Britain was not particularly *heavily* taxed in 1979, it is true to say that it was *badly* taxed. 'Bad' taxation arises not out of high levels of taxation *per se*, but out of the *distortions of relative prices* which are thereby induced (for an exposition of the excess burden of taxation see Musgrave and Musgrave 1980: 301–24). Important distortions can arise between the relative prices of work and leisure (caused by income taxation), consumption and saving (when certain forms of saving are tax-exempt, for example), and between different goods or classes of goods (for example, where housing receives favourable tax exemptions, as it does in many countries). Of course, all taxation (except the impractical lump-sum taxation) causes some distortion; the objective should be to keep this to a minimum, consistent with the government's revenue requirement.

A useful exposition of the problems of the British tax system at the beginning of the 1980s may be found in Kay and King (1986). Among a wide variety of problems we may cite three important examples.

First, *high marginal rates of taxation*: although average rates of taxation were not high, marginal rates were. The top rate on earned income stood at 83 per cent, and on unearned income at 98 per cent. The standard rate, applying to the vast majority of taxpayers, was 33 per cent. Although marginal tax rates on the very rich were extremely high, they did not raise much revenue because legal avoidance was relatively easy. A large profession of accountants and lawyers grew up, specialising in advising the wealthy on how to avoid tax.

Second, *ineffective taxation of capital gains*: one way that rich taxpayers could reduce the tax on their unearned income was to ensure that the income accrued in the form of capital gain (ie the rise in the price of an asset), which would be taxed at the relatively modest rate of 40 per cent, rather than 98 per cent. However, capital gains taxation (CGT) was also flawed, since it applied to nominal gains rather than real ones. For example, if inflation is running at 10 per cent and an asset appreciates in value from £1 million to £1.1 million, there is no increase in its *real* value; yet under the 1979 tax rules, £100,000 of its terminal nominal value would be liable for CGT. This was paid, however, only on the sale of the asset, so there was an incentive to hold on to it and thus defer taxation.

Third, *inconsistent treatment of savings*: some forms of savings were treated more favourably by the tax system than others. These were mainly of the institutional variety, such as life assurance policies and investment in owner-occupied housing. This favouritism often had undesirable side-effects, such as restricting the mobility of labour both between occupations (because of pensions tied to jobs) and geographically (because of rigidities in the housing market).

One can gauge the overall effects of the tax system from the following examples:

1 ineffective, high rates of tax, resulting in real resources being devoted to trying to avoid them, an economically wasteful activity;
2 distortions in people's choice of how to save, with decisions being made on the basis of tax considerations, rather than economic ones;
3 distortion of markets, among them the capital and housing markets.

How far have those problems been addressed during the 1980s? In many ways a lot of progress has been made in rationalising and restructuring the tax system. The main results of this process have been as follows.

First, marginal tax rates have been substantially reduced, to 25 per cent as the standard rate, and 40 per cent for higher income taxpayers. The objective of reducing the standard rate to 20 per cent has also been stated by successive Chancellors of the Exchequer, though this is unlikely to be implemented in the immediate future.

Second, although tax rates have been reduced this has not led to a fall in revenue, because of the buoyant growth in personal incomes in the mid- and late-1980s. Whether this growth was itself due to the lowering of tax rates and consequent increased labour supply is debatable (see eg Brown and Jackson 1990: 434–56 for a theoretical treatment; for evidence see Dilnot and Kell 1988; Brown 1988). Tax cuts have both income and substitution effects, which influence labour supply in opposite directions, so it is impossible to answer the question *a priori* (a point which politicians usually seem unaware of). The empirical evidence generally suggests that both income and substitution effects are small, and that they approximately cancel each other out. However, tax cuts may have had the effect of encouraging more people into the labour force (employment as well as unemployment grew during the 1980s), though taxation is not the only relevant factor here.

Third, during the same period, indirect taxes increased. VAT was raised from 8–12 per cent to a uniform 15 per cent (except for zero-rated items) in 1980, and to 17.5 per cent in 1991. Social security taxes (effectively equivalent to an income tax) were also raised during the early 1980s. These would offset the effective size of the tax cuts, and stunt the incentive effects.

Fourth, Capital Gains Tax was modified to apply only to real gains, though this was done imperfectly through a form of indexation of asset prices. Later, CGT was incorporated into the income tax system, so the incentives to derive one's income artificially in one form rather than another disappeared.

Attention has switched more recently to the taxation of savings, with greater incentives directed towards personal savings. Some of the distorting exemptions mentioned earlier were abolished, which broadened the tax base, but others were introduced. The Business Expansion Scheme (giving tax relief for investment in small businesses as long as the investment is held for five years or more) and Personal Equity Plans (giving tax concessions on shares, unit trusts and investment trusts which are held for a year or more) were introduced, to encourage personal savings and holdings of assets, but these have had limited appeal and are attractive mainly to the higher-rate taxpayer. The aim of these programmes, apart from encouraging savings generally, is to develop a 'popular capitalism' and to reduce the incidence of institutional forms of wealth holding. This complements the privatisation programme (see pp. 103–6), which also aims to increase personal direct holding of shares.

Taken together, these measures have simplified the tax system and made it more rational. The tax base is now wider, with fewer loopholes, and that allows personal direct tax rates to be lowered without revenue decreasing (tax revenue is, of course, the product of the tax base and the tax rate). This feature can also be seen in relation to corporate taxation, where the tax rate has come down from 52 per cent to 35 per cent, but capital allowances have been abolished. While many of these reforms are to be applauded, there is still some way to go. The taxation of saving is still not consistently levied, and some assets still receive special treatment (eg owner-occupied housing, agricultural land) as far as CGT applies.

Local taxation

We cannot leave the issue of taxation without mention of the Community Charge, or poll tax, as a basis for local taxation (see Department of the Environment 1986). Introduced in April 1990 (1989 in Scotland) as a replacement for the old local property tax ('the rates'), it proved a political disaster for the government and has now been abandoned. Its unpopularity was due to its perceived unfairness (a uniform tax per adult, regardless of income or wealth), and to the fact that tax bills proved much higher than anticipated. Local government finance is of interest because of the light it throws upon central government's attitude to the appropriate role of the state. In contrast to a number of European countries, Britain is a unitary state, which means that all power resides ultimately with central government. Local government's powers to tax and spend (and even exist) derive from central government. Thus while central government has been proclaiming the benefits of less government and of decentralisation, it has in many cases been *increasing* its own powers, at the expense of local government, viz.:

1   the increasingly strict limitations upon local spending, culminating in 'rate capping' and 'charge capping';
2   the abolition of the Greater London and Metropolitan councils;
3   the transfer of the proceeds of the property tax on business from local to central government;
4   the introduction of the right of schools to opt out of local government control and be funded directly by central government.

These important examples show how there has been a significant tendency to *centralise power*, in contrast to the stated aim of reducing the scope of government control. The recent review of the Community Charge (which resulted in its replacement by the 'Council Tax', a form of property tax with some relief for householders living alone) also took in the structure of local government, and further reorganisation, possibly involving the abolition of the higher tier (county) councils, is possible. In Britain, local government no longer acts (if it ever did to any great extent) as an alternative power base to central government, and its capacity to influence the local economic environment is much less than in many other European countries, such as the former West Germany.

Privatisation, regulation and competition policy

What would in earlier times have been called industrial policy has now given way to competition policy, which complements the large-scale privatisation programme of the last ten years. Central government no longer tries to 'pick winners' or to become actively involved in running industry; rather, it tries to set the appropriate framework within which firms can operate efficiently. This implies the minimum of government interference and low taxation. The government's current policy has been defined as follows:

The overall aim of UK competition policy is to encourage and enhance the competitive process.

(Office of Fair Trading, 1990)

This somewhat tautologous statement does at least illustrate how the government sees its role. In this section we shall look more closely at what the government has done, and whether the competitive process has in reality been enhanced.

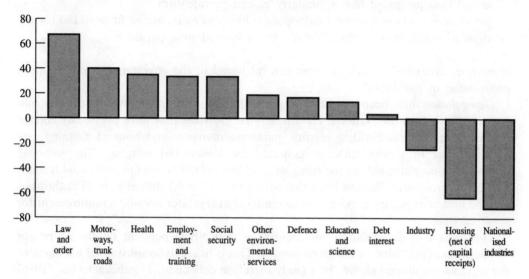

Figure 5.3 Percentage changes in government expenditure 1978–9 to 1989–90 (in constant price terms)
Source: *Treasury Economic Progress Report*, February 1990

Before doing so, it is instructive to see how these policies differ from what went before. Figure 5.3 shows trends in the distribution of public expenditure by programme, comparing 1978–9 and 1989–90. (Note that the *sizes* of the programmes are not shown: law and order is not the biggest programme, simply the one with the largest percentage increase.) The biggest losers have been industry (both private and public) and housing. The fall in the level of industrial support reflects the greater reliance on market forces, and the selling-off of many, formerly subsidised, nationalised industries. Reduced support for housing is again due to the sale of just over 1.2 million public sector dwellings, about 25 per cent of the stock of the 'council house' sector, which again used to receive substantial subsidies. Note that support for owner-occupied housing is not included in these figures; the major form of such support, tax relief on mortgage interest payments, reduces tax revenue rather than increasing expenditure. The overall effect on the government budget is the same, of course, but it does not appear as an expenditure item. Mortgage interest relief has grown significantly since 1980.

Privatisation

The most visible aspect of privatisation is the selling-off of state assets, but this is only part of the story. If one takes a wider definition of privatisation, to include any policy which reduces the size of the public sector or makes it more like the private sector, then one can add the following:

1 *deregulation* – introducing greater competition into already private industries, or allowing private sector competition into sectors of public monopoly

2 *raising prices and reducing financial deficits in the public sector* – this makes a public sector firm act more like a similarly placed private firm

3 *franchising* – where a natural monopoly is likely to exist, asking firms to bid for the right to supply the market, usually for a limited time period.

Numerous examples of each of these can be found in the government's privatisation programme of the 1980s.

Deregulation has been applied in particular to local government services and institutions such as the National Health Service. Services that were previously carried out in-house, such as building repairs, parks maintenance and hospital cleaning, are now put out to tender with, in general, the lowest bid winning. The in-house organisation may also bid for the contract, and this should be on fair and equal terms – that is, no cross-subsidisation from the authority is allowed. Initially, local authorities had the *option* of putting services out to tender, but this later became a requirement for some services.

The impact of deregulation will clearly be critically dependent on the scope for competition in provision of the given service. This is likely to be substantial for many of the services mentioned above. In a study of refuse collection, Domberger et al (1986) found tendering to generate significant cost savings (up to 20 per cent). Interestingly, the cost savings occurred even if the contract was won by the existing public sector supplier. Thus it is the existence of competition, rather than the public or private sector nature of the supplier, that appears to be the crucial factor.

Where a service or firm has remained in the public sector, the government has often had recourse to *increased prices* in order to reduce its deficit (or raise its surplus). There have been two main reasons for this policy: first, to help reduce the *overall* public sector deficit (or raise the surplus); and second, to make the firm more attractive to potential purchasers.

Council housing is one case where prices have been raised. Although the houses are owned by local authorities, it has been possible for central government to force up rents via reductions in the subsidies paid to the local authority under this heading. Rents have thus had to rise to balance the housing account. There is now virtually no general subsidy to public sector tenants, except in a few high-cost areas such as London. It has thus proved increasingly attractive to tenants to purchase their dwelling under the 'Right to Buy' legislation, at discounts of up to 60 per cent of the market price. Low-income tenants who choose to remain in the public sector receive help in the form of income-related housing benefit. This example reveals a number of features of government policy. First, targeted subsidies related to income are preferred to general subsidies to housing. This is consistent with the encouragement of individual choice and the avoidance of interference with the market mechanism. The glaring inconsistency, however, is that owner-occupiers continue to be subsidised via mortgage interest relief. When it comes to entitlement to subsidy, it appears that the status of being an owner is at least as important a qualification as being in poverty. Second, the policy of selling council houses ignores the problem of externalities, a familiar form of market failure. In this case the local authority has less freedom to manage the stock.

The pattern of turnover of council houses is dislocated, because many potential re-lets have been sold off (usually the better quality, more desirable dwellings), and new entrants hoping to rent from the public sector find their choice restricted.

Prices have also been raised for the remaining nationalised industries, to try to recover costs and reduce subsidies. This has been enforced through the imposition of *external financing limits* (EFLs) for each industry. These essentially limit the amount of public support available. Some EFLs (eg for the electricity supply industry prior to selling-off) have been negative – that is, the industry has been expected to make a profit. Previously applied principles for the operation of nationalised industries, such as marginal cost pricing (though this was in fact never strictly applied), have now been abandoned in favour of the use of EFLs.

External financing limits and higher prices have often been the precursors to selling-off. There seems to have been a presumption that the private sector would not buy a loss-making industry, so the government would have to restructure it first to make it profitable. This is a curious presumption in the context of the claimed superiority of the private sector in making profits and keeping costs down. The advantage of the public sector in terms of restructuring probably resides in a combination of informational asymmetries between public and private sectors and different degrees of risk aversion (ie the private sector is unwilling to take the risk of buying before it has reliable information about the true nature of costs in the industry).

Franchising is another technique which may be useful when the product market is not competitive. The franchisee earns the right to provide the goods or services for a limited period of time; examples are the ITV commercial television network (ten-year franchises) and British Telecom (twenty-five years). Franchising can be carried out in a variety of ways: the franchise can be sold to the highest bidder (who would then be able to act as a monopolist), given to the company prepared to supply at the lowest price (which would be at the competitive level, given sufficient bidders), or given to the company or companies offering the best guarantee regarding quality of supply.

Commercial television's regional franchises have in the past gone to companies offering to provide 'quality' television (for example, incorporating a local news service). The 1991 round of bidding was supposed to put greater emphasis upon who can pay the most, with the safeguard of some kind of quality threshold. (In the event, a number of bids failed because they were thought to be too high, and to overreach the financial capacities of the companies in question.) Of course quality is to a large degree a subjective matter, and standards are difficult to enforce except by awarding the licence to someone else next time round. This may be difficult if the incumbent firm has some built-in advantages, such as greater knowledge of the market, or has invested heavily in the appropriate technology. The fact that British Telecom (BT) holds a franchise shows that this may be combined with the sale of the assets themselves.

Sales of state assets may be considered the leading edge of the privatisation programme, and this brings up a number of interesting questions. As stated earlier in relation to contracting out of council services, the competitive environment into which the privatised firm enters is vitally important. There is little to be gained from turning a public monopoly, which is likely to be technically inefficient, into a private one, which is likely to be allocatively so.

This point poses a dilemma for government. From the point of view of consumer welfare, a competitive market is to be preferred. However, selling off a monopoly intact will raise more in revenue than seeking to substitute a competitive private industry for a public monopoly (the difference being the discounted value of future monopoly profits). Given the importance that the government places upon reducing the public sector deficit, this presents quite a problem.

In practice, the government appears to have preferred revenue to competition (see Kay and Thompson 1986), indeed to have been prepared to sacrifice competition simply in order to reduce the size of the public sector. There are numerous examples of this. BT was privatised as an entity rather than being split up in the way that AT&T was in the USA. Its only competitor up to now has been Mercury Communications, which is a very much smaller company. British Airways (BA) was privatised without any of its routes being reallocated to British Caledonian as recommended by the Civil Aviation Authority.

Regulation

Since the environment is in any case not always competitive, there is a need for some kind of regulation of those privatised industries which have a significant degree of monopoly power. In an influential report (Littlechild 1983) to the Department of Trade and Industry, Professor Stephen Littlechild recommended the '*RPI−X*' formula for BT, and this has subsequently been applied to other industries, with slight modification. Under the formula, the regulated firm is allowed to raise its prices each year by the rate of inflation *less* the amount X. For BT, X was originally set at 3 per cent for the years 1984–9, rising to 4.5 per cent thereafter (so that its prices had to fall in real terms by 3 per cent per year 1984–9). In September 1991 BT's X was raised again, this time to 6.25 per cent.

A number of advantages over the rate of return (on capital) form of regulation, much practised in the USA, are claimed for this method. The American system has proved open to 'regulatory capture' (see Stigler 1971), whereby the regulators end up defending the industry as much as regulating it. Because they set the rate of return (and hence effectively profitability), they then have to defend themselves and the firm against any charges of excess profits or consumer exploitation. And because the method requires detailed knowledge of the industry and its costs, regulators are often former (or future) employees of the regulated firm, creating a 'cosy' relationship between regulator and regulated. Rate of return regulation also provides an incentive for firms to increase their capital stock beyond the optimal level (the 'Averch-Johnson' effect) because this allows more profit to be made.

In contrast, *RPI−X* is claimed to be simple and transparent, and to give firms the incentive to be efficient, since lower costs imply higher profit. Matters are not quite that simple, however, because X has to be decided upon, and this can be done only in the light of the rate of return on assets being earned by the firm. On the other hand, excessive profits are likely to lead (as they did for BT) to a higher X value when the time for reassessment arrives (see OFTEL 1988).

The *RPI−X* formula for BT is expected to be temporary, pending the arrival of sufficient competition. The government has recently announced that it will consider favourably a licence application from *any* potential entrant, thus modifying the previous policy of licensing only two participants in the market.

In other industries, notably water, the regulation is expected to be permanent, since ownership of water supply and sewerage systems confers natural monopoly power. The formula for regulation in this case has been modified to $RPI-X$ plus a 'K factor', where the K factor represents additional costs which even efficient operation of the enterprise could not avoid. These might be the additional costs of higher water-quality standards imposed by outside bodies such as the government or the European Commission. The water authorities are allowed to pass these costs on to the consumer, once they have been independently certified. The regulator has to decide what increase in prices is justified on the basis of these unavoidable costs, and this inevitably means that he has to get more involved in the detailed operation of the water authorities. This negates some of the advantages of the $RPI-X$ formula in terms of simplicity and openness. An offsetting advantage for the regulator is that there are ten regulated regional water companies, so their levels of performance can be compared with regard to efficiency. For example, it is proposed that the X factor will be determined by the performance of the most efficient authority, and will then be applied to all. As yet it is too early to comment upon how the system works in practice.

Competition policy

Individual regulatory bodies for telecommunications, water, gas and electricity apart, a more widely applicable competition policy is required to deal with monopolies, mergers and anti-competitive practices. UK policy in this area has often been described as ineffective, for reasons which will become apparent.

Responsibility for competition policy is shared between the Office of Fair Trading (OFT), the Monopolies and Mergers Commission (MMC), and the Secretary of State for Trade and Industry. The first of these acts as a watchdog, and carries out initial investigations into possible breaches of the law. If it finds a possible case to answer, it refers it to the MMC for a fuller investigation. Having done that, the MMC makes recommendations in a published report. This advice, along with that of the OFT, is considered by the Secretary of State, who decides what action, if any, to take. This is a very broad outline of procedures (for more detail see OFT 1990), and the procedures may not run their full course in all cases. For example, in the case of an anti-competitive practice (such as a market-sharing agreement between firms) the OFT might accept undertakings from the relevant parties that the practice will cease, in which case no referral to the MMC will occur.

In these procedures, monopoly is not defined in the textbook fashion, but rather as any situation where a single supplier has over 25 per cent of the relevant market (defined as a 'complex' monopoly). A merger might attract the attention of the OFT and MMC if either the company being taken over has assets of over £30 million or the market share of the companies (post-merger) exceeds 25 per cent. An anti-competitive practice is defined as one which is likely to restrict, distort or prevent competition.

In all cases, a 'public interest' criterion is used to decide whether or not any remedial action needs to be taken. This is very broadly defined – effectively not defined at all since in principle it can incorporate anything – but the notion of competition is one of the key concepts. However, monopoly and allegedly anti-competitive practices are not considered bad *per se*, and individual cases are always considered on their merits. All this adds up to a great deal of uncertainty about the outcome of any investigation (or even whether one will take place), and a more tightly defined legalistic approach might be preferable.

The other major weakness of the policy is in relation to the penalties which are imposed for improper behaviour. Firms are simply asked or ordered to desist from the anti-competitive behaviour. This is analogous to a thief being told, upon conviction, that he must just stop stealing! He is not imprisoned or fined, nor does he even have to return the stolen property. It is no wonder, therefore, that the MMC has had, on occasions, to reopen a case where the monopolistic tendency or anti-competitive practice has recurred (eg that of film distribution).

A number of anti-competitive practices (of which the OFT keeps a register) are actually allowed, on the grounds that they are in the public interest. This book, for example, is covered by the Net Book Agreement, which forbids bookshops to sell it at less than the publisher's recommended price. The argument behind this restriction is that it allows smaller, specialist bookshops to survive, and makes a wider range of books available to the public. These advantages are assumed to outweigh the disadvantages of higher prices.

Competition policy is also affected by the provisions of the Treaty of Rome. Article 85 of the Treaty prohibits agreements affecting trade between member states which have the object of preventing, restricting or distorting competition. Article 86 deals with abuses of dominant position in a particular market. The Commission of the European Communities also has the power to control mergers, when they have a European dimension, but not if both companies are from the same country. The EC has the power to levy fines and penalties on firms, up to a limit of 10 per cent of turnover – a very formidable penalty. This presents a sharp contrast to the domestic UK situation.

In summary, UK competition policy is not particularly stringent. There has been a fair degree of success in getting rid of restrictive practices, but competition policy has not prevented a large amount of merger activity and the growth of large conglomerate enterprises. One study (Shaw and Simpson 1989) concluded:

> The evidence . . . suggests that the Monopolies Commission had only a minor impact on the competitive process.

Although this conclusion was drawn from cases dealt with between 1959 and 1973, the basis of policy has not changed much since then.

Government policy toward competition is sometimes contradictory. Despite privatising BA without acting to create a competitive environment (to BA's benefit), it has recently allowed the transfer of valuable landing rights at Heathrow from financially troubled Pan-Am (which has now ceased business) to the successful American company United Airlines, without gaining in return the right of entry into the US domestic market for BA. This behaviour could be interpreted as consistent, if it were supposed that government considered revenue to take precedence over competition.

Market failure

Against the background of the strong commitment of the Conservative government to the free market, it is instructive to look at a particular policy area where we might expect the market to fail, in the sense of not producing the optimal allocation of resources. The area we shall examine is environmental policy. The environment may not be well served by the market because of externalities and the absence of property rights over the natural environment (see Dasgupta and Heal 1979: 39–78, for an exposition). This may lead, for example, to an excessive quantity of pollution being produced and to excessive exploitation of natural resources.

Although an externality is an example of market failure, that does not mean that a market-based approach to the problem is not feasible. For example taxes and subsidies can be used to correct market prices for the externality. If the tax/subsidy is set correctly (and this is a big if, because of the amount of information required to calculate it) then an optimal allocation of resources can be achieved.

The government certainly appears to want to follow this type of approach, in line with its economic philosophy. An example of the use of prices to protect the environment is the tax differential between leaded and unleaded petrol, currently about 3 pence per litre, a difference of about 7 per cent. Initially the government relied only upon exhortation, but consumers showed little inclination on this basis to have cars converted, and the petrol companies did not make unleaded petrol widely available. It was only when a price differential sufficient to recoup the cost of conversion in a short space of time was established that unleaded fuel's market share became significant. The recent appointment of economist David Pearce as special adviser to the Secretary of State for the Environment suggests that the economic viewpoint will continue to be important in environmental policy.

Britain has often in the past been accused of having a poor environmental record. Examples of this are the poor quality of drinking water, the state of the beaches, and the trans-border pollution produced by coal-burning power stations. Domestic policy has not been vigorous in this regard, and it is likely that European legislation is going to become more and more dominant. This is indeed appropriate, since many environmental problems are international in scope. For example, a tax on carbon emissions in one country, while reducing emissions at home, may actually cause an increase in emissions abroad, offsetting some of the benefit (see Pearson and Smith 1990). It is better, therefore, if the tax is applied on the widest scale possible.

How is environmental policy affected by other government programmes, notably privatisation? This is a particularly interesting issue because some of the privatised industries – water, electricity and transport – are environmentally sensitive. The issue could become that much more important if plans to privatise the coal industry proceed.

The notion of market failure might suggest that privatisation would make the environmental situation worse, but this is not necessarily the case. We must also admit the possibility of *government failure* – the state might not always act in the best interests of the environment. The appalling environmental record of some Eastern European states should warn us of this. The key question is whether the government (which must ultimately be responsible for environmental regulation) will be tougher on itself as owner of nationalised industries, or on the private sector. There is some evidence for believing the latter. Within the framework of the privatisation programme for water supply, the National Rivers Authority has been established as the watchdog over the water authorities and over private companies, with regard to their waste discharges into rivers. Previously, the water authorities were responsible for monitoring the behaviour of both the private companies *and themselves*, and were among the worst offenders.

The nuclear power programme is another environmentally sensitive programme which suffered a set-back in the context of privatisation, in this case of the electricity industry. No one in the private sector was prepared to buy the nuclear plants once their true level of profitability became apparent, and they were withdrawn from the sell-off. Paradoxically, under public control, the industry had been able to hide its costs from government and to continue the programme. This may reveal one of the greater benefits of privatisation: close scrutiny of the given industry by an army of private sector analysts appears to be a lot more effective than overview by civil servants and government ministers. In so far as nuclear power is indeed an environmental hazard (and more so than other forms of energy production, such as fossil fuel power stations), privatisation will have had, perhaps inadvertently, a beneficial environmental impact.

The macroeconomy

The UK is one of the four large economies of the European Community. The overall structure of employment and output is similar to those of West Germany and France (see Table 5.1). The main difference with respect to Germany is that the UK is more specialised in services and less in manufacturing. Compared to France, the UK is less agricultural and has a larger extractive sector. GNP per capita in the UK is relatively low by comparison with other European Community countries and well below the level of the United States (see Table 5.2, line 9.)

Table 5.1 The structure of output and employment, 1986

	France		West Germany		United Kingdom	
	Output	Employment	Output	Employment	Output	Employment
Agriculture & mining	5.6	10.5	3.0	7.5	6.6	4.4
(of which mining)	(0.9)	(0.8)	(0.9)	(1.0)	(4.5)	(1.3)
Manufacturing	28.1	28.6	38.4	40.1	28.3	28.4
Electricity, gas & water	3.0	1.0	3.2	1.1	3.3	1.5
Construction	6.7	9.6	6.1	8.5	7.0	7.7
Transport	7.7	7.7	6.8	7.0	8.3	8.0
Wholesale, retail & catering	18.8	23.2	12.4	20.2	15.9	26.0
Financial & community services	30.1	19.3	30.0	15.5	30.7	24.0

Source: *OECD National Accounts* Vol. II: Detailed tables 1964–87

Table 5.2 puts the recent performance of the UK economy into international perspective. GDP growth through the 1980s was faster than for most other EC countries, but less than for Japan and the United States (see line 1). Labour productivity growth was relatively rapid, almost matching that of Japan (see line 2).

Line 3 gives total factor productivity (TFP) growth (that proportion of growth in output not attributable to factor input growth) for the 1970s and the 1980s. On this alternative measure, 1980s UK productivity growth is again high by international standards, and is also a marked improvement on the 1970s record. Explaining this productivity kick will be one of our major concerns in this section. The 1980s recovery is also reflected in the revival of investment growth (see line 4). On the negative side, UK unemployment was high throughout the decade (see line 5), and there was a substantial rise in long-term unemployment (see line 6). The causes of high unemployment and of the growth of long-term unemployment will provide another of our main themes, as will inflation, the rate of which remained above the average for the industrial countries in all but two years (see line 7).

Table 5.2 Selected comparative macroeconomic indicators

	France	West Germany	Japan	United Kingdom	USA
1 Average of annual growth in GDP, 1980 to mid-1990 (%)[a]	2.2	2.2	4.5	2.7	2.8
2 Average of annual growth in GDP per employed person, 1980 to mid-1990 (%)[a]	2.0	1.4	3.1	2.6	0.9
3 Total factor productivity growth:[b]					
(i) Average 1973–9	1.7	1.7	1.5	0.6	0.4
(ii) Average 1979–88	1.6	0.7	2.0	1.8	0.4
4 Growth of investment at constant prices (%):[b]					
(i) Average 1973–9	1.4	0.6	3.2	1.1	3.8
(ii) Average 1980–9	1.9	1.5	5.2	3.7	2.5
5 Unemployment rate (%) average 1980–9[a]	9.3	6.0	2.5	10.0	7.2
6 Long-term unemployment (> 1 year) as a percentage of total unemployment:[c]					
1980	32.6	17.0	16.0	19.2	4.3
1988	44.8	32.6	20.2	40.8	7.4
7 Inflation rate (%); consumer prices, average 1980–9[a]	7.0	2.9	2.5	7.1	5.4
8 Net public debt as a percentage of GDP/GNP:[b]					
1981	14.2	17.4	20.7	46.5	18.5
1990	24.7	20.7	6.1	27.9	28.2
9 GNP per capita in 1987 US$, 1987[d]	12,920	14,430	15,840	10,490	18,950

Notes:
[a] The source for lines 1, 2 5 and 7 is *National Institute Economic Review* 1/91. The unemployment rate data are OECD standardised rates.
[b] The source for lines 3, 4 and 8 is *OECD Economic Outlook*, no. 47.
[c] The source for line 6 is *OECD Employment Outlook*, 1987, 1989. Data for West Germany and the United Kingdom are from unemployment registers, while data for the other countries are from labour force surveys. Survey-based data give higher measurements of this proportion in all countries where comparison can be made.
[d] The source for line 9 is *World Bank World Tables* 1990/91.

For a more detailed analysis of UK progress through the 1980s, see Table 5.3. We find from the data cited that the UK experienced seven years of strong GDP growth following the recession of 1980/81. Over the same period employment growth (line 2) was much slower, with significant growth occurring only after 1986. This relatively slow rate of growth of employment is reflected in productivity and unemployment data. Productivity growth began to pick up at the mid-point of the recession, in 1981, and remained at historically high levels through to 1987, except for the mild recession year of 1984 (see line 3.) The upward trend in productivity growth was particularly strong in manufacturing (see line 4). The unemployment rate, at 4.9 per cent in 1979, more than doubled to 1982 and remained roughly at the same high level until 1987, when it began to fall (see line 5). This persistence of unemployment at high levels is almost unique in British data; for purposes of comparison, the unemployment rate in 1932, at the trough of the Great Depression, was 15.6 per cent,[1] but after that fell continually until 1937, when it stood at 7.8 per cent. The rate of inflation, 17.9 per cent in 1980, fell to 4.5 per cent in 1983 (see line 6), but remained above 4 per cent for the rest of the decade, except for 1986, the year in which oil prices almost halved. It began rising from then until late 1990, when it peaked at just over 10 per cent. Finally, in line 7, we chart the path of the current account of the balance of payments as a percentage of GDP. There was a large trade surplus in 1981, almost surely a cyclical phenomenon, which was gradually whittled down to current account balance by 1986. From 1987 onwards, there was a sequence of continually increasing deficits.

Table 5.3   Selected UK macroeconomic indicators, 1981–9 (percentages)

		1981	1982	1983	1984	1985	1986	1987	1988	1989
1	Growth in GDP	0.9	1.8	3.7	1.8	3.8	3.6	4.2	4.4	1.9
2	Growth in employment	4.7	2.2	1.7	0.8	0.9	0.0	1.0	3.2	2.5
3	Growth in GDP per employee, whole economy	1.8	3.8	4.4	0.9	2.5	3.2	2.8	1.5	0.3
4	Growth in GDP per employee, manufacturing	3.4	6.7	8.6	5.6	3.2	3.5	6.1	5.4	3.5
5	Unemployment rate	9.4	10.9	10.8	11.0	11.0	11.1	10.0	8.1	6.3
6	Inflation, retail prices	12.0	8.5	4.5	5.1	6.0	3.4	4.2	4.9	7.8
7	Current account of the balance of payments/GDP	3.0	1.9	1.4	0.7	0.9	0.0	−1.2	−3.9	−4.5

Source: *National Institute Economic Review* 1/91

So much for the facts. In this section we discuss each key macroeconomic variable – unemployment, productivity, the rate of inflation and the balance of payments – in turn, and offer a synthesis of views on the causes of the trends observed. Our initial task, however, is to outline the macroeconomic policy regime since 1979.

UK macroeconomic policy in the 1980s

It is generally recognised that the return to power in July 1979 of a Conservative administration, led by Mrs Thatcher, marked a large discrete change in the macroeconomic policy regime (see, inter alia, Buiter and Miller 1983; Bean and

Symons 1989). The change was, essentially, from a regime of Keynesian demand management, with a central focus on the level of employment, to what one might call a regime of Medium-Term Monetarism, where the main object of policy was the rate of inflation. This policy change was not unique to the UK; one can perceive a similar move in other countries at around the same time (see papers in *Economic Policy* no 5 1987). It is probably true to say, however, that in the UK the break with the past was more radical than elsewhere. To illustrate this point we shall start with a brief discussion of policy prior to 1979.

The economics of Keynes had been at least as influential in post-Second World War Britain as in the other industrial economies, possibly more so. The key idea in Keynes's work – that the government could and should take responsibility for the maintenance of a high and stable level of employment – first expressed officially in the Employment White Paper of 1944, became the cornerstone of macroeconomic policy through the 1950s and 1960s. Maynard (1988: ch. 1) discusses the means by which that goal was to be achieved – in essence fiscal policy, with a subordinate role for credit control and credit rationing. As far back as the early 1940s, when officials and their advisers were discussing the feasibility of demand management, doubts and worries were expressed about the control of inflation at low levels of unemployment (Jones 1987: ch. 3). It is clear that the idea behind the Phillips Curve was well understood in these quarters, many years before Phillips's paper was published in 1958. Interestingly, inflation was viewed then, as later, as a problem of excessive wage growth at given unemployment, caused by irresponsible bargaining by labour unions, rather than as a problem of excessive monetary growth. As it turned out, inflation and unemployment were both low in the 1940s and 1950s, apart from a brief outbreak of inflation during the Korean War. Both began to rise, albeit cyclically, from around 1960, to precipitate the famous shifting-out of the Phillips Curve, an international phenomenon of the 1960s and 1970s. One important policy response to this in the UK was the imposition of a sequence of incomes policies, which set recommended or mandatory maxima for wage increases, underlining the prevailing view that inflation could be lower, at a given level of unemployment, if wage bargainers, particularly union leaders, could be induced to be more reasonable. To that end, from the early 1960s, union leaders were increasingly incorporated into the policy-making process (see Jones 1987: chs 6 and 8).

The stagflation of the 1970s put severe political and intellectual strain on the Keynesian policy position world-wide, and especially in the UK, since domestic performance on counts of output growth, inflation and unemployment was among the worst of the industrialised countries. The new Conservative administration of 1979 was, as we have said, monetarist in its interpretation of the causes of inflation, and anti-interventionist in its general economic philosophy. It was this outlook that led the government to design policies aimed at deregulation, reduction of the size of the public sector, and reduction of the economic power of groups representing vested interests, especially the trade unions. It was considered that all of these policy elements would lead to improved supply-side performance, and ultimately to renewed growth with stable prices.

The centrepiece of the new macroeconomic policy stance was the Medium-Term Financial Strategy (MTFS), unveiled in 1980. The MTFS set out annually differentiated targets for the growth of selected monetary aggregates and for the Public Sector

Borrowing Requirement (PSBR), for four years into the future. The pattern of differentiation envisaged steady declines in monetary growth and government borrowing over the four-year period. The idea behind the plan to reduce monetary growth is straightforward. Although it is open to doubt whether the leadership of the Conservative Party was convinced by the theoretical and empirical work of monetarist economists on the causes of inflation, it is beyond doubt that it fitted well with their economic philosophy to perceive inflation to be caused by excessive money creation, as embodied in the slogan 'too much money chasing too few goods'. Targeting monetary aggregates was not new in the UK – the previous Labour administration had instituted this in 1977. It was the explicit medium-term perspective that was new. That new perspective was a signal not only that the primary priority had shifted from employment to inflation, but also that an attempt at a decisive break with the practice of short-run macroeconomic intervention was under way. This in turn would mean a move away from discretionary policy-making towards simple policy rules, a switch which was, at the time, being advocated by the new classical economists in the United States and elsewhere.

A convincing macroeconomic rationale for reduced public sector borrowing is less easy to find. The original stated purpose was to reduce the potential crowding-out effects on interest-sensitive private sector spending. (*Financial Statement and Budget Report* 1980–81), but as Bean and Symons (1989) argue, this is likely to be negligible in a small open economy with a high degree of capital mobility. Bean and Symons discuss and find unconvincing a number of other possible explanations, most of which invoke either the necessity of a fiscal contraction to bolster the credibility of the monetary regime, or the unsustainability of the 1979 level of public debt. In the end, however, they locate two substantial arguments. First, the steady reduction of public sector borrowing helped to reinforce the recognition that government spending and revenue raising must be considered together, so that calls for increases in government spending in one area should, as a matter of routine, be accompanied by proposals for raising the required revenue and/or proposals for spending cuts in other areas. Second, the announcement of a medium-term fiscal strategy helped to reinforce the break with the past, by signalling to private agents the government's intention not to expand aggregate demand in the face of price or wage rises likely to have adverse effects on activity levels.

Another break with the past was symbolised by the fact that this administration did not enlist the support of the unions in the fight against inflation. There were no more incomes policies after 1979, and few, if any, consultations with union leaders. Why? Maynard (1988: 30) has argued that incomes policy was abandoned because of its past ineffectiveness and also because controls over wages were incompatible with the aim of improving supply-side performance. While the success or failure of past incomes policy is a subject which we might reasonably leave the econometricians to fight about, the sources of incompatibility between incomes policy and supply-side strategy are germane to the present discussion. There were two sources of incompatibility. The first was microeconomic. Incomes policy in the UK had taken the form of norms for wage rises, usually percentage rises, and sometimes fixed money increases. It is straightforward to demonstrate that such norms, if enforced, would have led to distortions in relative wages and therefore misallocations of labour. The second source of incompatibility was more political. The administration was concerned to reduce union power, and subsequently did so by legislation which curbed various forms of activity during labour disputes, by reducing union immunity from the law, by introducing compulsory secret ballots on strike action, and through a number of other similar reforms. It is inconceivable that trade-union leaders would have co-operated over wage moderation with the government while these reforms, to which they were opposed, were being implemented.

It is also true that power within the unions had been devolving toward the shop-floor in the period before 1979. So even without this legislative programme, it is arguable that union leaders could not have delivered any wage moderation package to which they might have agreed.

The announcement of a target is one thing; meeting it is quite another, as anybody who has tried to give up smoking will readily agree. To what extent did the administration, re-elected in 1983 and again in 1987, manage to keep its macro-economic promises? On monetary growth there was mixed success. Initially a broad money aggregate, Sterling M3 (£M3), was the chosen target. (£M3 is conventionally defined M1 plus private sector sterling time deposits and public sector sterling deposits.) In the first two years of the MTFS, £M3 overshot its target growth by a large factor (18.4 per cent in 1980 against a target maximum of 11 per cent, and 16.3 per cent in 1981 against a target maximum of 10 per cent). This was due in most part to distress borrowing by commercial companies during the recession (Maynard 1988: 60). £M3 targets were revised upwards in response to the overshoot in 1982, and the new targets were met in financial years 1982/3 and 1983/4. After 1984 £M3 was again above target, but by this time the government was placing less emphasis on it, and more on the growth of M0, the monetary base. The reason for this change was that the relationship between £M3 and nominal-GDP turned out to be unstable, so that £M3 was a less reliable predictor of nominal aggregate demand, and hence of inflation, than had been hoped (Burns 1988). At the same time, the exchange rate began to play a role as a target of monetary policy, and, after 1986, appeared to be given increasing weight. This was for three reasons. First, it was recognised that reliance on one or two monetary aggregates could be misleading, so that a broader range of indicators should be taken into account. Second, there was a growing recognition among policy-makers world-wide that exchange rates could, and indeed often did, move a long way out of line with what might be called their fundamental equilibrium rate (defined as a rate compatible with internal and external equilibrium) for considerable stretches of time, with potentially damaging global macroeconomic effects (see Eastwood, Chapter 7 in *The European Economy*). Third, there was the issue of entry into the Exchange Rate Mechanism of the European Monetary System. Over the 1980s, the UK became increasingly committed to entry, although it has since been revealed that the government was deeply divided on the issue.

During 1988 and part of 1989, the then Chancellor of the Exchequer, Nigel Lawson, one of the members of the government in favour of ERM membership, appeared to be targeting the exchange rate exclusively, keeping sterling close to a parity of 3.1 deutschmarks for almost a year and a half. During this period even M0 overshot its target, growing at over 6 per cent annually, compared to a 1987 budget target of 1–5 per cent. By the end of the decade, it was clear that monetary policy had become increasingly pragmatic and more responsive to macroeconomic events, as was demonstrated by the lowering of interest rates after the stock market crash of October 1987.

On PSBR targeting, it is evident that the planned reductions in government borrowing were delivered much later than orginally envisaged. In 1987 the Public Sector Financial Deficit[2] finally fell below 1.5 per cent of GDP, the level which had been set in 1980 as the PSBR target for 1983/4.

Unemployment

The main negative feature of the UK macroeconomy during the 1980s was undoubtedly unemployment. The initial surge in unemployment from early 1980 to the end of 1982 was largely caused by adverse shifts in factors affecting aggregate demand. The direct effect of the monetary squeeze came through in the form of a sharp rise in interest rates. The Bank of England minimum lending rate rose from 12 per cent in April 1979 to 17 per cent in November of that year, with the short-term lending rates of the commercial banks rising by a similar amount. Minimum lending rate fell back to 12 per cent only in March 1981. The second demand factor was a severe loss of competitiveness. Between the end of 1978 and the end of 1980, the UK's nominal effective exchange rate appreciated by over 25 per cent and the real effective exchange rate by over 30 per cent. Why? Bean and Symons (1989) pinpoint two causes. It is important, first, to bear in mind that the second round of OPEC oil price rises were taking place at this time, *and* that the UK had recently become a net exporter of oil. The international capital market may therefore have taken the view that the medium-term prospects of the UK economy had improved considerably *relative* to the prospects of economies dependent on imported oil. Empirical studies of the appreciation of the pound over this period suggest that this might account for between one-third and one-half of its extent. The rest can probably be accounted for by the monetary squeeze itself, although as Buiter and Miller (1983) explain, there are some problems with fitting Dornbusch's (1976) celebrated overshooting model to the facts.

A fiscal contraction also contributed to the downturn. Layard and Nickell (1986) argue this in their study of unemployment, but do not hazard an estimate of how much of the demand contraction was fiscal in origin. The fiscal deficit did not fall, since tax revenues fall and transfer payments rise in times of recession, but there were important spending cuts. These cuts were not in general in the sphere of government consumption, although that grew less than in previous years (1.6 per cent and 0.3 per cent in real terms in 1980 and 1981 respectively, compared to an annual average of 1.8 per cent 1974/9). The fact is that government consumption is politically difficult to cut, as it often takes the form of support for specific programmes, such as the wage bills of the education and health services and the military. It was rather on public sector investment programmes that the axe fell dramatically. Consider the following data for 1980/1. Gross capital formation for the whole economy fell by 9.4 per cent, which accounts arithmetically for about 75 per cent of the fall in total final expenditure. Of that fall in investment, around 50 per cent was in public sector investment, which was cut by just under 17 per cent. Thus about 38 per cent of the fall in total final expenditure was attributable, in an arithmetical sense, to cuts in public sector investment programmes.

From 1982 onwards output growth revived. As we have seen, however, unemployment did not fall. Instead it gradually rose until it peaked in 1986 at over 3 million. The nature of the post-1982 upward trend was unusual. More than 100 per cent of the increase was due to a rise in long-term (greater than one year in duration) unemployment. That is, the number of people unemployed for less than one year actually fell from 1982 onwards. It is centrally important, therefore, to our understanding of the persistence of unemployment through the 1980s to explain why this growth in long-term unemployment occurred.

One apparently obvious explanation is that the recession caused a great increase in structural or mismatch unemployment. Jackman and Roper (1987) provide the most thorough search through the data for evidence on this. They devise a number of possible measures of mismatch, employing regional, industrial and occupational unemployment and vacancy data. Surprisingly, they find little evidence of a large increase in extent of mismatch. Most of their indices show only small, temporary changes during the period 1980–1. Although the measures used are inevitably open to criticism, it is striking that none demonstrates the posited relationship. So while we cannot rule out a structural explanation, it is sensible to seek alternative theories of the rise of long-term unemployment.

Neither the persistence of unemployment nor the rise of long-term unemployment through the 1980s was unique to the UK, as noted earlier and in Table 5.2. Similar developments unfolded in much of Europe, as well as in Canada and Australia. Macroeconomists world-wide have suggested various explanations. One simple theoretical device, that of splitting the work-force into 'insiders' and 'outsiders', has been a feature of a number of the explanations offered. Research in this area has mushroomed, but the work of Blanchard and Summers (1987), Lindbeck and Snower (1989) and Layard and Nickell (1987) provides useful starting-points. The key insight is this: there are insider forces in the determination of wages, such as pressure of product demand, profitability, retention and motivation of workers, and so on. There are also outsider forces, the most important of which is the threat which unemployed people can pose to incumbent workers as potential replacements.

The wage which emerges from bargaining between firms and workers is a function of both types of forces. Given the neo-classical proposition that demand for labour is decreasing in wages for profit-maximising firms (demand decreases as wages rise), then the aggregate level of employment, and hence of unemployment (for a fixed labour force), are also determined by the relative strengths of these forces. Now the relative strengths of these forces in turn depend on the extent to which insiders, the incumbent workers, can insulate themselves from outsider pressure, and also on the amount of pressure that the outsiders themselves can actually exert. In what is probably the most convincing story of this kind, Layard and Nickell (1987) contend that the key factor is the ineffectiveness of the long-term unemployed as job-seekers. They argue that this factor makes it possible for an economy to be shocked into a high unemployment, high average duration of unemployment equilibrium. What follows is a simplified exposition of their hypothetical mechanism.

Imagine a world where the long-term unemployed are deeply discouraged job-seekers, so that anybody unemployed for more than one year stops looking for work altogether. Take the short-term unemployed to be active job-seekers. Now envisage an unanticipated downturn in aggregate demand. Firms react to this by shedding labour, first by closing down vacancies, then by lay-offs. The withdrawal of vacancies from the labour market is vital, as it cuts sharply the probability of escape from unemployment for all the unemployed. Some of the newly unemployed or the previously short-term unemployed now become long-term unemployed and stop searching for work. When the economy revives the total number of people ready to take up work has fallen, and thus, one might postulate, outsider downwards pressure on wages has now decreased, leading to a higher wage, lower employment economy after the shock. Whereas it is perhaps implausible to suggest that this situation could go on forever, it is feasible that it could persist for some time. Of course, it all turns on the way wages behave. Nickell (1986) provides econometric evidence on the importance of the duration structure of unemployment in determining the overall effect of unemployment on wages for the UK in the recent past, and Crafts (1989) finds similar results on the basis of British data from the Great Depression period.

Unemployment began to fall in the UK after 1986. It fell fairly steadily through the boom years of 1987 and 1988, and by mid-1990 stood at about one half of its 1986 level, from whence it began slowly to climb again. It is too early to be definitive about the causes of the 1986–90 fall in unemployment. No doubt a large part will be attributed to the late 1980s boom, but it is possible that the positive efforts made to reactivate the long-term unemployed with the government's RESTART scheme, introduced in 1988, also made a significant contribution.

The productivity miracle

The first year of exceptional productivity growth was 1982, the year when the economy began to recover from the 1980–1 recession. The last year of high productivity growth was 1987 (1988 in manufacturing). The economy slowed into the current recession from 1989 onwards, with productivity growth slowing as well. This gives six years of high productivity growth. In this section we investigate the causes of this sustained phenomenon. We begin by describing and then casting doubt on five major hypotheses, and then turn to the most influential and controversial one – that there has been an important revolution in industrial relations.

Our first hypothesis is that the boom in productivity was a cyclical phenomenon. There is a mass of evidence to support the view that productivity is cyclical; in fact some Real Business Cycle theorists argue that it is possible to view the cycle as largely caused by exogenous movements in productivity. Prior to the emergence of these new theories it was conventional to view the cyclicality of productivity as due to sluggishness in labour force adjustment. If the costs of adjustment to firms are increasing in the size of the adjustment, then it will profit firms to spread the adjustment over time. If a firm faces predictable cycles in demand, then the cycle in employment will be damped relative to the demand cycle, and so productivity will appear to be pro-cyclical. To what extent could the 1982–8 boom be due to this effect? Most commentators agree that the length of the boom argues against the labour adjustment interpretation. To make the story convincing, either the costs of adjustment would have had to be improbably large, or firms would have to have been expecting a second recession throughout the mid-1980s.

Our second hypothesis is that exceptional investment growth caused the boom. As we saw in Table 5.2, investment growth did, indeed, revive in the 1980s. But it must be remembered that this was against a background of general economic recovery; in fact the ratio of investment to GDP did not change much. Another piece of evidence against this story is that TFP (total factor productivity) growth also revived. TFP growth is that element of growth in output not explained by *aggregated* factor inputs, therefore not directly linked with growth in the capital stock, net investment.

A third hypothesis that grows out of the last point is that the boom in TFP growth was due to measurement errors in relation to net capital growth. In the UK capital stocks are measured on fixed-life assumptions. Many economists have argued that these assumptions would be likely to give misleadingly high estimates of capital stocks for the period after the First Oil Shock in 1973–4, owing to the shortening of the economic lives of fuel-intensive machines. Wadhwani and Wall (1986) produced an alternative time series on the UK manufacturing capital stock for 1972–82, based on the historic cost accounts of firms, which suggests a cumulative overestimation in official figures of about 14 per cent for the period 1974–82. Now if the capital stock is overestimated for the mid- and late 1970s, then net investment and net capital growth are underestimated for the 1980s, leading to a falsely high reading for TFP growth. Muellbauer (1986) calculates, however, that, although significant, these errors in measurement account for only a small proportion of the apparent productivity boom of the 1980s.

Our fourth possibility is that the boom was caused by a technological revolution based on the proliferation of the micro-chip. This theory is severely weakened by international comparisons. The productivity boom was almost exclusively a British phenomenon. One would expect that, if it had been due to a technical revolution, that revolution would have been concurrently apparent in a number of countries.

The fifth hypothesis which we tentatively reject is that the recession of 1980/1 acted in an economically Darwinian way, closing down in the main less efficient firms, and therefore raising average levels of efficiency. The grounds for rejection are that one would expect this effect to have had a once-and-for-all impact on productivity, so that the hypothesis, like the first one, became less convincing as time went by and the growth in productivity was maintained. In any case, as Oulton (1987) showed, plant closures tended to be concentrated in larger firms, precisely those that tend to be more efficient. These results cast further doubt on the Darwinian hypothesis.

If we put these five possibilities to one side, we are left with the hypothesis that the organisation of production went through some kind of revolution. There was undoubtedly scope for this. Many commentators on the British industrial scene in the 1960s and 1970s remarked on the relative sluggishness of productivity growth, and blamed organisational factors for this, in particular bad management but also excessive trade-union power (see inter alia Maynard 1988). Trade-union membership grew from about 40 per cent of the work-force in the mid-1960s to over 50 per cent in 1980, and then fell back rapidly to around 40 per cent again by 1989. Is it possible that the productivity boom was related to this decline in the influence of trade unions? Many studies have looked for evidence on this. Blanchflower et al (1988) found that job losses during 1980–1 in unionised firms were larger than in non-unionised firms, while

Layard and Nickell (1989), among others, find that TFP growth was 3.8 per cent higher in unionised than in non-union firms 1979–85. Metcalf (1990) argues that the latter finding could be explained by the former; management in unionised firms took the opportunity provided by the recession to eradicate the overmanning which they had tolerated through the 1970s. The critical question, however, is whether something *more* than this happened, whether there was a change in the general industrial climate which saw trade unionists become more amenable to changes in working practice. At the level of individual firms it is certainly clear that, since 1979, organisational changes in the direction of greater labour flexibility have been more widespread and frequent than before (see Boakes 1988; Cross 1988).

If unions did indeed become more amenable to organisational change, thus facilitating higher productivity growth, we need to know why this happened. One possibility is that the recession of 1980–1, and the accompanying change in macroeconomic policy regime, had a shock effect on industrial relations. If the regime change was believed to be permanent, then for the first time in decades agents on both sides of industry would have to come to terms with a government committed not to undertake counter-cyclical demand management.

Another possible cause of change in industrial climate was the sequence of industrial relations legislation mentioned above. The government itself considers that those changes were important, citing the fall in strike activity (see W. Brown and Wadhwani 1990). Brown and Wadhwani (1990: 68) are, however, sceptical on the productivity effects of legislation. They argue that it was product market crises with origins in increased competition and/or technical innovations, rather than any direct weakening of the unions, that were responsible for many of the more dramatic changes in working practices. They cite evidence from Stewart (1987) which shows that the mark-up of union wages over non-union wages held throughout the 1980s, which suggests that while unions became more willing to accept changes in the organisation of work, they still had the negotiating muscle to gain compensation for those changes.

A final, related, factor which might have weakened union resistance to change is demoralisation following on the defeat of key unions in major industrial disputes. The two most important of these in terms of public impact were the coal strike of 1984–5 and the News International dispute of 1987. Both featured highly publicised violent clashes between police and workers, both produced heavy defeats for unions with reputations for militancy and solidarity (ie a commitment to resisting redundancies, whatever their grounds), and both were followed by major rationalisations and reorganisations of the industries involved, leading to massive productivity gains.

The 1989–90 decline in productivity growth offers new evidence against which to test our theories on 1980s trends in productivity. This decline is so recent that studies of it are as yet unavailable. It seems likely, however, that the following synthesis on productivity trends through the 1980s will finally emerge. The recession of 1980–1 was important, in part because it led to cyclical productivity gains during the subsequent recovery and in part because it shocked industrial relations out of the status quo. This, together with the heavy defeats of major unions in the mid-1980s, led to a period of rationalisation of working practices which lasted to the late 1980s. Once these rationalisations were complete, and as the economy slowed in 1989 and 1990, the growth of productivity went into decline.

Inflation

We have already seen that the rate of inflation fell fast in the early 1980s. But inflation was never fully eradicated, with the annual rate of price increase staying higher than the OECD average level for all but two years of the decade, and rising again through 1989 and 1990. In this section we shall not elaborate on the causes of the trends in inflation through the decade, but rather concentrate on some of the proposed remedies to what has been perceived, correctly in our view, as an enduring weakness of the UK economy since the mid-1950s.

Our first remedy locates the causes of high inflation, at least in the short run, in failures of the labour market. If we take the Keynesian view that changes in levels of unemployment in the short run are due predominantly to changes in aggregate demand, and hence susceptible to demand management, then high inflation at the target level of unemployment must have its origin in the battle for mark-ups between firms and workers. A number of economists (Bruno and Sachs 1985; Newell and Symons 1987; Calmfors and Driffill 1988) have investigated the idea that the short-run trade-off between inflation and unemployment is affected by the structure of wage bargaining. This line of research was prompted by the observation that some of the countries in which wages are negotiated centrally rather than at the microeconomic level of firms and unions, notably Austria, Norway and Sweden, managed to steer relatively safe courses though the troubled waters of the 1970s and early 1980s, especially with respect to inflation and unemployment. The argument runs as follows. In a highly unionised economy, where wages are negotiated at the microeconomic level, no individual set of bargainers is responsible for the macroeconomic consequences of their collective decisions. It is conjectured that if wages were set centrally, with appropriate adjustments for sectoral differences, then these macro-economic consequences, in particular in terms of unemployment, would become the clear responsibility of the bargainers. This theory, if valid, would be especially relevant to very open economies, such as the UK, where the maintainance of export competitiveness is vital to medium-term performance.

Despite the fact that governments of both main parties have in the past resorted to wage controls in their battle against inflation, the idea of wholesale reform of the system of wage negotiation has never been on the political agenda in the UK. There are probably good reasons for this, as it would require extensive reform of the union movement, which in the UK is a complex intermingling of craft- and industry-based organisations. For the Conservatives and the Labour Party alike, the political price of any attempted reform would be unacceptably high, given the uncertainty surrounding any possible improvement in performance. Although a reform along the lines suggested by the analysis of the previous paragraph is therefore not feasible for the UK, that analysis does provide a rationalisation for the popular view that British inflation is a problem of the wage-setting system.

Another possible institutional reform, aimed at the reduction of medium-term inflation, would take the form of the creation of a fully independent central bank. In the UK monetary policy is the province of the Treasury rather than the Bank of England. This stands in contrast to the situation in the United States and Germany, where the Federal Reserve and the Bundesbank respectively have much greater autonomy from the state in monetary matters. In an influential paper, Alesina (1989) demonstrates a strong negative correlation across the OECD countries between core inflation rates and an index of central bank independence. This correlation suggests that independent central banks may do a better job in maintaining price stability than governments. Why should this be so? One theory, developed by Rogoff (1985), highlights the importance of the credibility of policy-makers. At the core of the credibility problem lie the political pressures that could reverse previously announced policies. Suppose, for instance, that a government announces a low inflation target. If private agents perceive that the government is likely to indulge in a pre-election boom, then the announced target will lack credibility. Rogoff argued that policy-makers could enhance their credibility if they made it difficult to reverse policy, by delegating the control of inflation to an independent central bank (see also Eastwood, Chapter 7, and Sumner, Chapter 8 in *The European Economy*). This idea has attracted a number of followers recently, in the UK and elsewhere. In 1990 the New Zealand government moved in the Rogoff direction, and observers will be watching events in that country with renewed interest. Opponents to central bank independence in the UK tend to concentrate on the problem of public accountability.

An alternative anti-inflation measure is to fix the exchange rate against a low-inflation currency (see also Dyker, Chapter 11 in this volume, on Yugoslavia, and Sumner, Chapter 8 in *The European Economy*). Here the problem of credibility is less severe, as the exchange rate is much more easily monitored and interpreted than data on monetary growth. This was the option chosen by the UK government in the autumn of 1990, when the UK entered the Exchange Rate Mechanism of the European Monetary System. The Bundesbank is generally perceived to be the dominant central bank in the System, and it has a record of acting firmly against inflationary pressures. The question now is how much credibility UK policy-makers have bought by entering the System. In order to avoid a credibility-shattering realignment of exchange rates, the historical inflation differential, 6.5 per cent on average between 1973 and 1986 (and 7.7 per cent at late 1990), will have to be eradicated, and indeed reversed, at some point in the near future. If this does not happen, then the UK will be in the unsustainable position of continually declining price competitiveness *vis-à-vis* mainland Europe. A reduction of the inflation differential could occur in two ways. On the first scenario wage and price setters recognise that the devaluation route to the maintenance of competitiveness is no longer available – that is, they believe the commitment to keep the current central parity – and modify their behaviour accordingly. On the second scenario, an actual loss of competitiveness results in deep recession, with rising unemployment, which forces down rates of growth of wages and prices. At time of writing there were signs that private agents were beginning to recognise that their behaviour must adapt to the new regime. A sharp recession appeared nevertheless unavoidable.

The balance of payments

The steady decline in current account balances, from large surplus in 1980 to large deficit in 1989, is clear from Table 5.3. We have also seen that the rate of GDP growth in the UK was above that of its major trading partners through the 1980s. It is therefore tempting to explain the decline in the current account in terms of simple

Keynesian hydraulics. However, some other factors might have been at work. One could construct a partial explanation on the basis of the decline in oil exports from their peak in 1986. A more sophisticated alternative explanation of the recent deficits would run as follows. Mrs Thatcher's government removed exchange controls at the beginning of the 1980s. This, together with a strong pound, encouraged a flood of British funds into foreign securities. The great bull market of the middle 1980s then enhanced these assets. British holdings of foreign securities increased from £18.6 billion in 1980 to £147.5 billion in 1988, a swing of about one-third of annual GDP, most of which showed up as an increase in net foreign assets (see 1989 *Blue Book* p. 90). The British seemed intent on using up these windfall gains very quickly, and this inevitably had a substantial negative impact on the balance of payments in the latter part of the period. Considering the national economy as a household, this was analogous to, and as harmless as, buying a case of champagne after a successful day at the Derby. Having laid out this argument, it must be said that no econometric studies such as might shed light on the relative importance of the rival explanations for the behaviour of the current account in the 1980s are yet available.

Notes

1   See Feinstein 1976.
2   The Public Sector Financial Deficit differs from the PSBR in its treatment of asset sales flowing from the privatisation programme. The former measure treats these sales as negative capital formation, and therefore as belonging to the capital account, while PSBR treats them as negative current expenditure. It is argued that the Public Sector Financial Deficit is a better measure of the pressure imposed by the government on financial markets.

References

Alesina A (1989) Politics and business cycles in industrial democracies. *Economic Policy* **8** April
Bean C, Symons J S V (1989) Ten years of Mrs T. In Fischer S (ed) *NBER Macroeconomics Annual 1989*. Washington, DC
Blanchard O, Summers L (1986) Hysteresis and the European unemployment problem. In Fischer S (ed) *NBER Macroeconomics Annual 1986*. Washington, DC
Blanchflower D, Millward N, Oswald A (1988) *Unionisation and Employment Behavior*. London School of Economics, Centre for Labour Economics, Discussion Paper no 337
Boakes K (1988) *Britain's Productivity Miracle – More to Come*. Greenwald Montagne Gilt-Edged Economic Research Paper, May
Brown C V (1988) Will the 1988 income tax cuts either increase work incentives or raise more revenue? *Fiscal Studies* **9**(4): 93–107
Brown W, Wadhwani S (1990) The economic effects of industrial relations legislation since 1979. *National Institute Economic Review* **131**
Brown C V, Jackson P M (1990) *Public Sector Economics* 4th edn. Basil Blackwell
Bruno M, Sachs J (1985) *The Economics of Worldwide Stagflation*. Basil Blackwell
Buiter W, Miller M (1983) Changing the rules: economic consequences of the Thatcher regime. *Brookings Papers on Economic Activity* **2**

Burns T (1988) The UK government's financial strategy. In Ellis W and Sinclair P (eds) *Keynes and Economic Policy: The Relevance of the General Theory after Fifty Years*. Macmillan

Calmfors L, Driffill J (1988) Bargaining structure, corporatism and macroeconomic performance. *Economic Policy* **6** April

Crafts N F R (1989) Long-term unemployment and the wage equation in Britain, 1925–1939. *Economica* **56**(222)

Cross M (1988) Changes in working practices in UK manufacturing industry 1981–88. *Industrial Relations Review and Report* May

Dasgupta P, Heal G M (1979) *Economic Theory and Exhaustible Resources*. Cambridge University Press

Department of the Environment (1986) *Paying for Local Government*. CM 9714 HMSO

Dilnot A, Kell M (1988) Top rate tax cuts and incentives: some empirical evidence. *Fiscal Studies* **9**(4): 70–92

Domberger S, Meadowcroft S, Thompson D (1986) Competitive tendering and efficiency: the case of refuse collection. *Fiscal Studies* **9**(1): 69–87

Dornbusch R (1976) Expectations and exchange rate dynamics. *Journal of Political Economy* **84**

Feinstein C (1976) *Statistical Tables of National Income, Expenditure and Output of the UK 1855–1965*. Cambridge University Press

Jackman R, Roper S (1987) Structural unemployment. *Oxford Bulletin of Economics and Statistics* **49**

Jones R (1987) *Wages and Employment Policy 1936–1985* Allen & Unwin

Kay J A, King M (1986) *The British Tax System* 4th edn. Oxford University Press

Kay J A, Thompson D J (1986) Privatisation: a policy in search of a rationale. *Economic Journal* **96**: 1–17

Layard R, Nickell S (1986) Unemployment in Britain. *Economica* **53**

Layard R, Nickell S (1987) The labour market. In Dornbusch R, Layard R (eds) *The Performance of the British Economy*. Oxford University Press

Layard R, Nickell S (1989) The Thatcher miracle. *American Economic Review (Papers and Proceedings)* **79** May

Lindbeck A, Snower D (1988) *The Insider-Outsider Theory of Employment and Unemployment*. MIT Press, Cambridge, Mass.

Littlechild S (1983) *Regulation of British Telecommunications' Profitability*. Report to the Department of Industry

Maynard G (1988) *The Economy under Mrs Thatcher*. Basil Blackwell

Metcalf D (1990) Trade unions and economic performance: the British evidence. In Brunetta R, Dell'Aringa C (eds) *Labour Relations and Economic Performance*. Macmillan

Muellbauer J (1986) Productivity and competitiveness in British manufacturing. *Oxford Review of Economic Policy* **2**(3)

Musgrave R A, Musgrave P B (1980) *Public Finance in Theory and Practice* 3rd edn. McGraw-Hill

Newell A T, Symons J S V (1987) Corporatism, laissez-faire, and the rise in unemployment. *European Economic Review* April

Nickell S J (1986) Why is wage inflation so high? *Oxford Bulletin of Economics and Statistics* **49**

Office of Fair Trading (1990) *An Outline of U.K. Competition Policy*

OFTEL (1988) *The Control of British Telecom's Prices: A Statement Issued by the Director General of Telecommunications*

Oulton N (1987) Plant closures and the productivity miracle in manufacturing *National Institute Economic Review* 121

Pearson M, Smith S (1990) *Taxation and Environmental Policy: Some Initial Evidence* IFS Commentary 19. Institute for Fiscal Studies

Rogoff K (1985) The optimal degree of commitment to an intermediate monetary target. *Quarterly Journal of Economics* **100**

Shaw R, Simpson P (1989) *The Monopolies Commission and the Competitive Process* IFS Report **33**. Institute for Fiscal Studies

Stewart M (1987) Collective bargaining arrangements, closed shops and relative pay. *Economic Journal* **97**

Stigler G (1971) The theory of economic regulation. *Bell Journal of Economics and Management Science* **2**: 3–21

Wadhwani S, Wall M (1986) The UK capital stock – new estimates of premature scrapping. *Oxford Review of Economic Policy* **2**(3)

Walker W, Sharp M (1991) Thatcherism and technical advance – reform without progress? Part I – the historical background. *Political Quarterly* **62**: 262–72. Part II – The Thatcher legacy. *Political Quarterly* **62**: 318–37

CHAPTER 6

Benelux

JACQUES BUGHIN

Introduction

The Benelux countries – Belgium, The Netherlands and Luxembourg – often go unmentioned in economics textbooks, perhaps because their economies seem so small. In the context of this book and its companion volume, *The European Economy*, however, these three countries present much that is of special interest. In relation to the movement towards a single European market, in particular, the Benelux offers a long history of trade and exchange liberalisation and integration, and economic co-operation. This unique experience of three-cornered co-operation – going back to early 1948 – should provide some useful insights as to the likely success and possible difficulties attendant on economic integration on a larger scale. In this chapter, therefore, we concern ourselves especially with the experience of integration between the three constituent economies.

Having said this, we must also affirm that, for all the apparent strength of integration, each of the three economies has continued to exhibit its own, autonomous development trends, so that the different national experiences have been to a degree divergent. For this reason, our survey starts by looking at the main economic trends of the three countries separately. After that we turn the focus on to three issues that are critical for the whole of Benelux:

1 Against the background of high levels of unemployment, *employment patterns and labour market policies* are reviewed, and the general '1992' perspective thereon discussed.
2 Against the background of a growing tendency for financial markets to integrate, an overview of *capital and money markets* is presented, and recent single market reforms in this area explained.
3 In the context of the increasing strategic importance of technology for comparative advantage in international trade, the technology policies operating in the Benelux are discussed, with the '1992' dimension again to the fore.

Finally we look at the issue of *social security*, which has been heavily featured in the Benelux countries, and examine the implications for The Netherlands and Belgium of an integrated European social security system.

General economic trends

Selected background statistics

Table 6.1 presents some key statistics for the three countries of the Benelux since 1978. We can pick out the following general trends:

1   Luxembourg has reported the best GDP performance over the recent period. Its growth rate is approximately double that of either Belgium or The Netherlands.
2   Luxembourg has also performed better in terms of growth of capital formation and industrial production, and in terms of the rate of unemployment.
3   The economic trends for The Netherlands and Belgium are similar (particularly in relation to unemployment), but the Dutch current account is stronger, while Belgian unit labour costs show the highest yearly rate of increase, compensated to some extent by a higher rate of growth of labour productivity.

Table 6.1 demonstrates, then, the need to look at the three countries separately, in order to take account of these divergences. We take each now in turn.

Belgium: the key trends

Summary

In the early 1980s, following the various Oil Crises, Belgium was suffering from macroeconomic imbalances, ranging from growing unemployment and recurrent current account deficit to high inflation rates and substantial public-sector deficits. In 1982 the Belgian franc was devalued. This, and accompanying measures, led to a complete restructuring of the economy. As early as 1985, Belgium was back in current account equilibrium, while investment recovered in that year to grow steadily up to the threshold of the 1990s. Since 1987 the rate of inflation has decreased substantially. Developments in 1990 showed the same pattern, with sustained exports, a still favourable differential in the inflation rate, strong consumption demand, and a near-neutralisation of the 'snowball' effect[1] in the public sector.

Unemployment

Belgium has suffered from acute underemployment of labour, and this has been particularly marked in industry. Aggregate employment began to show positive growth again in early 1985, but the unemployment figure remains high, above the average for the OECD countries. (The unemployment–employment problem is discussed in greater detail on pp. 132–43.)

Current account

Like most small countries, Belgium is heavily trade oriented: thus in 1986 exports represented 45 per cent of total resources (GDP plus imports). A large proportion of exports goes to the EC: the main customers are Germany and France, and, of course, the other two Benelux partners.

Table 6.1 Selected statistics of economic performance in the Benelux (average annual percentage change)

	Belgium[b]	Luxembourg[c]	The Netherlands[d]
Private consumption[a]	1.7	2.2	1.1
Gross fixed capital formation	−0.6	1.6	1.3
GDP[a]	1.5	2.9	1.4
GDP price deflator	4.8	5.1	2.8
Industrial production	1.1	2.7	1.9
Employment	5.4	7.7	0.2
Wages/salaries	5.4	7.7	3.3
Labour productivity	1.7	2.2	1.3
Unit labour costs	3.8	−0.4	1.9
Unemployment (% of civilian labour force)	10.8	1.2	8.1
Balance of payments, current account	−0.9[e]	—	3.5

Notes:
[a] Constant prices, 1980 = 100
[b] 1979–87
[c] 1978–87
[d] 1979–88
[e] Belgium and Luxembourg Economic Union

Source: OECD country surveys

The current account improved significantly over the 1980s, and a 1980 deficit amounting to 6.9 per cent of GDP had been turned into a surplus of 0.2 per cent of GDP by 1987. To put this into perspective, the comparable change in the aggregated current accounts of Belgium's principal trading partners was much more modest – from a deficit of 2.2 per cent of aggregated GDP to a surplus of 0.9 per cent. The improvement in the Belgian current account over the 1980s was mainly due to performance on visible trade. On the export side, geographical orientation has been an important growth factor (the reunification of neighbouring Germany is a particularly good example of this). There have also been substantial gains on the import side.

Rate of inflation

A 5 per cent plus average annual inflation rate was the rule in Belgium at the beginning of the 1980s. The rate decreased substantially, however, towards the end of the decade, and had fallen below 2 per cent by 1989. Since then inflation has strengthened again somewhat, because of the combined effect of increased energy prices and the appreciation of the dollar. For 1991 the inflation rate was about 3.5 per cent, which is in line with the inflation rates of its principal neighbours (Germany, France and The Netherlands).

Public finance

One of Belgium's most prominent problems is that of budgetary balance. Through the 1980s the country faced a public sector deficit recurrently above the EC average, and although the situation has improved since 1985 the cumulative debt stood as high as 135 per cent of GDP in 1988. The burden of the stock of debt is so heavy that interest payments crowd out other categories of public expenditure and the scope for active fiscal policy becomes more and more limited. In the post-1985 period the primary budget (excluding interest payments) has been in surplus, which has made some contribution to the stabilisation of the public debt ratio.

Since 1988 the government has pursued the objective of reducing the net annual public sector borrowing requirement to 7 per cent of GDP. The objective had at time of writing (December 1991) been nearly attained, but transfer of power to Regions and (ethnically based) Communities (see next sub-section) may threaten it in the future. The recent trend towards *debudgetisation* (removal of items of public expenditure from the budget) poses another threat to sound public finances.

Other important developments

In August 1988 a *constitutional reform* was promulgated which transferred political power in relation to the environment, technology, employment, education, housing, energy and communications, among others, to an overlapping system of three Regions and three Communities. This reform leaves the Belgian system of public administration highly decentralised and highly complex, arguably running counter to the politico-integrative impetus of '1992'.

The old *two-tier exchange rate system* (see p. 143 on financial markets) was abolished in March 1990. Under that system the emphasis had been very much on use of the interest rate as a single policy instrument, and on keeping the rate of interest down, consistent with the EMS constraint, in order to ease the financing of the public sector deficit. In recent years there has been a shift in emphasis towards 'shadowing' the deutschmark.

Belgium has initiated a reform in the organisation of *financial markets*, featuring a programme of deregulation aimed at adjusting to the lowering of international barriers with the implementation of the single market (this topic is discussed in detail on pp. 145–7).

Luxembourg: the key trends

Summary

The steel and oil crises of the early 1970s induced a major restructuring of the Luxembourg economy. Diversification within manufacturing and a substantially expanded role for the services industry have allowed the Luxembourg economy to regain equilibrium and vitality. The unemployment rate has remained very low, and performance on inflation has been one of the best among OECD countries. Growth of

GDP has been above average, and the current account has been in steady surplus. The policy of diversification has greatly increased the weight of the financial sector within the economy, which presents an interesting challenge in the context of the financial integration which implementation of the single market programme will bring.

Unemployment

This topic is discussed in detail in the next section. Briefly, unemployment has been very low in Luxembourg, partly as a reflection of the timely diversification strategy, which expanded services as it shrank the steel industry, and clearly created a new comparative advantage for Luxembourg. But the low rate of unemployment has been equally a symptom of a very tight labour supply situation, conditioned by demographic factors, and by the attractions of employment abroad for Luxembourgers. This latter factor, an inevitable concomitant of the openness of the Luxembourg economy, imposes on the country the need to specialise in activities with high value-added per worker. This in turn places high priority on the development of effective human capital policies (see section on technology policy, pp. 149–50).

Current account

The external economic relations of the Grand Duchy have always been framed within some customs union with its principal neighbours – formerly the Zollverein and now the BLEU (Belgium and Luxembourg Economic Union). The BLEU, founded in 1922, has been progressively integrated into wider free-trade zones – the Benelux, the ECSC and the EEC. While Belgium was for many years Luxembourg's principal trading partner, Germany has been since 1958 the main customer for the Grand Duchy's exports. Luxembourg's current account is predominantly a function of external trade with these two countries, and, on a sectoral dimension, of exports of services.

Public finance

Government expenditure represents about 40 per cent of GDP. The budget has been in systematic surplus, in marked contrast to the experience of the other two Benelux countries.

Other important developments

Reform of the financial sector   Given the importance of financial markets for the well-being of the Luxembourg economy, it is vital that institutional structures should keep pace with the evolution of the international financial system. For detailed discussion see pp. 143–5.

The establishment of an *integrated technology policy*. Given the absence of any natural advantage other than the geographical situation of the country, and given the small size of the national territory, it is clear that economic growth will have to rely more and more heavily on the knowledge base. A recognition of this on the part of the authorities has produced a commitment to the development of technology policies sufficiently broad in scope to cover the whole structure of the Luxembourg economy. This aspect is discussed in greater depth on pp. 149–52.

The Netherlands: the key trends

Summary

Like Belgium, The Netherlands has suffered from a number of characteristic imbalances from the 1970s onwards. Among them, we may remark in particular a high unemployment rate, a big public sector deficit, and a deterioration in the profitability of capital. In an effort to grapple with these disequilibria, policy measures have been set in train focusing on control of real wages, tight budgetary policy, and price stability, through a policy of maintaining a stable exchange rate *vis-à-vis* the deutschmark.

Unemployment

High rates of unemployment have been the norm in The Netherlands during the 1980s: the reasons for this are discussed on pp. 132–5. There has been a concomitant upward trend in the number of unfilled vacancies in recent years, a clear symptom of misallocation of human capital (see pp. 140–1 for a discussion of education policies launched to counter this trend). Tight control over real wage increases remains the main element of policy to reduce unemployment.

Current account

The Dutch current account is heavily influenced by two factors: first, the role of natural gas in the economy, and second, the export trade to Germany. Natural gas contributes to the balance of payments most obviously as an export earner, but also as a substitute for alternative, imported energy materials. The import substitution effect of gas production in 1988 appears to have been almost exactly equivalent to the current account surplus in that year (EC 1990a).

Public finance

The economic forecasts of the Netherlands Central Planning Bureau envisage that the public sector deficit of the country could grow to about 6 per cent of GDP in the early 1990s. While the Dutch deficit is smaller as a proportion of GDP than the Belgian, the primary budget surplus in The Netherlands has not been high enough effectively to stabilise the ratio of public debt to GDP. This degree of budgetary disequilibrium has not been accompanied in the Dutch case by deficit on the balance of payments or serious inflation problems. But crowding out does threaten the economy, and it is this that lies behind the priority the government attaches to reducing the public debt burden.

Other important developments

The Dutch policy of maintaining a stable exchange rate *vis-à-vis* the deutschmark provides an illustration, in anticipation, of the monetary integration that should come with the establishment of the single market (see also Sumner, Chapter 8 in *The European Economy*, on monetary integration).

Employment and labour market policies

Introduction

European employment and unemployment trends since the early 1960s reveal a decisive break about the year 1975. A fall in growth rates of employment around that time broke the pattern of steady-state full employment. Huge labour market imbalances and high levels of unemployment were the result, typically in The Netherlands and Belgium, but with the Grand Duchy of Luxembourg presenting a notable exception.

It is commonly believed that the problem of unemployment can reasonably be decomposed in terms of the following elements (see Springer 1991):

1   an insufficient level of demand for goods and services
2   an insufficient rate of capital accumulation
3   a hysteresis effect
4   sectoral mismatch
5   rigidities in the wage formation process.

It is generally accepted among academic economists that these elements came to the fore following the Oil Shocks of the 1970s. This may help to explain why the Grand Duchy – with its tight labour market and international specialisation in financial services rather than manufacturing – has been so well insulated from major labour market imbalances. But the checklist of key issues is well worth developing in relation to The Netherlands and Belgium. After that we look at labour market policies in all three countries, before closing the section with an assessment of the likely employment effects of the completion of the single European market.

The problem of insufficient production capacity and demand constraints

Estimation of disequilibrium models for The Netherlands and Belgium reveals the existence of capacity constraints and demand constraints in both cases (Lambert 1988; Meersman and van der Meer 1990). These models indicate a growing incidence of capacity constraints for recent years, suggesting the need for a two-pronged policy approach based on co-ordinated stimulation of demand and supply.

The constraints estimated by these models are in general consistent with business survey data from the manufacturing sector, this clearly reflecting the dominant role of industry in the transmission of shocks through the economy as a whole. By way of illustration, Table 6.2 reports data on constraints from national business surveys, for the Belgian and Dutch manufacturing sectors respectively. The negative shock on the demand side around 1975 comes through strongly from these data. As time passed, however, capacities were adapted to the level of demand (mainly by scrapping). As a result, the recent economic recovery saw capacity constraints become binding, especially in The Netherlands.

Table 6.2   Demand Constraints (DC) and Supply Constraints (SC) as reported in business surveys (%)

	Belgium		The Netherlands	
	DC	SC	DC	SC
1965–70[a]	41	24	38	23
1971–74[a]	37	26	51	23
1975	67	17	79	13
1977	65	22	76	13
1979	71	24	41	48
1981	83	14	64	34
1983	79	20	83	16
1985	72	27	42	56
1987	81	17	31	65

Note: [a] Arithmetic mean of annual figures

Source: OECD business surveys and author's computations

The hysteresis effect

The so-called hysteresis ('a lag in variation behind the variation of the cause') effect originates partly from this shortage of capital, because excessively low increments to capital stock inhibits creation of new jobs under conditions of limited substitutability between capital and labour in the short run. In addition, however, hysteresis may flow from three other factors:

1   the impact of the duration of unemployment on human capital maintenance
2   the marshalling of insider power
3   the nature of the wage curve.

We now study these in turn.

The *human capital* argument holds that out-of work people lose, over time, their capacity to maintain and update their skills, which reduces their chances of getting back into employment. This line of reasoning receives support from the data for both The Netherlands and Belgium, particularly strongly in the latter case, where the proportion of long-term unemployed (out of a job for more than one year) to total unemployed is one of the highest in Europe, and is still growing.

The basic argument of the *insider-outsider theory* is that outsiders are no longer able

Table 6.3 Long-term unemployed as a proportion of total unemployed, selected years (%)

	1973	1979	1983	1985	1988	1990
Belgium	41	61.5	66.3	69.8	77.5	76.2[a]
The Netherlands	12.8	35.9	50.5	60.7	50	49.8
Reference: USA	—	4.2	13.3	9.5	7.4	5.7

Note: [a] Estimates

Source: OECD database on unemployment by duration and age group

to re-enter employment by underbidding because, for example, replacement of insiders involves excessively high turnover costs.

In most European countries legal restrictions on firing imposed by industrial relations regimes may, indeed, have largely prohibited the replacement of insiders and outsiders. What is more, the problem seems to be particularly acute in the Benelux. Bertola (1990), for instance, in his Europe-wide estimates of job security as a proxy for labour turnover costs, ranked Belgium second, directly after Italy (see Paci, Chapter 4 in this volume, on Italy), and ahead of France and Sweden. Furthermore, recent studies have shown that the Benelux countries have the highest level of short-term inertia in the adjustment of employment levels, another symptom of low flexibility in employment turnover (Heylen 1991).

Finally, the idea of the *wage curve*, brought back into fashion by Blanchflower and Oswald (1990), focuses on the way in which unemployment may act to depress the level of wages in heavily unionised economies.

The reasoning here is based on two key propositions. First, in bargaining situations involving firms and unions, high unemployment reduces the unions' fall-back (the outcome for the union if the negotiations fail) and weakens their negotiating strength *vis-à-vis* the firms. Second, there is a lower bound to this process of attrition of fall-back beyond which any increase in unemployment has no further effect on wage pressure because the probability of an unemployed person finding a job tends to zero.

This scenario, which produces a breakdown of the equilibrating forces within the labour market, may well be relevant to the Benelux, since high unemployment rates do coexist with high rates of union membership and coverage in that region. Tentative application of the wage curve theory to some sectors of Belgian manufacturing suggests a structural break in the wage–unemployment trade-off for observed industry unemployment rates on average five percentage points below the highest registered sectoral unemployment rate (Bughin 1991).

Sectoral mismatch

Comparisons at the sector level reveal a high degree of divergence in the balance of staffing, with some declining sectors reporting surplus labour while other, more dynamic sectors, suffer from shortage of labour. In every Benelux country we find that the job skills sought by firms – especially in booming sectors like chemicals and engineering – simply do not match those offered by job-seekers. This increasing diversity of labour market situations is also apparent at the regional level throughout the Benelux, with some regions persistently reporting a low level of unemployment, some a high.

Beyond that, *globally* high rates of unemployment, coupled with other economy-wide sources of labour market imbalances like low interprofessional mobility, tend to reduce intersectoral flows. This can be envisaged in terms of an outward shift in the Dutch and Belgian Beveridge Curves, as the mismatch between unfilled vacancies and job demands grows. Reding and Cabie (1990: Illustration 11) demonstrate a growing dispersion around the mean of Belgian provincial unemployment rates as the national unemployment rate rises.

Rigidities in the wage formation process

Finally, it is self-evident that wage inflexibility with respect to labour market imbalances may help to explain the persistence of unemployment. In terms of wage curve theory, the sensitivity of wages to the unemployment rate is particularly low by European standards in both Belgium and The Netherlands (van Poeck and van Gompel 1991). Going beyond that, the van Poeck and van Gompel study also reveals that a high degree of wage responsiveness to short-term productivity growth – a typical feature of the Belgian economy – significantly reduces the rate at which unemployment declines. On a slightly different tack, it is noteworthy that labour market performance, in terms of getting unemployment down, is positively correlated with an intermediate level of centralisation of the union–firm bargaining system, which is indeed a feature of the Belgian and Dutch economies (see Figure 6.1).

Labour market policies

The unemployment problem has been to a degree alleviated in recent years as a function of economic recovery and the falling rate of growth of the labour force. However, the rate of unemployment – however measured – remains at a high level in both Belgium and The Netherlands, and the search for remedies continues to attract high priority at the policy level. We now proceed to a broad review of that search for remedies as it has unfolded in Benelux, with special emphasis on Belgium and The Netherlands.

Belgium

Table 6.4 provides an overall picture of the Belgian labour market. It is apparent from the employment data that total employment did register positive growth from the mid-1980s onwards, especially in the services sector, following the recession of the early 1980s. Employment in industry grew marginally in relative terms in the late 1980s, while self-employment, always relatively more important than in neighbouring countries, has increased its share in total employment steadily since 1980. Public-sector employment, in contrast, fell in the late 1980s as the Belgian government sought to grapple with the budget deficit problem.

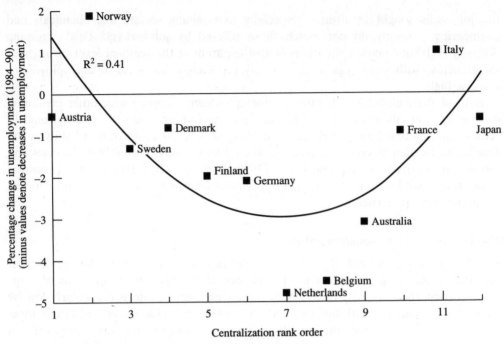

Figure 6.1   Percentage changes in unemployment 1984–90
Source: van Poeck and van Gompel 1991

The rate of increase in nominal wages fell significantly in the late 1980s, but rose again at the beginning of the 1990s. Taking account of trends in prices and productivity, the share of wages in GNP exhibits a slightly downward trend. These stylised facts provide the background to the array of labour market policies that has emerged.

A critical factor affecting growth in total employment in Belgium, which does not come through from the data in Table 6.4, is the development of *part-time employment*. Since 1975 part-time employment has nearly doubled as a percentage of total registered employment in Belgium. This form of employment is especially prevalent in the services sector, and among the female labour force. But while the upward trend in part-time employment is primarily a function of services-oriented restructuring and higher female participation rates, it has been boosted by specific government policies.

Policy towards part-time employment evolved continually from 1981 to 1986, and has now reached a 'steady state'. The strategic goals 1981–6 were twofold: on the one hand, to extend all the rights enjoyed by full-time workers (especially with regard to social security) to part-time workers; on the other to reinforce labour market flexibility by allowing increased freedom to management to vary working time as they saw fit. In addition, the use of temporary workers was facilitated by the Law of 24 July 1987.

The figures from business surveys on capacity constraints (Table 6.2) have already highlighted the acute problem of *shortage of capacity* in Belgium. 'Expansion laws' have accordingly been passed by the government with a view to encouraging capacity-widening investment (see EC 1990b). As a result, the trend towards destruction of employment has been largely reversed in Belgian manufacturing, which helps to explain the recovery in industrial employment trends in the late 1980s.

Active *incomes policies*, aimed at restoring business profitability, were elaborated as early as 1982, following on the devaluation of the Belgian franc. Strict wage controls were enforced between 1982 and 1986, after which they were removed in order to allow market forces to play a fuller role in wage negotiations. The wage-fixing procedure, now again decentralised, is based on the negotiation of two-year agreements between firms and union representatives, subject to the government regulations on the safeguarding of international competitiveness embodied in the Law of January 1989. These regulations allow for the imposition of restraint on the growth of nominal personal incomes.

Table 6.4 Key trends in the Belgian labour market

	1980	1982	1984	1988	1990
Labour force[a]	4,156	4,197	4,214	4,222	4,220
Domestic employment[a]	3,787	3,672	3,635	3,959	3,832
Employment by activity[b]					
Farm	3	2.9	2.9	2.7	2.6
Manufacturing	24.5	23.2	22.7	22	22.3
Trade and services	18.6	19	19.8	19.5	19.6
Government	19	20.1	20.4	20.5	20.3
Self-employed	14	14.6	15.2	15.7	16
Nominal wage per employee[c]	8.6	3.6	6.6	2.0	5.3
Labour productivity (Real GDP/employee)[c]	4.4	2.9	2.1	2.9	2.3
Share of wages in GDP[c]	−1.2	−2.4	−0.8	−2.8	−1.0

Notes:
[a] In thousands at 30 June (*Source*: Belgian Ministry of Finance and author's computations)
[b] Percentage share of total employment (*Source*: Belgian Ministry of Finance)
[c] Annual percentage increase (*Source*: EC 1990b)

Indexation is permitted, but is limited by royal decree to 2 per cent. It is triggered when the consumer price index rises above a critical level fixed by the government.

Overall, the government seems to have been fairly successful in moderating growth in real wages, with the real cost of labour rising less in Belgium than in partner economies over recent years.

The success of these policies notwithstanding, the Belgian labour market remains in serious imbalance, and part of the explanation for the fall in the unemployment figures must be sought in *labour supply containment* measures. The rate of growth of the labour force has been reduced by the introduction of new training schemes and early retirement packages. Education is now compulsory up to the age of 18 (half-time after 16); government aid makes it possible for workers retiring after 60, but before 65, to receive a full pension (as if they had gone on to 65), provided that employers guarantee to replace them with new workers. Other labour supply policies have contributed directly to the upgrading of labour as well as possibly reducing labour supply in the short term, notably those extending the apprenticeship system to several industrial sectors in which it had not previously existed and replacing the system of paid day release by paid education leave.

Other labour supply policy moves have included the following:

1 *Shortening of the working week*: the normal working week is now on average 38 hours, with overtime permitted up to a maximum of 65 hours a year.

2 *Provisions for the impact of technological change*: a law of 1973 requires that works councils be informed of any lay-offs resulting from technological change. Where a number of sectors are involved, all relevant representative bodies must be informed.

3 *Unemployment benefit*: Belgium used to provide unemployment benefit with virtually no time limitation. Now this is going to change. Entitlements will henceforth be dependent on past history of employment.

Luxembourg

The labour market is globally well balanced in the Grand Duchy, with an unemployment rate averaging about 1.5 per cent of the registered labour force (see Table 6.5). Job creation has proceeded vigorously, at a rate of nearly 3.5 per cent annually since 1986 according to OECD estimates, mainly in the credit, banking and insurance sectors. Employment in industry – dominated by the steel sector – has recovered since 1988, after the recession in steel in 1987.

Table 6.5 Key trends in the Luxembourg labour market

	1978	1981	1983	1985	1986	1987	1988
Labour force (thousands)[a]							
Unemployed	1.2	1.6	2.5	2.6	2.3	2.7	2.5
Employed	156.3	158.7	157.8	160.9	165.1	169.6	174.9
of which:							
Industry	46.0	42.9	40.5	39.8	40.3	39.7	—
Services	66.9	72.0	72.9	77.4	80.4	84.2	—
Self-employed	23.0	20.0	19.4	18.8	18.5	18.2	—
Unemployment rate (%)	0.8	1.0	1.6	1.6	1.4	1.6	1.6
Real personal income (per capita)[b]	—	−2.2	−1.7	−0.6	4.9	4.0	4.0

Notes:
[a] Including border workers
[b] Percentage change on previous year

Source: STATEC

Given the tightness of the domestic labour market, and the existence of the BLEU, it is not surprising that there has characteristically been a significant net inflow of labour into Luxembourg, gaining strength from the early 1970s. In 1990 about 30 per cent of the resident population was foreign.

After a decline in the early 1980s, average real wages per employee have now regained positive growth. The increases have been concentrated in sectors like banking, with much more modest wage settlements in industry, owing to the less favourable business climate.

With unemployment so low, employment problems have taken a fairly low ranking in policy terms in the Grand Duchy. But there has been government concern about employment trends in industry, and this has borne fruit in the form of measures to stimulate capital investment. These have been particularly aimed at the chemicals sector.

The government of Luxembourg has pursued the following main elements of policy in relation to labour supply and labour relations.

Reform of the education and training system   To prevent the emergence of acute skills shortages, a reform was promulgated as early as 1983 involving the setting-up of vocational guidance and induction courses for 15–17-year-olds, reform of secondary schooling, and a restructuring of the apprenticeship system; special policies have also been set in motion, in collaboration with foreign universities, on the training of high-level personnel (see pp. 149–50 on technology policy for details).

Employer–employee agreements on the implications of technological change   Sectoral agreements have been signed in the iron and steel industry which commit employers to the provision of information to workers' committees on the possible impact of new technologies on employment prospects.

Length of the working week   Unions and employers have agreed on a 38–40-hour week, with, in principle, no overtime.

Wage fixing   Bargaining is carried on at sectoral level. In 1986 automatic wage indexation and statutory minimum wage regulations were reimposed.

The Netherlands

Since 1985 employment growth in the business sector has been positive at about 1.5–2.0 per cent per year. The annual increment was expected to peak in 1990 at 85,000 worker-years. Government employment has remained roughly constant on a full-time equivalent basis since the mid-1980s. As in Belgium and Luxembourg the creation of new jobs has been concentrated in the services sector, more precisely in the retailing, hotel and catering, and financial services sectors. On average, from 1985 to 1990, total employment in The Netherlands grew more rapidly than in the European Community as a whole.

Turning now to wage costs, we note that growth in nominal wages per worker-year has moderated since 1986, while growth in labour productivity has recovered. As a result, the wage share in GDP has tended to fall, a typical feature of the Belgian economy too (Table 6.6). When measured in terms of people rather than on a full-time equivalent basis, total employment growth has been significantly faster than appears from Table 6.6, thus reflecting the increasing importance of *part-time jobs* on the Dutch labour market. As much as 30 per cent of total employment in The Netherlands is now part-time, with a big concentration in the services sectors, where the pace of part-time job creation has followed closely the rate of increase of female employment. While the rate of growth of part-time employment has slowed in recent years, it is still impressive, and the absolute increment in jobs was probably around 115,000 in 1990. Government policies have actively encouraged the development of part-time employment, from the original part-time experiment (*experimenteele regeling bevordering deeltijdarbeid*), set up by the Ministry of Social Affairs as early as 1980, to the March 1987 directive on the promotion of part-time employment as a means of absorption of excess labour supply.

Table 6.6 Key trends in the Dutch labour market

	1984	1986	1988	1989
Labour force[a]	5,773	5,864	5,980	6,030
Employment[b]				
Total	—	4,689	4,814	4,826
Government	—	742	744	743
Employment by activity[c]				
Farm	—	−0.7	−0.5	0.5
Industry	—	1.9	0.5	1.5
Services	—	2.4	2.0	2.5
Part-time unemployment[d]	830	904	1,005	1,020
Nominal wage per employee[c]	3.2	1.6	1.4	1.1
Labour productivity (whole economy)[c]	3.2	0.0	1.5	2.3
Share of wages in GDP[c]	−4.6	1.1	−1.9	−2.2

Notes:
[a] In thousands (*Source*: EUROSTAT)
[b] In thousands of worker (*Source*: Centraal Bureau)
[c] Annual increase (*Source*: Centraal Bureau and own computations)
[d] In thousands (*Source*: EC 1990a)

Although The Netherlands stood out in the early 1980s in terms of degree of state intervention in the process of *wage determination*, the policy since 1986 has been to limit such intervention in order to promote greater wage differentiation. Again, while automatic indexation was the rule in the past, the contemporary tendency is towards non-automatic annual settlements.

Government policies on *unemployment* have sought both to reduce the number of people seeking work – for example, through early retirement schemes – and to strengthen the incentive for unemployed people actively to seek re-employment. A replacement ratio which was almost certainly too high around 1980 had been reduced to 70 per cent by 1985 (cf Belgium, where it is still above 80 per cent), more or less in line with other European countries.

Nevertheless, and as in Belgium, the rate of unemployment remains high, with an increasing proportion of long-term unemployed within the total. This increase in the long-term unemployment rate is reflected in the problems that some Dutch enterprises have in recruiting skilled labour. But it seems more and more difficult to fill jobs demanding even only modest educational levels, suggesting the need for further initiatives aimed at restructuring the labour market. Measures adopted include establishment of vocational training in secondary schools, incentives for hiring young people, consultation between the world of work and the world of education, and the setting-up of sectoral training funds. Most recently, a Youth Work Guarantee Plan has been mounted, and special incentives for on-the-job training by enterprises established.

Other measures aimed at restructuring the labour market in The Netherlands have included reductions in the working week, which now ranges from thirty-six to forty hours with overtime limited to ten hours per week, measures to make it easier for firms facing slack demand to fire workers, and attempts to restrict eligibility to unemployment benefit by linking entitlement to personal employment history (see p. 157).

The future of employment patterns in the Benelux

Having mapped out the *historical* basis of employment and labour market policies in the Benelux, we proceed now to a discussion of the *prospects* for employment in these countries in the context of the completion of the internal European market.

While nearly everyone would agree that market integration should be a positive-sum game for the level of employment in the European Community as a whole, questions remain as to the likely distribution of gains by country and sector. We now draw on various simulation studies in order to highlight employment prospects for the Benelux countries, with special emphasis on Belgium and The Netherlands.

Market integration and gains in employment: some stylised facts

Strictly speaking, positive employment growth will result from the completion of the internal market only if the growth in GNP resulting from that process is greater than the corresponding gains on labour productivity, accruing through, for example, economies of scale and scope, rationalisation and capital deepening. A number of studies (eg Cecchini et al 1988) have shown, however, that while the single market programme will increase the number of jobs in the EC, the employment effect will not be linear, with the volume of employment decreasing in the short run and then rising again after some five years through the effect of faster economic growth.

The main general points to emerge from the simulation exercises applied to the Benelux countries are as follows:

1 The high degree of *openness to trade* of the countries in question should mean that the benefits from the removal of trade barriers with be that much greater. The high level of foreign direct investment, especially in The Netherlands, will also have important implications in the context of '1992'.
2 In the context of the special importance of the *financial sector* in Luxembourg, liberalisation of capital movements and the setting-up of monetary union will be more critical for the Grand Duchy than liberalisation of commodity trade.
3 The benefits for *public debt service* attendant on completion of the internal market will be especially relevant to the Benelux, given the large public deficits of both Belgium and The Netherlands (see pp. 145 and 148). This gain would accrue on the medium-term perspective, and could impact favourably on employment through a reduction in the strength of the crowding-out effect.

The likely impact on manufacturing

Broadly speaking, the evidence confirms the proposition that sectors which play an important role in international trade and make up a significant part of the given economy will be the first to benefit from completion of the single market. Since manufacturing is mainly export-oriented in both Belgium and The Netherlands, this suggests, *prima facie*, that there will be significant gains in employment in manufacturing as a whole in both countries. Table 6.7 presents data on the expected impact of 1992 for manufacturing as a whole, and by main sector of manufacturing.

Table 6.7 Estimated percentage change in turnover of sectors of manufacturing as a result of the completion of the single market

ISIC No	Branch of activity	Netherlands	Belgium	EC 12
311/2/3/4	Food, beverages and tobacco	—	4	6
321	Textiles	7	4	7
322/4	Clothing and footwear	7	12	7
323	Leather and leather goods	8	—	6
331/2	Wood and wooden products, furniture	9	9	7
341/2	Paper and paper products, printing	7	6	5
351/2	Chemicals	6	6	4
	Synthetic fibres	1	5	3
353/4	Petroleum refining	0	7	3
355	Processing of rubber products	4	0	5
356	Processing of plastics	7	8	6
361/2/9	Non-metallic mineral products	8	2	5
371/2	Production and initial processing of metals	5	9	4
381	Manufacture of metal products	9	5	6
382R	Mechanical engineering	7	10	6
3825	Office machines, EDP equipment	7	7	6
383	Electrical engineering	9	10	7
3843	Manufacture of motor vehicles	8	5	4
384R	Other vehicle manufacture	11	5	5
385	Precision engineering and optics	7	0	6
Total manufacturing industry		7	7	5

Source: Compiled from Nerb 1988

Table 6.7 confirms that Belgium and The Netherlands are likely to benefit by more than the average for the EC as a whole in relation to industry in the aggregate. In terms of specific sectors, the biggest turnover (and hence, *ceteris paribus*, employment) gains are likely to be made by high-technology sectors (eg mechanical and electrical engineering, EDP) and other automated sectors (eg chemicals). Clothing and footwear stands out for Belgium, as does the leather industry for The Netherlands. As confirmed by other studies (see eg Sleuwagen 1989) the sectors that are likely to benefit less from the completion of the internal market are the sectors in which export performance is poor, or which are highly protected by non-tariff barriers, eg textiles in Belgium.

Of course one must be very careful about interpreting these simulation exercises. The main conclusion is, however, a robust one – completion of the single market will be beneficial, in terms of added value *and* employment, for manufacturing in the Benelux, though there will have to be reallocation of labour between sectors on the basis of comparative advantage if all the potential benefits are to be realised.

Financial markets

Abolition of obstacles to the free movement of capital within the EC is a key requisite for the successful completion of the single market programme. In this section we look at financial markets in each of the three countries in the context of harmonisation of financial services regulations under the '1992' regime.

Luxembourg

The 1960s was the golden age of the Luxembourg financial services industry. The stock exchange grew rapidly, and became the listing place for Eurobonds. By the end of the 1980s about 120 foreign banks had branches or subsidiaries in the Grand Duchy. The vigorous development of Luxembourg's financial sector can be traced to two main factors – the two-tier currency system and the relative absence of regulation. We now look at these in turn.

The two-tier currency system

The single monetary zone established on the territories of Belgium and Luxembourg served as a vehicle for the two-tier currency system. Broadly speaking, the system distinguished two kinds of francs: one was regulated and supported by the Central Bank, and was used only for commercial transactions; the other, which was used for all types of financial transactions, was left to fluctuate freely in response to market forces. This gave the financial services sector the advantage of operating in a currency with no exchange restrictions whatsoever. (In 1991, under German pressure and in the light of its apparent incompatibility with the objectives of the EC, the two-tier currency system was abolished.)

Regulation

The influx of foreign banks into Luxembourg is largely explained by the absence of regulation. Luxembourg's development as a fund management centre was largely based on the invention of the *incorporated fund*, an innovation principally made possible by the combination of Belgian legal restrictions and the total lack of control on the part of the Luxembourg authorities. With the passage of time, a degree of regulation has been established. But there are still weighty reasons for banks to operate in Luxembourg, in terms of lightness of the corporate tax burden and the level of administrative costs. Furthermore the August 1983 legislation on investment funds anticipated various subsequent EC directives, and made it possible to set up a a new type of investment fund – the SICAV (*société d'investissements à capital variable* – variable capital investment fund). The SICAV has been a great success because it combines the tax advantages of an incorporated fund with greater flexibility in management. The number of investment funds in Luxembourg is currently about 500, and is still rising.

Prospects

The future for assets management and mutual funds will unfold within the structure of laws passed in 1988. The new legislation, which stipulates that the administration of such funds must be based in the country, also gives companies the right to market throughout the EC. This will no doubt ensure that the assets management business will continue to boom in Luxembourg.

The total capitalisation of the Luxembourg stock exchange, on the other hand, is not likely to increase sharply, in the face of stiff competition in securities trading from neighbouring countries like Germany. The stock exchange is, certainly, considering measures to modernise clearing and settlement procedures, and this could help to build the image of a top-rank securities trading market in the future. For the time being, however, the Luxembourg financial centre will continue to be dominated by banks.

Some idea of the *likely impact of EMU* can be gained by looking at the experience of the existing Belgium–Luxembourg zone of monetary union. Established in 1921, the BLEU is based on the principle of a single main currency, namely the Belgian franc, which coexists on the exchanges with a complementary currency, the Luxembourg franc. What is special about the BLEU is that it is a monetary union in which the exchange rate is fixed (one Belgian franc = one Luxembourg franc), *and* where the currency of one country is legal tender in the partner country.

Analysis of the operation of the BLEU reveals a number of interesting aspects. Because the nominal parity is fixed, the only possible source of real exchange rate fluctuations are differences in rates of inflation. Reding and Cabie (1990) confirm that the level of volatility of the real exchange rate has been lower between Belgium and Luxembourg than between Belgium and the Netherlands. This reduction in the scope for exchange rate fluctuations in turn reduces the magnitude and frequency of shocks on the two economies in general, which improves the business climate all round.

By establishing a wider zone of exchange, each partner country is less tightly constrained to adjust to external macroeconomic disequilibria on its own territory, *as long as* equilibrium in the zone as a whole is maintained. Furthermore, the establishment of a monetary union implies the abolition of capital controls, so that private investment expenditure becomes less tied to domestic savings. Reding and Cabie (1990) have shown that this is indeed the case for the BLEU.

Recent work on *seigniorage* (the 'income' in terms of real resources which a monetary authority derives from the issue of currency) tends to the conclusion that authorities in high-inflation countries will lose from the establishment of monetary union (Gros 1989). In the case of the BLEU the income from seigniorage has been generally no more than about 1 per cent of GNP, so that this has clearly not been a major instrument for financing the public sector in either country. The advent of EMU would therefore create no special difficulties for Luxembourg in this connection.

In the light of all this, the establishment of EMU would likely yield the following benefits and costs for the Grand Duchy (see One market, one money 1990):

1 Like other small economies, Luxembourg would generally benefit from the disappearance of transaction costs and exchange rate uncertainty.

2 The liberalisation of capital movements would favour Luxembourg as a financial centre, while on the other hand the disappearance of exchange rate uncertainty, and the harmonisation of banking legislation, would tend to reduce the volume of banking activity.

Belgium

According to OECD experts (OECD 1989) Belgian capital markets are influenced by two dominant factors – the huge public deficit and the scale of international transactions.

The public sector borrowing requirement

As for many countries, the First Oil Crisis triggered the emergence of great macroeconomic imbalances in Belgium. The high degree of exposure to international pressures meant that the country could not have escaped the impact of the crisis, though the impact was exacerbated by defective domestic policies. In the face of deteriorating terms of trade, measures of retrenchment were in order. In the event, wages were indexed to the price index, while an increasing social security bill (which in itself actually eased the budgetary situation) increased the burden on Belgian companies and eroded competitiveness. This in turn provoked an expansion in public-sector programmes as the government sought to prevent a landslide of bankruptcies in depressed sectors. Meanwhile, the high rate of unemployment imposed a growing encumbrance on the public exchequer.

The result was a huge public-sector deficit, of the order of magnitude of 15 per cent of national income in 1982. After peaking in the 1980s, the deficit has been attacked by successive governments, and the net borrowing requirement has fallen steadily to stand at about 7 per cent of GNP as of the beginning of the 1990s. The requirement remains substantial, however, and this means that government bond issues play a very major role on the domestic capital market.

There have been calls for better debt management as a means of reducing the cost of servicing the public debt. The recent decision by the Minister of Finance to liberalise regulations in the financial sector, partly in pursuance of EC directives but mostly to enhance competition among financial intermediaries, should help in this direction. It should lower interest rates on public debt and make them more stable in the face of external pressures.

The role of the banks

The structure of financial intermediation in Belgium is as follows:

1 private banks, the largest of which are the Banque Bruxelles-Lambert (BBL), the Kredietbank (KB) and the Générale de Banque (GB)
2 private savings banks, specialising mainly in domestic transactions (savings and loans)
3 public credit institutions like the Crédit Communal and the CGER (Caisse Générale d'Épargne et de Retraite – General Savings and Pension Bank).

The role of the banks in financial intermediation has remained fairly stable over the years. Belgian mutual funds have been in direct competition with Luxembourg, and have remained marginal because of the special advantages the mutual funds of the Grand Duchy enjoy.

Banks and other credit institutions play a key role in the domestic Belgian economy because the government deficit is financed in the short run by treasury bills which can be held only by domestic institutions. But Belgian banks are also active in international financial markets. The international side of their business has been boosted by the absence of regulations on capital movements. This helps to explain why the Belgian banking sector is one of the most internationalised among the OECD countries, lagging only behind Luxembourg and Great Britain. It also explains why around three-quarters of the banks operating in Belgium are foreign-owned, and why as many as 400 foreign securities are quoted on the Brussels stock exchange.

At the same time, the high degree of internationalisation leaves the Belgian banking sector vulnerable to external factors against the background of a relatively low rate of return on capital and a low share of equity within total assets. This vulnerability is illustrated by the hostile take-over attempt in 1989 by de Benedetti against the Générale de Belgique, a financial holding company which is part owner of Générale de Banque.

Prospects

The vision of a more integrated and competitive financial market at the European level poses the question of what future Brussels – with one of the smallest stock exchanges in Western Europe – may have as a major financial centre. There was a significant revival of levels of activity on the Belgian stock exchange after 1981, thanks to a number of fiscal concessions granted by the government to issuing companies and equity-holders alike. Further development, however, will be conditional on modernisation of the exchange itself. This would involve, first, opening up financial markets, second, restructuring public credit institutions, and third, cutting the tax burden on saving and lowering barriers to entry.

Opening up financial markets   The stock exchange has been dominated by three clearing banks, with comprehensive networks of subsidiaries and branches around the country. These banks are allowed to act as intermediaries to the extent of collecting orders for the purchase of stocks. But they are not allowed to execute the orders and operate on the exchange directly; that is the monopoly of brokers. The situation is now in flux. Negotiations on a modernisation plan have been going on with the Ministry of Finance since 1988, and it seems likely that this will result in the brokers' monopoly being ended, brokerage fees being put on to a regressive basis, and a stricter code of ethics for intermediaries being imposed. In September 1989 new regulations were introduced to prevent insider trading and protect Belgian firms from hostile take-overs. The futures market was reactivated in January 1989, and at the same time a computer-assisted trading system (CATS) was introduced for the most actively traded stocks. This should help to give Brussels a competitive edge by allowing an increase in the length of trading hours, and integration into the IDIS quotation system which displays up-to-date quotes from all European stock exchanges.

Restructuring public credit institutions   The Belgian government is planning to force these institutions to compete with the private sector. The necessary harmonisation of regulations will be effected by the Banking Commission.

Cutting the tax burden on saving and lowering barriers to entry   The threat of greater openness of financial markets has compelled the Belgian government to reduce the withholding tax on interest on bonds and dividends from 25 per cent to 10 per cent. New financial instruments would seem necessary if foreign savings are to be attracted. On the other hand, the domestic demand for many new instruments like options is relatively low because of very conservative attitudes on the part of institutional investors. Lowering entry barriers to make access easier for foreigners will no doubt increase the volume of business done on the Brussels stock exchange.

Finally, the possibility of paperless settlement creates new opportunities for the dematerialisation of financial markets. In this context *Euroclear*, a Morgan Guarantee Trust Company development based in Brussels, is likely to play an increasingly dominant role in domestic clearing activities.

As with Luxembourg, the *impact of the EMU* on Belgium can be assessed on the basis of experience with the BLEU. That experience suggests that the principal benefits for Belgium from EMU will be associated with reduced uncertainty on exchange rates and a lowering of interest rates, which will have a favourable effect on the public debt service situation. The loss of monetary discretion will mean that it will no longer be possible to resort to monetisation as a way of financing budget deficits. But by the end of the 1980s the role of monetisation in fiscal balancing had in any case been greatly reduced.

The Netherlands

The three-centuries-old Amsterdam stock exchange is ranked among the ten largest stock markets in the world, and is one of the most sophisticated. It has always been a very international exchange, although one-half of its total equity capitalisation is attributable to the four largest Dutch-based companies. The pace of internationalisation is evident from the link-up with the Tokyo stock exchange, the creation of the Amsterdam Interprofessional Market (AIM), and the installation of a very effective computerised trading system.

Amsterdam has responded to the increasingly sophisticated needs of investors by developing business in options and warrants (certificates which give the holder the right to subscribe to the shares of a company as from some future date at some stated price). The Amsterdam European options exchange was the first such exchange to be established in Europe, and has reinforced Amsterdam's vocation to play a major role in the development of European financial markets.

In its efforts to remain competitive, the Amsterdam stock exchange has, since 1986, accepted a range of deregulation measures, which have largely anticipated the EC directive on liberalisation of capital movements. The stock exchange, the European options exchange and the futures exchange are all now self-regulating. But a law of 1988 introduced safeguards against insider dealing, and imposed restrictions in relation to take-over bids.

Prospects

There have been no radical changes on the Amsterdam stock exchange over recent years. But as competition intensifies, changes are bound to appear. The bond market will probably see very little change, since the Dutch government, like the Belgian, will continue to fund its deficit in the primary market. The Eurobond market could expand, but only if fees on bond operations are reduced to the levels of other financial centres. The market is currently dominated by banks, but the market share of the banks will probably contract in the near future as other institutions increase their level of activity. The major challenge for the Dutch financial centre will be to retain its share of world capitalisation. In the quest for an internationalisation of attitudes, the commitment to operationalisation of the IDIS quotation system will, as in Belgium, play a key role.

The experience with the *de facto* monetary union between The Netherlands and Germany, with no realignment between the guilder and the Deutschmark since 1983, provides useful pointers to the *likely impact of EMU* (One market, one money 1990). The main benefits from the *de facto* union have been in the form of reduced transactions costs uncertainty for both countries, and lower inflation rates for The Netherlands. These benefits would be reinforced under EMU, with the additional benefit for The Netherlands of a lowering of the real rate of interest, in the context of a heavy public debt service burden.

Technology policy

As is demonstrated in Chapters 12–16 in *The European Economy*, the rate of technological progress has been a key element in West European growth trends in the post-war period, and is certain to be at least as important in relation to future growth trends. At national level, as at EC level, however, it has been recognised that maximisation of the rate of technological dynamism is dependent on the adoption of appropriate policies, not least in the Benelux countries.

Indicators of technological dynamism

Before surveying technology plans we look at some statistical comparisons of technological dynamism, as measured by R&D intensity, on an international scale (Table 6.8). We can see from the table that the Benelux countries lie on the EC average in relation to R&D expenditure, but lag significantly behind world technological leaders like Japan, Germany and the USA. (Note that the figures for Luxembourg are pushed up by one important Luxembourg-based chemicals firm, whose level of interaction with the industrial sector of the country is low; if we omit this outlier, R&D intensity coefficients for the Grand Duchy fall by half.) The same pattern is evident in relation to number of R&D personnel as a proportion of total work-force.

Table 6.8   R&D statistics: the Benelux countries in international comparison

	Netherlands (1989)	Luxembourg (1990)	Belgium (1988)	Germany (1989)	France (1989)	EUR12 (1989)	Japan (1989)	USA (1989)
GDE[a] (% of GDP)	2.17	2.04	1.53[c]	2.88	2.32	2.05	3.04	2.82
GDEE[b] (% of GDP)	1.32	1.79	1.18	2.10	1.40	—	1.98[d]	1.98
% of GDEE financed by state	42.7[d]	5.3	26.4	32.8	48.7	—	18.7	48.3
R&D personnel (per 1,000 of active pop.)	9.7[d]	9.1	8.9	14.3[e]	11.7[d]	—	13.8	—

Notes:
[a] Gross domestic R&D expenditure
[b] Gross domestic R&D expenditure by enterprises
[c] 1989
[d] 1988
[e] 1988

Source: Biname and Guene 1991

Another striking feature to emerge from Table 6.8 is the degree of divergence between countries in relation to the share of domestic R&D that is publicly financed. Generally speaking, it is low R&D-intensity countries that report low levels of public support for R&D (Japan is an obvious exception), and it is noteworthy that while public support for private R&D is relatively strong in The Netherlands, it runs at only half the Dutch level in Belgium, and is quite marginal in Luxembourg. Table 6.8 does not, of course, bring out trends over time in R&D intensity. Macq (1989) and Soete and Verspagen (1989) show that levels of publicly financed R&D have stagnated in Belgium in recent years, while there has been an upward trend in the level of privately financed R&D. In The Netherlands the opposite pattern has been observable.

At the policy level, then, the patterns that emerge from Table 6.8 point to two priorities:

1 boosting public financial support for private R&D, especially in Luxembourg, but also in Belgium
2 developing training programmes for R&D-oriented skills.

These two dimensions are discussed in detail on pp. 149–55.

Technology policy

Education and training

A major constraint here in the case of *Luxembourg* is the lack of a fully fledged university. The Grand Duchy possesses only two main centres of higher education – the Centre Universitaire (CRP-CU) and the Institut Supérieur de Technologie. This explains why so many Luxembourg students go abroad to study, mainly in neighbouring countries like Belgium, France and Germany. It also helps to explain why more than one-third of Luxembourg firms report difficulties in recruiting highly skilled labour (Biname and Guene 1991).

Faced with these problems, the government of the Grand Duchy has elaborated plans to set up new higher-educational facilities in the country. But debate continues on the question of whether a Luxembourg university should be set up, given the number of universities close at hand in neighbouring countries and the level of competition between universities which will inevitably follow '1992'.

The Luxembourg government does support research and training in business-oriented areas through individual grants. Projects can be carried out in a foreign university, or in a Luxembourg-based firm. The aim here is to build up a pool of highly skilled labour suitable for employment in high-technology sectors like chemicals, biotechnology, and so on. A major policy initiative was launched in March 1987 with the foundation of three public research centres (*centres de recherche publics* – CRP): the CRP-CU (mentioned above), the CRP Henri Tudor and the CRP-Santé. These centres have been given two tasks: first, to furnish a structure within which a core of public-sector research can flourish, and second, to organise technology transfer from centres of higher education to the private sector.

Although small in area, *Belgium* has an impressive university network. Endowment in highly educated personnel is often cited as one of its main comparative advantages. However, Belgium also suffers from shortages of skilled labour in certain high-technology sectors, which suggests a need to formulate new policy measures to promote education and training for a better match between labour supply and employment opportunities, and to stimulate research in high-technology areas.

On training, a number of policy initiatives have been set in motion to meet the needs of employed and unemployed people (see p. 137). Upgrading for those already in work has been encouraged through a working hours credit scheme, while for unemployed people the authorities have set up training programmes, mainly in booming sectors like computers and informatics in general.

In relation to the stimulation of research, the emphasis has been placed on university centres and public science-based institutions. Fundamental research is supported by government grants to the universities and to the FNRS (Fond National de Recherches Scientifiques), a public body which finances individual research projects. For applied research specific credits (*fonds de recherches spéciaux*) are allocated by university research councils, while supplementary funds are made available to those councils by the central government under the PAI (*poles d'attraction interuniversitaires*) programme.

The government of *The Netherlands* has elaborated a number of different action programmes aimed at making the education system more flexible, and more responsive to the need to recycle the Dutch labour force. These action programmes include the following.

The establishment of a Committee for Education and Labour Market Forecasts This committee concentrates on the monitoring of labour market gaps, and on forecasting labour supply and demand. It generates valuable quantitative assessments of the state of the Dutch labour market which are used by the government authorities in their evaluations of education and training policies.

The setting-up of a Vocational Training Refresher Programme   This programme was launched in 1987. It is aimed at lower, secondary and higher levels of vocational training. Some of its funds are very specifically earmarked, eg for the strengthening of the infrastructure at institutes of higher education.

Retraining for employed and unemployed people   Moneys have been set aside for the retraining of both categories of labour. A special fund has been established for the vocational training of unemployed people. Retraining of employed people is left largely to industry, but the government helps in the case of small and medium-sized enterprises.

Professional upgrading in new technologies   A programme has been organised by the various ministries of education for the training of vocational secondary schoolteachers in new technologies, mainly in the informatics area but also in new production technology, office automation and material technology.

Informatics stimulation plan   Launched in 1985, the plan serves general educational and specific training needs. Most of the national projects implemented under this rubric have been for employed people. (Note, however, that on the conclusion of the training programme the firms involved have to carry on the project at their own expense.) Training projects for unemployed people are organised through regional labour exchanges. At the more general level of education, the informatics stimulation plan provides courses in the fields of information auditing, construction informatics and computerisation in health care.

Scheme to stimulate the transfer of knowledge   The objective of this scheme is to promote the transfer of knowledge from research institutes to the private sector (subsidies can be provided for a maximum of four years) and to facilitate co-operation between universities.

Public support for private-sector R&D

The *Luxembourg* government has framed two main objectives in this area. The first and firmest commitment is to the provision of a favourable environment – in terms of tax regulations, borrowing facilities and expert assistance for initiatives coming up from private enterprises. The second priority is actively to encourage R&D activities, particularly in small and medium-sized businesses exposed to strong international competition, by creating pools of competence in booming new-technology domains.

The instruments for implementing these objectives fall into two main categories – *fiscal and financial incentives* and *logistic incentives*. Under the first heading come provisions for accelerated depreciation of assets used for R&D activities and subsidies covering up to 50 per cent of the cost of feasibility studies relating to R&D projects at the small business level. The latter provision is aimed at ensuring that small businesses *start* their R&D projects with a careful analysis of the chances of success. Advances of up to 30 per cent of total costs are also provided for the financing of the later stages of any R&D project resulting in a prototype or a new product. One-half of the advance is refundable, but only if the innovation is a commercial success. These advances constitute the major public sector contribution to private-sector R&D. Beyond that, the SNCI (Société National de Crédit à l'Investissement), a public institution, offers medium-term loans to supplement the above-mentioned advances. These loans are generally for a period of three to five years, with a rate of interest of 5 per cent. The volume of credit provided on this basis varies substantially from year to year.

Under the heading of *logistic support*, Luxinnovation, set by the the Economics Ministry as early as 1984, provides an R&D information service, and support for co-operative agreements between private firms.

The number of firms reportedly benefiting from these various schemes is relatively low, which confirms that Luxembourg still lags seriously behind most of the EC countries in public support of private R&D. In conclusion, we can 'question whether public facilities are adequate for the promotion of private R&D, especially in high-technology-intensive sectors' (Biname and Guene 1991: 43).

Table 6.9 An overview of R&D finance for a group of key sectors of the Belgian economy (billions of constant 1980 Belgian francs)

R&D expenditure minus public-sector financial support	1983	1984	1985	1986	1987	1988
Private firms	3,163	2,686	2,956	1,963	1,358	1,350*
Public authorities	−16,653	−16,165	−17,987	−16,813	−16,899	−16,990*
Private and public institutions	2,374	2,279	2,423	2,312	2,219	2,220*
Education	10,195	10,530	10,825	10,979	11,479	12,100*

Note: * Estimates

Sources: SPPS (Service de la Programmation et de la Politique Scientifique); Macq 1989; author's computations

Table 6.9 shows the pattern of R&D finance for a group of key sectors in *Belgium*. Table 6.10 focuses on individual key sectors, presenting statistics on their shares of total R&D and total public sector financial support for R&D. The most important points to emerge from Table 6.9 are that education is clearly the principal recipient of public sector financial support for R&D, while the proportion of total financial support that has gone to the private sector has steadily fallen. Table 6.10 shows that electronics and chemicals are the most R&D-intensive sectors of the Belgian economy, but receive relatively less financial support from the public sector.

These stylised facts can be traced in origin to specific aspects of Belgian R&D policy. At the beginning of the 1980s, and under the influence of the recession of that time, policy was mainly oriented to general economic objectives or to the promotion of applied research in the private sector. This has progressively changed, as the priority has shifted towards the promotion of university-level research, and towards the support of research in human and environmental sciences.

To cope with the new policy orientation, the Belgian authorities decentralised public support for industrial R&D to the Regions, while maintaining central control (with a degree of decentralisation to the Communities) over R&D finance for both public and private sector higher-education centres. Human science programmes focusing on management of social security and the health sector have been set up, while new environmental programmes have centred on climatic change, the energy problem, and so on.

Table 6.10   Distribution of R&D expenditure and public-sector contribution to that expenditure in 1988, by key sector, in percentages of total for whole economy

	R&D expenditure	Public sector financing of R&D activity
Electronics	30.6	27.2
Engineering	6.0	4.3
Metallurgy	4.9	4.9
Pharmaceuticals	10.1	8.7
Transport	4.0	9.4
Chemicals	25.8	14.8

Source: SPPS

The decentralisation of R&D programmes for private industry to Regional level poses the question as to whether R&D stimuli may thereby tend in the future to unevenness. Of course support must be concentrated on the high-tech industries – which are not evenly distributed among the regions – and measures will have to be taken to ensure that that priority is held sacrosanct. The instruments that exist at Regional level include the provision of subsidies (perhaps the most important), of advances, refundable where the given innovation is crowned with commercial success, and of loans, with a medium-term maturity and bearing a low rate of interest.

At the beginning of the 1980s R&D expenditure in *The Netherlands* was at a low ebb compared to the other OECD countries. Since then, however, the country has managed nearly to catch up, largely because of vigorous growth in corporate R&D spending during 1984–8: thus over that period the corporate R&D rate nearly doubled, to stand, in 1988, at about 1.4 per cent of GDP. This growth was in turn largely a reflection of the recovery in corporate profitability in Dutch industry, with Dutch public support to industry R&D remaining at a relatively modest level (15 per cent of total private industry R&D expenditure in 1988).

As in Belgium, R&D expenditure in The Netherlands is located mainly in manufacturing, but there is now a growth trend in R&D activity in services, mainly linked to information technology. The most highly R&D-intensive sectors are chemicals (R&D accounted for 12 per cent of sectoral value added in 1987) and the metals industry (about 9 per cent of value added in 1987).

The Dutch authorities are conscious that much will have to be done to reinforce government support for R&D in the coming years, because of the strategic role which it will play in the face of increased competition, including for small and medium-sized businesses. In this context a range of new, market-oriented policy instruments has been elaborated:

1   INSTIR programme
2   OMK programme

3 TOK programme
4 PTBS programme.

The status of these programmes in terms of eligibility for subsidy and project scope is laid out in Figure 6.2. The horizontal axis of the figure shows how easy/difficult it is to access funds under these programme heads, with approval barriers becoming lower as one moves to the right; the vertical axis indicates the stage in the innovation process that the given programme addresses, with movement down the axis bringing us closer to the stage of marketable new product or service.

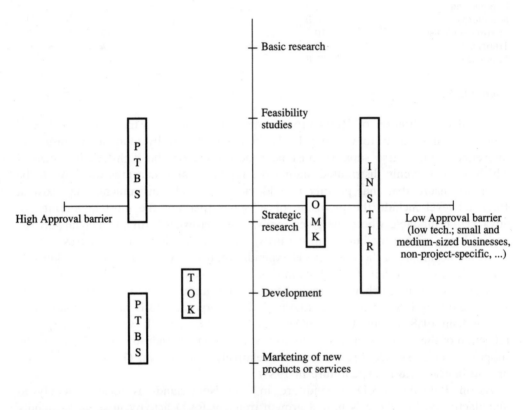

Figure 6.2 The Dutch technology policy instruments
Source: States General, Second Chamber 1990

The INSTIR programme is the most generally accessible one, offering subsidies against wage costs in R&D activity. The objective of the programme is to stimulate technological dynamism in small and medium-sized enterprises. The original INSTIR concept was reviewed in 1989, and new subsidy ceilings imposed. More than 80 per cent of INSTIR's beneficiaries have fewer than 250 employees. The OMK programme, which started in 1986, aims mainly to help small businesses with projects that have already reached the advanced strategic research stage. It is available only for projects not supported by PBTS (see p. 155). The TOK programme grants loans at a preferential interest rate of 5 per cent for the development stage of a specific innovation. The credit covers 60 per cent of the total costs involved, and has to be repaid if the development results in a commercially viable product or service. Finally the PBTS forms the core of the national technology programme. Its approach is broad and it has no predetermined priorities. Its objective is to stimulate medium-term growth by disseminating knowledge of new technologies. In principle support is temporary. Since 1989 the programme has focused mainly on improved construction materials. PBTS works in complementarity with well-known international programmes like Eureka (see Hobday, Chapter 14 in *The European Economy*, on the electronics industry).

A final perspective on R&D in the Benelux

In the light of all this, and in the context of the impact of '1992', we can draw the following conclusions:

1 Increased international competition as trade barriers are lowered will demand increased R&D effort. This is particularly important for the Benelux countries because they have historically lagged behind the OECD average on a number of key R&D indicators.
2 R&D effort to boost productivity and create comparative advantage requires favourable public policies. In this context the main message seems to be that governments in each country must take priority measures to create a new impetus here (in the Dutch case to consolidate the measures set in motion in the late 1980s).
3 Public support for R&D must be oriented to new technologies. It should be consistent with the revealed technology advantage that The Netherlands has, for example, in telecommunications and semiconductors, and Belgium in biotechnology (see Soete and Verspagen 1989).
4 Organisations in small countries usually operate at sub-optimal scale. This raises the question as to whether the new technology paradigm will allow a relaxation in the constraint of scale. If so, we can expect to see a reinforcement of Benelux policies favouring small and medium-sized enterprises.

Social security in the Benelux

The social protection of citizens is a major issue in the countries of the Benelux. Nearly 30 per cent of GDP is currently spent on social programmes.

Belgium

The history of the Belgian system of social security goes back to the creation of the Belgian state in 1830. It is essentially structured around three socio-professional groups – civil servants, wage-earners and self-employed people – though the health-care system is largely uniform across the three groups.

The *health-care* system is managed by a unifed national organisation, INAMI (Institut National d'Assurances-Maladie-Invalidité). INAMI stands at the apex of a system composed of a number of mutual funds which serve as intermediaries between their members and INAMI. The system has recently come in for much criticism as a source of cost inflation in the health-care system, and is currently being reformed under the auspices of the Ministry for Social Affairs (see below, on this page).

As far as other benefits are concerned, the main outlines of the system are as follows:

1   *Civil servants* have enjoyed a special legal status since 1844. Their pension funds are managed by the civil service itself.
2   For *wage-earners* unemployment benefit is provided by the National Employment Office. The office distributes benefit in collaboration with trade union workers and a public non-union institution CAPAC (Caisse Auxiliaire Publique d'Allocation de Chômage). In relation to industrial injuries, firms are free to subscribe to their own insurance schemes. But management in this area of insurance is ultimately controlled by FAT (Fonds des Accidents du Travail). Old-age pensions and family allowances are managed by specific national offices. Finally, the ONSS (Office National de Sécurité Sociale) manages the receipt of all social security contributions. This form of 'indirect labour cost' is set at one of the highest levels in Europe, amounting to some 35 per cent of gross earnings.
3   For *self-employed* people, pensions, family allowances, etc are managed by a special fund, INASTI (Institut National d'Allocations Sociales pour Travailleurs Indépendents). INASTI co-ordinates the various private funds to which self-employed people may choose to affiliate.

Each Belgian local authority runs a public centre of social assistance. These centres provide a minimum wage to people ineligible under the national system, or otherwise in poverty.

The aggregate financial burden of the social security system has increased sharply in recent years, to stand at about 25 per cent of GDP in 1990. Behind this trend lie a number of factors, not only the ageing of the population and the increase in the number of beneficiaries, but also possibly the overconsumption of social security services. Against the background of the huge budget deficit, measures have been taken to bring greater cost discipline into the system, particularly in relation to health care. Health-care cost containment plans have centred on the deindexation of costs, cuts in length of stay and number of beds in the hospital sector, and rationalisation of the ambulance service.

The Netherlands

Like Belgium *The Netherlands* have a long tradition of national insurance, with the first social protection measures being passed in the early years of the twentieth century. But the system remained fragmented and limited, except for civil servants, until it was enlarged, after the Second World War, consequent on the work of the Van Rhijn Commission.

The peculiarity of the Dutch system lies in the coexistence of a wage-earning-based social insurance system and a national programme for all residents of the country. The former is based on the 'equivalence principle' (benefits depend on contributions) and the latter on the 'solidarity principle' (benefits are uniform). As in Belgium, supplementary benefit is provided to residents whose entitlements under the two main schemes are either zero or insufficient to maintain a minimum living standard.

The social insurance programmes for wage-earners include the following.

1   The health insurance programme (ZFW – Ziekenfondswet), which guarantees 70 per cent of regular salary during periods of hospitalisation of up to one year.
2   The disability benefit programme (WAO – Wet Arbeidsongeschektheid), which provides the wage-earner who is disabled for more than one year with benefits which depend on earning history and degree of disability.
3   The unemployment benefit programme (WW – Werkloosheidwet): until recently this provided support for the first six months of unemployment irrespective of employment record. The provisions have now been changed so that benefits are extended only to people who have worked at least twenty-six weeks in the year preceding their unemployment.

The national programmes include the old-age pension and child allowance provisions. Currently a pension of 50 per cent of the net minimum wage is paid to all Dutch residents over 65 years of age. Child allowances are paid for each child of under 18 years of age, and vary according to the number of children in the family.

A typical feature of the Dutch economic scene is the size of its social insurance and social assistance programmes in relation to GDP. As in other countries with a strong commitment to social security, Dutch spending on this item has increased steadily from year to year, and stood at more than 30 per cent of GDP in 1990.

Both transfer payments and health-care costs have been factors in the increase in the budget deficit, and this has fostered a new priority on cost control. The most important measures of reform have included a change in eligibility rules for national programmes, a lowering of the minimum wage, and more market-oriented policies in the health-care sector. Contributions assessments have also been modified. According to the Dutch planning bureau, these measures should have helped the social security budget to attain balance in 1991 (*Ekonomisch beeld* 1991: 87–8).

Social security and the single market

The foregoing paragraphs underline the degree of divergence between the social security systems of Belgium and The Netherlands and the complexity of the system in each country. How will these systems stand up to the introduction of the internal market?

In this context, the idea of developing unified European social policies, with the drafting of the Social Charter at the December 1990 meeting at Strasbourg of the European Council, the recent EC directives on harmonisation of social security systems, and the related decisions of the Maastricht Summit of December 1991, are clearly of great importance. With the free movement of people within the Common

Market, how can losses by individuals moving from one system to another be minimised? Would it be preferable to harmonise social security system comprehensively in order to prevent unwarranted migration flows between countries?

Pedersen (1991) advances two propositions:

1   Taking into account the direct and indirect impact on production costs, a higher level of indirect labour costs induced by the rate of social security contributions leads to a lower hourly wage rate. Thus an *ex ante* harmonisation which raises social security levels requires greater wage flexibility in low benefit countries, if those are not to suffer a loss of competitiveness.
2   Tax harmonisation in the context of the single market programme will tend to lower the burden of indirect taxes. This will have implications for social security expenditure, since countries with a high rate of indirect to direct tax will tend to lose revenue. For countries with large budget deficits this is clearly a major problem.

On this basis we can conclude that the consequences of social security harmonisation for The Netherlands and Belgium would be

1   pressure to reduce social security spending because of an increased burden of budget deficit; in fact, as we have seen, the financing of social security in these two countries is based as much on employees' and employers' contributions as on the tax system, and this would mitigate the impact on social security of tax harmonisation;
2   positive impact on employment if *ex ante* harmonisation levels up social security provisions to the range of the high-benefit countries; this follows from the fact that the Benelux countries have among the highest rates of indirect labour costs, and hence among the lowest rates of direct hourly labour cost, in the EC.

Note

1   The 'snowball effect' describes the process whereby the stock of public debt may continue to increase as a proportion of GNP in the context of a surplus on primary budget, because of the burden of interest charges on the cumulative deficit inherited from the past (see Bogaert 1984).

References

Bertola G (1990) Job security, employment and wages. *European Economic Review* **34**: 851–54
Biname J P, Guene C (1991) Evaluation du potentiel R&D du grand-duché de Luxembourg. *Rapport de l'Institut de Recherches Economiques et Sociales* Louvain-la-neuve
Blanchflower D, Oswald A (1990) The wage curve. *Scandinavian Journal of Economics* **92**: 212–35
Bogaert H (1984) Déficit des finances publiques: l'effet balle de neige. *6ᵉ Congrès des Economistes de Langue Française* Commission 2, rapport préparatoire

Bughin J (1991) Industry wage curves for Belgium: does any switch exist? Mimeo, Université Catholique de Louvain, June

Cecchini P et al (1988) *The European Challenge: The Benefits of a Single Market*. Gower, Aldershot

EC (1990a) *Economic Papers: Country Studies The Netherlands* (81)

EC (1990b) *Economic Papers: Country Studies Belgium* (82)

Ekonomisch Beeld (1991) Centraal Bureau, The Hague

Gros D (1989) Seigniorage in the EC: the implications of the EMS and financial market integration. *IMF Working Paper*, January

Heylen F (1991) Long-term unemployment in the OECD countries. *SESO Working Paper* Universiteit van Antwerpen, May

Lambert J P (1988) *Disequilibrium Macroeconomic Models: Theory and Estimation of Rationing Models Using Business Surveys Data*. Cambridge University Press

Macq A (1989) Les déterminants de la recherche et développement dans l'industrie belge. Master's thesis, Facultés Universitaires Notre-Dame de la Paix, Namur

Meersman H, van der Meer T (1990) A disequilibrium model of the Dutch goods and labour markets. *Research Memorandum 89–21* De Nederlanse Bank, Amsterdam

Nerb G (1988) The completion of the internal market: a survey of European industry perception of likely effects. *The Cost of Non Europe* Basic Findings, Vol 3, EC, Luxembourg

OECD (1989) *Economic Surveys Belgium-Luxembourg 1988/89*

One market, one money (1990) *European Economy* (44)

Pedersen J H (1991) Harmonization of social security in the EC revisited. *Journal of Common Market Studies* **29**(5): 505–26

van Poeck A, van Gompel J (1991) The decline in unemployment (1984–1990) and the wage formation hypothesis. *SESO Working Paper* Universiteit van Antwerpen, May

Reding P, Cabie I (1990) Aspects d'une union monétaire: le cas d l'U.E.B.L. Mimeo, Facultés Universitaires Notre-Dame de la Paix, Namur

Sleuwagen L (1989) The European single market: implication for Dutch manufacturing industries. Mimeo, Katholieke Universiteit, Leuven

Soete L, Verspagen B (1989) Recent comparative trends in technology indicators in the OECD area. *MERIT Reseach Paper 89–007* Maastricht

Springer K A (1991) *From Micro to Macro in Disequilibrium Economics: a New Keynesian Analysis of the Dutch Unemployment Problem*. VU University Press, Amsterdam

States General, Second Chamber (1990) *Technology Policy Survey 1989–90*, The Hague

CHAPTER 7

Sweden

LARS PETTERSSON

Introduction

The deep business recession of 1952–3 may serve as the starting-point for our analysis of the development of the Swedish economy. In the course of that recession, much of the industry serving the Swedish home market, which had been favoured by the protected conditions of the 1930s and the war years, was eliminated. At the same time, the heavy fixed investment associated with the Korean War boom of 1950–1 had produced patterns which survived the recession to play an important part in shaping Sweden's post-war industrial alignment (Schön 1990: 73). Among other things, it meant that heavy industry increased its share in the economy after the recession. The public sector, too, began renewed growth at a faster pace. Thus the structure of the Swedish economy underwent radical change during the early 1950s. It is, indeed, possible to speak of a *structural shift* in the Swedish economy in 1952–3 (Krantz and Nilsson 1975: 200).

If we examine the trend of annual growth in Sweden's gross national product after 1952, we can discern, in addition to cyclical economic changes, longer-term structural changes (Figure 7.1). For example, we see how the general level of growth rates changed during the early 1970s. Average growth in 1973–90 was 1.9 per cent, as compared with 3.9 per cent in 1952–73. It seems as though the Swedish economy experienced a break of trend about 1975.

On a somewhat different interpretation of the figure we can detect during the period up to 1965 the recovery phase of a lengthy and possibly cyclically recurring fluctuation. The late 1960s and the 1970s would then represent the downward phase and the 1980s a new recovery, though a weaker one than that of the 1950s and 1960s. Later on in this chapter we shall see that such a long-term cyclical interpretation of growth may have something to be said for it. To anticipate the argument in brief, the interplay between material and non-material investment can, under the influence of the way in which the labour and education markets function, give rise to recurring long-term fluctuations in the economy.

In order to illustrate this interpretation we shall make a special study of certain key

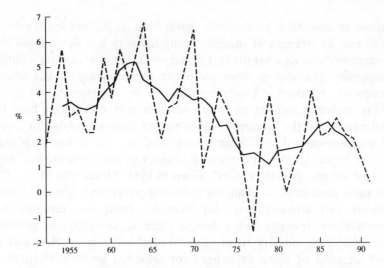

Figure 7.1   Economic growth in Sweden 1952–90 (annual percentage change)
Note: Continuous line: five-year moving average
Source: *Ekonomifakta* 1991 Näringslivets ekonomifakta, Stockholm

parts of the Swedish economy. We shall concentrate primarily on an activity which is exposed in large measure to foreign competition – *manufacturing industry*. Capital formation in manufacturing both influences and is influenced by capital formation in *housebuilding*, which belongs to the protected sector by virtue of the non-tradeability of the outputs it generates. Of the non-material categories of capital formation we shall pick out education and knowledge, in particular *engineering education*. This last choice can be justified in terms of the deference paid in modern growth theory to the role of knowledge in economic growth (Romer 1986). All these activities exhibit in addition fluctuations longer than those of the trade cycle, which indicates that they are important to any understanding of long cycles in growth.

We then widen the perspective. Structure-influencing economic policy, among other factors, is introduced into the discussion, which is then extended to embrace the whole of the competitive sector (the C-sector) and protected sector (the P-sector), and the whole of the vocational education sector. In all of this, the analysis concentrates on the 1980s. The primary aim is to explain why the economic recovery of the 1980s turned out to be relatively so weak.

First, however, we shall present some background. A description of manufacturing industry's capital formation trends over time is followed by a survey of the explanations of the long cycle of growth already in circulation.

Investment in manufacturing industry

Three phases of acceleration

As already mentioned, manufacturing industry is one of the activities in which capital formation exhibits fluctuations of greater duration than those of the trade cycle. It is an activity which has been and remains a strategic component of the Swedish economy.

Rates of increase in industrial productivity have been high. Sweden's economy is export-oriented, and its strength in manufacturing industry has determined in large measure its competitiveness *vis-à-vis* the rest of the world, and the country's faith in the future and propensity to invest in other sectors of the economy. It has often been within the framework of industrial enterprise that new development blocks have been initiated – that is, technical and organisational changes in manufacturing have created imbalances and tensions in the economy, which in turn have stimulated or forced the emergence of supplementary forms of entrepreneurial activity. It has been said that the industrial firm, in its capacity as creator and carrier of new technologies, has been 'the motor of the economic growth process' (Eliasson 1988: 13; see also Sharp, Chapter 12 in *The European Economy*, on changing industrial structures). On this view, even though agriculture and housebuilding, for example, have also reported massive progress in productivity, industry has a unique place as an engine of growth. The capacity of manufacturing industry to produce 'tradeables' – ie articles, and indeed services as well, capable of being exchanged for imported goods – strengthens the argument further. When the industrial sector shrinks relative to other branches of the economy, balance of payments problems arise which in themselves impose a restriction on the nation's economic activity.

How has industrial capital formation developed during the period under review? According to Figure 7.2, it has undergone three phases of acceleration: one up to 1961 inclusive, with very high volumes of investment in 1958, 1959, 1960 and 1961, a somewhat more modest one during the early 1970s, and one during the latter part of the 1980s.

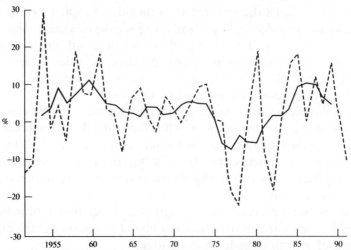

Figure 7.2   Annual percentage rates of growth of gross investment in Swedish manufacturing industry 1952–90
Note: Continuous line: five-year moving average
Source: *Ekonomifakta*

The industrial investment boom of the late 1950s and early 1960s was largely a *Grunder* period, when new places of work were being established, often to produce goods which had not been produced before and with a technology not previously used in Sweden. During these years industry's rate of investment in buildings increased

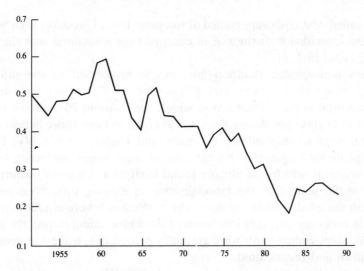

Figure 7.3 Investment in buildings as a proportion of total investment in manufacturing industry
Source: Unpublished working tables, Krantz O, Umeå University; *Industristatistik*,
SCB, Stockholm

relative to that of investment in machinery, which underlines the innovative and structure-transforming character of the boom (Figure 7.3).

The investment boom around 1975 was a different matter. The annual rate of increase in capital formation had slowed since 1962. Many export branches had been finding it more and more difficult to compete. Profits, and especially dividends, were falling. Mechanisation and mergers, coupled with attempts to exploit economies of scale, had become increasingly important elements in the process of industrial change. One symptom of this was a steady increase in the weight of investment in machinery (from 1962 onwards) compared with investment in buildings (Figure 7.3). At the same time government power and influence over investment decision-taking had been strengthening.

The boom started to develop in 1972–3. The initial impetus came from rising demand for raw materials and freight services occasioned by extensive stockpiling on the part of Sweden's customer countries. Both private and government decision-takers seem to have made up their minds that the structural problems of the 1960s had thereby been overcome. This somewhat optimistic line of thought resulted in large-scale investment in the shipbuilding, steel, forestry and chemicals industries; that is, in enterprises which had long functioned as profit-machines in the Swedish economy, around the mid-1970s. The idea was to take offensive action in what were believed to be the enterprise areas of the future (Örtengren 1981: 101). A proportion of the power supplies for these energy-hungry industries would be supplied by the two new nuclear power plants which were constructed during this period. In point of fact these investments were to a large extent wide of the mark, inasmuch as they were tax-financed, defensive investments in firms and operations which in a number of cases had already been knocked out of the game. The bottom was falling out of the international market for many of the products of the favoured industrial branches even while the expansion was going on.

The so-called cost crisis supervened at the same time. Unusually high wage increases more or less coincided with the rise in energy prices associated with the formation of the OPEC cartel in 1974.

The then non-socialist coalition government responded to the situation with a number of minor devaluations and a 'casualty ward' for sick industries in which subsidies constituted the medicine most widely used. About 30 thousand million kronor were paid out in subsidies during the years 1977–82 to keep those industries alive. Half of the total went to shipbuilding (Dahmén and Carlsson 1985: 64). This industrial policy, implemented against a background of high wage- and energy-costs, hit an industrial economy which had already found itself in a defensive posture even during the 1960s in the sense that the rationalisation of existing production units had been preferred to the establishment of new. The result was severe equilibrium problems in the Swedish economy and very low levels of fixed investment during the late 1970s and early 1980s. Shipbuilding yards were gradually phased out, while the steel industry was slimmed down and restructured.

In other words, the investment boom of the 1970s can be characterised as an artificial and ill-balanced re-ignition of the Swedish economy. In the short term, of course, it contributed to the growth of the GNP. But it was not long before it produced precisely the opposite effect, with severe cyclical fluctuations in levels of GNP and a very deep depression in 1977–8.

One reason why growth in the GNP level was not sustained was probably the subsidy policy, with its widespread effect of freezing labour and capital in doomed industries. It checked the emergence of 'new' enterprises more compatible with contemporary comparative cost conditions. The difficulties were then exacerbated further by the way in which the extensive programme of support measures aggravated problems of macro-equilibrium in the economy. What was originally a structural crisis developed into a government budgetary crisis as well.

The year 1978 represented a turning-point in the sense that the profitability of industry began to climb again – out of a very low trough. Manufacturing profit rates began to draw nearer to the yields on financial capital (Figure 7.4). The same year also marked a turning-point in fixed capital formation in manufacturing industry, though with a deep cyclical slump in 1982. The investment boom of the 1980s also brought a break in the tendency towards an ever-diminishing share of building and an ever-rising share of machinery within total investment which had lasted since 1962 (Figure 7.3). But there was no great boom in the laying down of industrial plant to match the one that occurred around 1960. Instead, another kind of capital formation accelerated during the 1980s, namely non-material investment. Investment in research, education, marketing and services increased substantially in manufacturing industry. This development gained real impetus as early as the crisis of the 1970s (Örtengren 1981: 120). Thus the picture of stagnating industrial capital formation during the late 1970s can be modified somewhat. While material investment was falling drastically, non-material investment was rising – and went on doing so throughout the 1980s. R&D expenditures in the private sector increased more rapidly in Sweden than in any other industrial country during the 1970s and the first part of the 1980s (L. Ohlsson 1990: 15).

All in all, this survey of industrial capital formation leaves us with an impression of two long, and in some degree spontaneous and 'successful', investment booms – the

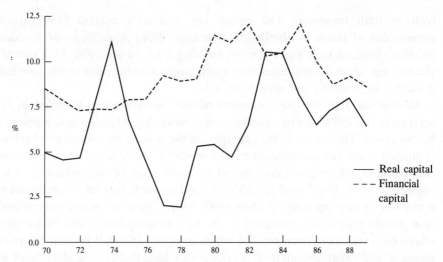

Figure 7.4   Returns to industry on real and financial capital 1970–89 (per cent)
Source: *Ekonomifakta*

first around 1960 and the second, more dubiously, around 1985 (Figure 7.2) – dubiously because the extensive capital formation of the 1980s did not have any counterpart in economic growth such as was recorded around 1960. The earlier investment boom was to a large extent based on the construction of new production capacities, through which the Swedish industrial apparatus was able to expand its markets. As examples of new products which were brought on stream during the 1950s we may mention transistor radios, TV sets, washing machines, excavators, power saws, outboard motors, torque converters, vibrating machines, freezers, beer-cans, moulding machines for plastics, and mining machinery, to cite only a few items from a long list. Even so, there are many who believe that the long-term growing power of industry and the pace of change could have been even stronger had it not been for a certain degree of conservatism with regard to the orientation of investment (Jörberg 1991: 47). A contributory factor here was the undeveloped capital market. Profits did not come on to it in sufficient volume, but remained with, and were ploughed back into, the firms which had made the profits.

In the second investment boom – the one in 1985 – a certain amount of investment in new production capacities also took place, with investment in buildings increasing somewhat as a share of total investment from 1983 (Figure 7.3). However, the question is whether the pattern of rationalisation of old enterprises was truly broken. The large-scale devaluation of 1982 meant (*inter alia*) that the crisis-stricken branches of trade and industry got a respite. Their international competitiveness was improved without any exertion on their own part. It is by no means certain, therefore, that the devaluation produced the kind of transformation and expansion of the competitive sector that was required. Moreover, much of the investment in new capacities, especially after 1985, was in the motor car industry, an old-established branch of Swedish industry. It is unclear to what extent those investments can be taken to represent renewal. The future will show whether they should be regarded as on the same footing as those in the shipbuilding industry during the 1970s. Certainly, the similarities in the decision-making processes are frightening. The degree of subsidy was high in both instances. The motor car industry's current (1991) problems are reminiscent of those in shipbuilding in the 1970s. A collapse of Sweden's vehicle industry could, in fact, make the shipbuilding crisis of the 1970s look minor indeed by comparison, since it constitutes that much larger a component of the Swedish economy than the shipbuilding industry ever did.

Having said that, the large element of 'soft' investment in knowledge, markets and services in the 1980s also means that new, knowledge-intensive development blocks can be discerned. There is one, for example, in the processing industry, where information technology and the accumulation of knowledge on a large scale have created new combinations. More generally, the wider application of electronics to new modes of organising work, to product specification and to the industrial environment has created a number of new openings (Schön 1990: 110). There are many indications, too, that new growth centres are springing up in the university towns and major conurbations, where networks have been created which integrate in novel fashion the purveyance of financial and other commercial services with high-technology R&D and production. The boom of the 1980s, we believe, did after all contain elements which went beyond the rationalisation of existing activities. But for various reasons – which we shall come to presently – the development blocks did not manage to mature fully.

Thus, the course followed by industrial capital formation can be summarised like this: boom until 1962; stagnation at a relatively high level 1962–75 with a boom that went wrong at the end of the period; crisis 1975–82; boom 1982–89; stagnation 1989–?. Alternatively, the penultimate turning-point can be placed at the absolute bottom point, in 1978, instead of in 1982 (Figure 7.2). If manufacturing industry is the growth machine we have assumed, this sequence of developments can explain a great deal about the pattern of economic growth in Sweden.

Explanations

The oscillations of Swedish industrial capital formation between boom, stagnation and crisis have been interpreted in a variety of different ways.

One interpretation takes as its starting-point the wide technological gap between Sweden and the United States, notably during the 1950s. The import of technology, it is argued, stimulated Swedish industry's vigorous campaign of new building and establishment of new enterprises during the late 1950s and early 1960s. New products, new technologies and new methods threw up attractive investment openings. The introduction of the transistor, for example, and the opportunities this opened up for transistorising processes and products, lay at the root of a considerable proportion of the investment activity during the period. Nuclear power was another imported technology which was brought into use later on. In the production of electrical goods, in medicine, in the iron ore and special steel industry and in shipbuilding, Sweden made its own contributions to technical progress, and these were indeed substantial. As to the rest, 'Swedish industry has attained its prominent position mainly by keeping well up with the application, further development and commercial exploitation of technologies and new techniques acquired from others' (Carlsson et al 1979: 187).

When by the early to mid-1960s the technological gap had been to a significant extent closed, investment became orientated, for want of anything better, towards rationalisation of existing activities and technology. Both the volume and share of industrial capital formation fell into the doldrums.

This mode of explanation can be extended to the 1980s by predicating that the boom of 1982–9 resulted to a considerable extent from the large-scale application and diffusion of information technology in Swedish industry – and in industry-linked enterprises – with the aid of technology developed mainly abroad.

In other explanations, some kind of industrial law of motion is formulated – often inspired by Joseph Schumpeter's view of economic change. According to this argument a period of diffusion of innovation, establishment of enterprises and boom (eg the period to 1962) is always followed, as a result of increasing competition for markets and productive resources, by rationalisation, slump and crisis. Alternatively the crisis comes about because a variety of established interests become entrenched once branches of the economy have grown strong, all with a strong motive for defending the established state of affairs in capital formation. New enterprises, which compete with the existing ones for productive resources of various kinds, are successfully fought off. That which is tried and trusted receives priority and favour. The articulation of established interests leads to expansion within old frameworks and rationalisation of the industrial structures already in existence (Krantz and Schön 1983). The reluctance to back fundamentally new economic enterprises leads to stagnation and crisis. The crisis weakens the established interests. It also eliminates the least competitive firms, liberates labour and capital, and then creates the conditions for a new period of diffusion of innovation and establishment of enterprises.

Developments of Arthur Lewis's model of the industrialisation of underdeveloped countries, emphasising the feature of 'unlimited supply of labour', have been applied as well. In this reading of the evidence, as long as the reserve of poorly educated labour, especially in agriculture, was large, and a constant flow of labour offered itself to industry and kept the share of wages in total costs low, the level of investment remained high (R. Ohlsson 1978: 7). When this flow dried up in the 1960s, profits diminished and investment with them. Industry went into a period of rationalisation, stagnation and eventually crisis.

This explanation can be extended to cover the industrial boom of the 1980s by focusing on the migration from the old 'semi-large' industrial centres to the major towns. During the 1980s the well-educated labour population of the old industrial districts, now driven out of business, became arguably a reserve work-force for the growth centres represented by university towns and large conurbations.

There is another way of interpreting things which places the emphasis on economic policy in a very broad sense. In one explanation which properly speaking applies to Europe as a whole, the importance of the economic integration of the 1950s and of the regeneration of capitalist institutions after the war is singled out as being of key importance. Beyond this, Keynesian-inspired claims by economists and governments to be able to administer effective demand in such a way that economic crises would be avoided created faith and optimism in the Western economies, and consequently high volumes of investment (Boltho 1982). Then, the argument goes on, when the integration process lost momentum during the 1960s and Keynesian financial policies showed their inability to solve the problems of macroeconomic equilibrium of the early and mid-1970s, faith declined. Industrial investment accordingly slowed down.

The recovery of the 1980s has likewise sometimes been explained in terms of 'faith'. The coming to power of Reagan and Thatcher and their assertion of free trade and other principles of competitive capitalism, it is said, restored faith in the system and so revived industrial capital formation. The boom in the countries where faith was growing swelled the demand for Swedish exports, following which industrial investment increased in Sweden as well.

All these interpretations include important fragments of a complicated reality. They are all consistent with the data, which makes it difficult to rank their appropriateness. All of them are mainly macro-oriented and for the most part focused on the supply side of the economy. It ought to be stressed, therefore, that the pattern exhibited by industrial investment was also influenced from the demand side, namely by the demand situation on the world market with respect to Swedish products. The boom around 1960 and the one around 1985 were both stimulated, among other things, by expanding foreign demand for Swedish products.

While not ignoring the role of demand, however, we shall in our own contribution to the debate confine ourselves chiefly to the internally determined supply conditions within Sweden. Our interpretation will be based (*inter alia*) on the way the labour market and education system have functioned and interacted, and the significance of this interaction for the supply of competence to, and accumulation of knowledge in, manufacturing industry and the building trade. The approach should be seen as a complement, rather than as an exclusive alternative, to the theories outlined above.

The need for key competence: a 'cyclical history'

Industrial installation generally requires personnel with special competence. We can therefore speak of complementarity between certain categories of industrial invest-ments and certain categories of educational investments. The handling of equipment, once installation has been effected, also demands appropriate competence. Even though technical and organisational change continually alters the required combina-tions of people and capital equipment, every era of industrial development is characterised by the need for certain 'key groups'. It may be a matter of skilled workers of particular kinds or technicians with specific trainings.

The important role of key groups in capital formation and production, and the constant changes in requirements in terms of competence, make plausible the hypothesis that the level of education and knowledge and degree of flexibility on the labour market of individuals are factors to which a central role ought to be assigned in any interpretation of fluctuations in rates of growth of productivity and GNP. In an era of development in which, more and more, the firm can be regarded as an institution which creates, develops and allocates knowledge, these factors will surely tend to become increasingly important.[1]

The most recent investment boom, the one that occurred during the 1980s, saw such key groups as systems analysts, financial economists, international sales people and others becoming more and more important. In other words, the non-material bias of investment and the increasing service element in production meant that non-technicians came through as key groups to a greater extent than before. For the sake of simplicity, however, we shall limit ourselves to the engineer category in our analysis. This category has been the vehicle for crucial elements of key competence throughout the entire period. We believe that the long gestation period required to produce such competence, combined with certain institutional peculiarities of the Swedish labour market, have influenced economic activity in Sweden in a systematic fashion. For ease of analysis we also assume at this stage that the Swedish economy consists only of manufacturing industry and housebuilding. The process can then be described as follows.

First, during the 1950s there was a boom in industrial capital formation, which brought with it expanding demand for complementary competence. Much of this demand was for technicians of various kinds – draughtsmen, designers, patent engineers, research engineers and others – and civil engineers, since the industrial capital formation of the period consisted to such a large extent of construction of new buildings.

Second, the growth in demand for building technicians – and building workers – was intensified by the migration which increasing capital formation brought in its train. New housing was required in new locations. The result was a stiffening of competition for capital and labour between industrial and housing construction. Industry found it difficult to get hold of building technicians for its new construction projects. Continual growth in subsidised housebuilding made the building of new industrial capacities more expensive, and even displaced it.

Third, the expanding demand for engineers after 1953 meant that both their absolute and relative wage levels increased. It was mainly starting wages that rose. This is not surprising. Older engineers are generally already well established on the labour market at the point when the economic upswing begins. They often have long-term contracts with their employer. Moreover their mobility, and therefore also their chances of raising their wages, are diminished by the collusion that goes on within the framework of employers' organisations. For example the metal trades employers' association (verkstadsföreningen) has taken elaborate measures to obstruct any change of employer by white-collar staff already in employment (Wadensjö 1988: 109). For engineers seeking an engineering job for the first time, there is more freedom of wage-determination. Their wage and/or level of appointment can therefore be raised quickly when excess demand increases. This form of wage increase was common during the late 1950s and early 1960s (Pettersson 1990: 33).

Fourth, whether aspirants to education looked at starting wages or aggregate lifetime earnings, or at more complicated measures of profitability, they grasped the point that the returns to investment in engineering education were rising. This meant that the flow to the technical upper secondary schools and colleges increased.[2] But despite the fact that the demand pull on both education and students was so strong, there was a lag in the expansion of the intake. There was a severe shortage of premises and teachers. School and college facilities were, certainly, gradually enlarged to admit increasing numbers of prospective engineers (Figure 7.5). But the supply of newly qualified engineers on the various sub-markets reached its peak only after a lag of five to ten years, because the expansion of school facilities and educational programmes took time, and because the need to gain practical experience, coupled with the demands of military service, meant that the gestation period for engineers was in any case extremely long.

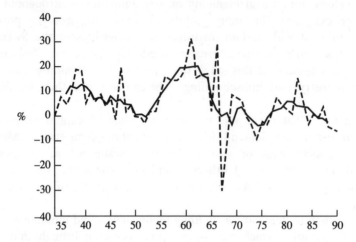

Figure 7.5   The 'Long Swing' in engineering education 1934–90 (annual percentage change in the number of new entrants to secondary school engineering courses (two, three- and four-year courses))
Note: Continuous line: five-year moving average
Source: Petterson L. (1983) *Ingënjorsutbildning och Kapitalbildning* Lund University; *SCB-statistik* Stockholm

Fifth, this lag gave rise to dynamic excess demand on the key group's labour market. At the same time the continuing competition between industrial construction and housebuilding pushed up costs on a wide front in both activities. The overhang of excess demand then grew so big as to become a major factor in checking the boom and precipitating a phase of industrial stagnation and rationalisation (after 1962). The whole trend was strengthened by the fact that to a certain extent the key groups were wage-leaders who pulled other groups' wages along after them (Holmlund 1990: 56). The share of wages increased at the expense of profits. This conspired to slow down industrial capital formation and steer it into new paths where the need for technicians was not as great.[3]

Sixth, it was during the ensuing period of stagnation that the expansion of education and the flow to the labour market really got under way. But the labour market situation suddenly became tight. From 1966, more and more newly qualified technicians and engineers were accepting work at a low level of appointment in industry, or applying for non-technical jobs. A 'reserve' of industrial key competence was now being built up in the form of young engineers in various branches working at relatively low wages. For the key groups as a whole, however, the adjustment of wages proceeded slowly. As has been noted, the older technicians were generally well established on the labour market. As a result, the downward adjustment of wages took place primarily via the outflow of new age cohorts from engineering employment and via starting wages in engineering employment (Figure 7.6). By the middle of the 1970s the reserve was well established, as it had also been at the beginning of the 1950s.

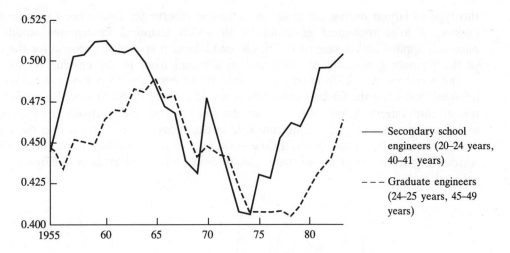

Figure 7.6   Wages of young engineers relative to wages of established engineers
Source: *Tjänstemännens löner* SAF-SIF-lönestatistik, Stockholm

Seventh, as growth of aggregate industrial investment fell away and the element of rationalisation investment within the total increased, there was a drop in the rate at which large production units in new locations were being created. Migration diminished and with it the demand for new housing. The so-called 'Million Programme' of housebuilding did in fact continue through the 1970s. But in 1974–5, to the surprise of the forecasters, the bottom fell out of housing demand. Vacant dwellings became a familiar sight in many Swedish local communities.

Eighth, the latter part of the 1970s merits the appellation of crisis period. Of course the faltering world economy and the massive misdirected investments made around 1975 played a part in the build-up towards this crisis. But they hit an economy in which the competition between industry and subsidised housebuilding had already rendered industrial capital formation more difficult and costly.

It is fair to say, however, that conditions for the next industrial recovery were already ripening during the crisis. The skilled labour force was now less in demand for the construction and on-streaming of new production units. Where the demand for skilled labour did become increasingly buoyant, however, was in the sphere of knowledge accumulation by firms. In-house training was able to expand. Networks of skilled personnel were able to prepare the ground for R&D and knowledge accumulation, and thus for potential leverage effects on productivity and growth. Thus activity aimed at maintaining and developing knowledge and competence across the spectrum of firms intensified during the crisis. This meant also that the scope for importing patents and technologies widened. The key role of young and relatively low-paid engineers in laying the foundations of recovery ensured that their wages began to rise again, even as early as the late 1970s, from a position about 1975 when their absolute and relative wages were very low. (Something similar had happened in the 1950s, when the wages of young engineers began to rise before the real boom got going.) But in the early 1980s engineers' wages were still low by international standards (L. Ohlsson 1985). Low wages meant that industrial firms had the option of 'storing' this type of labour during the crisis. As a labour reserve for future tasks, and as the creator of a technological environment in which technical innovations could be encoded, applied and disseminated, this stored labour prepared the ground for the use of the younger generation of engineers on a broad front in the ensuing boom.

The recovery after 1978 received an extra boost from the 16 per cent devaluation implemented when the Social Democrats assumed power in 1982; it was also subsumed into an international boom. But even so, the still low cost and relatively ample supply of key competence played a significant role in the recovery, just as it had in the early 1950s. Another factor was probably the slowdown in housebuilding during the 1970s, which mitigated the tendency of that sector to crowd out industrial activity (Figure 7.7).

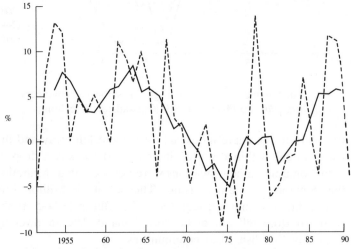

Figure 7.7   Gross investment in housing (annual percentage change)
  Note: Continuous line: five-year moving average
  Source: *Ekonomifakta*

Finally, the industrial recovery of the 1980s, like those of the 1950s and 1960s, quickly brought difficulties for expansive firms in terms of getting hold of technicians and engineers for their capital formation plans. In the event, the reserve was eaten up relatively rapidly, and the upward trend in wages accelerated. As far as building technicians are concerned, this resulted primarily from renewed overheating on the housing construction front in many towns – the boom of the 1980s, like previous booms, gave rise to migration. But other protected activities, too, were competing with industry for labour. Key personnel became increasingly expensive, or even simply impossible to get hold of, and this served little by little to change the character of the boom and precipitate its eventual collapse.

The argument has been presented here in terms of a Swedish economy consisting only of industry, technical education and subsidised housebuilding. The structural reality was, of course, more complex. Moreover, other influences – for example economic policy – have so far been omitted. However, the simplified argument does illustrate certain features and relationships which are significant for the pattern of Swedish economic growth:

1   the important role of educated key groups

2 the existence of a reserve of young, low-paid engineers during any given crisis which, coupled with the existence of a technological gap *vis-à-vis* other countries, is at the same time a necessary condition of the next recovery

3 the tendency for protected activities and industries – exemplified here by housebuilding and investment in engineering education – to be pulled into the boom in the competitive sector

4 the tendency to 'overshooting' in the capital formation activity of protected enterprises

5 the competition for labour and capital between the various sectors of the economy, and the tendency for this competition to raise the wage share at the expense of the profit share, so bringing capital formation to a halt

6 the tendency to 'long swings', explained by the fact that mutually complementary investments take varying lengths of time to implement – and by the above-mentioned tendency to overshooting.

It is now time to broaden the argument out, and to apply it to the whole of the competitive sector and the whole of the protected sector respectively. The latter includes the major part of both housebuilding and the public sector. We shall concentrate on the 1980s, while supplementing the argument with cross-references to other periods.

The 1980s recovery

The need for transfer

We have called manufacturing industry the 'engine of growth'. As we saw earlier, manufacturing industry constitutes the greater proportion of that part of the economy which is subject to foreign competition – the competitive (C) sector. That competitive environment can be assumed to be a significant driving force for productivity improvements. Thus it might be possible to define at least a part of the problem of achieving stable growth in terms of the need to transfer productive resources from the protected (P) sector to the C-sector, especially since a large and productive C-sector also makes it possible to resolve macro-equilibrium problems such as budgetary and trade balance deficits which block growth in various ways.

During the 1980s there was a particular need to switch the highly educated people who could function as resource-allocators and innovators into the research- and knowledge-intensive – and international – industrial environments which had now come into existence. In other words, it was a matter of transferring the categories which were capable of accumulating the knowledge that could function as a lever of productivity growth (Eliasson 1989: 36). Many of the people who possessed this knowledge in a readily accessible form were probably already employed in the expanding firms of the C-sector. But in construction, in defence, in colleges, in nationalised enterprises, in the rapidly growing local authority-owned companies sector and so forth, there was a significant body of personnel which could have activated such qualities within the framework of the C-sector in short order. The same applied to the large private services sector, with its relatively low level of productivity, which grew rapidly during the 1980s. To achieve results, key workers need to operate in an environment where their knowledge can be disseminated and developed, and this implies a need for supporting staff and apprentices capable of encoding the knowledge. So it was just as important to transfer skilled workers as to transfer technicians.

It is essential that it should be possible for this kind of transfer to take place, even when the economy's capacity ceiling has been reached and full employment reigns. If that does not happen, capital formation in the C-sector easily loses momentum – and/or goes over on to a more defensive and rationalising posture. However, an effective transfer mechanism requires that wages and profits be allowed to rise in the C-sector in order to enable it to attract labour and capital from the P-sector. It also requires that the P-sector be held in check and macroeconomic policy kept tight. If policy is too expansive, overheating comes too early, and tends to centre on strategic parts of the protected sector. Housebuilding, we recall, had on earlier occasions been a reliable inflationary hothouse within the P-sector, with steep wage-rises in boom periods.

The conditions for effecting transfer were not altogether bad in 1982, when the Social Democratic government came to power. The C-sector's prices relative to the P-sector, for example, had improved since 1978. This price relative can be regarded as the key parameter governing the flow of resources between the two sectors (Henreksson 1990). It may therefore be presumed that the flow of resources had switched towards manufacturing industry and other competitive activities. The shift in relative prices had also meant that the competitive segment of the economy was now able to produce goods and services at relatively lower costs than before, which improved international competitiveness. Profitability in the C-sector had accordingly improved too – compared with the catastrophic years 1977–8 (Figure 7.4). An international boom was on the way. Moreover, housebuilding had tailed off, albeit at a relatively high level. As we saw, the wage levels of industry's key groups had been very low at the end of the 1970s, which favoured the C-sector in the initial phase of the recovery, and were soon on the way up, as was necessary if that sector was to be able to attract resources even after overheating had set in. On top of all this came the Social Democrats' 16 per cent devaluation – in fact just a year after the 10 per cent devaluation carried through by the previous non-socialist government. Competitiveness vis-à-vis other countries accordingly improved further, which ought to have favoured the C-sector. Notable increases in industrial investment were also recorded for a few years (Figure 7.2). However, these increases were not reflected in GNP growth on the pattern of the 1950s and 1960s. Only in 1984 did the Swedish economy exhibit a rate of growth (4 per cent) corresponding to the pre-1973 average. What happened? Why was the growth effect of this recovery so limited?

The 'Swedish Model'

Before seeking to answer the above questions, we shall consider some aspects of the pattern of economic policy which resulted from the collaboration between 'big government, big unions and big business' under the rubric of the 'Swedish Model'.

At the Swedish Trades Union Congress (LO-kongress) of 1951, a comprehensive economic policy programme entitled 'The trade union movement and full employment' was presented. Its authors were two economists employed by the LO, Gösta Rhen and Rudolf Meidner. Their aim was to reconcile the aims of full employment and price stability while simultaneously stimulating growth. Restrictive financial policy, equal pay for equal work ('solidarist wage policy') and selective and mobility-promoting labour market policy were the chosen instruments for accomplishing these ends. The solidarist wage policy was considered necessary for price stability in the long term. It would prevent unjustified wage-differentials from driving up the general level of wages, and therefore of prices, in conditions of full employment. It was also believed that the wages equalisation policy would entail the elimination of firms with low productivity. These would be unable to cope with the high wages established under central agreements. With the aid of a central employment service, assistance with removals, training for skills which stood at a premium, and so on, the redundant labour could then be switched into the highly productive firms where the bottlenecks existed. Any tendency to wage drift in these firms would thus be curbed. The reallocation of labour and capital, it was thought, would make production more efficient, and the supply of goods on the market would expand. It would be the task of government to provide the labour market policy instruments, tax away the excess profits of highly productive firms, and pursue a restrictive financial policy. If regional difficulties arose in connection with the elimination of the less productive firms, the state could intervene with a range of selective regional policy measures.

For all this to work it was essential that there should be central agreements between disciplined parties on the labour market who could arrive at some sort of consensus as to what aggregate wages bill the national economy was capable of bearing. The programme was in the event implemented step by step during the 1950s and 1960s.

The industrial and housing investment booms of the 1950s and 1960s - in both the competitive and the protected sector – were able to accelerate in parallel for a fair period of time until shortage of labour and high wages brought the process to a halt in 1962. The obvious presumption is that this was indeed facilitated by the squeezing-out of less productive firms through the operation of the wages equalisation policy. However, research carried out in the field tells a different story. The mobility-promoting measures *were* having some impact on events by 1960. But the main provisions of the Rhen-Meidner economic policy seem not to have had any effect until some way into the 1960s (Svensson 1991). A more spontaneous rationalisation process, in which the 'death of textiles', the entry of women into the labour market and the rationalisation of agriculture were prominent ingredients, was probably of more importance in supplying the expanding industrial firms with labour, with this redistribution of the work-force going hand in hand with a frenzied expansion of industrial vocational education at the lower levels. This came through in terms of a rise in the absolute number of students in that category, and an increase in their weight within the vocational education sector as a whole (Figure 7.8). In point of fact the most serious bottleneck involved the higher-education categories – technicians and engineers. It did, in the event, prove possible to alleviate the shortage of competence to some extent by bringing in personnel with lower-level educational qualifications. In the long run, however, the shortage of technicians helped to bring the boom to a standstill.

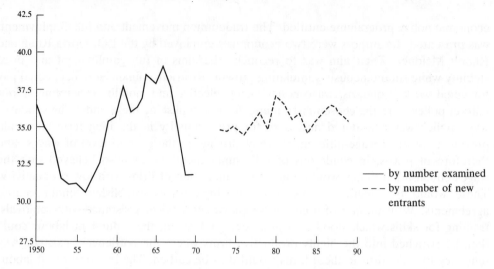

Figure 7.8   The percentage share of 'Industry and Crafts' in lower-level vocational education
Source: Unpublished working tables, Anders Nilsson, Department of Economic History, Lund University

Around the middle of the 1960s the Swedish Model was functioning well enough, in so far as transfer of labour from the rationalisation reserve to the more productive firms was taking place on a large scale. However, problems were emerging little by little. In 1965 the employees of a growing public sector were granted the right to strike, and this made discipline on the labour market more difficult. On top of that, the rationalisation reserve was diminishing. Furthermore, the rate of establishment of new firms and of growth in demand for labour from highly productive firms was so insignificant for long periods during the 1970s that the now stronger tendency for less productive firms to be eliminated simply brought unemployment and de-industrialisation.

By the beginning of the 1980s, de-industrialisation had proceeded so far, and the balance of payments deficit was so large, that the continued squeezing-out of industrial firms by means of the wages equalisation policy had become an increasingly unattractive option. Instead the protected sector, public as well as private, became an increasingly natural rationalisation reserve for those who thought in socio-economic terms. But the public sector does not automatically shrink under the pressure of excessively high wage claims, for these can be offset via taxation or borrowing. In any case, high wages in the P-sector were in conflict with the aim of shifting resources from P to C. Moreover, the situation had by the early 1980s changed in many other respects since the 1960s. On top of the balance of payments deficit there had been budget deficits for several years. Inflation was considerably higher than previously as well. It is true that by 1982 it was receding from the very high levels which had prevailed for some years (12–16 per cent). More precisely, Sweden had by that year arrived somewhere near the average for the OECD (about 9 per cent) and this moderated the pressure on export industries. However, the rate of inflation was still sufficiently high to lead to misdirected investment, undesirable redistribution etc.

Finally, the need to bring inflation under control imposed a constraint on macroeconomic policy. It became clear to responsible politicians that financial policy must now move in the direction of extreme austerity. But there were to be several occasions in the future when that constraint would prove to be insufficiently hard.

The Swedish Model takes 'The Third Way'

It was against this background that a package of 'aftercare' measures was launched, following the great devaluation of 1982. The initiative came from the same group in the Economics Department of the Ministry of Finance which had initiated the devaluation. It came to be dubbed 'the Third Way'. The name was meant to denote a middle course between the extremes of traditional accommodating financial policy – the scars left by the 1970s still inspired fear – and the shock-therapy approach to the stamping out of inflation. Of course it is true that a tight squeeze on effective demand of this latter sort would have brought down wage claims and price rises. But the likely cost in terms of unemployment was considered far too high. Besides, it was thought that such a policy would precipitate de-industrialisation, which would have serious repercussions on (*inter alia*) the balance of payments.

Much of the inspiration for the Third Way was drawn from the Rhen-Meidner Model of the 1950s. Once more strong trade unions, conscious of their responsibilities, would, it was hoped, conclude agreements which preserved the competitiveness and profitability of firms while simultaneously granting the wage-earners their well-deserved pay rises. And once more the Swedish Model would have demonstrated its capacity to reconcile low inflation with full employment.

But the government did realise that changed socio-economic conditions called for some new tricks. It was better understood now than it had been in the 1960s that accommodating financial policies leading to expansion of effective demand must be eschewed. Furthermore, there was a desire to develop an alternative to tough retrenchment during times of prosperity in the shape of those elements of supply policy which had, indeed, already been present in the 1950s model. Deregulation of various markets, for example, would lead to better allocation of resources and more efficient production. Stimulation of household savings would improve the supply of capital. On the labour market, efforts should be made to increase mobility. What this came down to was a revitalisation of the whole battery of measures that existed within the framework of the Rhen-Meidner Model, such as the various provisions for training and retraining, removal allowances, an active job-finding service etc. Of course there was also a socio-political aim here. The new rule that unemployed young people could not draw cash benefit for more than fourteen months was intended primarily to prevent them from ending up in an unemployment culture. But in putting unemployed people under heavy pressure to take the jobs offered or sign up for a training/retraining programme, the government was also counting on the downward pressure on wage claims, and thus on inflation, which the redeployment of unemployed people would bring. There was also the idea that specific inflationary bottlenecks in production could be overcome, and supply rendered more effective, via labour market policy. Subsequently (1988) a tax reform was initiated too, with a view to improving labour supply and mobility and rewarding entrepreneurial flair.

As has been observed, restraint in the financial policies of the state was an important element of the Third Way policy, just as it had been of the 1950s version of the Rhen-Meidner model. This time round, however, the tight macro-orientation derived not merely from solicitude for the value of money. In an economy with a competitive sector that was far too small, a substantial proportion of any given expansion of aggregate demand would be channelled towards the protected sector's goods and services, and exert upward pressure on prices and wages in that sector. If the desire to shift productive resources from P to C was serious, total demand had to be held in check.

Between 1982 and 1984 the C-sector did certainly grow at the expense of the P-sector – reckoned in value-added terms (Figure 7.9). After that, however, the reallocation process seemed to lose impetus. In 1985 the value-added position remained approximately unchanged from the 1984 level. Measured in terms of number of hours worked, the relative increase in the weight of the C-sector 1982–5 was marginal. Thus for a few years the Swedish Third Way seemed to have been a successful choice of route. The balance of payments deficit diminished, and investment in the competitive sector increased. But after 1985 the C-sector's downward trend continued.

If we scrutinise the structure of investment in industry during the period 1982–5, we see that it was mainly the relatively high-technology, research- and knowledge-intensive branches which increased their shares (L. Ohlsson and Vinell 1987: 75). The R&D efforts of the 1970s and 1980s, which had been very impressive by international standards, gave just such activities temporary comparative cost advantages in Sweden. The low level, in international terms, of the wage costs of technicians and scientists during the 1980s reinforced these advantages (L. Ohlsson and Vinell 1987: 238). For a short period it was possible for the knowledge accumulated and developed during the crisis within Swedish industrial firms to be put into practice very rapidly by technicians, scientists and other key groups, resulting in innovations, reallocation of resources and high productivity. The labour reserve which had been created at lower levels of appointment during the crisis now moved up into strategic positions in industrial firms, and helped to generate relatively high value-added levels in industry in 1984 and 1985. Besides this, the successes of the competitive sector improved the balance of payments and created an atmosphere of optimistic expectations. Commercial activity flourished throughout the nation. All of this served to confirm the proposition that conditions in the C-sector can encourage the growth of GNP in a number of different ways, indirectly as well as directly.

For all that, there was only one single year (1984) in which the pace of economic growth was normal according to the criteria of the 1950s and 1960s. As for the rate of inflation, it actually rose somewhat in 1982, and then stabilised at a level appreciably higher than the OECD average. In other words, there were cracks in the economic and political façade even during the early part of the recovery of the 1980s. The cracks were subsequently to become bigger and more numerous.

An over-expansive policy and an over-large protected sector

The Third Way policy involved the de-regulation of various markets – including credit markets. This de-regulation was all the easier to implement inasmuch as the internationalisation of the Swedish economy and the emergence of a 'grey' loan market had already made credit regulations obsolete. Deregulation did, of course, facilitate

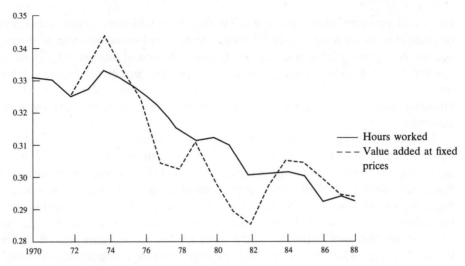

Figure 7.9   The C-sector's weight within the total economy 1970–88
Source: Henreksson 1990

the procurement of capital for the competitive sector. However, when the Riksbank, in 1985, stopped trying to control bank lending to households and private individuals, this led to what the then minister of finance called the Great Consumption Party. As well as giving an expansionist impulse to the economy that was incompatible with the struggle against inflation, the increasing volume of credit brought growth of the protected sector in its train. The demand for housing had, of course, already started to expand as a result of the migration occasioned by the boom. This upward trend was intensified by the credit expansion. The heavily subsidised construction of housing swiftly gained momentum, and became an increasingly serious competitor for the C-sector's building work-force – as well as a hotbed of inflation.

The financial sector, which enjoyed a boom following its deregulation in 1985, became a competitor for talent, knowledge and aptitudes of a somewhat different character. This was a forum of activity that surrounded itself with relatively complicated information technology systems, which may help to explain why the proportion of technicians employed in the 'rest of the financial sector' category (excluding banks and insurance companies) was by the late 1980s almost as high as the proportion of economists (L. Ohlsson 1990: 139). New opportunities for making use of the international arena for financial transactions, an easy credit market, and a substantial degree of inflation, were all factors which favoured share dealing and property speculation and the creation of a large sector handling securities and monetary transactions. Purely financial deals became increasingly popular compared with direct investment in production enterprises. Financial departments developed within large industrial firms which often earned more money for the firm than the production departments. Many economists, information technicians and engineers who would have been an asset in production activities opted during the latter part of the 1980s to devote themselves to financial transactions instead. This sector of the economy did, of course, also contribute to growth. A substantial part of it was subject to competition, too. However, because such a large portion of the financial sector's assets came to be tied up in real property whose value was swollen by inflationary expectations and easily obtainable credit, it formed a destabilising element within the national economy. It was ultimately to prove destructive, notably towards the end of our period. For some years, nevertheless, the financial sector made large profits. Successful brokers, information technologists and traders demanded and got very high salaries, which naturally attracted competence and talent – and had the effect of raising the level of wages generally.

Beyond this, it proved impossible to keep macroeconomic policy as tight as would have been desirable. Tax increases might have eased the pressure, but they were not an appropriate method in a country which already had the highest tax burden in Europe. Budgetary deficits fuelled inflationary expectations and thus contributed to the buoyancy of the P-sector. Overall, then, there were many factors operational during the 1980s which favoured the protected sector and raised prices and wages within it. Even within the competitive sector, growth tended to be concentrated in areas like financial services which had a destabilising impact on the competitive environment as a whole.

Longer-term trend changes worked in the same direction. The continual strengthening of rent-seeking interest groups can be counted among them. The problem came to the fore during discussions on the transfer payment system. Retrenchment here, which could have mitigated the expansionist pressure, turned out to be a matter of extreme difficulty. There were too many strong interests which could see advantages for themselves in continued loan-financed subsidies to the housing sector, compensation to pensioners for the effects of devaluation, increased child allowances, the upward adjustment of central government's contributions to county and district expenditure, and so on. Above all, the leadership of the LO would not accept any reduction in transfer payments to its members, nor the increase in unemployment figures which would inevitably have ensued from retrenchment. By the 1980s these interests were well organised, and had to a considerable extent 'colonised' the Swedish government. In trying to impose a squeeze, the Ministry of Finance found itself standing virtually alone (Feldt 1991: 210–15).

We can thus go a good way towards explaining the half-hearted character of the 1980s recovery by reference to the fact that the protected sector, both private and public, grew by degrees much stronger through the 1960s and 1970s. Furthermore, those who worked in it – on the public side at least – had also become better and better organised, as we have noted. It is true that when overheating set in, as did in fact happen as early as 1984–85, there *was* still room for wage rises in the C-sector. However, the strong trade-union organisations in the P-sector, with their massive bargaining power, were not prepared to miss the bus. The union negotiators encountered surprisingly feeble resistance from the employers' side, and wages in the P-sector maintained the 'correct' distance.

The then minister of finance has provided vivid and intimate pictures of the negotiations between the parties in the public sector in 1984. Suffice it to recall here that on an official occasion he called them 'a bunch of lunatics'. By this he meant, presumably, that both sides, employers and workers, had chosen a path other than the Third Way, and in so doing had taken up a position far removed from the realities of stabilisation policy as the finance minister saw them (Feldt 1991: 166).

Trends in the wage level in the protected sector must take their share of the responsibility for the fact that far too little growth-promoting change took place, especially after 1985. Far too large a proportion of the labour force remained in the old 'cosy' spheres of operations. It is true that industrial capital formation did continue to accelerate for a few more years. However, difficulties in getting hold of key personnel now conspired to channel investment more towards enterprises with less need for such personnel – the motor car industry, for instance. High demand for technicians now began to be replaced in some degree by high demand for skilled workers (Figure 7.10). Productivity gains were, however, slow to accrue to Swedish industry (Figure 7.11). One reason was that research-intensive branches of industry, which enjoyed big comparative cost advantages and in which a high rate of value-added was to be had if key competence could be obtained, were no longer able to replenish their reserves of such competence (L. Ohlsson and Vinell 1987: 159).

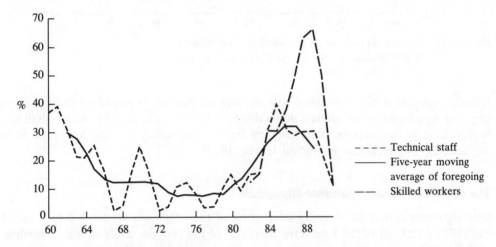

Figure 7.10   Proportion of firms in manufacturing industry with 'shortages' of technical staff and skilled workers respectively (per cent)
Source: *Konjunkturbarometern*, KI, Stockholm

We mentioned earlier that the price relative C/P (in terms of prices of outputs) epitomises the incentive which governs the flow of resources between the competitive and protected sectors. This price relative fell after 1985, which means that the costs of producing goods and services in the C-sector inevitably rose (Henreksson 1990: 25). The shortage of competent personnel and the rise in the cost of buildings, inputs and staff not only affected value added and productivity, but also meant it became increasingly advantageous to shift production abroad.

As a result of all this, the competitive sector's growth impetus was interrupted following only a short period of expansion after 1982. If the education of technicians and scientists had expanded vigorously during the 1970s the reserve of personnel would have been larger, competition for competence would have been less intense and the expansion would have been able to continue for a while longer. In fact, the only real expansion of highly trained personnel in that decade came in the case of graduate engineers, where the numbers qualifying continued to rise somewhat during the 1970s, although clearly, with the benefit of hindsight, insufficiently. The turnover of two-year

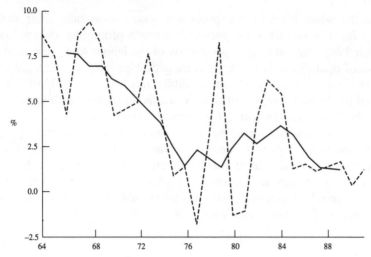

Figure 7.11   Growth of productivity in manufacturing industry
Note: Continuous line: five-year moving average
Source: *Ekonomifakta*

technical education had diminished sharply, and the overall growth of secondary school engineering education had slowed down during the 1970s (Figure 7.5). As we shall see, however, it is not certain that this can be blamed solely on the low returns to engineering and technical education in the 1970s.

The restructuring of vocational education

Our argument is that the ongoing adaptation of the education system led to what we can call, on account of the long-term character of the process, a 'structural "crowding-out" of competence'. Its mechanism may be described as follows.

When the industrial boom of the 1950s came, the protected sector formed a much smaller proportion of the total economy than it does today. Therefore, although the protected sector grew as well, the educational expansion which ensued was largely aligned towards the educational requirements of the competitive sector. The technical upper secondary schools grew more rapidly than the general upper secondary schools. And it was to these technical upper secondary schools that the 'reserve of talent' which existed among the children of workers and farmers by preference sought entry. As well as this there was a vigorous expansion at the lower levels of vocational education – aligned to a large extent towards the needs of industry (Figure 7.5). The immediate cause was that the returns to these types of education seemed high. But the flow was also facilitated by the generally positive contemporary view of technology and technological solutions to problems.

When the growth rate of industrial capital formation then slowed down during the 1960s and 1970s while at the same time the relative size of the protected sector became bigger and bigger, the demand for education began to focus increasingly on the labour market in the protected sector. The pattern followed by the proportion of cohorts of new entrants to lower vocational education accounted for by industry and crafts is an example of this (Figure 7.8). Social science courses expanded at the universities. In the upper secondary schools interest in natural science courses declined steadily right through the 1970s, as it did in relation to two-year technical training. This meant that the educational system was in no position to give the required support to the research- and knowledge-intensive industrial developments which offered a historic opening to the future in the 1980s in consequence of the very large investments in R&D which had been made during the 1970s. The reserve of personnel available in the early 1980s and capable of being turned quickly into key staff sufficed to initiate the boom. It was not enough to sustain it, against a background of severe competition for competence from other parts of the labour market.

The rapidly expanding output of economists during the 1970s might in itself suggest an expanding interest during that decade in the C-sector as a place of work. Those opting for an upper secondary or university education in economics were not, however, self-evidently inclined towards the competitive sector. A large number of economists in fact ended up in the public sector, and, on top of this, the *private* P-sector sucked in many newly qualified economists and social scientists. Indeed the abundant supply of social scientists, lawyers and economists has probably been a driving force behind the creation of large segments of the private service sector. Graduates lacking in either aptitude, opportunity or desire to work in industry have carved out their own niches in the P-sector instead.

The burgeoning wealth of alternatives to the C-sector as a labour market suggests that the displacement of the C-sector was more than just a reaction to trends in relative wages. The rejection of technical education by the youth of the 1970s, as also the difficulty of switching well-educated young people from the P- to the C-sector during the 1980s, was probably determined equally by working conditions and attitudes towards those conditions. The urbanised children of the welfare state have acquired attitudes to, and value-judgements about, education and working life, which differ markedly from those which still held sway in the 1950s and early 1960s. The change is sometimes described as a 'silent revolution'. Sociologists who have applied themselves to the subject tell us that young people have evolved an increasingly 'inner-world-orientated' mind set, which stresses scope for self-fulfilment, self-understanding and community of spirit relative to opportunities for material welfare and security. Above all, studies have shown well-educated younger people to have a 'post-materialistic' scale of values which includes (*inter alia*) an increasingly cosmopolitan attitude, but at the same time a diminished faith in the 'technocratic' society. Increased appreciation of the ecological view of society has also played an important role here (Hagström 1991: 18). It *may* have been difficult to reconcile such a value-profile with the conditions prevailing in the C-sector. (Let us note parenthetically that in the long run the new scale of values may have profound effects in another way. To the well-travelled and cosmopolitan youth of today, possible membership of the EC may not be the great and daunting step which it represented for Swedish opinion in the 1950s. The changed values of young people in this respect was one of the factors which made possible the Social Democratic government's application for membership of the Community in 1991.)

To sum up, then, on the structural problems of the 1980s: the large alternative labour market, in combination with the changed values of the younger generation, created problems for the C-sector. It was not only the recruitment of sufficient numbers of key personnel that was problematical: there was also a qualitative aspect. Many potential specialists, innovators and entrepreneurs probably preferred a more 'post-materialistic' – and quieter and more secure – existence in the large and variegated P-sector rather than in the more exposed C-sector, even though wages were higher in the latter. Thus the greater the proportion of the total economy made up by the P-sector, the harder it became for firms in the C-sector to attract the numbers and quality of employees they wanted, and the harder it became for the latter sector to fulfil its role as 'growth-engine'.

Conclusion

The Swedish economy has a tendency to long, recurrent fluctuations in economic growth. In what is an export-dominated economy these are, of course, determined to a large extent by international economic fluctuations. However, they are reinforced by mechanisms internal to Sweden itself. One of those mechanisms is conditioned by the interaction between fixed capital formation and investment in key competence. When fixed capital formation accelerates, investment in key competence is dragged along in its wake. It is difficult to access competence in time, however, and this creates a 'pig cycle', for example in terms of the interaction of industrial investment, the supply of engineers, young engineers' wages, the flow to engineering education, and so on, which in turn means periods of excess demand and supply on the labour market for engineers. As far as industrial investment is concerned, the duration of the recovery phase and its contribution to economic growth are affected by the magnitude and quality of the excess supply of personnel – the reserve of key competence – built up during the preceding crisis. But growth potential is also dependent on the scope for shifting personnel out of the protected sector and into the sector which is subject to foreign competition and whose conditions are specially significant for economic growth as a whole. The crux of the matter is to switch key competence, and other resources, over to those parts of the C-sector which for the moment have the most pronounced comparative cost advantages. That the recovery in industrial investment during the 1980s gave rise to such a relatively modest degree of economic growth was the result (*inter alia*) of difficulties in these respects. The difficulties were especially severe for the research-intensive part of industry, where the need for technical and scientific competence was particularly keenly felt.

It is true that industrial investment continued to accelerate up to and including 1988. However, it was concentrated increasingly on enterprises with less clear-cut comparative cost advantages, that is on sectors with relatively low historic R&D components, and in which the need for technicians was relatively modest. One reason was that the post-1985 credit expansion, against a background of little real restrictiveness on the fiscal policy side, tended to keep wages and prices buoyant in the protected sector. In any case, the Swedish tradition of wages equalisation made it easy to argue for high wage-rises in the P-sector as well. Thus it became difficult to tempt key groups – and indeed workers in general – into the C-sector. In addition, other domestic costs of producing goods and services in the C-sector rose because prices and wages in the P-sector were far too high. We have cited in particular the impact of subsidised housebuilding, which made building in the C-sector more expensive and to a degree displaced it. From as early as 1985, therefore, the C-sector started to decline again in terms of its relative weight within the economy, This, of course, in turn reduced its unit contribution to overall growth.

Certain trend changes were also important for the way events unfolded. One of these was the continuing increase in the protected sector's share of the total economy. Another, partly resulting from the former, was the steady strengthening of various interest groups, especially trade unions. A third was the change in young people's perceptions of education and working life. By degrees these trend changes have made it that much more difficult to get the required categories of highly trained personnel into the parts of the economy which drive growth. A large alternative education market and labour market, in the latter of which the working conditions were more compatible with young people's values and the wages of key groups were probably comparable to those in the competitive sector, displaced the parts of the Swedish economy which had strong comparative advantage and would have been capable of generating economic growth in a variety of ways.

Epilogue

The structural problems which were discernible for most of the 1980s have intensified little by little. From the spring of 1991 onwards we can speak about an incipient structural crisis, of the kind that first became visible during the 1960s. Protected sectors of the economy which were pulled along in the boom gradually jostled aside, or inflated costs in, the most innovative and growth-promoting parts of the economy. However, the current situation (December 1991) is in many ways more serious than was that of thirty years ago. One reason is that the protected sector covers so much larger a proportion of the economy now. Moreover, there are now more organised, rent-seeking interest groups. The difficulties that would attend pursuit of a restrictive economic policy such as might be capable of restraining the P-sector are formidable indeed.

During the 1960s the stagnation stage was fairly long drawn out, until an exogenous disturbance, in the shape of the formation of OPEC, turned stagnation into crisis. The crisis of 1990, by contrast, developed relatively rapidly. The reason was probably that the onset of stagnation was quickly followed by a classical financial crisis. The combination of deregulation of the credit market and inflation had multiplied values both on the Swedish property market and of Swedish-owned property abroad. Assets owned by banks, insurance companies, private persons, local authorities and others came in varying degrees to be held in the form of just such high-value real estate. Underlying the high values were expectations of continued inflation. The incipient structural crisis put a damper on actual price rises, however. The unilateral linking of the Swedish krona to the ECU in May 1991 did the rest, in that it sidelined devaluation as an instrument of adjustment in favour of lower wages and/or higher unemployment, thus lowering inflationary expectations. Suddenly the overvalued properties simply looked overvalued. The first visible evidence of an incipient financial crisis was when scrip-issuing property management companies started going bankrupt. This posed problems for the institutions holding such scrip as well. Banks especially have begun running into difficulties, which in practice means that banks will be exceedingly cautious with credit in future. A classical 'credit crunch' is developing, with all that that entails in terms of further credit retrenchment and bankruptcies.

The Swedish Model has not, then, been entirely successful. Neither during the 1950s nor during the 1980s did the government succeed in maintaining a sufficiently restrictive macroeconomic policy to avoid inflation, and the rate of increase of prices has been above the OECD average all through the 1980s. The Swedish Model's wage equalisation policy probably facilitated the procurement of labour for the most expansive firms during the 1960s. During the 1980s, however, this tradition of wage determination tended if anything to impede the elimination of bottlenecks in the most productive firms. What we are witnessing now (December 1991) is probably the collapse of the Swedish Model.

Notes

1   There are similarities between the traditional concepts of human capital and knowledge. But whereas the human capital concept has been used primarily for analysing the macro-influence of formal education on productivity and income, the debate about knowledge has revolved principally around the question of how knowledge has been utilised in the production process – at the micro-level. It has been said that behind the innumerable innovations, reallocations of resources, training decisions and so on which serve continually to unlock the productivity of physical production factors in a firm, there lies a knowledge base which can function as a 'lever' for other factors of production. This effectively allows the latter to function under conditions of increasing returns. The unique role of the knowledge base stems from the fact that knowledge does not easily deteriorate with use. It is tied to an organisation and is activated and deepened, created and re-created, in and through the production process itself. Human capital, in contrast, is regarded as tied to the individual and therefore depreciates.

2   People starting their working life at a relatively high level of appointment or wages tend to have a higher wage throughout their working life than a person starting off further down the structure. The relative starting wage of an educational category, in this case engineers, can therefore be regarded as an approximation of the lifetime returns to qualifying as an engineer.

3   Entry upon a phase of stagnation and rationalisation, and ultimately of crisis, is probably hastened by the inflation, and also the balance of trade and balance of payments problems, to which the high wage share contributes. More precisely, inflation and equilibrium problems create international mistrust of the economy's performance, and this affects the flow of foreign funds. The discount rate has to be raised in order to prevent an outflow of currency reserves, and the resultant high real interest rates affect capital formation.

References

Boltho A (1982) Growth. In Boltho A (ed) *The European Economy – Growth and Crisis*. Oxford University Press

Carlsson B et al (1979) *Teknik och Industristruktur – 1970-talets Ekonomiska Kris i ny Belysning*. IUI/IVA, Stockholm

Dahmén E, Carlsson B (1985) Den industriella utvecklingen efter andra världskriget. In *Sveriges Industri* Industriförbundets förlag, Stockholm

Eliasson G (1988) *The Knowledge Base of an Industrial Economy*. IUI, Stockholm

Eliasson G (1989) *The Dynamics of Supply and Economic Growth – How Industrial Knowledge Accumulation Drives a Path-Dependent Economic Process*. IUI, Stockholm

Feldt K O (1991) *Alla Dessa Dagar . . . I Regeringen 1982–1990*. Norstedts, Stockholm

Hagström T (1991) *Ungdomars Livsstilar – Arbetslivets Krav* Arbetsmiljöinstitutet, Solna

Henreksson M (1990) Devalveringens effekter på den svenska ekonomins struktur. Unpublished contribution to the conference *Devalveringen 1982. Rivstart eller Snedtändning?* Stockholm

Holmlund B (1990) *Svensk Lönebildning – Teori, Empiri, Politik* Allmänna förlaget, Stockholm

Jörberg L (1991) *Den Svenska Ekonomiska Utvecklingen 1850–1990*. Department of Economic History, Lund University

Krantz O, Nilsson K A (1975) *Swedish National Product 1861–1970*. Gleerups, Kristianstad

Krantz O, Schön L (1983) Den svenska krisen i ett långsiktigt perspektiv. *Ekonomisk Debatt* 7: 478–86

Ohlsson L (1985) Industrisysselsättning och sysselsättningspolitik. *Ekonomisk Debatt* 5: 347–56

Ohlsson L (1990) *Kunskapsbildning för Industriell Förnyelse*. Norstedts, Stockholm

Ohlsson L, Vinell L (1987) *Tillväxtens drivkrafter*. Industriförbundet, Stockholm

Ohlsson R (1978) *Ekonomisk Strukturförändring och Invandring*. Gleerup, Lund

Örtengren J (1981) Kapitalbildning i svensk industri under efterkrigstiden. In *Industrin inför 80-talet* Almqvist & Wicksell International, Stockholm

Pettersson L (1990) *Svenskt Ostadsbyggande 1862–2005 – en Cyclisk Historia*. BFR, Stockholm

Romer P M (1986) Increasing Returns and Long-Run Growth. *Journal of Political Economy* 94: 1002–37

Schön L (1990) *Elektricitetens Betydelse för Svensk Industriell Utveckling*. Vattenfall, Vällingby

Svensson L (1991) Kvinnliga privattjänstemäns relativa löner 1960–1990. Unpublished working paper, Department of Economic History, Lund University

Wadensjö E (1988) Arbetsmarknadspolitiken och arbetsmarknadsorganisationerna. In Dahlberg Å (ed) *90-talets Arbetsmarknad*. Allmänna förlaget, Stockholm

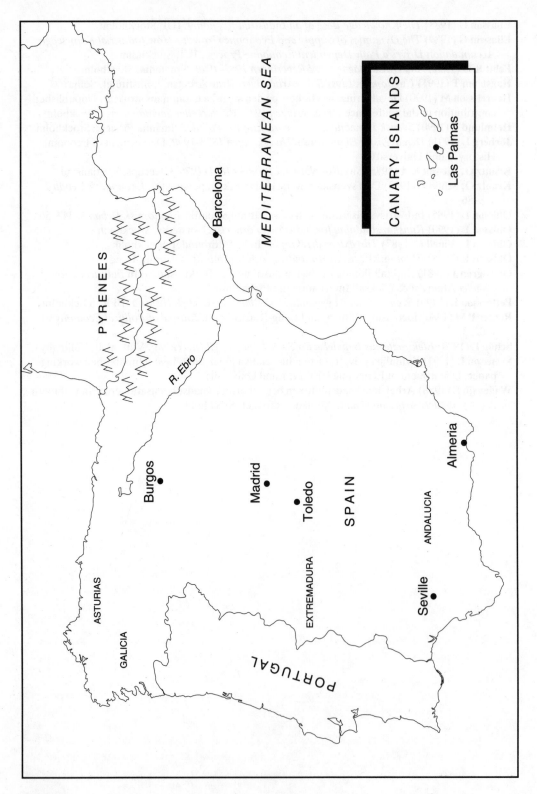

CANARY ISLANDS

Las Palmas

MEDITERRANEAN SEA

Barcelona

PYRENEES

R. Ebro

SPAIN

Burgos

Madrid

Toledo

Almeria

ANDALUCIA

Seville

EXTREMADURA

ASTURIAS

GALICIA

PORTUGAL

Map 8.1

CHAPTER 8

Spain

JOSEPH HARRISON

Introduction

Measured by Western European standards, Spain is traditionally portrayed as a prime example of economic backwardness. Not until the mid-1960s did the proportion of the active population employed in industry come to exceed that of the agricultural labour force. Historically, Spanish economic development was held back by the continued existence of a high cost and inefficient agrarian sector, the main feature of which was the extensive cultivation on dry lands of the traditional monocultures of wheat, olives and the vine. Low agricultural yields, which resulted in chronically low per capita incomes among the great mass of rural consumers, in turn acted as an obstacle to industrial development. Thrown back on the domestic market after the loss of Spain's American colonies at the beginning of the nineteenth century, industry was largely confined to a few isolated pockets on the periphery. Foremost among these islands of progress were Catalonia, centre of the nation's cotton textile industry, the Basque Country, with its metallurgical and shipbuilding interests, and the coal-mining region of Asturias. Recent research indicates a hitherto unsuspected advance in the Spanish countryside during the first three decades of the twentieth century, not least in livestock farming, fruit and horticulture. Even so, on the eve of the Spanish Civil War, cereals and legumes accounted for three-quarters of the cultivated surface and generated as much as 45 per cent of agricultural income (Grupo de Estudios de Historia Rural 1983; Tortella 1984; Harrison 1989).

Early-twentieth-century Spain could also stake a claim to possessing the most closed economy in Western Europe. After a short-lived experience of free trade begun in 1869, the final years of the nineteenth century saw a pronounced drift in the direction of autarky. A protectionist tariff introduced in 1891, owing much to pressures from the wheat farmers of old Castile, Catalan textile manufactures and Basque ironmasters, was reinforced in 1906 and 1922. A mood of economic nationalism gave rise to a plethora of interventionist measures which sought to secure the domestic market for Spanish producers (García Delgado 1984). During the international depression of the 1930s, Spanish commentators maintained that the country's relative economic retardation and isolation from the main currents of world trade helped it to weather the worst excesses of the inter-war slump (Servicio de Estudios del Banco de España 1934; Harrison 1983). It is generally agreed that the most serious problems facing Spain's fledgling Republic between 1931 and 1936 were not the outcome of coincidental external circumstances, but the product of long-standing basic internal problems such as agriculture. Thus, the strains and stresses which were to explode in a bloody civil war originated above all in the Spanish countryside (Fontana and Nadal 1976).

The triumph of the reactionary forces led by General Franco in 1939 heralded a renewed and more emphatic attempt at self-sufficiency. Urged on by the victorious Nationalist army, which feared an invasion of the peninsula by the wartime Allies, and the xenophobic, semi-fascist Falange, the single party of the New Order in Spain, Franco and his economic ministers embarked on a quest for autarky which was to bring disastrous results.

The pursuit of self-sufficiency

The Franco regime's attempt to reconstruct the Spanish economy after three years of internecine strife turned out to be a long-drawn-out process: this is clearly illustrated by a glance at the major economic indicators. It was not until 1950 that the index of industrial production overtook the peak year of 1929, while agricultural output remained below that year's level until 1958. Moreover, Julio Alcaide's revision of the national income estimates, at constant 1964 prices, demonstrates that the pre-civil war level of 1935 was not attained again until 1951 (Alcaide 1976). Indeed, the first decade of Franco's New Order was characterised by almost unalleviated economic stagnation. Chronic shortages of basic foodstuffs and essential raw materials led to widespread hunger and perennial bottlenecks to production throughout the economy. A drastic reduction in real wages, decreed by the Francoist authorities, provoked a drop in living standards unparalleled in contemporary Spanish history. The spectre of mass starvation was narrowly averted only by huge imports of foodstuffs from the pro-Axis regime of Juan Domingo Perón in Argentina (see p. 193). Albert Carreras's recalculation of national income estimates for 1941–5 shows an average increase of 1 per cent per year, with substantial fluctuations over the period, partly depending on the level of the harvest. This poor overall achievement was less than satisfactory compensation for an average yearly fall of 6 per cent during the period 1936–40, which included the civil war. For the quinquennium 1946–50, Carreras's index of industrial production reveals a 10 per cent rise. However, this figure has to be seen in a wider perspective. Compared with the performance of other Mediterranean economies such as Italy, Greece and Yugoslavia, whose industrial output shot up by between 70 per cent and 110 per cent, Spain's modest achievement appears less impressive (Carreras 1984; Carreras 1989; García Delgado 1987).

Official explanations of Spain's miserable economic performance in the 1940s invariably seek to place the blame on factors beyond the control of the country's policy-makers. Above all they emphasise three factors:

1 the damage wreaked upon the Spanish economy by three years of civil war

2   the so-called enduring drought (*La pertinaz sequía*) which persisted throughout the
    1940s
3   the United Nations' resolution of December 1946 which urged member states to
    recall their ambassadors from Madrid, and to suspend economic relations with the
    erthwhile ally of Nazi Germany and Fascist Italy (Arburúa 1956; Suanzes 1963).

Not surprisingly, the consensus of opinion among Spain's economic historians rejects
these interpretations as *post hoc* excuses.

In terms of the destruction of physical capital, the First Development Plan of 1964
claimed that the 1936–9 conflict caused the ruin of 250,000 dwellings, while a similar
total were rendered unfit for human habitation. The railways too suffered heavy losses:
41 per cent of all locomotives, 40 per cent of goods wagons and 61 per cent of
passenger carriages were destroyed. In addition, one-third of the merchant marine
(225,000 tonnes) was sunk (Comisaría del Plan . . . 1965). This document failed to
provide detailed information on the loss of industrial plant and equipment. In fact the
textile, chemical and metallurgical sectors of Catalonia were hardly touched by the
fighting. Furthermore the refusal of the Basque Republican government to
contemplate a scorched-earth policy, along with the desire of the Nationalists to take
over the region's industry intact, meant that it too was spared the destruction suffered
by the manufacturing centres of the belligerent nations during the Second World War.

In the absence of adequate supplies of rainfall south of the Pyrenees, economic
commentators contend that the requirements of Spain's farmers might have been more
usefully served by a realistic irrigation policy, together with the allocation of larger
amounts of foreign currency by the authorities to purchase vital supplies of chemical
fertilisers and farm equipment. In fact, the Franco regime's proclamations of irrigation
schemes were largely for propaganda purposes, and produced few concrete results.

Finally, the UN boycott of Franco's Spain after the end of the European war, which
certainly denied Spain much-needed economic aid, must be seen as a direct response to
the regime's refusal to carry out even the most basic democratic reforms, its execution
of political prisoners, the banning of trade unions and opposition of political parties, its
refusal to sanction a free press, and so on (Clavera et al 1978; González 1979; Catalán
1989).

Many scholars stress the high cost of Francoism, particularly if the limited progress
of the Spanish economy after the Civil War is contrasted with what might have been
expected had political and economic conditions remained much as they were before
1936 (Comín 1986; Fontana 1986; Tortella 1986). It seems reasonable to argue that a
democratic Spain would have obtained a similar rate of growth to Italy after 1945.
Political liberalisation, ruled out by Franco, would surely have secured for Spain the
considerable benefit brought elsewhere by Marshall Aid. Economic co-operation with
the rest of Europe, followed by integration into the expanding markets of the EC,
might also have been expected, if Franco had stepped down as Head of State. The best
opportunity for such an eventuality occurred in 1946 when a group of monarchist
generals petitioned the *Caudillo* to restore the Spanish monarchy under the more
liberal figure of Don Juan, an option which had considerable support among the
Truman and Attlee administrations (Tusell 1988).

Spain's undistinguished economic record throughout the 1940s has generally been ascribed to its inefficient and outmoded economic system which was based on arbitrary bureaucratic controls down to the level of the most trivial decisions. Matters were not helped by the dictator's own crass ignorance of economic affairs, along with the general incompetence and widespread venality of ministers and civil servants. In dealing with corrupt administrators, bribery was often deemed the only effective way of getting hold of precious supplies. To put it bluntly, the dispassionate advice of Spain's tiny band of professional economists was ignored while the country was run like a military barracks. Ministers were obsessed with ill-thought-out interventionist schemes. Many of the economic institutions founded after 1939 were inspired by models developed in Hitler's Germany or Mussolini's Italy. Above all, economic recovery south of the Pyrenees was constantly subordinated to the priority task of ensuring the political survival of the Franco regime (Fuentes Quintana 1984; Velasco 1984; Viñas 1984; Fusi 1985; Tedde 1986).

In the countryside, state interference, intended to regulate prices and production, served mainly to create a thriving black market (*estraperlo*). In the case of wheat, the black market grew to be even bigger than the official market. Meanwhile, livestock farming received minimal official backing, and the development of products such as citrus fruit, which enjoyed a comparative advantage in the newly emergent export markets, faced a variety of obstacles (Barciela 1981; 1983; 1986). Despite the regime's strident advocacy of rural values, designed to placate ex-combatants from Franco's overwhelmingly peasant army, state intervention after 1939 was soon directed at fostering industrial development. The cornerstone of industrial policy, which attained its apogee between 1946 and 1951, was import substitution. Spearheading the messianic quest for industrial self-sufficiency was the *Instituto Nacional de Industria* (INI), a state holding company set up in 1941 on the model of the Italian organisation IRI (*Istituto per la Riconstruzione Industriale*). Presided over until 1962 by Juan Antonio Suanzes, a naval engineer and boyhood friend of the *Caudillo*, INI's brief, set out in Article I of its charter, was to 'encourage and finance, in the service of the nation, the creation and resurgence of its industries, especially those whose aim was the resolution of problems imposed by the requirements of the defence of the country or were aimed at increasing Spain's degree of self-sufficiency' (Schwartz and González 1978).

During the late 1940s and 1950s INI's component companies, paramount in the fields of electricity supply, chemicals, iron and steel, non-ferrous metals, engineering and automobiles, built up the requisite infrastructure for the subsequent process of development which followed the 1959 Stabilisation Plan. Nevertheless many of the Institute's projects were undertaken with scant regard to their opportunity cost. Public-sector borrowing to finance some of INI's pet projects was to exert strong inflationary pressures on the economy by the end of the 1950s (Donges 1976; Braña et al 1979).

Protectionism, already in the ascendancy before the outbreak of civil war, was augmented after 1939 by an arsenal of interventionist measures and devices. Exports were thwarted by an overvalued peseta, while the option of devaluation was repeatedly rejected. Meanwhile, imports of raw materials that were to be found in the peninsula, were generally banned, irrespective of their quality or extraction costs. In addition, the authorities resorted to the use of import licences and quotas to tackle Spain's ever-present trade deficit.

By the end of the 1940s it was patently obvious to all except the blinkered ideologues of the regime that Spain's autarkic policies had failed. Writing in 1948, Britain's commercial counsellor in Madrid reported insurmountable economic problems characterised by marked inflationary trends, basic shortages of foodstuffs, raw materials and equipment, declining efficiency of road and rail transport (Walker 1949). Echoing the views of Spain's leading industrial bank, the Banco Urquijo, Britain's representative contended that no recovery was possible in either agricultural or industrial production without a massive increase in imports of basic raw materials and capital goods. Yet where were the necessary funds to come from? Exports were far from buoyant. Notwithstanding frantic machinations in Washington on Spain's behalf by a well-orchestrated 'Spanish Lobby' of influential American Catholics, anti-communists, military planners and business people with interests in the peninsula, the Franco regime remained firmly excluded from the European Recovery Programme. Fortunately for Spain, the Iberian power obtained between 1947 and 1949 $264 million in credits from Argentina, which were largely utilised to purchase cereals and other foodstuffs. However in January 1950 Argentina, itself in economic difficulties, suspended all credit sales to Spain (Schneidman 1973; Viñas 1982).

Although formally bound by the UN resolution of 1946, the Truman administration chose not to oppose credits granted to the Spaniards by US commercial banks. Hence it did not intervene in January 1949 to prevent a loan of $25 million to the Franco regime from the Chase National Bank. This advance, which carried an annual rate of interest of 2.5 per cent, was for a period of two years only. Finally, in September 1950, at the instigation of a group of US politicians led by Senator Pat McCarran, a joint committee of Senate and Congress granted a credit to Spain of $62.5 million via the Export-Import Bank to finance imports of American goods. The terms of this loan were far from unfavourable. Spain was to repay nothing for five years, after which it was allowed a further twenty-five years to pay off the loan, which bore an annual rate of interest of 3 per cent. On the advice of the United Nations, the Truman administration delayed payment until 1952. Even so, its approval marked a watershed in Spain's post-war international economic relations (Viñas 1981; Fanjul 1980).

The outbreak of the Korean War in June 1950 led to rising international demand for Spanish supplies of such items as wolfram, iron ore and mercury. More importantly, despite the well-known antipathy shared by Harry Truman and his Secretary of State Dean Acheson towards General Franco, the conflict in Asia and the Cold War in general led to a growing *rapprochement* between Spain and the United States which was to culminate in the early days of the Eisenhower administration in 1953 in the signing of a bilateral military and economic agreement (Whitaker 1961). At long last Spain was to be allowed back into the fold. Its ostracism was over, with all that that implied in terms of international capital flows (Whitaker 1961).

Growth, instability and timid liberalisation

After the disappointing performance of the Spanish economy in the 1940s, a number of indicators bear witness to the high degree of economic growth and structural change which took place over the next decade. Between 1950 and 1959, national income, measured at constant 1964 prices, rose by 54 per cent, from 425 billion pesetas to

653 billion. Over the same period, the proportion of the active labour force employed on the land fell sharply from 49.9 per cent to 42.5 per cent. Albert Carreras's index of industrial production shows an average increase of 6.6 per cent a year for the period 1951–5 and 7.4 per cent a year for 1956–60, despite a pronounced deceleration in 1959–60, due to the deflationary impact of the Stabilisation Plan. These figures compare favourably with the industrial performance of other Mediterranean nations although Spain's industrial expansion, unlike that of its Southern counterparts, was not achieved without a simultaneous rise in inflation from 1954 onwards together with a serious deterioration in its balance of payments after 1956 (Carreras 1984; García Delgado 1987). Spain's commendable rates of industrial growth did not, furthermore, obscure important structural weaknesses in the manufacturing sector. As late as 1958, enterprises employing fewer than five workers accounted for 85 per cent of the total number of companies. Small firms predominated even in such sectors as chemicals, basic non-ferrous metals, machinery and equipment. As a result of consequent losses of economies of scale, Spain's manufacturing sector was plagued by low productivity, lack of competitiveness and a lamentable level of export achievement (Rogers 1957; Donges 1971).

The improvement in Spain's economic fortunes after 1951, precarious as it was, coincided with a decision by the *Caudillo* amidst popular protests in the big cities, to reshape his Cabinet. The critical new appointment in the economic sphere was that of Manuel Arburúa to the Ministry of Commerce, now separated from the Ministry of Industry. Much controversy surrounds the contribution to Spanish economic development of Arburúa, who replaced Suanzes, the arch-exponent of autarkic development. Some scholars portray Don Manolo as the originator of a Spanish NEP, struggling to put an end to the prevailing orthodoxy of self-sufficiency (Viñas et al 1979). Other commentators highlight his confused thinking, all too obvious in his rambling speeches, his indecisiveness, and his loss of momentum after the passage of a spate of legislation during his first two years in office. Even this notable achievement, his detractors argue, was carried through with an eye to securing offers of credit from the Americans (Clavera et al 1978). Few would deny Arburúa's entrepreneurial flair, which at times verged on corruption: witness his wheeling and dealing over the ministerial telephone on such topics as the granting of import licences, which became legendary (Franco Salgado Araujo 1976; Anderson 1970; Payne 1986).

The centrepiece of Arburúa's economic strategy was an attempt to facilitate an increase in specific types of imports. First, in an endeavour to remove the most glaring excesses of the black market in the countryside, as well as to stabilise food prices, he launched a crash programme of foodstuff imports. Luckily for him, this initiative coincided with a succession of abundant harvests at home, apart from 1953. Thus this particular aspect of his plans did not end up draining away large amount of Spain's foreign reserves, as his critics had feared (Banco Urquijo 1954). Second, Arburúa tried to tackle a variety of problems, including poor agricultural yields, low industrial productivity, energy shortages and inadequate transport facilities, by means of imports of much-needed raw materials and capital equipment. Between 1951 and 1955 imports of machinery, including vehicles, and metals rose by more than two-thirds, to stand at 26 per cent of the figure for total imports. After 1955, there was a sharp acceleration in imports of semi-manufactures, itself an indication of the consolidation of the manufacturing sector. Yet, disappointingly for economic liberals, Arburúa remained staunchly committed to the policy of import substitution. In consequence, Spain's industrialisation policy continued to be underpinned by an assortment of protectionist measures, exchange rate manipulations, and so on.

As Arburúa himself recognised, the task of finding new export lines, particularly manufactured goods, which satisfied the needs of the expanding international market, would prove a difficult and protracted business. Moreover, since at that time the terms of trade were moving relentlessly against suppliers of foodstuffs and raw materials, Spain was under extreme pressure to extricate itself from a situation where agricultural products (fruit, vegetables, wine) accounted for as much as three-fifths of its total exports. No amount of exchange rate manipulation and other artificial stimuli, however, could compensate for the lack of competitiveness of Spanish manufactures.

US aid

Spain's failure in the 1950s to generate a significant increase in export earnings to finance its economic reconstruction served only to underline the importance of United States support for the beleaguered Spanish economy. This was especially true during the middle years of the decade. Between 1951 and 1957 the United States provided the Iberian nation with $625 million of aid. Thanks to the USA's generosity, the ailing Franco regime gained a crucial breathing space without which it might well have succumbed (González 1979; Viñas et al 1979). In spite of the meagreness of the sums involved, American aid contributed to Spanish economic development in a number of vital ways. First and foremost, it offset part of the trade deficit which resulted from the ineffectiveness of Arburúa's export drive (Torres 1956). United States representatives in the peninsula constantly reiterated that US aid secured higher living standards for the population as a whole and, initially at least, helped combat inflation (Sausse 1957; Shearer 1959). In addition, the terms and conditions of American support were intended to strengthen the bargaining position of economic liberals within the Spanish Cabinet. Article II of the Defence Support Programme, for instance, committed the recipient nation to stabilisation of its currency, establishment of a realistic exchange rate, tight fiscal discipline, eradication of monopolistic practices, stimulation of competition in the domestic market and encouragement of international trade. However, up to 1956, when the US Ambassador to Spain openly criticised the Franco regime for its restrictive attitude to foreign investment, the Eisenhower administration appeared more concerned with the military and strategic implications of the 1953 agreement than in opening up the Spanish market to new competition (Cuesta Garrigós 1955; Fernández Valderrama 1964).

Pre-stabilisation 1957–9

By the winter of 1956 Arburúa's plans to liberalise the Spanish economy were in disarray. Exports, particularly of industrial products, were simply inadequate to pay for the necessary imports crucial to the success of his industrial programme. The drying up of US aid after the mid-1950s posed an increased threat of rampant inflation and balance-of-payments difficulties. In the long run, earnings from foreign tourism and emigrant remittances would help ease the latter problem. In the late 1950s, however, a growing number of bankers and industrialists, especially in Catalonia, looked to foreign investment as a way out of Spain's seeming impasse. Yet with the political and economic disintegration of his regime looming, Franco, along with his second in command Rear Admiral Luis Carrero Blanco, remained deeply imbued with an almost allergic mistrust of foreigners (Navarro Rubio 1976).

As rumours circulated in the Spanish capital of a report, written by Arburúa, claiming that Spain's gold reserves had fallen to as little as $40 million, Franco opted for action. Faced with the threat of national bankruptcy, Arburúa had recommended a package of stringent austerity measures. The *Caudillo*, fearing popular unrest, decided to sack his discredited minister. In the Cabinet reshuffle of February 1957, out went Arburúa in company with a coterie of old-guard Falangists. To the key economic portfolios of Finance and Trade, Franco appointed two politically inexperienced technocrats, Mariano Navarro Rubio, a director of the Banco Popular, and Alberto Ullastres, a professor of economics. Both men were closely associated with the Catholic lay group *Opus Dei*, as was another personality who was to play a prominent role in Spanish economic life during the 1960s, Laureano López Rodó. The latter, a former professor of public administration, had already been appointed Technical Secretary-General to the Presidency in December 1956. Ideologically these men were economic liberals who looked to Europe for Spain's salvation. Personally, all three were austere, hard-working and business-like (Anderson 1970). The new appointments were ably supported by a group of talented economists, including Juan Sardá at the Bank of Spain, Manuel Varela at the Ministry of Commerce and Juan Antonio Ortiz García at the Ministry of Finance (Fuentes Quintana 1984; 1986). Together they embarked, hesitantly at first, on the obstacle-strewn path from autarky to the introduction of market mechanisms. Needless to say, Spain's technocrats never considered that economic liberalisation should be accompanied by great political freedoms, the legislation of trade-union activity or a more progressive taxation system (Merigó 1982).

From 1957 to early 1959 the authorities pursued a series of cautious initiatives, largely through the modification and adaptation of existing instruments. This period was subsequently dubbed 'pre-stabilisation', though it is difficult to discern any deliberate line of policy. In April 1957 the system of multiple exchange rates was simplified and the peseta devalued, though not by enough. Large amounts of short-term capital flowed out of the country. Moreover, a plethora of economic controls was retained or extended. To protect industry from the effects of inflation, new subsidies and deposit techniques were introduced. In an attempt to peg prices, the rediscount rate was raised from 4.25 per cent to 5 per cent in July 1957, while interest rates on deposit accounts were frozen. To bring in extra revenue, a series of tax reforms was carried out in December. Later, in 1958, as the policy-makers began to run out of steam, attempts were made to attach Spain to a number of international institutions which were later to underwrite the Stabilisation Plan. In January 1958 Spain joined the Organisation for European Economic Co-operation (OEEC), soon to become the OECD (Organisation for Economic Co-operation and Development). In July 1958 it also became a member of the International Monetary Fund (IMF) and the World Bank

(Viñas et al 1979; Muns 1986). These bodies provided important technical aid to Spain's liberal reformers and facilitated the acceptance of new ideas and methods. Their support and encouragement was especially critical at this stage since many influential figures, not least Franco himself, were still emotionally attached to autarky. Both INI and the Industry Ministry strongly favoured industrialisation and inflation in preference to stabilisation and economic liberalisation. Only when Finance Minister Navarro Rubio briefed the dictator on Spain's profound and destabilising balance-of-payments crisis did the latter relent. Even then, many of the leading participants could hardly believe their luck when the *Caudillo* agreed to back the reform proposals. The abandonment of self-sufficiency was, it seems, a price Franco was in the end prepared to pay for his regime's political survival (Navarro Rubio 1976; Fuentes Quintana 1984).

Indeed, the Stabilisation and Liberalisation Plan of July 1959, which many considered to be mistitled, was introduced against a background of near-insolvency. Spain's balance of payments, in perpetual crisis since 1957, gave cause for extraordinary concern during the first half of 1959 when the Bank of Spain's gold and foreign currency reserves, net of short-term liabilities, showed a negative figure. During the six-month period from December 1958 to May 1959 Madrid was the scene of hectic activity, involving, among other matters, deliberations with missions from the OEEC and IMF. A handful of high-level dignitaries visited the Spanish capital, among them Jacques Rueff, author of France's recent Stabilisation Plan, and the director-general of the Fund, Per Jacobsson. The latter is credited with a decisive role in getting the Spanish Stabilisation Plan accepted. It was approved by the Cabinet on 30 June 1959, after which it was sent as a Memorandum to the IMF and OEEC. On 20 July 1959 it was finally published as a decree-law (Muns 1986).

The years of development

During the decade and a half following the Stabilisation Plan of 1959, Spain experienced unprecedented rates of economic growth. From being a laggard, the country suddenly discovered itself near to the top of the international growth league. Among member states of the OECD, only Japan enjoyed faster and more sustained growth in this period. After an initial set-back to economic activity in 1959–60, due largely to the unanticipated deflationary impact of the Plan, Spain's GDP, at constant prices, grew by 7.5 per cent a year between 1961 and 1973. There was a remarkable burgeoning of foreign trade. Between 1959 and 1973 Spain's export–GDP ratio more than doubled, from 6.1 per cent to 14.1 per cent, while the import–GDP ratio rose form 6.9 to 15.9 per cent. Furnished with increased imports of raw materials, capital goods and semi-manufactures, Spain was able to speed up the process of economic transformation, begun in the 1950s, from a traditional agricultural economy to a modern industrial state. The proportion of the active labour force still on the land tumbled from 41.9 per cent in 1959 to 24.1 per cent in 1973. During this period the contribution of agriculture to GDP fell from 20.0 per cent to 11.4 per cent, while that of industry (including construction) rose from 29.9 per cent to 42.9 per cent (García 1976; Banco de Bilbao 1983; Banco Bilbao Vizcaya 1989).

While ministers attributed Spain's impressive growth performance to official planning policy, other commentators, while acknowledging that government policies may have had a marginal impact, ascribed the country's loudly trumpeted 'economic miracle' to a fortuitous set of trends in the Western economies as a whole. Above all, critics of the exaggerated claims of the planners stressed that Spain had been capable of financing the massive increase in imports which made possible its rapid economic growth during the 1960s and early 1970s thanks largely to three crucial developments:

1   a staggering increase in earnings from foreign tourism
2   emigrant remittances from more than 1 million Spaniards working abroad, the great bulk of whom had left Spain since 1959
3   a renewal of overseas investment in the Spanish economy (Anderson 1970; Fontana 1986; Estapé and Amado 1986).

A second determining factor in Spain's spectacular upsurge was the presence of a pool of reserve labour in the countryside whose marginal productivity on the land was close to zero. During the phase of expansion, about 1.5 million Spaniards quit the countryside for the towns, thus providing a cheap and abundant source of labour for the industrial and service sectors. In geographical terms, the main net losers of population were Andalusia, Extremadura, Castile and Galicia. Catalonia, Madrid, the Basque Region and the País Valenciano were the principal net gainers. In addition, it has been estimated that during the 1960s a further 1 million women joined the labour force. Thus industrial employers were spared the costs of inflationary wage settlements as a condition of attracting more labour (Martínez Serrano et al 1982).

Third, and of the utmost significance in the long run, Spain's industrial boom and the simultaneous improvement in living standards was made possible by cheap and abundant supplies of energy, not least of imported oil. Between 1960 and 1973 demand for energy rose by 7.8 per cent per annum. As a late starter in the industrialisation stakes, the country came to rely heavily on oil not only in providing motive power for industry but also in transportation. Moreover a number of Spain's leading industries (iron and steel, metallurgy, cement) were energy-intensive. Hence, by 1973 Spain ranked above France and West Germany with respect to energy consumption per unit of industrial production (Sudrià 1987).

The Stabilisation and Liberalisation Plan of 1959

The Spanish Stabilisation Plan had two essential objectives. Internally, it aimed to restore financial stability by carrying out a series of monetary and fiscal measures designed to restrict demand and limit inflation. Additionally, the plan set out to liberalise external trade and promote foreign investment.

In order to bring down domestic inflation, the authorities imposed savage cuts in public sector expenditur, while direct advances by the Bank of Spain to public institutions were frozen at their 1958 level. The significance of this latter action lay in the fact that the central and private banks provided not only the state but also autonomous institutions such as INI and the state railways (RENFE) with a sizeable share of their funds. In the case of the Bank of Spain, finance to the public sector was drastically reduced, from 11 billion pesetas in 1958 to 3.4 billion in 1959. To balance the budget for the public sector as a whole, the regime announced price increases of up to 50 per cent for transport and public utilities, while taxes on petrol and tobacco, both state monopolies, were raised. In the short run, serious harm to business activity resulted from raising of the Bank of Spain's rediscount rate from 5 per cent to 6.5 per cent. This unnecessarily restrictive action soon led to increases in interest rates throughout the system.

Yet the most far-reaching measures concerned Spain's foreign trade and payments system. Multiple exchange rates were abolished and the peseta fixed at a par of 60 to the US dollar. Quotas and other restrictions were removed from about 30 per cent of imports from OECD countries. In addition, legislation was introduced which offered substantial incentives and guarantees to foreign investors. Among other initiatives, proposed or implied in the plan, were a long-overdue revision of Spain's antiquated tariff legislation, measures against restrictive practices, a reform of the inadequate and regressive taxation system, and the introduction of long-range economic planning. All of these proposals eventually passed into law, though three at least were to prove a disappointment to economic liberals. The new tariff of 1960 was still strongly protectionist; it was not until 1963 that a feeble anti-monopoly law was enacted; the tax reforms proposed in 1959 did not come into operation until June 1964 (Naharro 1960; González 1979; Anderson 1970).

In the short term the Stabilisation Plan undoubtedly yielded some positive results. Most encouragingly, the rate of inflation fell dramatically. Significantly, this was achieved despite the devaluation of the peseta, which adversely affeced import prices. A sudden spurt in exports, along with escalating receipts from foreign visitors, foreign investment and the repatriation of capital, contributed to healthy balance-of-payment surpluses in 1959 and 1960. Nevertheless, many commentators consider the policies carried out during the second half of 1959 to have been excessively harsh. The fact that they did not trigger off a severe contraction in economic activity was largely due to unplanned-for developments, not least the beginnings of mass tourism. During 1959 real income fell by 2.5 per cent and real investment by as much as 11 per cent. Many entrepreneurs were frightened off by the sudden change in economic policy and set about reducing their commodity stocks (Rubio Jiménez 1968; Burgos López 1973; Gámir 1980).

Whatever its short-term consequences, there can be little doubt that in the long run the Stabilisation Plan provided a stimulus to economic activity which brought Spain closer to the market system and began to expose domestic producers to outside competition. Between 1959 and 1963 the so-called 'first technocrats' actively pursued liberalisation policies. Indeed, these five years saw a far greater degree of coherence, realism, imagination and ambition in the formulation of economic policy than at any previous time during the Francoist era (Ros Hombravella 1979).

Indicative planning

As we have seen, the Stabilisation Plan of 1959 contained a commitment on the part of Spain's policy-makers to the introduction of long-range economic planning. Due to prevailing uncertainies, it was over a year before the regime invited the World Bank to dispatch a mission to Spain to assist in the preparation of a long-term development plan aimed at the expansion and modernisation of the Spanish economy, the amelioration of living standards and financial stability (International Bank for Reconstruction and Development 1963). In February 1962, the same month that Spain applied unsuccessfully to join the EC, López Rodó was appointed Commissioner for the Plan. The Bank's report, solicited by Navarro Rubio, was delivered to the new Commissioner in August. López Rodó carefully censored the document in an attempt to win over the support of Carrero Blanco (Cotorruelo Sendagorta 1963; Fuentes Quintana 1963; Burns 1965; González 1979).

The Spanish system of planning, in operation from 1964 to 1975, was closely modelled – some contended it was copied lock, stock and barrel – on the French model of indicative planning in force since 1946. While the public sector was compelled to meet targets set by the planners, the authorities tried to direct the activities of the private sector through a range of indirect methods. These included credit and fiscal measures, as well as the application of a process known as concerted action, involving agreements between individual firms and the relevant ministry, aimed at securing a fixed level of production.

Three plans were implemented during the period, which coincided with the final years of the ailing dictator. These covered the years 1964–7, 1968–71 and 1972–5. Their main objectives are summarised by Rosa Alsina.

1   Economic development, defined in terms of a continuous rise in national income, though not based on significant structural transformation, nor institutional changes, nor a substantial improvement in the distribution of wealth.
2   The promotion of a market economy, though with the participation of the public sector.
3   An opening-up of the Spanish economy and a greater degree of integration into the world system, more specifically the EC. Hence the emphasis on improvements in productivity aimed at making the Spanish economy more competitive.
4   The relegation of social objectives to a secondary position (although considerable differences existed between plans) (Alsina 1987).

All three plans aimed at securing large increases in production and encouraged investment at the expense of consumption. Thus industry was given a much greater priority than agriculture, especially in the First and Third Plans. Yet whereas these two plans called for short-term growth and rapid industrialisation, the Second Plan, while not ignoring these objectives, laid greater stress on achieving stability. The First and Third Plans set out to attain sharp increases in imports, partly financed by increased earnings from exports. In contrast, the Second Plan tackled the trade deficit inherited from its predecessor. Indeed, given the incompatibility of their many goals, the planners were forced to establish a list of priorities, the least important of which could be sacrificed to suit the circumstances. Thus, for example, in the First and Third Plans, López Rodó and Industry Minister Gregorio López Bravo saw inflation and a deteriorating trade balance as the price which had to be paid for obtaining high rates of economic growth.

How far were the planners' objectives achieved? In the event, their stop-go policies brought about an average annual increase of 6 per cent in GDP, at current prices, between 1964 and 1975. Gross capital formation expanded by an average of 7.7 per cent a year. Yet economic growth was accompanied by a considerable level of inflation together with persistent trade imbalances. Moreover, none of the Planning Commission's forecasts was borne out by subsequent developments. This was notoriously so during the Third Plan which, among other difficulties, was adversely affected by the world slump after 1973 (Alsina 1987).

It is hard to judge what the fate of the Spanish economy might have been without the planning experience. Bearing in mind the favourable international context, at least before the onset of the Oil Crisis, Spain would almost certainly have grown come what may. Indeed, Spain's highest rates of growth were achieved during the period 1961–3, before the planning process got underway. Manuel-Jesús González, a forthright opponent of Spanish planning, criticises the so-called Men of Development (López Rodó and López Bravo) for their politically motivated concern with increasing the level of state intervention and seeking greater discretionary powers. Had Spain pressed on with the liberalisation process initiated by Navarro Rubio and Ullastres the results would undoubtedly, González argues, have been faster growth, lower inflation and less inefficiency during the subsequent decade (González 1979). Another critic, José Luis Sampedro, argues that the adoption of the planning process provided the regime with a ready-made excuse for refusing to carry out fundamental structural reforms which would have offended powerful sectional interests (Sampedro 1967). Elsewhere, it has been claimed that the plans introduced a more rational element into the process of decision-making, influenced the expenditure patterns of private companies and offered incentives to regional development (Álvarez Rendueles 1975).

Tourism, emigrant remittances and foreign investment

Three main exogenous variables – income from foreign tourists, emigrant remittances and foreign investment – earned Spain the necessary foreign currency to pay for essential imports after 1959. These variables were to play decisive roles at different stages over the next decade and a half, allowing the country the luxury of accumulating a series of trade deficits.

While the number of tourists visiting Spain rose eightfold, from 4.19 million to 34.56 million between 1959 and 1973, receipts increased from $126 million to $3,091 million. Over the same period, income from tourism offset 87.6 per cent of the trade deficit. According to an OECD report, as early as 1961 Spain's dependence on earnings from foreign tourism in its balance of payments was greater than any other European nation. Tourism also had important spin-off effects on the material economy. To attract large numbers of visitors, two-thirds of whom came from France, Britain and West Germany, much-needed infrastructural developments were initiated in the coastal regions affected by the holiday boom. As well as providing motorways, railway lines, airports, water, public utilities and improved health facilities, tourism also attracted a sharp movement of labour away from agriculture and fishing towards hotels, the construction industry, transport and commerce (Organisation de Coopération et de Développement Economiques 1962; Alcaide 1968; Cals 1974; Figuerola Paloma 1978).

The movement of vast numbers of Spaniards to France, West Germany, Switzerland, The Netherlands and other expanding economies was encouraged by the Stabilisation Plan, which made it easier to leave the fatherland in search of work. Between 1959 and 1974 the flow of emigrants exceeded 1.3 million, with an estimated net exodus of 700,000 persons. During the period 1960–6 the volume of emigration accounted for one-fifth of Spain's agricultural labour force and one-eighth of the non-agricultural working class. One calculation shows that in 1966–7 migrant workers sent home about one-quarter of the sum which the country earned from foreign tourism (García Fernández 1965; Alcaide 1968; Román 1971; Rubio 1974).

Throughout the 1960s imports of foreign capital accounted for approximately one-tenth of gross capital formation and one-fifth of gross industrial investment. They made their most significant contribution to Spain's balance of payments between 1962 and 1969, bringing in $2,634 million. This compared with an accumulated trade deficit on goods and services of $2,245 million (Varela Pareche and Rodríguez de Pablo 1974). Official statistics for the period 1960–72, which relate only to companies for which foreign investment accounted for more than half of the paid-up capital, show that 80 per cent of the total originated from five countries – the United States, Switzerland, West Germany, France and the United Kingdom. Over the same period, 72 per cent of all incoming capital thus measured went to three main regions: New Castile (mainly Madrid), Catalonia and the Basque Country. In contrast, relatively little foreign capital was directed to those parts of Spain most starved of funds, for example Andalusia, Extremadura, Galicia and the Canary Islands.

The extend of overall foreign control in a particular industry often bore little relation to the quantum of external investment flowing into it. Between 1959 and 1973 the lion's share of foreign investment (26.3 per cent) went to the chemicals industry. However, foreign concerns held only 36.8 per cent of the paid-up capital of large chemicals companies. Conversely, in the motor-vehicle sector, which received 9.2 per cent of total foreign investment, 56.7 per cent of the paid-up capital came from outside Spain (Cuadrado Roura 1976; Muñoz et al 1978; Lieberman 1982).

Criticisms of the role played by foreign capital in Spain during these years and afterwards focus on its concentration in a limited number of sectors, including chemicals, metallurgy and foodstuffs, which tended to reduce its multiplier effects, and the failure of the policy-makers to co-ordinate foreign investment with regional policy. Nevertheless, these disadvantages were more than outweighed by a host of important gains, not least the injection of capital, the incorporation of the most up-to-date technology, the expansion of new sectors, the appearance of more dynamic forms of entrepreneurship, productivity increases, and an extension of the market (Cuadrado Roura 1976; Muñoz et al 1978).

The Spanish economy, already suffering the effects of inflation and balance-of-trade problems, was severely hit by the fourfold increase in the price of crude imposed by the oil producers after 1973. In 1974 the nation's bill for imported oil and other sources of energy rose by an alarming 210 per cent from 72.9 million pesetas to 225.8 million. The share of energy in total imports soared from 13 per cent in 1973 to an average of 27.4 per cent for the period 1974–8. After the Second Oil Crisis of 1979 the situation deteriorated further. By 1981, 42.4 per cent of Spain's total import bill (1,259 million pesetas) was given over to these items. This represented a staggering 66.7 per cent of the value of Spanish exports (García Alonso 1983).

By the end of 1974 the First Oil Crisis had put an end to a decade and a half of economic growth. In the following year the rate of growth of GDP, at constant prices, fell from 5.3 per cent to 0.6 per cent. Over the period 1976–8 growth rates recovered a little, averaging 2.7 per cent a year. Even so, these rates represented only one-third of the growth achievement of the boom years. Following the new round of OPEC oil price increases in 1979, growth rates tumbled to an annual average of 0.8 per cent for the period 1979–82. As oil prices soared, so too did Spain's trade deficit. A shortfall in the country's balance of trade of $3,545 million in 1973 had almost quadrupled by 1980, reaching $13,424 million as the full impact of the Second Oil Crisis was felt (Banco de Bilbao 1980; 1983; Banco Bilbao Vizcaya 1989).

It was Spain's misfortune that the economic crisis of the second half of the 1970s hit the country as it embarked on the lengthy and convoluted process of political transition from dictatorship to democracy. There is little doubt that the Spanish economy was the victim of a high degree of political uncertainty, especially during the critical phase from the death of General Franco in November 1975 to the first free general election in June 1977. The inherent weaknesses of the new monarchy at this time gave rise to timid and occasionally irresponsible government (Rojo 1987). The centre-right government led by Adolfo Suárez which triumphed at the polls in 1977 inherited a host of unresolved problems. Most glaringly, Spain's annual rate of inflation stood at 26 per cent. Hourly wage rates before tax in the manufacturing sector had risen by 30 per cent in the previous twelve months. Furthermore, important basic industries, including steel, shipbuilding and textiles, faced severe structural crises. The understandable desire of the new administration to maintain levels of employment (unemployment then stood at 6 per cent) meant that these and other sectors needed to achieve substantial reductions in real wages. While elsewhere in Western Europe governments embarked on the familiar path of restrictive policies, the authorities in Spain chose to tackle the deteriorating economic situation with a mixture of gradual readjustment coupled with an attempt to find some form of social consensus (Leal 1982).

In October 1977 the Suárez government, along with the opposition Socialist and Communist parties, signed the so-called Moncloa Pacts, which provided for a 22 per cent wage ceiling. It was hoped that this would be accepted by the nascent trade unions in return for important institutional and economic reforms. For its part, the government declared its intention of bringing down the level of inflation to 15 per cent by the end of 1978, an objective which it only narrowly missed. In retrospect, it has to be stated that in their determination to avert serious social and political problems, the nation's leaders permitted real wages to rise far too quickly in relation to productivity growth. The result was stagflation, together with a sharp increase in the number of unemployed people. Any improvements in economic performance achieved by the Moncloa Pacts were swept aside by the oil price rise after 1979. Over the next three years, before the Socialist Party won power, there were few encouraging signs. The authorities failed to bring down the level of inflation by any significant amount, while Spain suffered a series of chronic trade deficits. Meanwhile, as the employers struggled to reduce wage costs, Spain's jobless total passed 2 million, representing 16.5

per cent of the labour force by 1982. The government's attempts to safeguard 'lame duck' industries by pouring funds into the public sector brought a trebling of the public sector deficit from 1.7 per cent of GDP in 1979 to 5.5 per cent in 1982 (Fuentes Quintana and Requeijo 1984; Rojo 1987; Banco Bilbao Vizcaya 1989).

The Socialists in power

Felipe González's Socialists come to power in October 1982 with a specific electoral commitment to create 800,000 new jobs. However, the disastrous experiences of inflation in Mitterrand's France, together with the political impact of the attempted coup led by Colonel Tejero in the previous year, helped push Spain's first peacetime Socialist government towards economic orthodoxy. In fact the three Socialist administrations (1982–6, 1986–9, 1989–) accelerated the process of gradual readjustment initiated by the Suárez government in 1977. Under finance ministers Miguel Boyer and Carlos Solchaga, the main planks of Spain's economic policy have been sound finance, attempting to reduce the level of inflation, industrial restructuring, and bringing public expenditure under control.

During its first period in office, the González government was enormously helped by the moderation of the socialist trade-union movement, the *Unión General de Trabajadores* (UGT). Despite fierce competition for members from the Communist-led Workers' Commissions (*Comisiones Obreras*), the UGT refrained from submitting excessive wage claims for fear of throwing the government's economic programme off course. Even so, the loyalty of the UGT rank-and-file and many of the Socialist Party's 40,000 militants was severely tested as employers were given increased powers to hire and fire. Despite the early promises to provide new jobs, 21.6 per cent of the labour force was out of work by 1985, the poorest record at that time anywhere in Europe. From the beginning of 1987, working-class frustrations, in the face of persistently high levels of unemployment, sparked off a wave of industrial unrest. The workers' protests reached a climax during the twenty-four-hour general strike of 14 December 1988, when two-thirds of Spain's 11 million workers struck work, bringing the country to a standstill. After the Socialists scraped home with the tiniest of majorities in the general election of 1989, losing 800,000 votes, they quickly announced that they wanted to make peace with the trade unions. Finance minister Solchaga's take-it-or-leave-it attitude to workers' demands was dropped. Meanwhile, official figures demonstrated that 600,000 new jobs were created in 1989, with unemployment coming down to 16 per cent.

Unemployment aside, the Socialists could, up to 1989, claim a fair degree of success in bringing the economy under control. During their first term in office they halved the level of inflation, while growth rates rose slowly if not spectacularly. Spain's rate of growth of GDP, at constant prices, expanded steadily from 1.4 per cent in 1982 to 3.0 per cent in 1986. From 1987 to 1989, despite the government's inability to maintain a social pact with the unions, Spain once more enjoyed a respectable level of economic growth as GDP rose at an annual average rate of 5 per cent. More disturbingly, inflation crept upwards, from 4.6 per cent in 1987 to 6.9 per cent in 1989.

Threatened with an overheated economy running out of control, the Spanish authorities started to apply the brakes after the summer of 1989. In an attempt to curb credit and dampen down domestic demand, they displayed a marked preference for monetary rather than fiscal measures. Hopes of a relaxation in government policy were dashed by the publication of the trade statistics for 1989. These showed an estimated balance-of-trade deficit of $29 billion in 1989, compared with a shortfall of $17.6 billion in 1988. More worrying for the authorities was the current account deficit of $11.6 billion, as against $3.6 billion in 1988. Optimists pointed out that nearly half of Spain's huge trade bill in 1989 related to capital goods. The bulk of these items, they contended, were destined for Spanish factories, where they would contribute to the modernisation of the production process, thereby making the industry more competitive (Banco Bilbao Vizcaya 1989; *Financial Times* 24 February 1989; 21 June 1989; 19 February 1990).

Spain and the EC

Spain became a member of the European Community on 1 January 1986, twenty-four years after the Franco regime first petitioned Brussels for entry. In the early years, the hopes of Spain's negotiators were essentially twofold: to remove those obstacles blocking the country's access to the markets of the 'Six'; and to bring about a general productivity increase for the economy as a whole. Yet all Spain achieved while the ageing *Caudillo* remained in power was a preferential agreement, as a result of the Luxembourg Accord of 1970. With the demise of the dictator in 1975, together with the simultaneous collapse of the authoritarian regimes in Portugal and Greece, there was a recognition on the part of the EC of the need to strengthen democracy in the former dictatorships by welcoming them into the fold. What Spanish negotiators had earlier perceived as an essentially economic problem now took on an important political dimension. The fact remains that in 1978, when Suárez appointed Leopoldo Calvo Sotelo as minister in charge of relations with the EC, 48 per cent of Spain's exports and 72 per cent of its industrial exports were destined for the markets of the 'Nine' (Donges 1980).

Negotiations for full membership were reopened in February 1979. However, discussions among member states soon became bogged down over agriculture, fisheries and the movement of workers. The fisheries issue entailed protracted negotiations which began only in March 1983, while Spanish entry became inextricably linked with the escalating costs of the European Agricultural Guidance and Guarantee Fund (FEOGA). It was only after months of crisis-ridden debate that the date for the entry of two Iberian nations was finally fixed. This date (1 January 1986) came towards the end of the Socialist Party's first term in office.

Under these circumstances Spain came to sign a punishing treaty of accession with the EC. This was partly due to the virtual absence of national debate, since all the main political parties, including the Communists, favoured entry. So too did between 65 and 70 per cent of the Spanish electorate, according to the opinion polls. Not surprisingly, with a general election due in 1986, Prime Minister González chose to portray membership as a major political achievement of his administration. Few commentators appeared over-concerned with the fine print of the treaty. Thus Spain committed itself to opening its markets to EC competitors and to bringing down its external tariff on industrial goods from third countries to the Community average of 5 per cent within a period of seven years. In return, it would take ten years for the most competitive sectors of Spanish farming (fresh fruit, vegetables and olive oil) to be phased into the Common Agricultural Policy. Moreover, EC rights on the free movement of labour between member states were withheld from Spaniards for a period of seven years.

Agriculture and fisheries

In 1988 agriculture and fisheries employed 13.4 per cent of Spain's active population and contributed 5.9 per cent of GDP, well above the EC average. Unlike Spanish industry, which made great strides during the 1980s, the agricultural sector remains highly uncompetitive by European standards. Significant changes are required if the nation's farmers are to compete on equal terms with their EC partners. On average, Spanish farmers spend just over half the sum which their Western European counterparts spend on such items as seeds, plants, fodder, chemical fertilisers, tools and repairs.

Some of the blame for Spain's poor agricultural showing can be put down to an unfavourable environment. For example, the country has the second highest average altitude in Europe after Switzerland. Some 20 per cent of the land surface is more than 1,000 metres above sea level. In the interior, African summers often give way to Siberian winters. As such, a large part of the territory – perhaps 40 per cent of all agricultural land – is subject to heavy erosion. A further problem afflicting Spanish agriculturalists is that many areas receive far from adequate rainfall. It has been estimated that four-fifths of the peninsula suffers from an arid climate which permits only low levels of agricultural productivity. In general, the average level of yields in Spanish agriculture is reckoned to be two-fifths of neighbouring France. Unfortunately, the chances of increasing the productivity of agriculture by irrigation are thought to be limited. The maximum area suitable for irrigation is calculated to be no more than 4.75 million hectares, or 23 per cent of the cultivated land surface. Large parts of the interior languish under severe water shortages. Violent fluctuations in the size of the wheat harvest are but one indication of the hazards facing cultivators on dry lands.

Another widely recognised problem with deleterious effects on agricultural output is the fragmentation of land holdings (parcelisation) and the number and size of farms. According to the 1982 agrarian census, the average size of farms in Spain was 18.9 hectares, compared with 15.6 hectares in 1962. Yet 60 per cent of Spain's 2.34 million holdings were less than 10 hectares in size, and 23 per cent of holdings were smaller than 1 hectare. The multitude of tiny plots, which is characteristic of Old Castile and Galicia, makes the introduction of machinery largely unprofitable. Between 1962 and 1982 513,000 small and medium-sized plots disappeared, mainly as a result of migration. Even so, for the farmlands of the so-called *minifundio* zone to become economic, three out of every four peasants will have to leave the land so that landholdings can be consolidated (Naredo 1971; 1988; Leal et al 1975).

At the opposite end of the spectrum are the large estates (*latifundios*) of central and southern Spain. A survey in 1969 showed that Spain possessed at that time 5,722 holdings over 500 hectares in size. Such holdings have been attacked for their low yields, the high incidence of absentee landlordism, and the consequent wide variations in income distribution among the rural community and flight of capital to the cities. Large landowners have often shown themselves reluctant to introduce irrigation systems or to farm their estates intensively. For the agricultural labourer, the heavy reliance on seasonal work ensures that the *latifundio* belt suffers from one of the highest levels of unemployment in the peninsula.

Only along the eastern and southern littoral and the Ebro Valley has Spanish agriculture fulfilled its potential. Over half a million hectares of land, three-quarters of it irrigated, is devoted to the cultivation of fruit, vegetables and other horticultural products. Yields of such items as tomatoes, iceberg lettuce, cucumbers, strawberries and flowers have been raised spectacularly by growing them under elongated, plastic-covered, tent-like structures, which permit cultivation all year round. Thus farmers and market gardeners have been able to offer out-of-season produce at premium prices. Areas such as the coastal plain of Almería are ideally suited to this method of cultivation. That zone enjoys average temperatures of 18°C, and is virtually frost-free, with 3,000 hours of sunshine a year. On the debt side, the sinking of increasing numbers of artesian wells to obtain water for the plants has caused a serious drop in the water table. Another problem has been the intrusion of salt water into the wells. The combined effect of these two external diseconomies eventually forced the authorities to limit this type of cultivation, which was competing successfully with its European rivals.

It was widely felt at the time that, in their dealings with the EC, Spain's negotiators made temporary concessions on agriculture so as to win a better deal for their fisheries sector. This strategy made good sense for many reasons. At the time of entry, Spain was among the leading fishing nations in Western Europe, with the fourth largest annual catch after Norway, Denmark and Iceland. The industry provided a livelihood for 100,000 fishermen, while 700,000 jobs were dependent on fishing, many of them in the politically sensitive regions of Galicia and the Basque Country. Under the Common Fisheries Policy, Spain was granted an immediate 40 per cent increase in the number of its vessels allowed to fish in Community waters. The EC also agreed to provide aid for the restructuring of the Spanish fishing industry leading to the modernisation and gradual reduction in the size of the fleet.

Industry

By the end of the 1980s Spain ranked as the eighth largest industrial nation in the Western world. In 1988 30.7 per cent of the active labour force was engaged in industry and construction, contributing 37.4 per cent to the country's GDP. Yet in the wake of the crisis of the 1970s the sector was not without its problems. Following the timorous and gradualist policies of their predecessors, not least the use of INI as a giant 'dustbin' to cater for private sector bankruptcies, socialist ministers were determined to implement some harsh decisions.

To the growing anger of the trade unions, Boyer and Solchaga chose to speed up the run-down of many of the nation's basic mature industries. Between 1984 and 1989 the government's Industrial Restructuring Programme axed nearly 85,000 jobs in steel, shipbuilding, textiles and electrical engineering. At the same time, incentives were offered to growth sectors, such as food processing, office equipment, electrical goods and defence systems. The restructuring of the industrial sector inevitably hit certain regions more than others, including regions like Asturias, Cantabria and the Basque Country, which were socialist strongholds.

Some of the most satisfying results have been achieved by multinational companies, which were actively encouraged to invest in Spain. For example, in order to persuade the West German Volkswagen Group to take a 51 per cent stake in the state-owned car manufacturer SEAT, the government were prepared to assume $1.2 billion of the latter's debt. By 1988 Spain was producing 1.73 million cars annually, 929,000 of which were exported, as Spain overtook the United Kingdom both in terms of output and foreign sales.

Among Spanish companies there are still blatant examples of poorly managed, under-capitalised firms, often family concerns, especially in the clothing and leather goods sectors. In the cotton textile sector of Catalonia, many small firms were unable to survive owing to cut-throat competition from the developing countries. Other Spanish companies perceived that the only feasible solution to their predicament was to shed labour and re-equip their plant with the latest machinery.

As Spain entered the 1990s, complaints that domestic producers lacked an exporting mentality were widely heard, while the Socialist government was accused of doing little or nothing to encourage one. Spanish companies were said to go to export markets in order to overcome economic problems at home, and not to stay in them. Industry remained too fragmented and companies too small. The lack of critical mass meant economies of scale required to enter large markets, where prices are as important as quality, could not be achieved (*Financial Times* 30 March 1990). Nevertheless, there are outstanding examples of enterprising Spanish companies which have acquired for themselves a niche in world markets by concentrating on intermediate technology. This is particularly the case in such sectors as machine tools, avionics and air traffic control equipment, batteries and meat processing.

Tourism

In the mid-1960s receipts from foreign tourism were a determining factor in Spain's so-called economic miracle. By the early 1990s, the country faced cut-throat competition in the package-holiday market from Greece, Turkey and Yugoslavia, as the strong peseta made Spanish holidays relatively expensive for its traditional clients. Yet tourism was still the basis for about 10 per cent of economic activity south of the Pyrenees and one in every ten jobs. In 1988, when the number of foreign tourists exceeded 54 million, Spain overtook the United States as the world's most visited nation. Income from tourism, which stagnated during the first half of the decade, rose by 47 per cent at current prices in 1986, 24 per cent in 1987 and 14 per cent in 1988.

In recent years, the Spanish Ministry of Tourism, while not discouraging low-budget holidays along the Mediterranean coast, has begun to target North American and Japanese visitors. Instead of emphasising Spain's ubiquitous sunshine and cheap alcohol, potential visitors are now informed of the country's cultural diversity and rich history. Benidorm, which, it was widely claimed in the mid-1960s, boasted more hotel beds than Yugoslavia (*sic*), now has to make way for Seville, Toledo and Burgos on the tourist posters. Spain's best hopes of maintaining its revenues from foreign tourism lies in improving both quality and variety so as to attract smaller numbers of wealthier visitors (Banco Bilbao Vizcaya 1989; *Guardian* 10 August 1990).

Acknowledgement

The author wishes to thank the Nuffield Foundation for an award to carry out research on this topic in Madrid and Barcelona.

References

Alcaide A (1968) El turismo español en los años sesenta: una consideración económica. *Información Comercial Española* **421**: 43–8

Alcaide J (1976) Una revisión urgente de la serie de Renta Nacional española en el siglo xx. In Instituto de Estudios Fiscales, *Datos básicos para la historia financiera de España 1850–1975*, 2 vols, Madrid, **1**: 1,127–50

Alsina Olive R (1987) Estrategia de desarrollo en España 1964–75: planes y realidad. *Cuadernos de Economía* **15**: 337–70

Álvarez Rendueles J R (1975) La planificación del desarrollo en España. *Información Comercial Española* **500**: 58–70

Anderson C W (1970) *The Political Economy of Spain: Policy Making in an Authoritarian System.* Madison, Wis.

Arburúa M (1956) *Cinco Años al Frente del Ministerio del Comercio; Discursos y Declaraciones.* Madrid

Banco de Bilbao (1980) *Informe Económico* 1979. Bilbao

Banco de Bilbao (1983) *Informe Económico* 1982. Bilbao

Banco Bilbao Vizcaya (1989) The Spanish economy in 1988 and 1989. *Situación* 18, international edition

Banco Urquijo (1954) *La Economía Española 1952–53.* Madrid

Barciela C (1981) El 'estraperlo' de trigo en la posguerra. *Moneda y Crédito* **151**: 17–37

Barciela C (1983) Intervencionismo agrario en España 1939–71. In Martín Aceña P, Prados L (eds) *La Nueva Historia Económica en España.* Madrid

Barciela C (1986) Los costes del franquismo en el sector agrario: la ruptura del proceso de transformaciones. In Garrabou R, Barciela C, Jiménez Blanco J I (eds) *Historia Agraria de la España Contemporánea. 3. El Fin de la Agricultura Tradicional.* Barcelona

Braña F, Buesa M, Molero J (1979) El fin de la etapa nacionalista: industrialización y dependencia an España 1951–59. *Investigaciones Económices* **9**: 151–217

Burgos López J I (1973) El estado y el proceso económico. In Velarde J, Fraga M, del Campo S (eds) *La España de los Años 70.* Madrid

Burns A (1965) Economic Development in Spain. *De Economía* **89**: 805–21

Cals J (1974) *Turismo y Política Turística en España: una Aproximación.* Barcelona

Carreras A (1984) La producción industrial española 1842–1981: construcción de un índice anual. *Revista de Historia Económica* **2(i)**: 127–57

Carreras A (1989) Depresión económica y cambio estructural durante el decenio bélico 1936–45. In García Delgado J L (ed) *El Primer Franquismo: España Durante la Segunda Guerra Mundial: V Coloquio de Historia Contemporánea de España.* Madrid

Catalán J (1989) Reconstrucción y desarrollo industrial: tres economías del sur de Europe 1944–53. *IV Congreso de la Asociación de Historia Económica, Universidad de Alicante, 18–20 diciembre de 1989*, pp 213–32

Clavera J, Esteban J M, Monés M A, Montserrat A, Ros Hombravella J (1978) *Capitalismo Español: de la Autarquía a la Estabilización 1939–59.* Barcelona

Comín F (1986) El presupuesto del Estado tras la guerra civil: dos pasos atrás. *Economistas* **21**: 24–32

Comisaría del Plan de Desarrollo Económico y Social (1965) *Economic and Social Program for Spain 1964–67.* Baltimore, Md

Cotorruelo Sendagorta A (1963) El informe del Banco Mundial y el plan de desarrollo español. *Boletín de Estudios Económicos* **59**: 209–25

Cuadrado Roura J A (1976) *Las Inversiones Extranjeras en España: una Reconsideración.* Málaga

Cuesta Garrigós I (1955) Los convenios entre España y Estados Unidos. *Moneda y Crédito* **52**: 39–52

Donges J (1971) From an autarkic towards a cautiously outward-looking industrialisation policy: the case of Spain. *Weltwirtschaftliches Archiv* **107**: 33–72

Donges J (1976) *La Industrialización en España: Políticas, Logros, Perspectivas.* Vilassar de Mar

Donges J (1980) La industria española ante su integración en la Comunidad Económica europe. *Cuadernos Económicos de ICE* **14**: 85–93

Estapé F, Amado M (1986) Realidad y propaganda de la planificación indicative en España. In Fontana J (ed) *España bajo el Franquismo.* Barcelona

Fanjul E (1980) El papel de la ayuda americana en la economía española 1951–57. *Información Comercial Española* **577**: 159–65

Fernández Valderrama G (1964) España–USA 1953–64; los convenios hispano-norte americanos de 26 de setiembre de 1953 con especial referencia a sus aspectos económicos. *Economía Financiera Española* **6**: 14–25

Figuerola Palomo M (1978) El turismo y la balanza de pagos. *Información Comercial Española* **533**: 127–35

Financial Times 24 February 1989 Spain

Financial Times 21 June 1989 Spain: banking and finance

Financial Times 19 February 1990 Spain

Financial Times 30 March 1990 After the fiesta, inertia sets in

Fontana J (1986) Reflexiones sobre la naturaleza y las consecuencias del franquismo. In Fontana J (ed) *España bajo el Franquismo.* Barcelona

Fontana J, Nadal J (1976) Spain 1914–70. In Cipolla C M (ed) *The Fontana Economic History of Europe.* London **6**(ii): 460–529

Franco Salgado Araujo F (1976) *Mis Conservaciones Privadas con Franco.* Barcelona

Fuentes Quintana E (1984) El plan de Estabilización económica, veinte cinco años después. *Información Comercial Española* **612–13**: 25–40

Fuentes Quintana E (1986) La economía española desde el plan de Estabilización de 1959: el papel del sector exterior. In Martínez Vara T (ed) *Mercado y Desarrollo Económico en la España Contemporánea.* Madrid

Fuentes Quintana E (ed) (1963) *El Desarrollo Económico de España: Juicio Crítico del Informe del Banco Mundial.* Madrid

Fuentes Quintana E, Requeijo J (1984) La larga marcha hacia una política económica inevitable. *Papeles de Economía Española* **21**: 3–39

Fusi J P (1985) *Franco: Autoritarismo y Poder Personal.* Madrid

Gámir L (ed) (1980) *Política Económica de España.* Madrid, 2 vols

García J (1976) La economía española en el período de transición de un sistema agrícola a una economía industrial y urbana moderna. *Revista Española de Economíe* **6**: 79–148

García Alonso J M (1983) La energía en la economía española: una visión de conjunta. *Papeles de Economía Española* **14**

García Delgado J L (1984) La industrialización española en el primer tercio del siglo xx. In Jover J M (ed) Los comienzos del siglo xx, vol. 37 of *Historia e España Menéndez Pidal.* Madrid

García Delgado J L (1987) La industrialización y el desarrollo económico de España durante el franquismo. In Nadal et al (1987)

García Fernández J (1965) *La Emigración Exterior de España*. Barcelona

González M-J (1979) *La economía política del franquismo 1940–70: dirigismo. Mercado y planificación*. Madrid

Grupo de Estudios de Historia Rural (1983) Notas sobre la producción agraria española 1891–1931. *Revista de Historia Económica* **1**(2): 185–252

Guardian 10 August (1990) The highway to the Spanish byways

Harrison J (1983) The inter-war depression and the Spanish economy. *Journal of European Economic History* **12**: 295–321

Harrison J (1989) The agrarian history of Spain 1800–1960. *Agricultural History Review* **37**: 180–7

International Bank for Reconstruction and Development (1963) *The Economic Development of Spain*. Baltimore, Md

Leal J L (1982) *Una Política Económica para España: lo Necesario y lo Posible Durante la Transición*. Madrid

Leal J L, Lequina J, Naredo J M, Tarrafeta L (1975) *La Agricultura en el Desarrollo Capitalista Español*. Madrid

Lieberman S (1982) *The Contemporary Spanish Economy: A Historical Perspective*. London

Martínez Serrano J A, Mas Ivars M, Paricio Torregrosa J, Pérez García F, Quesada Ibañez J, Reig Martínez E (1982) *Economía Española 1960–80: Crecimiento y Cambio Estructural*. Madrid

Merigó E (1982) Spain. In Boltho A (ed) *The European Economy: Growth and Crisis*. Oxford

Muñoz J, Roldán S, Serrano A (1978) *La Internacionalización del Capital en España 1959–75*. Madrid

Muns J (1986) *Historia de las Relaciones entre España y el Fondo Monetario Internacional 1958–82: Veinte Cinco Años de Economía Española*. Madrid

Nadal J, Carreras A, Sundriá C (eds) (1987) *La Economía Española en el Siglo xx: una Perspectiva Histórica*. Barcelona

Naharro J M (1960) El plan de Estabilización en la economía española. In Mayor P (ed) *La Economía en 1960*. Madrid

Naredo J M (1971) *La Evolución de la Agricultura en España: Desarrollo Capitalista y Crisis de las Formas de Producción Tradicionales*. Barcelona

Naredo J M (1988) Diez años de agricultura española. *Agricultura y Sociedad* **46**: 9–36

Navarro Rubio M (1976) La Batalla de la establilización. *Anales de la Real Academia de Ciancias Morales y Políticas* **53**: 173–202

Organisation de Coopération et de Développement Economiques (1962) *Le Tourisme dans les Pays de l'OCDE*. Paris

Payne S (1986) *The Franco Regime 1936–75*. Madison, Wis.

Rogers T E (1957) *Economic and Commercial Conditions in Spain*. London

Rojo LA (1987) La Crisis de la Economía Española 1973–84. In Nadal et al (1987)

Román M (1971) *The Limits of Economic Growth in Spain*. New York

Ros Hombravella J (1979) *Política Económica Española 1959–73*. Barcelona

Rubio J (1974) *La Emigración Española a Francia*. Barcelona

Rubio Jiménez M (1968) El Plan de Establilización de 1959. *Moneda y Crédito* **105**: 3–38

Sampedro J L (1967) Le Plan de développement espagnol dans son cadre social, in L'Espagne a l'heure du développement. *Revue Tiers Monde* **8**: 1,033–41

Sausse O L (1957) Algunos aspectos de los programas de cooperación económica hispano-americanos. *Revista de Economía Política* **8**: 35–45

Schneidman J (1973) *Spain and Franco 1949–59: Facts on File*. New York

Schwartz P, González M-J (1978) *Una Historia del Instituto Nacional de Industria 1941–76*. Madrid

Servicio de Estudios del Banco de España (1934) *Ritmo de la Crisis Económica Española en Řelación con la Mundial.* Madrid

Shearer E B (1959) Significado para España de la ayuda económica norteamericana. *Revista de Economía Política* **10**: 989–1006

Suanzes J A (1963) Franco y la economía. In *Ocho Discursos.* Madrid, pp 121–51

Sudrià C (1987) Un factor determinante: la energía. In Nadal et al (1987)

Tedde P (1986) Economía y franquismo: a propósito de una biografía. *Revista de Historia Económica* **4**: 627–37

Torres M de (1956) *Juicio de la Actual Política Económica Española.* Madrid

Tortella G (1984) La agricultura an la economía de la España contemporánea 1830–1930. *Papeles de Economía Española* **20**: 62–75

Tortella G (1986) Sobre el significado histórico del franquismo. *Revista de Occidente* **59**: 104–14

Tusell J (1988) *La Dictadura de Franco.* Madrid

Varela Pareche F, Rodríguez de Pablo J (1974) Las inversiones extranjeras en España: 1959–74: una vía de desarrollo. *Información Comercial Española* **493**: 13–20

Velasco C (1984) El 'ingenierismo' como directriz básica de la política económica durante la autarquía 1936–51. *Información Comercial Española* **606**: 97–106

Viñas A (1981) *Los Pactos Secretos de Franco con Estados Unidos: Bases, Ayuda Económica, Recortes de Soberanía.* Barcelona

Viñas A (1982) La primera ayuda económica norteamericana a España. In *Lecturas de Economía Española: 50 Aniversario del Cuerpo de Téchnicos Oficiales del Estado.* Madrid, pp 49–90

Viñas A (1984) *Guerra, Dinero, Dictadura: Ayuda Fascista y Autarquía en la España de Franco.* Barcelona

Viñas A, Viñuela J, Eguidazu F, Pulgar C F, Florensa S (1979) *Política Exterior de España 1931–75.* Madrid, 2 vols

Walker J (1949) *Economic and Commercial Conditions in Spain.* London

Whitaker A P (1961) *Spain and Defense of the West: Ally and Liability.* New York

CHAPTER 9

Hungary

PAUL G HARE

Introduction

At least since the days of the Austro-Hungarian Empire, Hungary has regarded itself as part of the West. This conviction was not shaken by four decades in the Soviet bloc, which involved the nationalisation of most productive activity, the establishment of a central planning system, and largely unsuccessful and ineffective efforts to integrate eastwards. Under the Soviet-type economic system, Hungary did develop quite rapidly and, from the late 1950s, living standards rose steadily. But growth was slowing down by the late 1960s, Hungary's technology in many branches lagged increasingly behind the best Western levels, and by the 1980s the country was facing severe crisis, both political and economic. Eventually, it became clear that the only way out of the crisis required the end of communist rule, with a commitment to transform the country's ailing economy into a market-type system. Against this background, the consistency of Hungary's international stance was clearly signalled by the new, non-communist government, elected in 1990, which was quick to announce its intention to seek membership of the European Community for Hungary.

Unfortunately, the legacy of communist rule cannot be undone rapidly, or without pain. For the whole structure of the economy is still very much geared to central planning, despite some major economic reforms introduced in stages since the late 1960s. Much of the economy is oriented towards the Soviet market, and relatively few productive branches can yet be regarded as competitive in Western markets. Moreover, the country is carrying a tremendous burden of hard-currency debt accumulated during the 1970s and 1980s. As Hungary begins the transition to a market-based economic system, it also faces severe domestic problems of inflationary pressure and unemployment.

This chapter starts by providing some basic facts about the Hungarian economy, about the main growth trends experienced in recent decades, as well as in relation to the economic structure as it has developed over the post-war period. The next two sections examine in some detail a range of important domestic and international issues facing the Hungarian economy and make reference to various stages of Hungary's economic reforms. The story is then brought up to date, and looks ahead to some extent, by focusing on the most significant features of Hungary's transition to a market economy. These include tax reform; extensive liberalisation of trade, prices and production; privatisation; convertibility of the forint; as well as several other important, though perhaps less critical, policy domains. The concluding section provides a short overview of the main findings, and briefly assesses Hungary's prospects for the 1990s.

Economic structure and trends

By the mid-1980s Hungary was a medium-developed country which had attained a per capita GNP of just over $5,700 (in 1980 international prices – UN International Comparisons Project). In 1950 the corresponding figure had been $2,208 (UN ICP) so that over the whole thirty-five-year period Hungary's per capita GNP grew at an annual rate of 2.78 per cent. Since the country's population grew by only 13.8 per cent between 1950 and 1985, this implies an average annual growth rate for total GNP of just 3.06 per cent. By comparison with most OECD countries, or with the more successful developing countries, this is not especially impressive. However, there has been, within the overall average, substantial variation in the growth rate between different periods, but with a strong overall tendency for it to decline as we approach the present, as shown in Table 9.1

The table also reveals that ICP data and the official Hungarian figures differ

Table 9.1 Growth rate[a] of GDP and its expenditure components

Component period	GDP (ICP)	GDP (H)	Consumption (household)	Public cons.	Investment	Exp.	Imp.
1950–60	4.54	5.88	5.43	3.62	9.67	11.9	10.2
1960–5	4.01	4.42	3.31	6.85	5.20	9.30	11.5
1965–70	2.97	6.28	5.72	5.68	9.33	10.5	8.96
1970–5	3.31	6.42	5.11	5.96	6.29	7.28	9.41
1975–80	2.06	3.68	2.71	4.33	1.74	3.94	7.04
1980–5	0.75	1.76	1.39	2.14	−3.38	1.03	4.89
1985–9	—	1.30	0.5	0.8	2.29	1.43	1.99
1990[b]	—	−4.0	—	—	−8.0	—	—

Notes:
[a] All growth rates are computed at constant prices relevant to the period or sub-period concerned
[b] Estimated

Sources:
Column 1: International Comparisons Project (Western GDP concept)
Columns 2–7: *Népgazdasági Mérlegek 1949–1987*, Központi Statisztikai Hivatal, Budapest, 1989; *Statisztikai Évkönyv*, various years, Központi Statisztikai Hivatal, Budapest; *Iparstatisztikai Évkönyv*, various years, Központi Statisztikai Hivatal, Budapest. (CMEA concept of national income for 1950–60; Western GDP thereafter; trade data based on volume indexes)
Last row: *Konjunkturajelentes 1990/3*, Kopint-Dátorg, Budapest, 1990 (provisional data, based on January–July)

substantially, especially for the 1960s. Given that the former are based on a methodology common to the large number of countries included in the ICP, it is a pity that the more detailed data required for this study are available only from Hungarian sources. Despite some differences of methodology, however, it is probably the case that Hungarian data do, for the most part, indicate the real trends, and also give a reasonable picture of shares and proportions. Accordingly, we use these data both to complete Table 9.1 and in the subsequent tables. It is perhaps worth adding here that although the differences between ICP and Hungarian data are, indeed, rather large, a detailed study of East European GDP statistics found that, both methodologically and in terms of the systems of data collection and processing being used, Hungarian data should be considered the most satisfactory in the region (Marer 1985). There remain, nevertheless, large differences between alternative GDP figures for all the East European countries, including Hungary, which I imagine will be removed only as they adopt Western conventions and procedures, and remove the grossest distortions in their tax and price systems.

Turning to the individual components of national income, we note that while all show considerable growth over the period being studied, the patterns of growth are very different for each component. Public consumption, which is in any case a relatively small component (as shown in Table 9.2), shows the steadiest and most consistent pattern, usually growing at a rate very close to that of GDP as a whole and therefore maintaining a roughly constant share of GDP. Household consumption exhibits a broadly similar pattern, though, especially in the 1950s, consumption growth was sustained only because of fluctuations in other variables: thus within that decade, public consumption initially grew very sharply, only to be cut back by two-thirds in the mid-1950s, and net investment also collapsed in the crisis year of 1956. Thereafter, the communist government displayed a strong commitment to maintaining the growth of living standards, as part of its tacit *modus vivendi* with the Hungarian population.[1] In order to sustain this commitment through the 1980s, the government was obliged, eventually, to allow investment to fall substantially to release the necessary resources. By the end of the 1980s it was no longer possible to maintain the crumbling façade of steady economic progress and steady improvement in living conditions, as a period of economic stagnation gave way to actual decline.

In the early 1950s investment grew at enormous rates as Hungary's socialist industrialisation on the Stalinist model got under way, only to collapse briefly in the mid-1950s before resuming growth. From the mid-1960s until the mid-1970s there was a decade of very rapid investment growth, followed by stagnation and decline. Rapid growth in investment was intended to lay the foundations for a significant technological upgrading of the economy, and with an increasing emphasis on export-oriented development. Much of the new investment was organised around a number of so-called central development programmes. As we shall see in later sections, the effort was only partially successful.

The trade data in Table 9.1 need careful interpretation because on an initial inspection they appear to show reasonably strong performance, with imports usually growing substantially more slowly than exports, exports generally growing faster than GDP (as in most small open economies in the post-war period), and apparently implying an increasing trade surplus. But the reality behind the figures is, unfortunately, much less satisfactory. (A fuller picture of Hungary's trade performance, distinguishing between dollar and rouble trade, is provided in Table 9.4, which we discuss below.) What emerges strikingly from Table 9.1 though, is the close correlation of the trends exhibited with the accumulation of a truly enormous hard-currency debt by Hungary. Within each sub-period, the growth rates in the table are based on constant prices; but of course the prices change between periods. And what has happened over the last few decades is that Hungary's terms of trade have gradually deteriorated, so that increasing amounts of goods have had to be exported to pay for any given volume of imports. Part of the deterioration can be explained by exogenous shocks, notably the increases in world oil prices in 1973 and 1979 (Hungary's response to these shocks was very weak, as we note in later sections). But much of it simply reflects the performance of an economy which is failing to compete in world markets. Despite all the reforms, Hungary was simply not improving its economic performance fast enough to keep pace with its principal trade partners and competitors.

How was this pattern of development reflected in the structure of the economy? Table 9.2 presents some data on the shares of the main components of expenditure in GDP, as well as the most important components of output (measured in value-added terms, of course), while Table 9.3 contains further data on growth rates according to a detailed sectoral breakdown of the economy, but this time only for the period since 1970.

On the expenditure side, Table 9.2 reveals no major surprises. As investment rose in the early years, its share of national income also rose *pari passu* with the declining share of household consumption. Conversely, the government's commitment to

Table 9.2 Expenditure and output shares in GDP (selected years)[a]

Component	1950	1960	1970	1980	1985	1989
Expenditure						
Consumption (household)	62.9	65.9	58.4	61.2	62.8	59.7
Consumption (public)	12.4	8.5	10.3	10.3	10.1	10.8
Investment	22.6	27.8	33.6	30.7	25.0	26.1
Trade balance (X–M)	2.1	−2.2	−2.3	−2.2	2.1	3.4
Output						
Industry	48.3	50.0	37.1	33.8	34.0	30.3
Construction	6.7	6.9	8.1	7.4	7.2	5.7
Agriculture	25.2	22.7	18.2	17.1	16.1	17.9
Other material branches	19.7[b]	6.0	21.0	18.9	19.2	18.9
Services, etc.	—	11.6	11.6	12.3	13.6	13.8
Balance of indirect taxes[c]	—	2.9	4.0	10.5	9.9	14.0

Notes:
[a] All figures are expressed as a per cent of GDP in year shown
[b] Including material services; columns may not sum to 100% due to rounding
[c] This is the aggregate difference between indirect taxes and subsidies on consumption and production

Sources: As for Table 9.1; 1950: based on CMEA concept of national income (ie excl. non-material services); other years: based on usual Western GDP concept

Table 9.3 Growth rates of national income by sector[a]

Branch	1970–5	1975–80	1980–5	1985–8[b]
Industry				
Mining	2.75	−0.85	−3.36	−1.42
Electricity	7.59	8.64	−0.48	2.20
Metallurgy	4.70	1.54	−5.07	2.67
Engineering	9.27	4.91	5.49	2.80
Building materials	5.32	5.46	1.64	3.60
Chemicals	11.60	6.44	6.38	2.92
Light industry	6.61	2.94	3.83	1.40
Food industry	5.81	4.74	−0.11	0.63
Industry – total (incl. other)	7.53	4.41	2.36	1.91
Construction	6.56	3.20	−1.37	0.37
Agriculture	3.26	1.97	3.00	1.95
Transport and communications	5.34	2.90	1.60	—
Trade	8.15	2.73	1.47	—
Water supply	4.65	4.61	1.17	—
Other services	5.51	4.18	3.21	—
Economy – total	6.25	3.55	2.24	1.75

Notes:
[a] Data for years prior to 1970 are not available in the same form; all figures represent growth rates per annum, at constant prices
[b] Based on gross output rather than value added

Sources: As for Table 9.1

consumption and its willingness to tolerate a decline in investment, reversed these trends in more recent years. As a result, contemporary expenditure shares, at least in terms of the broad aggregates, are not greatly different from what they were in 1950. However, this is evidently not the case for output shares, as the second part of Table 9.2 indicates. After a short-lived rise, corresponding to the push for industrialisation in the 1950s, the share of industry has now declined to the low 30s in percentage terms, not greatly out of line with what might be expected in a country with Hungary's level of development. Agriculture's share has steadily declined over the period as a whole, again as one would expect, though there is clearly room for further decline as productivity improves. Services, on the other hand (which includes part of 'other material branches') has not increased its share very much since 1970.

Turning to Table 9.3 it is immediately apparent that, within industry, chemicals has been the leading sector for most of the 1970s and 1980s. In contrast, mining has been in decline since 1975, largely because of the poor quality and high cost of Hungary's resources (other than bauxite) rather than because of the wider economic problems facing the country. By the 1980s several important branches were in decline, including metallurgy, the food industry and, outside industry, the construction sector (this last simply reflecting the decline in investment).

Table 9.4 Foreign trade in the main markets[a]

| Year | Dollar trade[b] | | | Rouble trade[c] | | |
	Imports	Exports	Balance	Imports	Exports	Balance
1970	57.9	52.2	−5.7	55.3	51.9	−3.4
1975	122.2	97.2	−25.0	115.1	101.4	−13.7
1970–9	111.6	93.9	−17.7	96.0	91.9	−4.1
(ann. av.)						
1980	163.5	160.2	−3.3	136.4	120.8	−15.6
1981	170.6	167.8	−2.8	143.7	131.6	−12.1
1982	166.2	183.1	16.9	158.6	141.4	−17.2
1983	191.1	214.0	22.9	173.9	160.1	−13.8
1984	207.7	236.9	29.2	182.8	177.1	−5.7
1985	217.2	222.9	5.7	193.0	201.7	−8.7
1986	226.4	206.0	−20.4	213.3	214.3	1.0
1987	253.2	235.8	−17.4	209.9	214.4	4.5
1988	268.9	296.2	27.3	203.5	207.9	4.4
1989	322.7	355.4	32.7	200.8	215.9	15.1

Notes:

[a] Figures represent trade in current prices in billions of forints

[b] Dollar trade refers to trade conducted in convertible currencies, mainly with Western countries and developing countries; however, some trade with CMEA member states was conducted in convertible currencies too (see text)

[c] Rouble trade covers the bulk of trade between CMEA member states, conducted in the so-called transferable rouble

Source: *Statisztikai Évkönyv*, various years

Table 9.4 traces the development of Hungary's trade in dollars and transferable roubles since 1970, while Table 9.5 shows the structure of trade by country and main product group in 1988 (this year being chosen to show a recent year, prior to the major changes going on since 1989). Table 9.6 presents some data on the evolution and current burden of Hungary's hard-currency (dollar) debt.

Since Table 9.4 refers only to the trade balance (but after taking proper account of insurance, transport, etc), it cannot give a complete picture of even the current balance of payments. Until very recently, for instance, the dollar results were improved each year by a significant surplus on the tourism account, though in 1989, a year when foreign travel and control over hard currency available to the population were both eased, a deficit was recorded here. In 1990, with a tighter regime in force again, a renewed surplus was likely. Nevertheless, for much of the 1970s and the start of the 1980s, dollar trade deficits were recorded, and while restrictive domestic policies led to better trade results in the 1980s, surpluses were insufficient to service and amortise the already accumulated debt: hence the debt went on rising through the 1980s, as shown in Table 9.6. On the other hand, rising hard currency exports since 1986 have led to a significant decline in the debt-service ratio.

Table 9.5   Trade structure in 1988, by product and partner (%)

Item/Trade direction	Imports	Exports
Product groups		
Energy	13.1	2.4
Raw and basic materials	13.4	8.0
Semi-finished goods	25.5	19.4
Spare parts	12.0	6.6
Machinery and other inv. goods	16.8	26.9
Industrial consumer goods	11.7	15.9
Agricultural products	2.3	7.5
Food Industry products	5.2	13.2
Total	100.0	100.0
Partners		
Europe	86.3	83.3
of which		
EC	26.0	22.6
(W Germany	13.9	10.9)
CMEA 6	18.7	17.0
(E Germany	6.4	5.3)
Soviet Union	25.0	27.6
Asia	6.5	9.4
Africa	1.4	2.5
The Americas	5.6	4.5
of which		
USA	2.2	2.9
Australia and Oceania	0.2	0.2
Total	100.0	100.0

Source: Statisztikai Évkönyv 1988

In the rouble account, trade deficits are recorded for most years, but substantial surpluses on the tourism account have enabled Hungary to avoid accumulating a significant debt in that direction; indeed by the end of the 1980s Hungary had accumulated an unwanted rouble surplus of around Rb 1 billion. With the collapse of the CMEA, and the conversion to hard currency trading from 1 January 1991, Hungary has had to enter into negotiations with the Soviet Union to convert this surplus to an 'equivalent' dollar balance. It has been reported that Hungary will be credited with about $920 million as a result of this, a better outcome than might have been expected. On the other hand, the Soviet Union wishes to spread the payment over several years while Hungary would prefer to receive it in 1991; negotiations are continuing on this issue at the time of writing (March 1991).

It is worth adding here, though we do not report in a separate table, that Hungarian trade data are published both according to countries of origin (imports) and destination (exports), the main distinctions here being between socialist and non-socialist

Table 9.6 Hungary's international debt

Year	Gross debt ($bn)	% Official (incl. IMF and IBRD)	Debt-service ratio	Reserves as % of imports
1981	8.70	6	42	20
1982	7.95	9	37	18
1983	8.25	21	36	33
1984	8.84	24	45	41
1985	11.74	24	58	54
1986	15.09	21	67	47
1987	17.73	20	52	30
1988	17.31	18	57	27
1989	20.6	18	49	20
1990 (prov.)	21.7	—	65	28

Note: The debt-service ratio is defined as the total interest and amortisation liability on medium- and long-term debt in the given year, expressed as a percentage of that year's export earnings

Source: *Financial market trends* **45**: OECD, Paris 1990

countries; and according to the currency employed in the transactions concerned, giving rise to the dollar and rouble accounts as reported in Table 9.4. In practice, these classifications cut across each other, since some socialist country trade has been conducted in dollars (and a small amount of developing country trade has been conducted in transferable roubles). To illustrate the orders of magnitude involved, about 11 per cent of dollar imports in 1988 were from socialist countries, while about 16 per cent of dollar exports was delivered to socialist partners. From 1991, of course, all trade will be conducted in convertible currencies.

Turning to employment and incomes, we display the evolution of Hungary's employment structure since 1950 in Table 9.7, while Table 9.8 shows the development of nominal wages, consumer prices and real incomes over the same period. The striking feature of Table 9.7 is the rapid increase in the share of the labour force working in industry, and the even sharper decline in the share employed in agriculture. However, even by the end of our period of study, the latter remains very high compared to the most developed Western economies. From Table 9.8 it is apparent that real incomes grew rapidly for two decades, from the mid-1950s to the mid-1970s. But recent growth has been far slower, and recent years have been characterised by a marked stagnation of real incomes.

Domestic issues

As we saw in the last section, the 1980s can be characterised as a period of economic stagnation for Hungary. Nevertheless in terms of economic reform the period was far from static, with many new measures being introduced, including some important institutional changes. Although not on the whole immediately successful, these

Table 9.7 Employment and employment structure in Hungary

Year	Total labour force (millions)	% employed in			
		Industry	Agriculture	Construction	Other
1950	4.107	19.4	52.0	3.1	25.5
1955	4.470	24.9	43.7	4.8	26.6
1960	4.735	28.4	38.7	5.6	27.3
1965	4.649	34.3	28.7	6.0	31.0
1970	4.980	35.9	25.2	7.3	31.6
1975	5.086	35.6	21.3	8.2	34.9
1980	5.074	33.5	20.5	8.0	38.0
1985	4.913	31.3	21.1	7.3	40.3
1986	4.892	31.4	20.2	7.1	41.3
1987	4.885	31.2	19.3	7.0	42.5
1988	4.845	30.9	18.8	7.1	43.2
1989	4.823	30.4	18.4	7.0	44.2

Source: *Statisztikai Évkönyv 1989*

Table 9.8 Wages, consumer prices and real incomes

Year	Average wage (nominal, fts)	Consumer price index	Real income per capita
1950	683	100	100
1955	1,141	159	115
1960	1,575	161	154
1965	1,766	165	181
1970	2,139	173	245
1975	2,881	199	306
1980	4,014	270	333
1985	5,866	374	360
1986	6,291	394	369
1987	6,808	428	372
1988	8,817[a]	496	367
1989	10,018[a]	581	376

Note: [a] These figures are affected by the introduction of personal income taxation in Hungary in 1988

Source: *Statisztikai Évkönyv 1989*

developments have undoubtedly put Hungary into a better position to manage its transition to the market than most of its Eastern European companions. Moreover, the Hungarians built on a reform process that began in a serious way in 1968 (and even earlier in agriculture: see Swain 1985), with the introduction of the so-called New Economic Mechanism (Hare et al 1981; Marer 1986a). Very importantly, the whole experience of reforms during the 1970s and 1980s served to convince the Hungarians of two things: first, that partial economic reforms, however apparently radical, could not succeed without fundamental changes in the role, structure and functioning of the central agencies of economic management; and second, that a market-type economy could be created only in a new political environment.

In the 1960s almost every country in Eastern Europe (including the Soviet Union) introduced economic reforms (Hare 1987). Some of these reform attempts were relatively cautious, extending only as far as simplifying the plan indicator system, forming groups of enterprises into associations, or reforming prices to remove the most glaring irrationalities. Others, like the 1968 reforms introduced in Czechoslovakia and Hungary, were rather more ambitious and radical. Both of these latter two reform programmes started in similar ways, by abandoning the traditional practice of breaking down detailed annual plans to enterprise level. They shared many other features but, unfortunately, the Czechoslovak programme was brought to an abrupt halt (and soon partly reversed) by the Soviet (formally Warsaw Pact) invasion of the country, which headed off a process of democratic political reform and reinstated a more traditional, hard-line Communist leadership (on the comparison between Czechoslovak and Hungarian economic reforms and associated political developments, see Batt 1988). Thus Hungary was left as the only country of the Soviet bloc with an operational programme of radical reform.

Aside from ending plan breakdown to enterprise level, the Hungarian reforms of 1968 were radical in several other respects. They introduced profits as the sole success indicator for enterprises, reinforcing its pivotal role with a profits tax – previously, profits above the planned level had normally been paid into the state budget (directly, or via the relevant branch ministry), implying an effective marginal tax rate on profits of 100 per cent. In addition, there was a price reform accompanied by a significant but far from complete liberalisation of price formation (Hare 1976); a partial decentralisation of investment decisions and the system of allocating credit (Hare 1981); extensive reforms of foreign trade (at least in the hard-currency, mainly Western markets), with important steps towards a unified exchange rate and an increasing number of organisations and enterprises in Hungary granted independent foreign trading rights (Marer 1981; 1986b); and a number of lesser measures, including some relaxation of controls over the labour market. The whole set of financial and fiscal instruments through which economic policy was to be exercised was referred to as the system of economic regulators.

At the time of its introduction, the New Economic Mechanism represented a real breakthrough in reform thinking, in that it explicitly recognised the inadequacy of earlier, partial reforms and was introduced all at once rather than step by step (Friss 1969). At the same time, there were clearly some major compromises involved in securing the political acceptance of such a reform package. Over time, these compromises turned out to be so diluting that the main thrust of the reforms, namely to encourage Hungarian enterprises in all branches of the economy to be active participants in their respective markets and to respond to market signals as one would expect in a Western economy, was undermined.

The main compromises were as follows. First, although staffing levels in the ministries and other central institutions were cut, the basic structure of the top levels of the system of economic administration remained intact. Hence most of the large state enterprises could feel that their security was not seriously threatened by the reforms. Second, while the tax system was supposed to become more uniform, numerous special taxes or subsidies were imposed (or allowed to stay, if they were already in place) both on domestic production and on imports and exports, to avoid either forcing many enterprises into rapid bankruptcy or disrupting established transactions. These so-called 'financial bridges' were intended to be temporary, but skilful lobbying and political pressure ensured not only their survival, but also their gradual proliferation. Third, the leading role of the Communist Party (Hungarian Socialist Workers' Party – HSWP) was not challenged, at least not openly, and the party continued to operate in every significant production unit.

Conceptually, the reform also made some serious mistakes, though this was far from apparent at the time. For around 1968 most observers, both inside and outside Hungary, were so impressed by the efforts to decentralise control over so many areas of economic life, breaking down some of the worst features of the Stalinist system, that they failed to see, or attach much significance to, certain omissions from the reforms. Not only that, but also in so far as there was an accepted theory of reforms, it seemed to imply that the Hungarian type of economic decentralisation should be sufficient to bring about a sustained improvement in economic performance.

As is clear from the above summary, the 1968 reforms concentrated attention on product markets, having relatively little to say about the labour market and virtually nothing about the capital market. Indeed, despite increased opportunities for enterprise-level initiatives in the investment area it was envisaged that the centre would retain substantial influence over the structure and direction of investment. The idea was that firms could concentrate on current production, while higher levels of the system would be more concerned with investment. But such a neat division of labour was doomed to failure, essentially because enterprises' need for resources controlled by the centre in the area of investment (credit, foreign exchange, technology licences, and so on) made them unavoidably dependent in other areas too.[2] This was the first mistake.

The second was the lack of provision for new entry in most branches, while the third mistake was the failure to put pressure on existing firms to improve their profitability, since there were no adequate procedures for bankruptcy or enterprise reorganisation before the mid-1980s, and in any case the government was completely unprepared to contemplate any major business failure. The final 'mistake', though in this instance an unavoidable one because of the prevailing international political environment within which Hungary had to operate, was the attempt to work with two foreign trade systems based on completely different principles – the CMEA system, dealing in the so-called transferable rouble, and the system operational with most other countries, dealing in US dollars or some other convertible (hard) currency (see pp. 227–31).

The net effects of all this were that enterprises continued to be highly dependent on, and protected by the central agencies; that much of the old planning system survived in order to deal with Hungary's CMEA links; that many firms had to reconcile CMEA trade controlled by state orders with more market-oriented trade with the West; and that those factors facilitating structural and organisational change, such as easy entry into and exit from various markets and activities, were almost completely lacking. Moreover most of these points, although initially suggested by a re-examination of the 1968 reforms in the light of Hungary's subsequent development experience, remained valid right up to the end of the 1980s, despite further stages of economic reform during that decade.

That the reforms did bring some worthwhile benefits to Hungary, whatever their shortcomings, hardly needs saying. For the most part, these benefits took the form of improved flexibility and better product mix, with smaller or less persistent shortages in many markets.[3] Since the late 1970s, serious shortage of everyday commodities has been quite unusual in Hungary, in contrast to the situation elsewhere in the region. Only certain durable items like telephones (requiring large infrastructural investments), cars and housing were subject to continuing and substantial unsatisfied demand. On the other hand, shortages of materials or problems with quality of components continued to be endemic at intra-industry level. Aside from the general improvement in market equilibrium (especially in consumer markets), there was a noticeable improvement in Hungary's growth rate, though this did not last.

It was implied above that the 'theory of reform' prevalent in 1968 turned out to be wrong. Explicitly or implicitly, this theory was based on Western theories of economic equilibrium according to which efficient resource allocation requires a reasonably rational price system (implying at least the removal of major distortions) with respect to which enterprises are encouraged to maximise profits. However, both practical experience in Hungary and other countries, and concrete calculations using general equilibrium models of Hungary (Zalai et al 1989; Hare et al 1990) indicate that the gains from improving the *static* allocation of resources are actually rather small (though they are certainly positive, of course).

Indeed, according to Murrell (1990), one cannot really claim that the socialist countries have been especially inefficient in this static sense, given their resource endowments of labour and capital at any given time. In his view, what really matters is the set of factors which stimulate better economic performance over time, which improve the *dynamic* allocation. Murrell argues that these have been non-existent or at best very weak, and that even the most radical reforms of the 1960s did little to address this weakness. So what are these dynamic factors? Essentially, they have to do with organisational change, based on a Schumpeterian view of the economy. For dynamic efficiency, it is critical for an economy to have effective procedures and arrangements both for closing down or reorganising inefficient production units (e.g. persistent loss-makers), as well as for expanding the most effective units and starting up new ones. In all these areas, Hungary has had a very poor record, right up to the end of the 1980s (as we noted above). This is a point we shall return to later when we consider the prospects for successful reforms in the early 1990s.

Although Hungary's 1968 reform package started well, it was already being undermined by new centralising tendencies by the early 1970s. This change arose partly for domestic reasons, stimulated by perceptions of widening income differentials resulting from the reforms (as, of course, was to be expected – but this did not make it any more welcome to conservatively inclined political leaders); and partly as a reaction to the more hostile international situation which followed the suppression of economic reforms and political dissent in Hungary's neighbour, Czechoslovakia. Concretely, in

1971 about fifty of Hungary's largest enterprises were placed under what was euphemistically described as 'closer state supervision', while central control over prices, wages, investment and so on was tightened. This was directly contrary to the original reform intentions, which had envisaged a gradual liberalisation in all these areas.

Rather than extending the reforms, Hungary's political leaders in effect opted for a strategy of accelerated growth based on high rates of investment, involving substantial inflows of Western capital to finance the expansion. In the event (as we saw on pp. 214–17) this strategy succeeded to the extent that growth rates did hold up well in the 1970s. However, very large hard-currency debts had been accumulated by the end of the 1970s, and these could not be serviced in the absence of the expected expansion of Western exports. Consequently, domestic policy had to shift over to a more restrictive mode, damping down demand in order to restrain imports. (Much more will be said about this critical issue in the next section.)

The strategy of pursuing growth as a substitute for reform was very like that followed in Poland over the same period (though with less disastrous effects than in the latter case). In both countries the politicians appear to have seen radical reforms – quite correctly – as a threat to their entrenched positions in the ruling hierarchy, and also perceived that Soviet attitudes were no longer so tolerant as they had been in the late 1960s. In contrast, their alternative of engineering an investment boom to promote faster growth required no major changes in the economy's institutional arrangements and, through use of external finance, could be done in such a way that consumption and living standards continued to rise steadily. Thus it is easy to understand the attractions of this approach, ironically made even easier (albeit less advisable) by the First Oil Crisis of 1973 (following the Arab–Israeli war of that year) which flooded Western financial markets with 'petro-dollars' looking for somewhere to invest.

By the end of the 1970s it was increasingly evident that the strategy was a failure, not least because the hard-currency debt was becoming unmanageable, exports were not expanding as had been hoped, and growth of total output was proving ever harder to sustain. Politically, the result was to strengthen the hand of the reformers, who were able to revive Hungary's reform programme and give it some new impetus, starting in 1979 and continuing through the 1980s. Although this second attempt at radical reform did not take the form of a single, comprehensive package, an important lesson had been learned from the shortcomings of the 1968 measures, namely the need to include *institutional change* as a central element in any new reforms. Accordingly, from 1979 onwards, there was a steady stream of institutional measures, as well as some significant changes in the original set of economic regulators. Interestingly, although almost all the new measures can be seen as sensible steps in a process of transition towards a market-type economy, their net effect by the end of the 1980s had been disappointingly modest, for reasons that we come to later on. Nevertheless, the foundations have been laid for a much faster transition in the 1990s.

The second wave of reform began with some rearrangment of functions among the central management bodies, the merger of three branch ministries to form a single Ministry of Industry, some attempts to break up certain trusts and large enterprises into their constituent parts, and new legislation to make possible a wide range of forms of small businesses (Hare 1983). These forms included small enterprises (essentially, state firms that would not be subject to all the rules applying to larger firms), small co-operatives, several types of economic working group (often used by groups of workers within existing state firms to escape state wage controls), as well as associations and partnerships. Most importantly, while for the more standard state enterprises it was still the relevant minister who had to approve the formation of a new unit, for these small economic units approvals could be given at lower levels of the system and were virtually automatic (unless the proposed activity was already illegal). Similarly, in the case of closures, the minister had to approve such a decision for the traditional types of economic unit (and this was done very rarely indeed), while for the new ones it was made clear that there would be no subsidies to cover losses and no restrictions on closures. Hence at least for this sector of the economy, there was a reasonable likelihood that competitive conditions would obtain.

From the point of view of getting people accustomed to the disciplines of a market-type economy, this was a very useful step, though most probably all that Hungary's leaders had in mind at that time was to enhance the general flexibility of the economy. It is doubtful whether they saw these measures as a significant step towards the overthrow of the socialist system in Hungary, for otherwise they would surely never have accepted them in the first place.

Subsequently during the 1980s there were further institutional reforms at every level. The most notable measures were the creation of a bond market in 1982 to trade bonds issued both to individuals and to other firms; a banking reform (which split the National Bank into a conventional central bank and five new commercial banks); a price reform promulgated under the banner of so-called competitive pricing, which sought to retain central controls over prices while simulating the world market at least for firms engaging in hard-currency trade; the introduction of bankruptcy and liquidation procedures in 1986; and the formation of enterprise councils, to devolve management away from ministerial control. In addition, in 1988 Hungary implemented a major tax reform to make the country's tax system conform more closely to Western patterns: VAT and personal income tax systems were introduced simultaneously, and some of the earlier very differentiated taxes were discontinued or reduced in scope (for details of these measures, see Hare 1990; Newbery 1990). Finally, towards the end of the 1980s and despite the very difficult balance-of-payments position, there were gradual moves to liberalise both prices and imports.

From the point of view of preparing the ground for a market-type economy (whether wittingly or not), those aspects of Hungary's reforms which have been most important relate to the development of agriculture, and the promotion (or, at times, merely the toleration) of various forms of small business, including a wide range of so-called second-economy activities. We conclude this section with some remarks on each of these topics.

Agriculture is important for several reasons. First, it is the principal source of the country's food supply, particularly significant in societies like Hungary which have industrialised only relatively recently. Given Hungary's tight balance-of-payments constraint, it is reassuring for both government and population that virtually no food has to be imported, other than luxuries like tropical fruits that cannot be produced domestically. Second, by being flexible about the use and size of private plots, and about the management and organisation of the collective farms themselves, Hungary has brought about a situation in which modern methods of farming could be applied successfully throughout the country (Swain 1985). Thus agriculture was the first sector in which traditional planning was abandoned in Hungary, and the good results achieved were often cited as a reason for extending reforms more widely.

Third, the symbiosis between private and collective production has resulted in stable supplies of a good range of foodstuffs, distributed reasonably competently through private and state-owned markets and shops. This legacy will prove a great strength of the economy in the 1990s, since even when real incomes decline in the early stages of the transition to a fully fledged market economy, the population's food supplies will not be at risk. One may contrast this favourable position with the sorry state of Soviet agriculture and food distribution, which is already proving to be a major impediment on the road to serious reforms.

Growth of small business and the second economy has been particularly significant in agriculture (as implied above), as well as in services to the population and parts of the construction industry (Galasi and Szirácki 1985); it has, however, also played a part in industry, though never providing more than 2 or 3 per cent of total output from that sector. Aside from contributing to the overall flexibility of the economy and improving supply, especially of services, these activities (which in one form or another are practised by a substantial fraction of the population) have also helped to make people in Hungary aware of market behaviour and conscious of market disciplines. Contrary to the present position in several other East European countries, Hungarians have also, as a result of second economy/private activity, become accustomed to paying relatively high prices for services and some goods, and clearly prefer this to the alternatives of queueing or sheer unavailability. All these features will prove helpful in the coming transition to a fully developed market-type economy.

Hungary's external economic relations

As indicated earlier, Hungary's external economic relations in the post-1950 period have been dominated by the need to operate in two separate trading systems, namely the CMEA and the Western system. Hungary's trade performance has also been strongly influenced not only by its own efforts and policies, but also by the unexpectedly successful entry on to the world market of many developing countries, especially the so-called newly industrialising countries (NICs) like Taiwan, Hong Kong and Singapore. The external debt which Hungary has accumulated during the 1970s and 1980s is the result of a mixture of external shocks and domestic policy errors, as we shall see.

Within the CMEA, most trade in any given year was determined on the basis of government-to-government (usually bilateral) negotiations between the member states,[4] as part of the normal cycle of annual planning (Kaser 1967; see also Alan Smith, Chapter 6 in *The European Economy*, on integration in Eastern Europe). Given this starting-point in the planning process, with its emphasis on economy-wide material balances (Cave and Hare 1981), demand for imports from CMEA countries tended to be based partly on the previous year's demands (on the reasonable assumption that most transactions would stay the same or change only slowly) and partly on shortages revealed in the first round of material balancing. Similarly, the proposed supply of exports would depend partly on the previous year's deliveries, partly on surpluses identified in the material balancing process. Through detailed negotiations and several iterations, these imports and exports would have to be revised to achieve an approximate overall balance in financial terms (ie in terms of the transferable rouble). Once this was done, orders to enterprises to supply particular commodities to CMEA partners would be issued as part of the annual plan, and other enterprises would be ordered to receive the agreed quantities of imports and distribute them within Hungary.

As a set of procedures for organising international transactions, this system had several features that set it apart from the trading arrangements that are more usual in market-type economies. One of the key features of the CMEA system was that, within each member state, there was a state monopoly over foreign trade. The extent of this monopoly varied from country to country, in the sense that different numbers of organisations and enterprises were accorded independent trading rights. Even in Hungary, for instance, the 1968 reforms only decentralised trade to the extent of expanding the list of organisations with such rights. In none of the CMEA countries was it possible for all enterprises to arrange their own foreign trade deals directly with the relevant foreign partner. This was, moreover, the case not only in relation to CMEA trade, but also in respect to most Western trade. Since most CMEA trade was organised through intermediaries above enterprise level (state trading organisations, or the Ministry of Foreign Trade itself), with little or no enterprise-to-enterprise contact, it is not surprising that it was inflexible, unresponsive to changing needs and preferences, and highly inefficient.

The inefficiency was exacerbated by a second feature of these procedures – quite simply the absence of any serious concern for efficiency in the planning process outlined above. The question was usually one of balancing, rather than of efficiency, and in any case it is doubtful whether the information was available to the government negotiators to enable them to make judgements about efficiency in anything other than a very rough and ready way.

One reason for the lack of relevant information relates to a third feature of the CMEA's trade practice, namely the structure of prices employed (for a detailed account of this, see van Brabant 1989). This was always a problem for the CMEA countries because each member, including Hungary, knew that its own domestic price system was distorted in various ways and could not provide a sound basis for valuing international transactions. In practice, all that could be done was to make use of the prices prevailing in Western world markets, with suitable adjustments to eliminate fluctuations and 'monopolistic distortions'.[5] To fit in with the five-year planning cycles, CMEA trade prices were, up to the early 1970s, fixed for five-year periods, the prices for a given period depending on an average of world market prices over the preceding five-year period. However, following the First Oil Crisis of 1973, the CMEA went on to a system of annual price revisions, with each year's prices being based on an average of the preceding five years of world market prices. In both periods, of course, this approach to price determination provided at best a very rough guide, and there were many deviations from the 'rules'. Even so, it is apparent that in periods of rising world prices the Soviet Union, which was Eastern Europe's main source of oil and several other basic materials, effectively provided massive subsidies.

Fourth, an astonishing feature of CMEA trade was its almost exclusively bilateral character, scarcely more sophisticated than the most primitive barter. We have already seen that trade flows themselves were determined through bilateral negotiations between the governments concerned; it was also the case that balances with one trade partner could not usually be offset by any opposite-sign balance with another. Thus the transferable rouble was not really transferable at all. Hence, strictly speaking, Hungary had to deal not with two trade balances (one for hard currency trade, another for CMEA), but with several, including a separate balance with each CMEA partner. It is not easy to imagine a system more conducive to inefficiency.

The final point to make about the CMEA trading system concerns its impact on investment and longer-term efficiency. At times the CMEA did see itself as a promoter of economic co-ordination and co-operation within the region, this being taken to include technological collaboration, too. Thus within certain industries, such as vehicles and electronics, there were attempts to divide up production (and hence the required investments) among the member states: this is one factor which led to Hungary's dominance in the bus market, with the firm Ikarus as the principal supplier. On the other hand there were strong countervailing forces embedded in each country's national planning system which created pressures towards autarky. These pressures, together with the traditional Stalinist (over-)emphasis on heavy industry led to massive expansion of mining, steel production, engineering and related branches throughout the region, irrespective of local comparative advantage. Moreover, even where co-operation within the CMEA framework was agreed, it frequently failed to live up to expectations. Thus in the case of Hungary's buses, several important components should have been produced by other CMEA members. In the event quality was often unacceptably low, deliveries were late, or the partner country was simply unable to fulfil its side of the agreement. Such difficulties strengthened the tendency to 'go-it-alone', or encouraged Hungarian firms to seek Western partners who were technically more advanced, and usually proved to be more reliable partners.

The parallel development of very similar industrial structures in virtually all the CMEA member states (actually, not quite to the same extent in Hungary as elsewhere) had some interesting effects on trade patterns and payments within the CMEA. One such effect was the emergence of a distinction between so-called soft and hard commodities (see Alan Smith, Chapter 6 in *The European Economy*). The latter category included certain basic goods in whose production most of the socialist countries experienced persistent difficulties. Meat was one such commodity, and since Hungary's agriculture was far more successful than that of the other countries in the region it was able to benefit from this classification; certain consumer goods were also included, and again Hungary had an advantage. Essentially, the hard commodities were those which could be sold for hard (ie convertible) currency in Western markets. Increasingly, these commodities were sold for hard currency within the CMEA area, too. It was for this reason that, over time, a small but rising share of Hungary's CMEA trade, especially with the Soviet Union, came to be conducted in hard currencies.

Overall, Hungary's membership in the CMEA system undoubtedly led to the creation of large stocks of plant and equipment whose only useful purpose was to produce goods for the Soviet and other East European markets. And the country's adoption of central planning of the Soviet type also resulted in the development of branches quite unsuited to Hungary's natural advantages. Under market conditions, much of this production will quickly be revealed as inefficient and wasteful, and many firms will have to close if they are unable to adapt their specialisation. Unravelling this legacy will take some time, and will prove extremely painful, but it is an essential element in Hungary's intended transition to a market-type economy.

Hungary's position in the CMEA has been examined at some length because the CMEA system is so different from that prevailing in the West. We can be far briefer in reviewing Hungary's Western trade. Essentially, this has been conducted along much more familiar lines, though the pattern and volume of transactions have been subject to a variety of restrictions, both internal and external. Internally, most firms until recently had to deal with the Ministry of Foreign Trade (renamed the Ministry of External Economic Relations in 1990, following a short period when it had been merged with the Ministry of Internal Trade), or with approved trading organisations, and had only limited powers to deal directly with Western suppliers and customers. And even when there was some formal decentralisation, central control was maintained through a system of export and import licensing. Nevertheless, the internal controls over Western trade were less detailed and less comprehensive than anything that applied to CMEA trade. Externally, Hungary's exports faced restrictions (quotas) in many important markets, such as in the export of agricultural products and a substantial range of industrial products to the European Community. There were also restrictions on Hungary's imports, especially of high technology products deemed to have actual or potential military significance. These were based on the lists of prohibited or restricted commodities prepared by COCOM, though in practice the controls were administered by individual Western governments. Sometimes governments imposed controls that were even stricter than the COCOM lists required, for instance the USA, operating through the Export Administration Act (for details of these controls, and their economic impact on East and West, see Hanson 1988; Macdonald 1990).

During the 1970s Hungary was subject to two shocks which affected the whole world, namely the huge oil price increases of 1973–4 and 1979. In fact the real impact on Hungary of these shocks was somewhat delayed because of the lags built into CMEA prices, since almost all Hungary's oil was supplied by the Soviet Union. However, marginal supplies could be – and sometimes had to be – purchased on the world market at the prevailing price, either directly for hard currency, or in exchange for certain hard goods like meat (as in some transactions with Middle Eastern countries). Despite this, the country's domestic price of energy hardly changed in the mid-1970s, whether to firms or to households: hence there was no particular incentive for anyone to invest in energy-saving equipment, and Hungary's level of energy intensity failed to show the improvements secured in almost all the developed market-economy countries. Even after the Second Oil Crisis, when CMEA prices adjusted more rapidly and when more oil supplies had to be found on the open market, the Hungarians were surprisingly reluctant to make oil and other forms of energy expensive domestically. There was, certainly, a more serious attempt to raise producer prices, but most consumers continued to benefit from highly subsidised energy.

Aside from the last decade and a half of inefficient production (and investment) resulting from this failure to make such an important set of prices correspond to the real opportunity costs revealed in external markets. Hungary encountered more pressing problems in its external trade as a result of the Oil Crises. These were greatly exacerbated by the parallel and, to Hungary, completely unexpected rise of the NICs, and their emergence as major exporters of increasingly sophisticated goods. The dash for growth in the 1970s, based on a huge investment programme but without restraining the growth of domestic consumption, had required substantial imports of Western capital (as noted in the last section). These capital flows could be managed only if the associated investment did indeed produce the additional hard currency exports to enable the debts to be serviced. Unfortunately, this did not happen, at least not to a sufficient extent (as is evident from Tables 9.4, 9.5 and 9.6), despite extensive use of preferential credits directed towards those investments promising higher hard-currency exports.

Thus the really vital question about Hungary is why the country's trade (especially that with hard-currency countries) was not more dynamic during the 1970s and 1980s. It is, as usual, easy to point to external factors as part of the explanation. One instance is provided by the various Western restrictions already referred to. It should be noted, however, that these did not strengthen over the period, while many of them applied to other countries, too. It is also true that at certain times the Western world market was in recession, which obviously depressed the demand for Hungarian products. But on average, Hungary has lost market share in the world market steadily throughout the 1970s and 1980s and no short term-factors can convincingly explain that.

Factors internal to Hungary must consequently bear the main burden of explanation. Despite the reforms already referred to, many of which clearly shifted the economy towards a market-type structure, it appears that too much of the old system survived. This was partly attributable to the central institutions of economic management, several of which (like the planning office, the price office) underwent very little change before 1990, and partly to the relationships between these bodies and enterprises. Contrary to frequently stated reform intentions, there was no general move towards a more normative approach to the financial management of the economy. Instead, very differentiated financial controls were used to protect some firms while others were heavily taxed, as discussed in the very detailed study by Kornai and Matits (1987). The result was that most enterprises could be sure of survival even if they performed badly, whereas if they managed to earn very high profits (whether from domestic sales or exports), they could also be sure that much of their gain would be taxed away to help others. As a result, enterprise incentives to innovate, to enter new markets, to take risks, and to cut costs were almost invariably muted.

In particular, despite constant exhortation and the availability of suitable credits, there was no effective incentive to develop export markets aggressively. At the same time, imports were held in check by continuing direct controls, so that even the threat of import competition was hardly taken seriously by most firms. It is fair to say that among large state enterprises the *forms* of the market were present in Hungary, without the *substance* (in other sectors, particularly in agriculture and small-scale business, the market was more of a reality; this is what gives Hungary such a good start in its transformation towards the market).

Reconstructing a fully fledged market-type economy

The new government elected in the spring of 1990, a coalition led by the Democratic Forum, is Hungary's first non-communist government since the 1940s. It has stated its intention to transform Hungary into a Western-style market economy, though its early months in office were spent working out a very broad range of policies, and many observers felt that real progress was very slow. Nevertheless, it is gradually becoming clearer what the government will do in the main policy fields, and the experiences of Poland already offers some useful guidance about the likely impact of certain policies. In this section, I focus on proposed measures in macro-policy, to do with banking and financial markets, the foreign exchange market, the treatment of the foreign debt issue, and the government's internal budgetary balance. In the area of micro-policy, I outline measures in price reform and price liberalisation, tax reform (this has both macro and micro aspects, of course), trade liberalisation and privatisation.

Macro-policy

As noted above, Hungary will have to contend, in its conduct of macro-economic policy in the immediate future, with external problems, notably the possibility of Western recession, and the redirection of trade resulting from the collapse of the CMEA (including the need to pay for oil in convertible currency). According to the budget for 1991, the government intends to shift at least half the net costs of these shocks on to enterprises and households in the first year, through subsidy reductions and planned price increases. The removal and reduction of subsidies will also help to restrain the budget deficit. Further measures along the same lines are expected in subsequent years.

The 1991 measures were expected to result in a rate of inflation approaching 40 per cent, partly because of the planned price increases, but also as a result of associated adjustments in money wages. The real wage was expected to fall by up to 7 per cent in that year, but it was unclear whether existing policies, such as the tax on wage increases, would prove sufficiently strong to enforce such a decline. While the inflation can be rationalised as part of a necessary process of relative price adjustment, it evidently creates a climate of great uncertainty for investors, and also generates worrying inflationary expectations in the general population. How these expectations might be changed again and inflation brought back under control, as the government intends after 1991, is clearly a key question.

Under present conditions in Hungary it is not easy to answer that question, since the price system seems to lack a firm 'nominal anchor'. Thus for reasons of competitiveness, the government is inclined to allow the exchange rate to decline gradually, rather than fixing it and using it as a means of imposing price and cost discipline on domestic agents. In addition, although there are proposals for a new law on the National Bank to give it some degree of independence from the government and a remit to use monetary policy to control the price level, no concrete measures to this end had been taken at the time of writing (March 1991). In recent years, it has proved all too easy for the government to require the Bank to finance government deficits in ways that could hardly avoid contributing to inflation. At the same time, it would be hard for the government itself to reimpose price discipline, since it lacks credibility in this area: hence it would probably have to enforce a string of bankruptcies and impose substantial unemployment before it would be believed, and it is doubtful whether it is politically strong enough to do this.

In these circumstances, it may be necessary for various forms of external pressure to be brought to bear on the Hungarian government – from the IMF, the European Commission or the European Bank for Reconstruction and Development – to impose the required monetary discipline. But however it is done, it probably cannot succeed without some initial pain. For the brute fact is that Hungary has to direct more resources into its external account to cover the servicing of the hard-currency debt (it is a different, and important, matter how far this debt should be cancelled or otherwise eased for Hungary) and to accommodate the recent shocks: hence domestic components of expenditure, including both private and public consumption and perhaps investment as well, will have to fall for a time – at least until the economy is able to start expanding again.

Micro-policy

Continuing the trend of recent years, Hungary is gradually relaxing all controls over prices and price formation, with the exception of a small residue of restrictions on certain strategic items. Beyond that, it is now virtually certain that the price office will be transformed into an office concerned with monopoly and competition policy.

Imports, too, were almost completely liberalised by 1991, in the sense that formal quantitative restrictions and licensing requirements had almost disappeared. On the other hand, the requirement on most importers to deposit the cost of their imports with the National Bank for a period (sometimes even with a surcharge) (like the UK import deposit scheme of the 1960s) will obviously continue to act as a deterrent, as will the depressed level of demand within Hungary. These are the factors that explain why the actual level of imports has grown so slowly in the last few years, despite the relaxation that has already occurred. Nevertheless most goods, whether imported or domestically produced, are readily available in Hungarian shops – so the present policy does not, on the whole, prevent people from getting the goods they desire (at a price).

On tax reform, the 1988 measures to introduce VAT and personal income tax, while simultaneously eliminating many of the older, more differentiated (by agent and commodity) taxes, now seem to be functioning well. The income tax rises rapidly to rather high tax rates, and since the schedule is not being indexed fully in line with inflation (indeed not at all, according to the 1991 budget), it will become increasingly unpopular. But it is undoubtedly an effective tax. Many of the remaining special taxes and subsidies on various activities will be phased out over the next two to three years, leaving Hungary with a tax system very much in accord with Western models.

Finally, it is essential to mention the government's privatisation plans which, after some delay, are now moving ahead rapidly (on this important topic, see Hare 1991; Grosfeld and Hare 1991). The new State Property Agency (SPA) is now established as the body which nominally 'holds' state assets, and it has the task of supervising the privatisation process. In a first round of privatisation, twenty of the more successful of

Hungary's large companies were offered for sale towards the end of 1990, and by mid-December more than two hundred offers or expressions of interest had been received; the actual privatisation of these companies was programmed to take place in the course of 1991. The SPA is expected to offer another batch of companies for sale every two to three months, and Hungary's approach also allows potential purchasers of Hungarian companies (whether Hungarian or foreign) to come forward with their own proposals.

Early 1991 also witnessed the launching of a so-called pre-privatisation initiative, involving the sale or leasing of virtually all small businesses like shops, restaurants and other service units (many of which had already been leased to existing managers from the early 1980s, unlike anywhere else in Eastern Europe). This is expected to be popular, and to go well. While foreign buyers or participants are welcomed in connection with the larger companies, most of the pre-privatisation activity is likely to be confined to Hungarian buyers or leasers.

There is every expectation of success with these initial privatisation measures. Later stages in the privatisation process, when less successful firms are put up for sale, could prove more problematic, and some backruptcies and major reorganisations can be expected at that stage. Overall, the government's present intention is to sell off about half the existing state sector within three years, a very ambitious objective.

This plan implies, of course, that even in 1994 half the economy will remain in the public sector. Hence, from the point of view of bringing about a general recovery in the economy, it is obviously important to develop policies towards such a large block of firms. So far, policy has not been very well developed in this area. It seems to be expected that there will be a mixture of management changes, reorganisation and perhaps some closures, but without much sign of a definite strategy to assist judgements about the long-term viability of the firms concerned. In my view, though, the need to improve the performance of these firms will soon be recognised by the government and begin to receive the attention it deserves.

Hungary's prospects for the 1990s

In summing up, and assessing Hungary's economic prospects in the next few years, it is useful to draw up a simple balance sheet: on one side can be listed the positive or helpful factors favouring a successful transition to a market-type economy, on the other, the negative or problematic factors. Such a balance sheet is shown in Table 9.9.

Table 9.9 makes clear that while Hungary has a number of factors in its favour, factors that will undoubtedly facilitate and probably help accelerate the transition to a market-type economy, there remain some very serious negative factors, too. Some of the latter are the result of poor or misjudged macroeconomic managment in the past, and are therefore a legacy of the *Ancien Régime*. Externally, the hard-currency debt falls into this category, and it is at least questionable whether the new government should be required to shoulder the entire burden of this legacy. In the short run, the collapse of the CMEA and the shift to the principle of hard-currency trading in the East from 1991, together with the unification of Germany, will both make the management of Hungary's hard-currency balances even harder. Because of its sharply worsened terms of trade with the Soviet Union, and the loss of some of the previous

Table 9.9 Balance sheet: assessing Hungary's economic prospects

Positive factors	Negative factors
Democratic political environment	Inexperienced government and senior officials
An end to enterprise party cells	Large hard-currency debt
Two decades of reform experience	Collapse of CMEA trading system
Experience of free markets, including a very active second economy	Large internal government deficit
Good education, training and research	Political dangers associated with inflation and unemployment
Favourable location in Europe	Re-unification of Germany
Clear commitment to EC association and eventual membership	Legacy of decades of interventionist government

East German trade, Hungary's trade balance may initially suffer to the extent of around $1 billion–2 billion per year. At the same time, the inability to sell certain goods at all for hard currency will obviously raise unemployment substantially, at least for a time. To mitigate these difficulties, it would be highly desirable, in my view, for the West to consider a substantial degree of debt reduction for Hungary so that its development through the 1990s is not unduly burdened by the errors of the past.

Internally, the effects of a long period of interventionist government will not dissolve overnight. Indeed, the need to help change in this area, as well as to help an inexperienced government cope with the transitional problems, presents a powerful case for Western aid of the technical assistance variety, a substantial volume of which is already coming forward through various channels (EC, OECD, World Bank, individual governments, private sector organisations, and so on).

As the IMF and other Western agencies will no doubt impress upon the Hungarian government, it will be essential to bring the domestic budget deficit under control in order to reduce inflationary pressures and release sources for exports, investment and possibly consumption. As many Western countries have discovered, however, the easiest way of cutting public spending is to cut back investment or delay some large projects. But given the need for investment in Hungary's infrastructure, this may not be a very desirable strategy. Instead, some current spending may have to be cut back, or service charges introduced where publicly provided services are still completely free.

The other route to restore balance in the budget is, of course, to raise taxes. In Hungary's case, though, a general rise in tax rates would be most undesirable, since the personal income tax schedule already rises quite quickly to marginal rates that would be considered excessive in Western countries, and the tax rates on enterprises are also high. What is far more appropriate, in my view, is to use the existing pressure on the budget as an opportunity to restructure the tax system to eliminate the bulk of existing subsidies both on production, consumption, and international transactions as rapidly as possible. In this way, significantly more revenue can be assured without a general increase in tax rates.

The key factor for Hungary's successful transformation is obviously, in the last analysis, the political one: can the government manage the economy in such a way that inflation remains under control and unemployment does not reach unacceptable levels? The problem is that for internal reasons the government is likely to want, or be obliged, to proceed fairly slowly and gradually with its reform plans, including the implementation of its privatisation programmes. But external factors dictate that restructuring should proceed rapidly so that exports can rise sharply while consumption is held down for a time. This will make possible the servicing of the existing debt, but is also important from the point of view of signalling to potential investors from abroad that Hungary is serious about reform and really determined to create a market-type economy. Unfortunately, what line of policy would almost certainly result in greater unemployment for a time than a more cautious approach. Thus a very delicate balance has to be struck between external and internal pressures. Given the positive factors shown in Table 9.9, Hungary could already be developing very successfully by the mid-1990s if it is able to make the right choices in the next year or two.

Addendum (January 1992)

The concluding section of the chapter identified positive and negative factors which could facilitate or hinder Hungary's transition to the market. Here I take the opportunity to add a few remarks on these factors in the light of Hungary's economic performance in 1991 and expectations for 1992.

First, it is important to ntoe that Hungary was more successful than expected in 1991 in shifting trade from the former CMEA region to Western (mainly EC) markets. This, together with an increase in deposits in convertible currency accounts by the population and an inflow of direct foreign investment of more than $1 billion, ensured that Hungary's balance of payments in 1991 was stronger than had been anticipated, despite substantial debt service obligations.

Second, in December 1991 Hungary joined Poland and Czechoslovakia in signing association agreements with the EC which envisage the removal of many trade barriers on both sides over a five-year period. While the terms of the agreement, which has still to be formally ratified by the Hungarian government, are less generous than many had hoped, it is clear that Hungary's industrial exports to the EC can now expand rapidly, including areas which were formerly constrained. However, special provisions have been made in the agreement for the 'sensitive' sectors of textiles and steel, and also for agricultural products.

Third, the government's overall financial position continues to give cause for concern. Although the central government budget is showing only a modest deficit, after cuts in subsidies and other measures, various off-budget funds (e.g. those for social security and housing) are in a more difficult position. This means that inflationary pressure could well persist, creating further uncertainty for investors.

Lastly, privatisation proceeded more slowly in 1991 than planned. However many small businesses were successfully privatised, and several hundred large and medium-sized state-owned enterprises were either prepared for privatisation or actually sold off. What this means is that Hungary is now poised for a period of very rapid privatisation over the next two years. The process is likely to be more rapid than elsewhere in the region, and is likely to be accompanied by a substantial amount of genuine restructuring. This will put the firms which survive in a much stronger position to compete in both domestic and international markets.

Notes

1   The government was led after 1956 by the re-formed Communist Party, which was named the Hungarian Socialist Workers' Party (HSWP). In 1989 the party became the Hungarian Socialist Party (HSP), and it lost badly in the 1990 parliamentary elections. The new government was formed by a coalition led by the Hungarian Democratic Forum which can be characterised, broadly, as a centre-right, nationalist party.
2   Interestingly the same misconception arose in the management of nationalised industries in the UK. For an illuminating discussion of the UK situation as it was perceived in the 1960s, see Dell (1973).
3   It is worth noting here that these benefits are unlikely to be reflected in published statistics on consumption or production, because the usual way of measuring these items in the national accounts *assumes* that markets are always in equilibrium, and hence fails to pick up the extent of *forced substitution* by households or firms, to use a term employed extensively in Kornai (1980).
4   Note that I use the past tense in this section to refer to CMEA arrangements because from the beginning of 1991 all trade in the area was conducted in hard currencies at world market prices (aside from a limited number of contracts involving straight barter or where long-term agreements to use the rouble remain in force). Hence CMEA trade will no longer be clearly distinguishable from normal trade between market-type economies.
5   This inevitably calls to mind the old joke about socialism, now rather dated by the collapse of communism in Eastern Europe, but still of some historic interest. Even when the World Revolution succeeded and socialism triumphed (it ran) it would be necessary to retain at least one capitalist country so that the socialist countries would know what prices to trade at.

References

Batt J (1988) *Economic Reform and Political Change in Eastern Europe: A Comparison of the Czechoslovak and Hungarian Experiences*. Macmillan
Brabant J van (1989) *Economic Integration in Eastern Europe*. Harvester-Wheatsheaf
Cave M, Hare P G (1981) *Alternative Approaches to Economic Planning*. Macmillan
Dell E (1973) *Political Responsibility and Industry*. Allen & Unwin
Friss I (ed) (1969) *Reform of the Economic Mechanism in Hungary*. Akadémiai Kiadó, Budapest
Galasi P, Szirácki Gy (eds) (1985) *Labour Market and Second Economy in Hungary*. Campus Verlag, Frankfurt
Grosfeld I, Hare P G (1991) Privatization in Hungary, Poland and Czechoslovakia. *European Economy* Special edition No. 2: 129–56
Hanson P (1988) *Western Economic Statecraft in East–West Relations*. RIIA/Routledge & Kegan Paul
Hare P G (1976) Industrial prices in Hungary. *Soviet Studies* 28 (2 and 3): 189–206; 362–90
Hare P G (1981) The investment system in Hungary. In Hare et al (1981) ch 5
Hare P G (1983) The beginnings of institutional change in Hungary. *Soviet Studies* 35(3): 313–30
Hare PG (1987) Economic reform in Eastern Europe. *Journal of Economic Surveys* 1(1): 25–58

Hare P G (1990) Reform of enterprise regulation in Hungary – from 'tutelage' to market. *European Economy* **43** (March): 35–54

Hare P G (1991) Eastern Europe: the transition to a market economy. *Royal Bank of Scotland Review* **169**: 3–16

Hare P G, Radice H K, Swain N (eds) (1981) *Hungary: A Decade of Economic Reform*. Allen & Unwin

Hare P G, Revesz T, Zalai E (1990) Trade distortions in Hungary. Paper prepared for European Commission (DGII), Brussels, mimeo

JEC (1986) *East European Economies: Slow Growth in the 1980's*, vol 3, *Country Studies on Eastern Europe and Yugoslavia*. Joint Economic Committee, USGPO, Washington, DC

Kaser M (1967) *Comecon*. Oxford University Press

Kornai J (1980) *Economics of Shortage*. North Holland, Amsterdam

Kornai J, Matits A (1987) *A Vállalatok Nveresgégének Bürokratikus Újraelosztasa*. Közgazdasagi és Jogi Kónyvkiado, Budapest

Macdonald S (1990) *Technology and the Tyranny of Export Controls*. Macmillan

Marer P (1981) The mechanism and performance of Hungary's foreign trade, 1968–79. In Hare et al (1981) ch 8

Marer P (1985) *Dollar GNPs of the USSR and Eastern Europe*, Johns Hopkins University Press for the World Bank, Baltimore, Md

Marer P (1986a) Economic reform in Hungary: from central planning to regulated market. In JEC (1986) 223–97

Marer P (1986b) Hungary's balance of payments crisis and response, 1978–84. In JEC (1986) 298–321

Murrell P (1990) *The Nature of Socialist Economies: Lessons from Eastern European Foreign Trade*. Princeton University Press, Princeton NJ

Newbery D M (1990) Tax reform, trade liberalization and industrial restructuring in Hungary. *European Economy* **43**: 67–96

Swain N (1985) *Collective farms which work?* Cambridge University Press

Zalai E, Révész T and Csekó I (1989) Trade redirection and liberalization in Hungary: application of the HUMUS model family. Discussion paper, *Karl Marx University of Economic Sciences*, Budapest

CHAPTER 10

Poland

MARK E SCHAFFER

Introduction

In January 1990 Poland launched a path-breaking economic reform programme. Authored by a team led by Finance Minister and Deputy Prime Minister Leszek Balcerowicz, the programme launched Poland into the transition from socialism. The Polish experience in transition has attracted much attention in the international community, and has provided lessons, both positive and negative, for reformers in other post-communist economies. The timing of the writing of this chapter (December 1991) is fortunate, because it provides an excellent vantage point for an initial assessment of the Balcerowicz Plan, two years after the start of the programme, and just following the first fully free parliamentary elections of the new democracy.

The first part of the chapter outlines the basic features of the Polish economy, the pattern of economic growth and performance in the communist period, and the market socialist system that existed in Poland from 1982 to 1989. The second part is concerned with the Polish economy in transition. I shall discuss the Balcerowicz Plan, the transition economic system, economic performance in 1990–1, and the challenge of structural adjustment and privatisation. A complete survey of the Polish economy since 1945 is of course not possible in a single chapter. I have chosen to focus on the enterprise sector in Poland, for three reasons. First, the central weakness of the socialist economic system lay in the failure to achieve levels of productivity and rates of innovation comparable to those in the developed West (cf Dyker, Chapter 12 in this volume, on the Soviet Union). A detailed look at the enterprise sector will highlight the causes of this failure. Second, the economic system established under the market socialist reforms provided the starting-point for the transition to capitalism. As we shall see later, the characteristics of the system that existed when the transition began have shaped to a major extent the transition path itself. Third, privatising the enterprise sector is the key challenge of the transition from socialism.

Basic features of the Polish economy

The Poland that emerged from the destruction and disruption of the Second World War had most of the characteristics of a developing country. The population was rural-based and a majority of the labour force worked in agriculture. Educational levels were relatively low. The birth-rate, the death-rate, the rate of population growth and of infant mortality rate were all high. In addition, much of the fixed capital of the country had been either destroyed or damaged during the war. The loss of a high portion of the intelligentsia meant a big loss of human capital as well. At the end of the forty-five-year period of communist rule, Poland was largely but not entirely industrialised, and had most of the peculiar characteristics of industrialised communist countries.

Table 10.1 charts Poland's progress according to basic social indicators over the period 1950–89. By 1989 the population was mostly urban-dwelling, but still contained a large (nearly 40 per cent) rural component, with about one-quarter of the labour force engaged in agriculture. Population growth had slowed considerably, and the infant mortality rate had fallen dramatically to near-developed economy levels.[1] Education levels had also increased substantially. According to these social indicators, Poland in 1989, though classified as a lower-middle income country, had the characteristics of upper-middle income or high income countries according to World Bank definitions (World Bank 1991).

Many of the other basic features of the Polish economy at the end of the 1980s were specifically typical of industrialised communist countries. Labour participation rates, though falling, were still very high by international standards, especially among women, who comprised 46 per cent of the work-force. Unemployment was negligible (according to official statistics). Industry's special priority under communism was evident in its large share of nonagricultural economic activity and in the small size of the service sector (Tables 10.2 and 10.3). And of course the ownership structure of the economy was dominated by the state, though here Poland differed somewhat from the standard communist pattern in a number of respects.

As is typical in a communist country, economic activity came under three different categories: state, co-operative and private. The state sector consisted of enterprises formally owned by the state. The co-operative sector consisted of enterprises formally owned by the co-operative members, although a large proportion of the fixed assets that they used (eg buildings) were owned by the state. The state sector and the co-operative sector taken together were referred to as the 'socialised sector' of the economy. In the 1980s co-operatives accounted for about 15–20 per cent of socialised sector employment, the bulk of it in retail trade and industry. In practice, the treatment of co-operatives by the state with respect to the running of the economic system did not differ much from that meted out to state-owned enterprises; they were treated by planners as coming within the ambit of the planned economy.

Poland was unusual among communist countries in that it did retain a large private sector throughout the communist period. But this was simply because agriculture remained largely private. The non-agricultural private sector accounted for a very small portion of economic activity (about 3 per cent of all employment) until the 1980s, when some of the restrictions on private sector development were lifted. In 1989 9 per cent of total employment was accounted for by the non-agricultural private sector

Table 10.1   Social indicators 1950–89

	1950	1960	1970	1980	1989
Population (millions,					
mid-year)	24.8	29.6	32.5	35.6	38.0
% urban	36.7	48.0	52.0	58.4	61.3
Per 1,000 inhabitants					
Live births	30.7	22.6	16.6	19.5	14.8
Deaths	11.6	7.6	8.1	9.9	10.0
Rate of natural increase	19.1	15.0	8.5	9.6	4.8
Infant mortality rate	111.2	54.8	33.4	21.3	15.9
(per 1,000 live births)					
Employment[a]	12.4	13.9	16.4	17.8	17.6
(millions, end-year)					
Participation rate[b]	85.5	85.3	89.7	83.8	80.2
Men	98.0	95.7	93.9	88.4	84.3
Women	73.9	75.1	85.2	79.1	75.8
Share of women (%)					
in working population	44.7	44.3	46.8	46.3	45.7
in socialised sector	30.6	33.1	39.4	43.5	46.7
employment					
Educational level of full-time					
socialised sector employees					
(%)					
Higher		3.8[c]	5.3	8.1	9.9
Secondary		11.2[c]	19.2	27.2	31.2
Basic vocational		8.2[c]	17.0	24.2	28.7

Notes:
[a] Employment is number of working people, including self-employed farmers
[b] Participation rate is defined as number of working people divided by population of working age
[c] 1958

Sources:
RS90: xxxii–xxxiii, xlvi–xlvii, 50
RS89: 93
RS87: 59
RS73: 83–4
Polska: 31
RSPraca90: xxviii–xxix, xxxii–iii, 27

(about half of which was in industry), compared with 64 per cent by the non-agricultural socialised sector (Table 10.2).

Market structure in Poland was relatively concentrated, another typical feature of communist economies. Both enterprises and establishments in the socialised sector tended to be large, but even more striking was the near absence of small socialised enterprises and establishments. Even at the establishment level, about 95 per cent of all employment in socialised industry in 1987 was in units with 50 or more employees (RSPrz 1988: 40). Those small establishments that did exist in the socialised sector were

Table 10.2 Economic structure 1950–89 (per cent)

	1950	1960	1970	1980	1989
Employment[a]					
industry	20.7	25.5	29.3	30.3	29.0
building	5.0	6.5	7.1	7.7	7.8
agriculture	53.6	43.3	34.3	29.7	26.8
transport and commun.	4.5	5.6	6.2	6.5	5.8
trade	5.3	6.0	6.9	7.5	8.7
education	n.a.	3.0	3.9	4.3	5.5
health and social welfare	n.a.	n.a.	2.8	3.5	4.7
Socialised sector	47.4	58.0	68.0	73.4	69.9
Private sector	52.6	42.0	32.0	26.6	30.1
of which agriculture	49.5	39.3	29.0	23.1	21.1
Non-agricultural socialised sector	43.3	54.0	62.8	66.8	64.2
Non-agricultural private sector	3.1	2.7	2.9	3.5	9.0
of which industry	n.a.	n.a.	1.3	1.6	4.3
Share of NMP produced Industry	24.3	34.5	44.0	50.9	47.9
Share of NMP distributed Net fixed investment	11.5	16.1	20.5	17.3	12.3
Foreign trade turnover (current prices)					
Share of total turnover with					
Socialist countries	58.9	63.1	66.2	55.7	40.4
Non-socialist countries	41.4	36.9	33.8	44.3	59.6
Share of exports to					
Socialist countries	56.5	62.6	63.9	55.9	40.6
Non-socialist countries	43.1	37.4	36.1	44.1	59.4
Share of imports from					
Socialist countries	61.1	63.5	68.6	55.6	40.1
Non-socialist	38.9	36.5	31.4	44.4	59.9

Note: [a] Employment is number of working people, including self-employed farmers, annual average, full-time equivalent

Sources:
RS90: xxxii–iii, 93–4
Polska: 35
RSPraca90: xxviii–xxix, 23–5
RSHZ90: 2–6

frequently grouped together in co-operative enterprises, and so the number of establishments per enterprise in the co-operative sector was relatively high compared to the state sector (Table 10.4). This pattern could be seen in an extreme form in retail trade. The bulk of this sector consisted of very small establishments (shops, restaurants) organised into very large cooperatives. For example, in 1986, 57 per cent

Table 10.3 GDP in 1987 (current prices)

	Billion zloty	Distribution (%)
Total	16,939.9	100.0
By source:		
Industry	7,054.5	41.6
Construction	1,783.6	10.5
Agriculture	1,859.6	11.0
Transportation and Communication	995.8	5.9
Trade	2,357.3	13.9
Housing	407.4	2.4
Education	443.6	2.6
Culture and Art	60.1	0.4
Health and Social Welfare	326.4	1.9
'Satisfying society's needs'[a]	723.2	4.3
By use:		
Consumption	11,673.8	68.9
General Government	1,516.4	9.0
Private	10,157.4	60.0
Investment	4,883.5	28.8
Fixed Investment	382.1	22.6
Changes in stocks	1,062.5	6.3
Total expenditure (C+1)	16,557.3	97.7
Exports	3,625.2	21.4
Imports	3,218.1	19.0
Resource gap (X−M)	407.1	2.4
Unallocated items	−24.5	−0.1

Note: [a] This may refer to defence

Source: World Bank 1990: 92–3

of shops and 79 per cent of eating establishments in the socialised sector were managed by two giant co-operatives (*RSHW 1980–86*: 12 and 212; *RS 1987*: 395). Much of the non-agricultural private sector was organised in very small establishments; average employment in the 1980s was just over two persons per establishment (Table 10.4). By the end of the 1980s, however, a large-scale private sector had become fairly well established, with perhaps one-fifth of employment in private industry in 1989 located in enterprises with fifty or more employees.

But the key feature of the Polish economy at the end of the period of communist rule, to which we can attribute the ultimate abandonment of the system, was the low standard of living enjoyed by the population. The levels of national income per capita and productivity achieved in Poland by the end of the 1980s were strikingly low compared to those achieved in Western Europe and North America.

Two methods are commonly used to compare levels of output and income across

Table 10.4 The structure of the Polish industrial sector 1986

	State	Co-operative	Private
Employment (thousands)	3,684	539	475
Enterprises	3,116	2,348	
Establishments	9,806	17,708	210,150
Average labour force per enterprise	1,182	229	
Average labour force per establishment	378	30	2.3
Establishments per enterprise	3.1	7.5	

Sources:
RS87: 251
RSPrz88: 2–3, 38–40

countries. First, commercial exchange rates, perhaps with adjustments, may be used to convert figures into a common currency; this is the method used by the World Bank, for example. The second method takes product-specific exchange rates, or 'purchasing power parities', and aggregates them to yield a single exchange rate which can then be used to convert figures from one currency into another. The UN International Comparison Project (ICP) is the best-known example of this second approach. In practice the second method generally yields relatively higher estimates of output and income for less developed countries than the first (see also Dunford, Chapter 9 in *The European Economy*).

The first method is simple and straightforward to use, but suffers from several drawbacks, most notably that commercial exchange rates are determined by a diverse set of factors, some bearing only a tenuous relationship to production conditions. A particular problem here is that the exchange rates used by the communist countries were often very artificial. Commercial exchange rates are also more influenced by the relative prices of tradeable goods than of goods generally. The purchasing power parity method is theoretically preferable for the purposes of comparing national product and income, but suffers from some practical drawbacks. Most importantly for our purposes, attempts to calculate purchasing power parities for communist countries have been criticised for failing to capture fully the differences in quality between similar goods in Eastern and Western countries.

Table 10.5 presents 1989 figures for GDP and GDP per capita in US dollars for Poland, West Germany and the USA, calculated according to both methods. It is clear that by the end of the communist period Poland had reached a level of national income per capita that was still only a small fraction of that achieved in the leading Western industrial countries – about one-tenth using the exchange rate method, and about one-quarter to one-fifth using the purchasing power parity method. And if we take into account the excessive levels of pollution and environmental damage suffered in Poland, and not captured in GDP, the comparison is even more unfavourable.

Economic growth and performance in Poland 1945–89

Poland's economic record in the communist period can be divided into three periods: the era of the standard communist strategy of extensive growth and catching-up, until

Table 10.5 GDP and GDP per capita 1989 (US dollars)

	GDP (US$ billion)	GDP per capita (US$)
ICP		
Poland	188.7	4,980
W. Germany	943.6	15,220
USA	5,147.7	20,690
World Bank		
Poland	68.3	1,800
W. Germany	1,189.1	19,180
USA	5,156.4	20,730

Source: World Bank 1991: Tables 1, 3 and 30

1970; the import-led growth experiment, 1970–9; and crisis, reform and renewed crisis, 1979–89.

The communist strategy for economic development sought to access two main sources of growth. First, like any other newly industrialising country, the level of technology in Poland following the Second World War was far behind that of the Western industrialised countries. Poland was therefore able to grow by taking advantage of readily available technology. This is evidenced at the macroeconomic level by rates of growth in productivity that were in excess of those of the technological leaders among Western countries, and at the microeconomic level by the diffusion through the economy of goods and technologies practically all of which were invented elsewhere. This process of 'catching-up, or 'convergence' has been commonly observed in capitalist and communist countries alike (Gomulka 1986).

The second source of growth during this period was the rapid growth of inputs of capital and labour, deliberately engineered. This is sometimes referred to in the literature under the heading of 'extensive growth' and is peculiar to the communist development strategy. Investment rates were raised at the expense of consumption and fixed investment grew rapidly. The industrial sector was favoured heavily and expanded rapidly ('forced industrialisation'). The labour force was growing moderately quickly during this period (about 2 per cent per year), and labour was furthermore redeployed from agriculture to industry.

A third source of growth in the period immediately following the war derived from the nature of post-war reconstruction. The repair and recommissioning of damaged fixed capital takes fewer resources than laying down new fixed capital from scratch. This growth reserve was probably mostly exhausted by the mid-1950s.

The 1970s saw a modification of the development strategy, as Poland experimented with 'import-led growth'. Large amounts of machinery were imported from the West, using money borrowed from the West. The plan was to pay back the debt using the increased export earnings made possible by the new fixed capital. At the end of the process, Poland would have paid off the debt and be left with a modernised capital stock and a higher standard of living for its population. The experiment went badly wrong, however. The necessary increase in exports to the West did not materialise, partly because some of the Western credits were used to import consumption goods rather than investment goods, partly because of the failure to manage the new investment projects efficiently or complete them on time, and partly because of the world-wide recession in the 1970s, when export markets were depressed and interest rates (by the late 1970s) high, increasing the foreign debt burden. As external imbalance deepened, domestic macro imbalances also intensified. This process culminated in the economic and political crisis of 1979–82.

The events of 1979–82 are well known and do not need re-elaboration here (see Tables 10.6 and 10.7). The crisis and its resolution was extremely costly to Poland. At the beginning of 1982 the country was under a regime of martial law imposed by the communist authorities. CIA statistics put the fall in GDP from 1979 to 1982 at 8.5 per cent; according to official statistics, the fall in NMP was over 20 per cent. Price stability had been lost, with inflation peaking at over 100 per cent in 1982. The hard currency debt was over $25 billion, and Poland stopped repayments of principal on the debt to commercial banks and stopped servicing altogether the debt to official creditors (the Paris Club).

Despite these adverse circumstances, the authorities began in 1982 to implement a major decentralising economic reform, to which I shall return shortly. The reform was, however, relatively unsuccessful. Some economic growth took place over the period 1982–9, but this did not amount to much more than recovery from the preceding crisis; by 1989, for example, the official figure for NMP and the CIA figure for GDP had both just about returned to their 1979 levels (Table 10.6). Hard currency exports did grow during the 1980s, and primary external balance was re-established, but the hard currency debt continued to grow, reaching $40 billion by the end of 1989.

Macro-control was re-imposed in the early 1980s, and then lost again in 1987 when a co-ordinated realignment of wages and prices went badly wrong (Table 10.7). Inflation accelerated to 60 per cent in 1988 and over 100 per cent (annualised) in the first half of 1989. At the same time control over wages was lost, and the so-called 'statistical real wage'[2] increased 14 per cent in 1988 and a further 8 per cent in 1989. The result was simultaneous rapid inflation and widespread shortages, a remarkable achievement for an economic system in which most prices were subject to central control. Organised labour unrest also increased at this time, and the scene was set for another economic and political crisis. The Round Table talks between the communist government and the Solidarity opposition in early 1989 was followed by partially free elections in June 1989, the advent of near hyperinflation in August after food prices were freed, and the fall of the communist government and the installation of a Solidarity prime minister and government in August–September 1989.

How should we assess the economic record of Poland during the communist period? The economic growth rates achieved by the traditional communist development strategy of 1950–70 and the import-led growth strategy of 1970–9 were relatively impressive, but could not be sustained. Growth in the 1980s was slow by international standards; output and productivity were growing at rates comparable to those in the countries of the developed West. By the 1980s, therefore, catching-up had more or less stopped. Poland had achieved what Stanislaw Gomulka has called the 'equilibrium technological gap' (Nelson and Phelps 1966; Gomulka 1970).

Table 10.6 Growth performance 1950–89

	Average annual growth rates					Levels (1979 = 100)					
	1950–60	1960–70	1970–9	1979–82	1982–9	1950	1960	1970	1979	1982	1989
Labour force[a]											
(Total)	2.0	2.0	1.4	−0.5	−0.1	59.1	72.0	88.1	100.0	98.6	97.8
Non-agricultural	4.1	3.5	2.2	−0.9	0.6	39.0	58.0	82.2	100.0	97.5	101.7
Material sphere[b]	1.7	1.7	1.2	−0.8	−0.6	64.3	76.3	90.1	100.0	97.5	93.3
of which, industry	4.1	3.5	1.8	−1.6	−0.3	40.3	60.3	85.0	100.0	95.2	93.5
Productive fixed capital	3.7	5.2	8.4	3.5	2.8	20.2	29.2	48.5	100.0	110.7	134.3
in industry	7.9	7.3	9.7	3.4	3.4	10.1	21.4	43.3	100.0	110.7	140.1
NMP produced[c]	7.6	6.1	6.7	−7.9	3.7	14.9	30.9	55.6	100.0	78.2	101.1
in industry	10.1	8.3	7.9	−7.9	3.6	8.7	22.7	50.6	100.0	78.2	100.1
NMP distributed[c]	7.8	5.8	6.9	−9.0	3.7	14.7	31.1	54.8	100.0	75.3	97.1
Consumption	10.0	2.7	7.0	−4.8	3.1	15.9	41.5	54.2	100.0	86.2	107.0
Investment	13.8	3.2	6.3	−21.9	6.0	11.5	41.9	57.5	100.0	47.6	71.4
Net fixed investment	15.1	4.5	8.1	−23.2	4.8	7.8	31.9	49.5	100.0	45.3	62.7
Exports	7.6	10.3	8.7	−5.5	5.7	8.5	17.7	47.2	100.0	84.4	124.0
Socialist countries	8.7	10.6	9.6	−4.3	5.8	7.0	16.0	43.7	100.0	87.6	130.2
Non-socialist countries	6.1	10.0	6.9	−6.2	5.4	11.7	21.3	55.0	100.0	82.5	119.0
Imports	8.4	9.2	9.5	−11.1	6.0	8.2	18.3	44.2	100.0	70.4	105.6
Socialist countries	8.8	10.0	7.4	−3.2	3.6	8.7	20.2	52.6	100.0	90.6	116.4
Non-socialist countries	7.7	7.6	13.2	−21.6	9.1	7.5	15.7	32.8	100.0	48.2	88.7
CIA estimates											
GNP		4.2	4.5	−2.9	1.5		44.5	67.5	100.0	91.5	101.3
in Industry		7.0	4.6	−5.8	1.2		34.0	66.7	100.0	83.6	91.0

Notes:
[a] Labour force is number of working people, including self-employed farmers, annual average, full-time equivalent
[b] Material sphere employment, productive fixed capital, and NMP are roughly comparable in coverage in that they all exclude 'unproductive' activities in the Soviet/Marxist definition
[c] NMP = Net Material Product

Sources:
RS90: xxvi–xxix
RS90: xxxii–xxxiii, xlii–xliii, 93–4
RS87: xxxiv–xxxvii
RS72: 391–2
Polska: 35
RSPraca90: xxviii–xxix, 23–5
RSHZ90: 8
CIA 1990: Table C–15
HES various years

Table 10.7   Macro balance and imbalance 1971–89

Year	Gross hard currency debt (US$ billion)	Hard currency trade balance (US$ million)	Inflation (official consumer price index)	Statistical real wage (1970 = 100)	Government budget surplus (+) /deficit (−) as a % of government spending
1971	1.1	124.8	−0.1	105.6	3.4
1972	1.6	−289.3	0.0	112.4	1.8
1973	2.8	−1,292.1	2.8	122.2	0.9
1974	4.6	−2,101.4	7.1	130.1	0.9
1975	8.0	−2,540.2	3.0	141.6	3.4
1976	11.5	−2,884.3	4.4	147.9	10.5
1977	14.0	−2,143.5	4.9	151.4	12.3
1978	17.8	−1,923.2	8.1	148.0	11.4
1979	22.7	−1,679.1	7.0	151.1	4.0
1980	25.1	−995.5	9.4	157.3	−2.1
1981	25.5	−95.8	21.2	160.9	−8.5
1982	24.7	1,433.3	100.8	120.7	−3.3
1983	26.4	1,437.8	22.1	122.1	−1.0
1984	28.8	1,531.1	15.0	122.8	−2.0
1985	29.3	1,060.0	15.1	127.5	−0.9
1986	33.5	1,072.2	17.7	130.9	−1.1
1987	39.2	1,234.5	25.2	126.3	−2.1
1988	38.5	1,009.2	60.2	144.5	0.8
1989	39.8	767.3	251.1	156.6	−10.6

Note: The coverage of government revenue varies slightly in the statistical sources used; the figures for the budget surplus for 1971–4 are the author's estimates

Sources:
HES 1981: 41
HES 1982: 54
HES 1983: 46
CIA 1990: Table C–1
RSHZ90: 7
RS80: 344
RS84: xxxvi–xxxvii, 395
RS87: xxxiv–xxxv, 413
RS91: xxiv–xxvii, 179

Prior to this point, catching-up had been feasible, and had actually taken place: the growth rate of productivity had exceeded that observed in the technological leader (the United States) and was close to those observed in other developed Western economies. But catching-up based on borrowing of technology cannot yield productivity growth rates that exceed indefinitely those of the technologically leading countries; a follower cannot pass the leader without becoming the leader himself. As the productivity level of the follower increases, the productivity growth rate of the follower falls so that the differences in productivity levels between the leaders and the follower stabilises. If the economic system in Poland had been the same as that in the West, we would have expected catching-up to cease when productivity levels were not far short of those in the West; that is catching-up would have stopped when technological 'convergence' had been achieved. But the socialist economic system in pre-transition Poland suffered from major static inefficiencies. At the point when catching-up would have stopped altogether (under a continuation of the socialist system), the technological level of the Polish economy would still have been far behind that of the developed West. Growth would have continued, but at relatively low levels, with the gap between Poland and the West more or less constant. It is likely that, by the mid-1980s, Poland was not far away from its equilibrium technological gap. The communist growth strategies – traditional, import-led, and reformed – had simply exhausted their potentials.

The economic system: market socialism in Poland, 1982–9

By the end of the 1940s Poland had established a more-or-less standard Soviet-type centrally planned economy. Attempts to change the system began very soon thereafter, with a major reform project in 1956. The decentralisation measures introduced at that point were short-lived, however, and the old system reasserted itself after a short period. The second major attempt at reform began in 1974. This time, decentralisation took the form of the transfer of economic power from the centre *and* from enterprises to large horizontal conglomerates. This reform attempt failed as well, and again the old system reasserted itself. The Polish economic system at the start of the 1980s could be characterised as essentially a standard centrally planned economy, with some inconsequential modifications (on the prehistory of reform in Poland see Zielinski 1973; Nuti 1981).

The economic crisis of 1979–81 was the catalyst for the 1982 reform. Wide-ranging discussions and debate led to the formulation of many different reform plans. These were considered by a Party-Government Commission on Economic Reform assisted by 500 economic experts and politicians. Preparation of the reform plan was completed by mid-1981. The laws necessary to implement the reform were enacted over the next six months, and the new enterprise system came into force on 1 January 1982. Implementation of the new system was, however, complicated to some extent by the declaration of martial law in mid-December 1981 (for a more detailed discussion of the reform, see Gomulka and Rostowski 1984; World Bank 1987).

A central feature of the reform was that enterprises should be independent, self-financing and self-managed (the '3-S principle', after the Polish initials). Independence meant that enterprises were to choose what to produce, how much to produce, how to produce it and using what means, etc, without direct administrative guidance from the centre. Self-financing meant that the income of an enterprise and its employees were to be determined by the enterprise's financial performance (in Kornai's terminology, budget constraints would be 'hard'). Financial discipline would be enforced and ailing enterprises allowed to go bankrupt. Self-management meant that large powers were to be given to workers and workers' councils.

While enterprise autonomy was to be enhanced, central planning would be maintained, though in a different form. Central allocation of materials and goods was to be largely abandoned, and price flexibility and regulated competitive markets introduced. The centre would guide the economy through the use of a wide range of indirect instruments – taxes, subsidies, prices, investment priorities, incomes policies, and so on.

The Polish economic reform as it was originally described was to be introduced gradually. Gomulka and Rostowski (1984) point out that, had these measures been implemented in full, the Polish reform would have been the most radical in Eastern Europe. As we shall see, however, the reform was neither implemented in full nor successful in achieving its goals of market equilibria and improved economic efficiency.

Under the reform, central allocation of materials and targets were supposed to be phased out, and the Plan to take on a purely indicative, forecasting role. The reality was somewhat different: traditional central planning did disappear, but direct central control over certain economic activities persisted, though its scope gradually decreased during the course of the reform.

Direct central control took three forms (see World Bank 1987: 118–22).

1 *Centrally allocated material inputs*   In 1982 70 per cent of all inputs by value were centrally allocated; by 1987 this had fallen to 35 per cent. Centrally allocated inputs were still allocated using the traditional method of material balances.

2 *Key investment programmes*   These were essentially islands of traditional command-economy planning, involving priority access to inputs in order to fulfil central commands. In 1982, key investment programmes covered fourteen sectors; by 1987 this figure had fallen to two.

3 *Government contracts*   Enterprises would sign contract to deliver final, intermediate or capital goods to government agencies. As with the key investment programmes, government contracts entitled enterprises to guaranteed input supplies, and so enterprises actually competed for these government orders.

In the early part of the reform central allocation of materials, key investment programmes and government contracts were used by the centre to safeguard supplies of key goods (military goods, key raw materials and industrial products) during a period of considerable economic dislocation and hardship. As the economic crisis of the early 1980s subsided, these formal, direct planning instruments were gradually withdrawn.

Equilibrium in the goods markets was to have been achieved by allowing a measure of free pricing by enterprises and by setting some centrally controlled prices at market clearing levels. The scope of free pricing in the economy under the reform did in fact remain limited; by one estimate, even at the start of 1989, the last year of the reform system, only about 30 per cent of transactions in the economy (by value) were completed at uncontrolled, free market prices. For the most part it was the prices of economically crucial and politically sensitive goods that were centrally set, for example energy, raw materials, food and rent. These prices were typically held below market-clearing and world price levels.

As is typical in a socialist economy of this type, state-administered pricing in Poland was accompanied by a complex system of turnover taxes (ie commodity taxes) and product subsidies. Enterprise financial independence required such a system, since enterprises were not supposed to be penalised simply for producing goods with low state-set prices (or rewarded in the opposite case). Subsidies were also used as part of the foreign trade system – enterprises producing certain goods for export would enjoy unit subsidies, much as EC farmers do under the CAP.

Anecdotal evidence suggests that turnover taxes were in fact used more or less parametrically, in the sense that they were set centrally rather than being tailored to fit the requirements of specific enterprises. The same cannot be said of enterprise subsidies, however. Econometric evidence based on the balance sheets of the 500 largest Polish industrial enterprises (Schaffer 1990a) shows that subsidies were adjusted to suit the requirements of individual enterprises, the main criterion being the enterprise's profit or loss. A loss-maker whose loss increased would be compensated with a nearly matching increase in its subsidy, while a profit-maker whose profit fell might be compensated but to a much more limited extent. Protracted loss-making by enterprises led to protracted subsidisation; bankruptcy in fact never occurred during the reform period. The 'self-financing' aspect of the reform was a failure; enterprise budget constraints remained obstinately 'soft'.

Enterprise profit, after the subtraction of turnover taxes and the addition of subsidies, was subject to an enterprise income or profit tax. This tax was intended to be linear at a rate of 65 per cent. In fact exemptions and extra payments were possible on a wide variety of grounds, and few enterprises actually paid tax at the standard rate. Enterprises that granted wage increases in excess of a centrally set figure were also liable to an additional wage tax. This tax was the central tool in the government's incomes policy, and was also intended to protect enterprise profits, and thus self-financed investment, from excessive wage claims. As it turned out, the authorities were reluctant to use the tool, and wage growth rates typically exceeded targets. What was left after these two taxes (minus contributions to and/or plus withdrawals from the enterprise's reserve fund) constituted the enterprise's retained profit. This was divided into three funds: the bonus fund, the social fund and the development fund (for financing investments).

Most investment in the early period of the reform was centrally funded. This proportion steadily decreased, and by the end of the reform period the bulk of investment was being funded by enterprises, either through retained profits or by borrowing from the state banks. Credit was offered to enterprises at subsidised (in real terms negative) rates of interest.

As noted above, enterprises were to be 'self-managed' under the new system, and a prominent role was given to workers' councils in the reform blueprints. Introduction of self-management got off to a poor start, as workers' councils were suspended following the introduction of martial law in December 1981. They were reactivated in 1983 but never built up any substantial influence. They had a deciding role in the allocation of the enterprise social fund but only a consultative role on other matters. And in the larger enterprises (accounting for most of the country's employment) they were not even consulted on the appointment and dismissal of enterprise directors (Gomulka and Rostowski 1984). Survey evidence from this period suggests that workers' councils were involved in few enterprise disputes, mostly because of their weak position *vis-à-vis* management and the centre (Kwasniewski 1985).

Although formal central control of enterprises was not to be a feature of the new system, the centre did, in fact, retain substantial powers over enterprise activity. Informal guidance by ministries was commonplace, and could be enforced through a wide variety of formal and informal measures (Kasperkiewicz 1985). As indicated above, enterprise tax liabilities and subsidy entitlements could be manipulated by the centre. Access by the enterprise to scarce industrial supplies could also be controlled by the centre. Ratchet-effect problems (see Dyker 1991: ch. 2) were therefore widespread; enterprises were discouraged from revealing their true productive capacity, since this would make it more difficult to negotiate a larger subsidy, tax break, level of supply of inputs, and so on. At a more basic level, the salary scales of enterprise directors were set centrally, and the appointment of directors controlled or guided by the centre.

Though the reform of the socialised sector did not prove successful, the liberalisation of the private sector did achieve significant results, especially after the start of the 'second stage of the reform' in 1987. The size limitations on private enterprises were gradually eased in the course of the 1980s, and the formation of private joint stock companies made easier. In response to these changes the non-agricultural private sector grew increasingly quickly. From end-1982 to end-1989 the number of people working in the private sector outside agriculture increased by over 1 million, from 667,000 to 1,780,000, with about 60 per cent of this increase taking place in 1988–9 (*RS*, various issues). Most of the increase in activity was located in industry and building. As the size of the total labour force was roughly constant and there was no virtually no unemployment in this period, this growth must have come at the expense of the socialised sector.

The results of the 1982 reform in terms of growth rates of industrial output, employment and productivity can be seen in Table 10.8. At first glance, the performance of the state-owned sector seems reasonable, with output growing at a rate of 3.9 per cent per year in the 1982–9 period and labour productivity growing even faster. This is misleading, however, since a good deal of this growth is attributable simply to the slow recovery from the crisis of 1979–82. The performance trend of the co-operative sector diverged little from that of the state-owned sector. The case of the private sector is rather different. At the start of the 1980s the private sector was extremely small, accounting for about 2 per cent of industrial output and 7 per cent of employment. Output and employment in private industrial firms grew quite rapidly compared to the state sector, but by 1989 these firms still accounted for only 7.4 per cent of total sales and 15 per cent of employment.[3]

Partial but still important reforms were also introduced in the financial sector and the foreign trade system. In 1988 the monobank system was replaced by a system based on a central bank, nine separate commercial (but still state-owned) banks, which took over dealings with the enterprise sector, and several other specialised banks (also state-owned). In January 1989 a new banking law made it possible for private individuals to set up banks. Some decentralisation of foreign trade took place, and enterprises began to market their exports directly. Regulations regarding the holding of foreign exchange were also liberalised somewhat, though the market for foreign exchange remained heavily distorted. Individuals were allowed to hold foreign currency and to deposit it in special hard currency bank accounts. A hard currency retention scheme was set up for the enterprise sector, so that exporting enterprises could also maintain hard currency bank accounts. The government introduced at the same time a system of inter-enterprise trading in hard currency. In 1988 it became legal for private individuals to set up licensed currency exchange bureaux (*kantory*), and by early 1989 many such

Table 10.8 Industrial growth by ownership category 1970–89

	Average annual growth rates		
	1970–9	*1979–82*	*1982–9*
Output[a]			
All	8.1	−4.6	4.0
Socialised	8.1	−4.9	3.7
State	8.0	−5.4	3.8
Co-operative	8.4	−2.1	1.0
Private	7.6	11.3	14.1
Employment[b]			
All	1.8	−1.6	−0.6
Socialised	1.8	−2.3	−2.4
State	1.5	−2.0	−1.9
Co-operative	3.6	−2.1	−1.5
Private	2.3	9.0	12.6
Labour productivity[c]			
All	6.3	−2.9	4.6
Socialised	6.3	−2.6	6.1
State	6.5	−3.4	5.7
Co-operative	4.8	0.0	2.5
Private	5.3	2.3	1.5

Notes:
[a] Output 1970–82 is global product (total transactions); output 1982–9 is sold production, except for private sector which is global product
[b] Employment is full-time equivalent annual average
[c] Labour productivity is based on output and employment figures

Sources: RS and RSPrz, various years

firms were operating. But the government maintained an official exchange rate that was highly artificial, and the zloty/dollar free market rate in 1988 and 1989 was typically four to five times the official rate. The increase in the rate of inflation during this period, combined with the negative real interest rate offered to savers, led to a movement into dollars by households and in effect a dollarisation of the economy (Fan and Shaffer 1991).

The 'Balcerowicz Plan' and the 'Big Bang' of January 1990

In September 1989 the Solidarity Government took office. Under the direction of Finance Minister Leszek Balcerowicz the new economic team set to work on a reform plan. The plan was organised around three themes: stabilisation, liberalisation and price correction, and systemic reform/structural adjustment.

When the new government took over, inflation was running at a rate of over 30 per cent per month. Macro-stabilisation of the economy was an urgent priority, and the assistance and support of the IMF was seen as crucial. Liberalisation of the economy was also seen as an urgent as well as important task, and the team decided to enact a large-scale radical liberalisation of the economy simultaneously with the implementation of the stabilisation measures. Systemic reform and structural adjustment (including the transformation of the system of ownership) was by contrast seen as an inherently longer-term process, to be achieved over a period of years and with the financial assistance of Western nations and international organisations such as the IMF, the World Bank and the EC.

The Balcerowicz Plan was hurriedly drawn up during September–December 1989, and a Letter of Intent signed with the IMF in December. Implementation of the stabilisation measures and many of the liberalisation and price correction measures started in October 1989, with a large dose at the beginning of January 1990. The stabilisation measures consisted of a package of tight fiscal and monetary policies. The stabilisation programme would be based on the establishment of three 'nominal anchors': the total amount of credit, the wage rate and the exchange rate.

Stabilisation measures

Fiscal policy

In 1989 Poland's budget deficit amounted to 8 per cent of GDP. The government's programme was to bring the 1990 budget into rough balance, mainly through drastic reductions in the scope and size of subsidies and tax exemptions (Gomulka 1990: 135). Subsidies were to be cut from 14 per cent to 6 per cent of GDP, that is to a level comparable to that in some West European countries (Schaffer 1990b).

Nominal anchor 1: total amount of credit

Monetary policy in 1989 was highly accommodating, the budget deficit being monetised by the central bank. In the second half of the year, when inflation accelerated sharply, the real rate of interest paid by the enterprise sector went strongly negative and the consequent implicit interest rate subsidy was so large as to be of the same order of magnitude as budgetary subsidies (Gomulka 1990). In 1990, under the Balcerowicz Plan, interest rates were to be positive and monetary growth kept under strict control. High interest rates would be used to protect and rebuild foreign exchange reserves and restore confidence in the zloty, which would return to its role as the main currency in use ('de-dollarisation').

Nominal anchor 2: tax-based incomes policy (TIP)

Enterprise wage increases above a certain government-set level were to be taxed at punitive rates. The TIP would be used to bring the 'statistical real wage' down about 30 per cent from its unsustainable 1989 level. The tax was not new – it had been introduced as part of the 1982 reforms – but was intended to re-emerge as an effective policy instrument in 1990.

Nominal anchor 3: a fixed unified nominal exchange rate

The exchange rate of 9,500 zloty per US dollar for all current transactions would serve as a basis for the establishment of 'internal convertibility' (convertibility on current but not capital account). Foreign exchange could now be bought and sold by enterprises and by the population without restriction, but the foreign currency retention scheme for exporters was dropped. Henceforth enterprises would have to surrender foreign exchange receipts to the central bank.

These stabilisation measures were accompanied by a unilateral suspension of debt service to commercial banks from 1 January 1990.

Liberalisation measures

The main aims of the liberalisation portion of the Balcerowicz Plan were to free the greater part of the domestic price system, correct prices remaining under state control (notably energy prices), remove the state from large-scale detailed direction of the economy, and provide a satisfactory environment for the growth of private enterprises. Some progress in liberalisation had already been made prior to January 1990. As we saw, most of the formal vestiges of central planning had been abandoned during the 1982–9 reform (eg central distribution of materials). The removal of the Communist Party from power and the collapse of the *nomenklatura* system caused the informal counterparts to formal central planning to disappear. Specific liberalisation measures introduced in January 1990 included the following.

Price liberalisation

Prior to August 1989, only about 30 per cent of all transactions in the economy took place at free prices; the freeing of food prices in that month raised this to roughly 50 per cent. As of January 1990, most of the remaining price controls were to be abandoned, leaving only about 10 per cent of all output selling at controlled prices.

Establishment of a free trade regime

Quotas on Western imports were to be replaced by a tariff-based system. Restrictions on the right to engage in foreign trade were to be lifted. The domestic economy would thus be exposed both to foreign competition and to international relative prices.

Legal requirements

There was liberalisation of legal requirements for the setting-up of private enterprises.

Systemic reform

In an important sense, radical reform of the economic system began months before the specific systemic reform measures of the Balcerowicz Plan were enacted. A key failing of the old economic system had been the absence of clearly defined 'rules of the (economic) game' and an unwillingness or inability on the part of the central authorities to play according to any such rules. The way in which the Solidarity movement assumed power in September 1989 (formation of a parliamentary majority following elections), and the manner in which the new government exercised this power, helped establish the rule of economic law in Poland immediately. A second key element of systemic reform that was also already in place by January 1990 was the institution of a strict financial regime for state-owned enterprises. Tax and subsidy rules would now be applied strictly, and bargaining between the centre and enterprise over taxes/subsidies would be abandoned. Enterprises that could not pay their bills would not be rescued by the state but would be allowed to go bankrupt. With these exceptions, however, the pace of systemic change and structural adjustment has been slow. In particular, privatisation of state-owned enterprises was seen in the Balcerowicz Plan as a medium-term goal, and no immediate changes to the formal system of state ownership were introduced. The legal status of workers' councils was also left unchanged by the Balcerowicz measures.

The 'Big Bang'

The wide scope of the Balcerowicz Plan measures and the sudden introduction of many of the stabilisation and liberalisation measures in January 1990 has led some to give this as the date of the Polish 'Big Bang'. The period since the Big Bang has, by contrast, seen a fairly slow pace in the design and implementation of reform policies. This does not mean that the pace of transition has been slow; indeed, by some measures (the growth in private sector employment, the growth in hard currency exports) it has been rapid. Rather, the strategy of the Balcerowicz team was, in general terms, to stabilise the economy quickly, to introduce as many liberalisation measures as technically feasible at the same time, and to introduce or support whatever systemic change could be accomplished in such a brief period. The measures not immediately introduced were those that were inherently time-consuming and slow, namely much of the anticipated systemic changes. Thus the Balcerowicz Plan gave the economic system of the Polish 'transition economy' its *basic* operating features almost right away, and these features have been more or less stable since the Big Bang.

The economic system: transition

At time of writing (December 1991) Poland can be characterised as a 'transitional socialist economy'. The bulk of state assets remain formally in state hands. Nevertheless, the economy has made substantial progress in the transition to a West European-type market economy in terms of how markets, economic agents and economic policy-makers operate. The direct price controls that figured so prominently under the previous system have been largely abandoned, and the scope of state-set pricing is about the same as in Western Europe.[4] The 'rule of economic law' has been clearly established. Government economic policy is subject to parliamentary oversight. The set of instruments used to implement economic policy in Poland, and the terms under which they are employed, now resemble those used in West European states more than those of the pre-1989 system.

The centre–enterprise relationship has also been transformed radically and has moved much closer to that prevailing in West European economies, despite the fact that most enterprises remain state-owned. As part of the Balcerowicz Plan, cost-plus subsidies were cut dramatically and the negative real interest rate subsidy disappeared. Pressures on the government to bail out ailing enterprises have so far been largely resisted. These pressures were relatively light in the early part of the Balcerowicz programme, in part because it was a workers' movement (Solidarity) that put the government in power, and in part because profitability in state-owned enterprises was surprisingly high (see pp. 261–2). As the Solidarity movement fractured and the financial situation of enterprises worsened, these pressures increased, though at the time of writing they were still being successfully resisted. In short, to use Kornai's terminology, state-owned enterprises in transition Poland have had to operate under a fairly hard budget constraint.

With decentralised price setting has come equilibrium in the markets for goods and services. Shortages and queues are a thing of the past, and goods are available in shops for those who want to buy them and who can afford them. The free trade regime has helped bring the structure of domestic prices closer to world market prices for tradeables. A labour market has also emerged, albeit a peculiar one. Open unemployment is now a major feature of the labour market, trade unions are active, and labour demand and wage determination in the private sector is more or less along Western lines. Labour demand and wage setting in the state sector is definitely not, however, because of the power of workers' councils (see below in this section). Finally, a capital market is emerging, but is developing only slowly. Investment finance from state-owned commercial banks is available, and new private banks are being established steadily, though they do not account for much of the market for credit. Large-scale capital transactions are rare, and the Warsaw Stock Exchange, which formally opened in April 1991, trades in very few companies (nine quoted companies as of December 1991). Small-scale capital transactions are rather more common, as evidenced by the ongoing expansion of the private sector and the progress of the government's small-scale privatisation programme (eg sale of shops).

One of the more curious features of this transition economic set-up is the system of ownership and control of state-owned enterprises and the role of workers' councils. As part of the 1982 reform, workers' councils were established in most state-owned enterprises. Though the powers of these councils were intended to be large, they were in practice not very influential in the running of enterprises. The *nomenklatura* system and the informal steering methods used by the state to guide enterprises meant that decisions taken by enterprise management reflected the interests of the state, tempered by trade unions (official and unofficial). The collapse of the communist system in mid-1989 and the assumption of power by the Solidarity government led to a fundamental change in decision-making at the enterprise level. The retreat from direct guidance of enterprises combined with the introduction of the rule of law meant that the hitherto moribund workers' councils became a leading force in enterprise decision-making.

Their previously only *de jure* rights became *de facto* rights. These rights included the appointment of the enterprise director, and in fact since the start of the transition workers' councils in many enterprises have replaced their directors (and those directors who were not replaced knew they could be). In short, Polish state-owned enterprises, while remaining state-owned, became to a considerable extent 'worker-controlled firms'. This is a wonderful 'Polish Paradox': one of the initial achievements following the collapse of communism and the arrival of a democratic government bent on transforming Poland into a West European-type capitalist economy was to create an economy dominated by worker-controlled firms – what some would call 'true socialism'.

With these changes, both in the economic environment in which state enterprises operate and in their governance, have come changes in the behaviour and attitudes of enterprise management and workers. State-owned enterprises are in general more market-oriented than before. Many have reacted to the sudden changes by trying to cut costs (including substantial labour shedding) and find new markets for their products (though this is not to say that they have achieved the levels of performance of their privately owned counterparts). Just how deep these changes in state enterprise behaviour are is debatable; enterprise-level studies (Dabrowski et al 1991; Jorgensen et al 1990; Krajewski and Krajewska 1990) suggest considerable variation between enterprises.

Another result of the introduction of the rule of law was the 'privatisation' of the entire co-operative sector. Co-operatives under the communist system were 'co-operatives' in law but not in fact. The return of the rule of law meant that the state no longer treated these co-operatives as if they were state-owned; in effect, members of the co-operatives became their owners in fact as well as in law. In 1991 co-operatives were formally reclassified in the official statistics as part of the private sector. Since at the end of 1989 the number of people working in the non-agricultural co-operative sector actually exceeded the number of people working in the non-agricultural private sector (1.9 million vs 1.8 million – *RS 1991*: xiv–xv), the establishment of the rule of law practically doubled the number of people employed in the non-agricultural private sector, and raised the private sector's share of total employment in the economy to nearly 50 per cent. I should add, however, that the effect on the volume of fixed assets owned by the private sector was much less dramatic, because most of the fixed assets used by co-operatives were state-owned.

Economic performance in transition, 1990–91

The title of this section could well have been 'The Start of the Great Recession'. The economic contraction in 1990–1 was huge: according to official statistics, GDP in 1991 will be about 20 per cent down on its 1989 level. Growth will resume only in 1992 or even later, and pre-1990 levels of GDP will probably be regained only in the second half of the 1990s. In this section I shall chart the development of the recession (see Table 10.9) and its proximate causes.

It is convenient to begin with a summary of macroeconomic developments in 1990 following the Big Bang of 1 January 1990 (see Gomulka 1991a; 1991b; Schaffer 1991).

Output

In 1990 GDP (measured in constant 1984 prices) fell by 12 per cent according to official statistics.[5] This was substantially greater than expected; the IMF-agreed programme anticipated a drop of only 5 per cent. The decline was basically all in the non-agricultural socialised sector, with industry particularly hard hit (output down about 25 per cent). The remarkable feature of this fall in the level of economic activity is that most of it took place almost all at once, in January–February 1990. Activity was then roughly flat for the rest of the first half of 1990, followed by a moderate pick-up in the second half.

Prices

There was a large burst of 'corrective inflation' at the start of the stabilisation programme – 79.6 per cent per month in January 1990, 23.8 per cent in February.[6] Inflation then subsided, but persisted at average levels of about 4–5 per cent per month for the rest of the year. The extent of the 'corrective inflation' was substantially greater than expected – the programme had assumed an increase of 45 per cent in January. The persistence of inflation was also a surprise; it had been hoped that inflation would be under control by mid-1990.

Money and credit

Monetary policy was extremely contractionary in 1990. In the first half of 1990, the real money supply fell by 42 per cent (compared to an expected 25 per cent in the IMF-agreed programme) and real credit to the non-government sector by 18 per cent (compared to no change as expected in the programme) (Gomulka 1991a: 74). The squeeze on credit caused enterprises to sell much of their hard currency holdings; households kept their hard currency but accumulated new savings in zloty. The effect of this was to de-dollarise the economy substantially (Gomulka 1991b: 13).

Employment and wages

Recorded employment fell by about 6 per cent – 1.1 million people – in the course of 1990, the fall being wholly accounted for by the socialised sector. Private sector non-agricultural employment increased by 555,000 (a 9.5 per cent rise) (*MRS 1991*: 276–7). Registered unemployment increased steadily during the year, from virtually zero to about 1.1 million, an unemployment rate of almost 9 per cent (measured as a percentage of the non-agricultural labour force) by the end of the year; this compares with the 400,000 initially budgeted for in the government's programme. Average real wages for the year fell by about 30 per cent, to 1982–4 levels, around what was anticipated in the IMF-approved programme (Gomulka 1991a: 74). The pattern of the fall was unexpected, however. From December 1989 to February 1990 the nominal,

Table 10.9   Economic performance 1988–91

	1988	1989	1990	1991
Annual CPI inflation (%) (December to December)	73.9	639.6	249.3[a]	60.4
GDP growth (%)	4.1	0.2	−11.6	8 to −10
Industrial sales growth (%)				
Total	5.3	−0.5	−24.2	−11.9
of which:				
Private sector (old definition, co-ops excluded)	15.8	22.0	8.9	48.6
Investment growth (%)	5.4	−2.4	−10.1	about −8
Statistical real wage growth (%)	14.4	9.0	−24.4	about 2
Enterprise profitability (%)[b]	19.0	45.5	29.4	9.4 (Jan–Nov)
Hard currency trade balance ($m)	1.009.2	767.3	3,765.7	−29
Export growth (%)	9.1	0.2	13.7	−1.4
Import growth (%)	9.4	1.5	−17.9	39.0
Registered unemployed (thousands, end-year)	4.6	9.6	1,126.1	2,155.6
Government budget surplus (+)/ deficit (−), % of government expenditure	0.8	−10.6	1.3	−12.6
Annual interest rate (%)[c]	6.0	61.3	103.8	53.9
Zloty/dollar exchange rate				
Official (NBP)	431	1,446	9,500	10,559
Free market	1,979	5,565	9,570	10,731
Number of commercial law partnerships	1,275	11,693	29,650	45,077
Individual businesses (unincorporated):				
Number (thousands)	659.6	813.5	1,135.5	1,420.1
Employing (thousands)	n.a.	1,475.5	1,915.5	about 2,600

Notes:
[a] About half of the increase in the consumer price index in 1990 took place in January and February; the CPI increased by 122 per cent from December 1989 to February 1990; from February 1990 to December 1990, by 57 per cent
[b] Enterprise profitability is 'gross financial result' divided by 'costs of sales of own production' (in %)
[c] Interest rate is the rate of refinanced credit

Sources:
BS, various issues
RS, various issues
SP, various issues
Corrochano and Barbone 1991
Informacija o sytuacii spoleczno-gospodarczej kraju: rok 1991. [GUS, January 1992]
Author's estimates

monthly wage in the state sector increased only slightly (about 8 per cent). The burst of 'corrective inflation' during this period thus meant that the 'statistical real wage' fell by about half at the start of the year. From March through the rest of the year, real wages increased at a rate of about 3.5 per cent per month; by December real wages were about 40 per cent higher than in March. This was possible despite the government's tax-based incomes policy because the massive cut in real wages in the first two months of the year, combined with a feature of the scheme that allowed enterprises to carry forward the unused portion of the wage 'norm', meant that the TIP became binding for most enterprises only around the start of the fourth quarter of 1990 (see Schaffer 1991).

Foreign trade

Following the devaluations and the trade liberalisation, exports to the hard currency area were up substantially on the previous year (by 40 per cent measured in constant zloty and by 39.4 per cent in dollars): hard currency imports for 1990 were up just slightly (after a sharp drop in the first half of 1990). This made for a substantial dollar surplus. Exports to the rouble area were down (by about 7–10 per cent) but imports were down much more (about 35 per cent), again making for a substantial surplus. Overall, total exports increased by about 15 per cent, and total imports fell by about 15 per cent, over 1989.

Enterprise profitability

Despite the depth of the recession and the cutting back of subsidies, enterprise profitability was quite high in 1990. Very few enterprises made losses either before or after taxes/subsidies, and there were virtually no bankruptcies. Investment also kept relatively high (it fell less than output).

*   *   *   *   *

It is still too early for a full explanation of the macroeconomic events of 1990, but a partial picture has emerged (see Gomulka 1991a, 1991b; Schaffer 1991). First, both monetary and fiscal policy were extremely contractionary at the beginning of the programme, much more so than intended. The enterprise sector suffered a severe liquidity squeeze starting in January 1990, and responded by sharply reducing real wages and economic activity. The NBP nominal interest rate on refinancing credit was raised from 140 per cent per year (about 8 per cent per month) in December 1989 to 36 per cent per month in January 1990 – high in nominal terms though actually still negative in real terms in January, with positive real interest rates starting in February. Enterprises responded in January by increasing only slightly their borrowing of turnover credits from banks in nominal terms. The larger-than-expected burst of corrective inflation in January (the price level nearly doubled from December to January) thus meant that the real stock of credit held by enterprises fell by almost 50 per cent. A large portion of hard currency holdings by enterprises were converted into zloty in January as enterprises sought to increase their liquidity, but hard currency holdings were concentrated in the export sector and so liquidity for most of the enterprise sector was sharply down. This led directly to a decrease in wages and economic activity by enterprises and was a major contributor to the sudden recession.[7] With respect to fiscal policy, the government budget was in substantial (8 per cent) surplus in the first half of the year (*BS* nos 1–3 1991: 34), when only approximate balance had been intended.

The second major element behind the 1990 recession was the large drop in aggregate demand caused by the huge drop in real wages in January–February. There were probably two factors behind this. First, enterprises, suffering from severe liquidity problems, did not have the money to pay higher wages. Second, the economic environment at the time was extremely uncertain, and the general expectation was that many enterprises would be in severe difficulties and would face bankruptcy. These being 'worker-controlled firms', workers were apparently willing to accept a large cut in real wages to help ensure the survival of 'their' enterprise (Schaffer 1991; Dabrowski et al 1991). The real wage cut was so large that in March, after inflation had subsided, the average enterprise monthly wage was well below the limit imposed by the TIP.

By March–April the liquidity position of enterprises had eased considerably, and it was becoming clear that enterprise profitability was in general quite healthy (largely as a consequence of the huge fall in real labour costs). Furthermore, as noted earlier, the TIP scheme adopted allowed enterprises that undershot the TIP constraint to carry forward the accumulated undershoot and pay it later in the year. Enterprises responded by starting to increase wages in real terms beginning in March, and the accumulated undershoot was mostly used up by around October. This steady increase in real wages, combined with a loosening of monetary policy in the second half of the year, fuelled a moderate increase in economic activity in the third quarter of 1990 and contributed to the persistence of inflation. The relative financial health of the enterprise sector was also partly responsible for the apparent ease with which the government was able to impose 'hard budget constraints' on enterprises; requests for subsidies and so forth could be more easily refused to enterprises that were making profits.

The picture of the labour market in 1990 is somewhat less clear. Employment in the socialised sector fell by 1.6 million, with about one-third of this decrease located in the co-operative sector. Recorded employment in the private sector increased by 555,000, with the increase concentrated in retail trade. Later in the chapter I shall argue that the distribution of the changes in employment is closely related to the process of ownership transformation that took place in 1990. Of the 1.1 million registered unemployed people at year's end, only 16 per cent had been laid off as a function of 'mass lay-offs' (*RS 1991*: 106). A large part of the shrinkage of state-sector employment was apparently achieved through attrition, which was to be expected, given the degree of workers' control; labour turnover data show that severances increased marginally in 1990, whereas hirings dropped sharply (*MRS 1991*: 151).

The persistence of inflation is explained by the failure of two of the nominal anchors of the stabilisation programme to act as anchors for most of 1990, combined with the loosening of monetary policy that occurred in the second half of the year. Real wages increased steadily during 1990 because the TIP was failing to bind. The over-devaluation of the zloty meant that the fixed nominal exchange rate, instead of acting as a nominal anchor to hold back increases in the domestic price level, actually contributed to domestic inflation via the price level of imports. The boom in exports to the West was also a clear consequence of the extent of devaluation, and the central bank failed fully to sterilise the surplus, which resulted in an unplanned increase in the supply of money. Note that the failure of these two nominal anchors was also a factor behind the maintenance of reasonable levels of profitability in the enterprise sector, and that kept employment levels from dropping even faster. According to one member of the Balcerowicz team, this strategy – risking persistent inflation in exchange for avoiding an East German-scale employment catastrophe – was deliberate, but went further than anticipated (Gomulka 1991b).

Macroeconomic trends in 1991 have been quite different from those of 1990. Details at time of writing are still incomplete, but here is a rough summary:

1 *Output* GDP fell by more than 8 per cent in 1991. The decline took place gradually over the first half of the year, in contrast to the sudden drop in 1990.

2 *Prices* The monthly inflation rate was 12.7 per cent in January due to administrative price increases, and then gradually subsided to about 2–4 per cent by the end of the third quarter.

3 *Monetary policy* In the first half of 1991 monetary policy was tightened and then gradually relaxed as inflation subsided.

4 *Employment and wages* Employment continued to fall steadily, and unemployment continued to increase. Unemployment reached 16 per cent (measured as a percentage of the non-agricultural labour force) by the end of 1991. In marked contrast to 1990, the TIP was a binding constraint on enterprise wages from January onwards. As a result, the upward trend in real wages was actually reversed; real wages dropped about 8 per cent in the first quarter of 1991 and another 7 per cent in the second quarter (*BS* no 10 1991: 12).

5 *Foreign trade* Total exports in 1991 fell slightly compared to 1990, with a very large fall in exports to the ex-CMEA countries (about 40 per cent) mostly offset by increased exports to hard currency countries. Imports, by contrast, increased by nearly 40 per cent. The large trade surplus of 1990 turned into approximate trade balance in 1991. The zloty was devalued in May 1991 by 17 per cent and pegged to a basket of currencies. In October the government instituted a crawling peg system.

6 *Enterprise and government finance* The loss of CMEA markets, the appreciation of the real exchange rate, and the increase in wages dating from the end of 1990, combined to decrease enterprise profitability sharply. This development conspired with the fall in the level of economic activity to cause a substantial shortfall in government tax revenue. A large government budget deficit emerged (on the order of 4–5 per cent of GDP), and a revised budget, with spending cuts, had to be drafted.

The causes of the large drop in GDP in 1991 are more or less clear, though it is still too early to give precise estimates of the scale of the different effects. Much attention has been focused on the collapse of exports to the ex-CMEA, but I think the effects of this factor have been somewhat exaggerated. Ex-CMEA exports did, as we have seen, drop by about 40 per cent in volume terms. These exports had, however, already lost much of their importance – they amounted to about 5 per cent of GDP in 1990 – and in any case most of the decline in ex-CMEA exports was offset by an increase in non-CMEA exports. The dominant effect is rather the large increase in imports caused mainly by the real appreciation of the zloty. In current prices the trade surplus in 1990 was 7.5 per cent of GDP. For 1991 trade ended up roughly in balance, mostly because of the increase in the volume of imports. Back-of-an-envelope calculations on the basis of the

Table 10.10 Structure of foreign trade 1989

| | Imports in 1989 (current zloty) | | | | |
	All	Socialist countries	of which CMEA	Non-socialist countries	of which EC
All	100.0	40.1	32.7	59.9	33.8
of which:					
Food, drink and tobacco	11.7	1.6	0.9	10.1	5.3
Crude materials (inedible)	8.4	2.5	2.1	5.9	2.1
Mineral fuels	12.7	9.6	9.5	3.1	0.4
Chemicals	10.9	2.4	1.6	8.5	6.2
Machinery and transport equipment	33.4	14.8	13.0	18.6	11.4
Other manufactured goods	22.9	9.2	5.6	13.7	8.4

| | Exports in 1989 (current zloty) | | | | |
	All	Socialist countries	of which CMEA	Non-socialist countries	of which EC
All	100.0	40.6	35.1	59.4	32.1
of which:					
Food, drink and tobacco	11.3	1.3	1.1	10.0	6.7
Crude materials (inedible)	6.0	1.1	0.9	4.9	3.0
Mineral fuels	9.7	2.6	2.5	7.1	3.6
Chemicals	7.7	3.1	2.6	4.6	2.5
Machinery and transport equipment	33.6	22.0	19.8	11.6	4.7
Other manufactured goods	31.7	10.5	8.2	21.2	11.6

Source: RSHZ90: 123–5

national income identity tell us that the disappearance of the trade surplus translates into a fall of about 6 per cent in GNP from the increase in imports and one of about 1 per cent from the fall in exports. Domestic absorption in 1991, therefore, fell much less than GDP, and in fact it appears that consumption in 1991 was at about the same level as in 1990. Any fall in GDP not directly attributable to foreign trade trends can be explained by multiplier effects arising from the fall in exports and investment, and on the tightening of monetary policy and the decrease in real wages in early 1991. On the other hand, the impact of these developments would have been softened by the expansionary effect of the budget deficit.

The large increases in exports to the West in 1990 and 1991 are of course very good news. As noted earlier, the 1982–9 socialist reform included some limited liberalisation of the foreign trade system. Table 10.10 shows that by 1989 Poland had made considerable progress in reorienting its foreign trade toward the West, and toward the EC in particular. These changes accelerated in 1990–1, spurred on by the collapse of the CMEA system. By 1992 Poland will be conducting about three-quarters of its foreign trade with non-CMEA countries, most of it with EC countries. This reorientation has taken place while total trade volumes have been increasing, so it is certainly a significant achievement. It is particularly encouraging to discover that state-owned enterprises, which dominate the export sector, are capable of responding significantly to changes in incentives and economic environment.

The drop in real wages in early 1991 is a direct consequence of the failure of the TIP to bind for most of 1990. The large undershoot in the first half of 1990 was carried over in the form of a large overshoot in the second half of 1990. But this meant that the enterprise sector as a whole ended 1990 with an average wage that was about 30 per cent above the December 1990 wage norm. The January 1991 norm was based on the December 1990 norm plus a bit for inflation, and so suddenly the TIP constraint began to bite, and very hard indeed. Even with the fall in real wages in early 1991, average wages exceeded the TIP wage norm by a considerable margin. The large punitive taxes thus incurred by many enterprises led to considerable industrial unrest in early 1991, which threatened to topple the government. However, the collapse in enterprise profits and the sharp drop in output combined to reduce wage pressure and the government survived the difficulties.

The collapse in enterprise profits is one of the most important developments of 1991. It was caused by the increase in unit labour costs (aggregate real wage costs were higher, aggregate real output lower than in 1990), the appreciation of the real exchange rate, and the fall in economic activity. Profit taxes are a major source of government revenue, and it is the collapse in profits, combined with the fall in economic activity, that has led to the emergence of a large government budget deficit. Cutting the deficit will be very difficult politically; indeed, the profit collapse is testing the government's ability to maintain hard budget constraints and resists pressures to rescue key enterprises. It is in this context that the collapse of the CMEA becomes important. The reason is that CMEA exports were concentrated in enterprises specialising in this market. These enterprises were hit extremely hard by the trade collapse, and have been lobbying hard, and not without justification, for special assistance from the government.

During the run-up to the October 1991 elections, the government's economic programme was strongly criticised by a number of parties that argued forcefully in favour of reflation. The elections resulted, moreover, in a very fragmented parliament. It will be difficult for the new government to bring the budget under control. If it does not do so, Poland will be heading for another episode of high inflation. Such an episode would prove extremely costly for Poland, and not just for the obvious reasons. On 18 April 1991 the IMF approved a three-year Extended Fund Facility (EFF). On 19 April 1991 the Paris Club reduced the Polish official debt of $33.3 billion by 30 per cent ($10 billion), with a reduction of a further 20 per cent in three years' time, conditional upon a successful implementation of the conditions of the EFF (Gomulka 1991b: 8). Unless the new government is able to regain control of the budget, the IMF requirements will likely not be met and the second tranche of debt reduction may be lost.

Privatisation and structural adjustment

Like all the transition economies, Poland faces a huge structural adjustment task. The services sector is relatively small, industry is large, and the transition from an agriculture-based society is not yet complete. The capital stock embodies outdated technology, energy- and material-intensive techniques are in common use, and pollution control and environmental protection are rudimentary. The foreign trade orientation bequeathed by the CMEA trade system had to change. And, most important of all, the system of ownership must be completely transformed.

A critical role in structural adjustment will be played by market forces and the domestic reallocation of labour and capital. It is the decisions of economic actors to reallocate resources that underpin this process. We expect the 'indigenous' private sector to be the most entrepreneurial in this regard, the privatised (formally socialised) sector second most, and the (still) socialised sector least. The success of structural adjustment is therefore intimately dependent upon the process of ownership transformation. That is why I shall concentrate on the role of ownership transformation within the process of structural adjustment. But first I want to discuss briefly the role of foreign capital.

The scale of foreign direct investment in Poland during the two years following the start of the transition has been relatively limited compared to, say, Hungary. The reasons for this are not entirely clear. Initially there were legal restrictions on foreign investment. This changed in June 1991 with the passage of a new foreign investment law, described by the OECD as 'quite liberal and comparable to FDI regimes in most OECD countries' (*Warsaw Voice* 1 September 1991: L1). Polish wage costs are quite low – about $1.50 per hour in October 1991 – and so we must look for other reasons why foreign investors have been discouraged. These include the uncertainty regarding the large foreign debt (at time of writing an agreement with the London Club of creditor commercial banks had still not been reached); perceived political instability and the spectre of renewed inflation; and the well-known capacity of the Polish work-force to mount industrial action (an advantage under the old system – it enabled the Polish people to bring down two communist governments in under a decade – but an advantage no longer).

By contrast, foreign official lending institutions have been very active. Here the World Bank has played the leading role, with large-scale lending concentrated on modernising the economic infrastructure. In 1990 the World Bank committed about $1 billion to projects in Poland, and was planning to invest a similar amount in 1991 (*Warsaw News* 29 September 1991: 83). The main constraint here is the absorptive capacity of the Polish economy; only a relatively small amount of these funds had actually been disbursed by mid-1991.

We can distinguish between two separate processes of ownership transformation. The first is privatisation proper: by this I mean the transfer of existing assets and/or organisations from the socialised sector to the private sector. The second process arises from the differential growth rates of the *indigenous private sector* (consisting of private firms that are newly established or already existed at the start of the transition process), the *privatised sector* (consisting of formerly socialised firms), and the *public sector* (consisting of firms that remain in state hands), with the last growing more slowly than the first two. I shall refer to this form of ownership transformation as 'growth privatisation'; its best-known proponent is the Hungarian economist Janos Kornai (1991). In the remainder of this section I shall discuss first privatisation proper and then growth privatisation in Poland. As we shall see, however, a clear distinction between these two ownership transformation processes is not always possible.

Table 10.11 Ownership and distribution of economic activity in 1989 and 1990

	NMP [a]		Labour [b]		Fixed Capital [c]	
	1989	1990	1989	1990	1989	1990
All [d]	100.0	100.0	100.0	100.0	100.0	100.0
State	69.9	67.7	52.8	50.0	71.0	64.8
Private	30.1	32.2	47.2	50.0	29.0	35.1
Previously private	19.2	23.1	33.3	38.9	21.2	23.4
Co-operatives etc	11.0	9.1	13.8	11.1	7.8	11.7
Non-agriculture:	86.9	92.4	71.5	70.6	72.4	77.0
State	67.4	66.0	49.5	46.9	63.9	59.4
Private	19.5	26.4	22.0	23.7	8.5	17.5
Previously private	9.7	18.0	10.1	14.1	3.2	7.2
Co-operatives etc	9.8	8.4	12.0	9.5	5.3	10.3
Agriculture:	13.1	7.6	28.5	29.4	27.6	23.0
State	2.5	1.7	3.4	3.1	7.1	5.4
Private	10.7	5.9	25.1	26.3	20.5	17.6
Previously private	9.5	5.1	23.3	24.7	18.0	16.2
Co-operatives etc	1.1	0.8	1.9	1.6	2.5	1.4

Notes:
[a] NMP = Net Material Product
[b] Labour is number of working people, including self-employed farmers, end year
[c] Fixed capital is productive capital only
[d] Numbers may not sum to 100 because of a small residual category

Source: RS91: xiv–xv

Poland held an initial advantage on ownership transformation compared to the other socialist countries, with the possible exception of Hungary. At the time the transition began, about one-third to a half of all economic activity originated in the private sector, depending on the measure used (see Table 10.11). The explanation for this situation is threefold.

First, as noted earlier, Polish agriculture was not collectivised as in the other socialist countries. Although steadily shrinking during the socialist period, private agriculture still employed 4.1 million people, 23.3 per cent of the labour force, at the end of 1989. Resourcing and productivity levels in private agriculture are quite low, however, and so this sector accounts for rather less in terms of capital and especially of output.

Second, the non-agricultural private sector was allowed to expand significantly as part of the socialist economic reform of 1982–9. The number of people working in the non-agricultural private sector nearly doubled over the period 1982–9. At the end of 1989 1.8 million people were employed in the sector, 10.1 per cent of the work-force. About half of this employment was in industry.

Third, as we saw above, the introduction of the rule of law at the beginning of transition effectively resulted in the instant privatisation of the entire co-operative sector along with some other miscellaneous economic organisations. At the end of 1989, 2.4 million people were employed in this sector, 13.8 per cent of the entire work-force. Most of these (2.2 million) were co-operative members. But since much of the fixed assets used by co-operatives were owned by the state, the privatisation of the co-operative sector did not privatise as much capital as it did labour or output.

Taking these three sectors together, fully 8.3 million people, 47.2 per cent of the entire work-force, were employed in the private sector at the end of 1989. Private sector shares of national income and fixed capital in 1989 were rather less – about 30 per cent and 29 per cent, respectively (Table 10.11). One may reasonably argue, however, that the scale of the task of ownership transformation is captured best by measures that relate to the economic disruption and social costs involved. In this context the amount of labour that must be reallocated is the most useful measure, and here the starting-point in Poland was clearly superior to that of any of the other East European countries.

The process of privatising state-owned enterprises and assets may usefully be divided into 'large privatisations' – eg the sale of a big state-owned enterprise, usually as a going concern – and 'small privatisations' – the sale or leasing of small elements of state capital, eg shops. I shall first describe the progress of the large privatisation process, and then turn to small privatisation and its relationship to ownership transformation via growth privatisation.

The process of privatising large state-owned enterprises proper has proceeded slowly, and the number of large privatisations in 1990 was quite small. The Balcerowicz Plan as originally formulated envisaged privatising by selling off shares:

> *The basic design of privatisation is likely to be along the lines carried out by some Western countries in recent years*: auctions of enterprise shares, with special purchase rights reserved for those directly affected by privatisation, i.e. workers and managers.
>
> (Government of Poland 1989; emphasis in the original)

A privatisation law passed in July 1990 defined the conditions under which sales of state-owned enterprise would take place, and a Ministry of Ownership Transformation was established (initially as a small division within the Ministry of Finance). Pilot privatisations of five state-owned enterprises were then carried out, with shares being sold by public auction in November 1990.[8] In April 1991 a stock exchange opened in Warsaw, trading in these and other privatised and publicly quoted firms. The foreign ownership provisions of the privatisation law were liberalised in 1991 with the passage of a new foreign investment law (see p. 266).

By about mid-1990, however, it had become clear to the government's economic team that privatisation via public auction would take much too long. The excessive concentration of Polish industry (the largest 300 state-owned manufacturing enterprises accounted for over half of all sales in socialised manufacturing in 1989) did make the task of privatisation somewhat easier. But if the pace of privatisation that took place under Mrs Thatcher – fewer than twenty public enterprises in ten years – was pursued in Poland, it would take about a century and a half to dispose of these 300 firms. And unlike Britain, the private capital needed to purchase these enterprises was not present in Poland. While sales of large state-owned enterprises, by public auction and to foreign investors, continued, then, the emphasis shifted to 'mass privatisation' as the main means of transforming the ownership structure of the economy in a short period of time: in 1991 the government set the goal of privatising 50 per cent of state assets in three years (ie by 1994).

The mass privatisation scheme of December 1991 envisages a two-stage process. First, selected large state-owned enterprises will be 'commercialised' – converted into joint stock companies with the state treasury as the sole shareholder. About 200 such enterprises (against 400 planned when the scheme was first announced) will be commercialised in the first wave. The shares in the commercialised enterprises are to be distributed as follows: 60 per cent of the shares will be transferred to twenty or so 'National Wealth Management Funds' (NWMFs), 10 per cent will be given to the workers in the form of shares in their privatised enterprise, and 30 per cent will be retained by the state. The National Wealth Management Funds are essentially investment trusts.[9] Shares in individual enterprises are to be concentrated in individual NWMFs as 'active investors'. In the second stage of the mass privatisation programme, shares in the National Wealth Management Funds will be distributed to all adult Poles. After a period of transition, trading in shares of enterprises and National Wealth Management Funds will begin. The idea behind this privatisation scheme is essentially to establish quickly and *de novo* an ownership structure similar to that found in the West, where financial intermediaries in the form of large institutional investors predominate.[10]

The transformation of state-owned enterprises into privately owned firms via commercialisation and privatisation will remove the special powers of workers' councils. Most importantly, managers will become accountable to the shareholders rather than to workers. Incentives for workers and workers' councils to acquiesce to the surrender of their formal powers have been put in place. As just noted, a portion of the shares of privatised enterprises will be distributed to the workers in those enterprises. The TIP was also formally abolished for all private enterprises in 1991 (existing and newly established private firms as well as privatised enterprises) and eased for commercialised enterprises.

The mass privatisation programme is still in its early stages, and it is difficult to predict how it will work out. The NWMFs will be run with the assistance of foreign financial firms, but the fund managers will be appointed by the President of the Republic. To whom the fund managers will be responsible is unclear. Another point of uncertainty concerns the relatively small number of enterprises to be put into the NWMFs. At time of writing it seems likely that the NWMFs will be successfully established, but whether shares in the funds will be distributed to the entire adult population is less sure. The costs of such an exercise are large, and with a limited number of enterprises in the funds it is not clear that a mass distribution of shares would be sensible. There is therefore a strong possibility that many Polish state-owned enterprises could occupy the transitional status of 'commercialised but state-owned' for some time.

In contrast to the slow pace of the large privatisation process, the small privatisation process has moved quickly. One technique frequently used by smaller state-owned enterprises has been liquidation of the enterprise. As of 12 August 1991, the liquidation process had been started in 504 state-owned enterprises, largely in services. About half entered the liquidation process under the State Enterprise Act because of their bad financial situation. These enterprises were closed at the request of supervisory councils, banks or even employees, and their assets usually auctioned off. The liquidation of the other half took place under the Act on Privatisation of State Enterprises. This did not involve physical closure of the enterprise, but simply a change of management and administration. The assets of the enterprise were usually leased to private companies composed of the employees of the former state enterprise. These liquidations have essentially been employee and/or management buy-outs, and have been proving an increasingly popular means of 'privatisation from below' (*Uncensored Poland News Brief* no 12 1991: 10; *Warsaw Voice* 20 October 1991: B5).

At first sight, growth in the private sector in 1990 was relatively impressive, given the overall economic climate. Using the old definition of the non-agricultural private sector (excluding co-operatives), recorded employment increased in the course of the year by 32 per cent. Growth in the trade sector was particularly impressive: employment increased by roughly four times in the course of 1990. And of course these figures do not capture the growth in unrecorded activity, the magnitude of which is unknown. I would argue, however, that the pace of this 'growth privatisation' in 1990 is directly traceable to the collapse of the co-operative sector. The reassertion of the private sector status of co-operatives upon the re-establishment of the rule of law was followed in 1990 by a drastic fall in co-operative employment. And where the fall in co-operative employment was most drastic – in retail trade – private sector (non-cooperative) employment increased the most.

The explanation is apparently as follows. Co-operatives have been dissolving via administrative and/or spontaneous methods. Thus when local authorities, which owned the shops used by retail trade co-operatives, put a shop up for sale or lease, a private enterprise was typically the new occupant. Whether it was more common for this private enterprise to be the co-operative unit that previously occupied the premises, re-formed as a private firm, or alternatively a new private enterprise, is not clear. Another possibility is that co-operative units withdrew from the large co-operative union and thereby lost their co-operative status. In any case, what we are seeing is the recreation of the small private business sector, and this process has been fuelled to a large extent by the shrinking co-operative sector.

Figures on employment by sector and ownership category are given in Table 10.12. The table shows quite clearly that the co-operative sector shed a huge amount of labour in 1990 – employment fell about 25 per cent. About one-third of this shed labour – approximately 290,000 jobs – was in the trade sector. It was in that sector also that the decline in employment in state-owned enterprises was steepest (34.4 per cent) and the increase in the 'previously private' sector greatest. In fact, about 80 per cent of all new employment in the previously private sector was in trade. Taken together, the decline in co-operative and public sector employment in trade is about the same in absolute numbers of employed as the increase in the previously private trade sector. For the economy as a whole, the decline in co-operative employment was about the same as the increase in the (non-cooperative) private sector.

Redeployment of co-operative assets could proceed at a rapid pace because the basic

Table 10.12 Employment[a] by ownership category and economic sector 1989–90

| | Post-1991[b] and pre-1991[c] ownership classification systems | | | |
	end-1989	end-1990	change	% change
Total	17,558.0	16,476.5	−1,081.5	−6.2
State	9,277.8	8,243.5	−1,034.3	−11.1
Private	8,280.2	8,233.0	−47.2	−0.6
Previously private	5,848.6	6,403.7	555.1	9.5
Co-operatives, etc	2,431.6	1,829.3	−602.3	−24.8
Socialised	11,709.4	10.072.8	−1,636.6	−14.0
Previously private	5,848.6	6,403.7	555.1	9.5
Agriculture	5,004.9	4,847.1	−157.8	−3.2
State	594.7	510.9	−83.8	−14.1
Private	4,410.2	4,336.2	−74.0	−1.7
Previously private	4,082.6	4,075.1	−7.5	−0.2
Co-operatives, etc	327.6	261.1	−66.5	−20.3
Socialised	922.3	772.0	−150.3	−16.3
Previously private	4,082.6	4,075.1	−7.5	−0.2
Non-agriculture	12,567.2	11,629.4	−937.8	−7.5
State	8,683.1	7,732.6	−950.5	−10.9
Private	3,870.0	3,896.8	26.8	0.7
Previously private	1,766.0	2,328.6	562.6	31.9
Co-peratives, etc	2,104.0	1,568.2	−535.8	−25.5
Socialised	10,787.1	9,300.8	−1,486.3	−13.8
Previously private	1,766.0	2,328.6	562.6	31.9
Trade	1,449.0	1,459.0	10.0	0.7
State	396.2	259.9	−136.3	−34.4
Private	1,052.8	1,199.1	146.3	13.9
Previously private	140.6	574.1	433.5	308.3
Co-operatives, etc	912.2	625.0	−287.2	−31.5
Socialised	1,308.4	884.9	−423.5	−32.4
Previously private	140.6	574.1	433.5	308.3
Industry	4,971.7	4,430.5	−541.2	−10.9
State	3,523.1	3,030.0	−493.1	−14.0
Private	1,448.6	1,373.5	−75.1	−5.2
Previously private	824.6	901.6	77.0	9.3
Co-operatives etc	624.0	471.9	−152.1	−24.4
Socialised	4,147.1	3,501.9	−645.2	−15.6
Previously private	824.6	901.6	77.0	9.3

(**Table 10.12** Employment[a] by ownership category and economic sector 1989–90 – continued)

	Post-1991[b] and pre-1991[c] ownership classification systems			
	end-1989	end-1990	change	% change
Building	1,229.3	1,090.9	−138.4	−11.3
State	769.9	631.3	−138.6	−18.0
Private	459.4	459.6	0.2	0.0
Previously private	409.7	424.9	15.2	3.7
Co-operatives etc	49.7	34.7	−15.0	−30.2
Socialised	819.6	666.0	−153.6	−18.7
Previously private	409.7	424.9	15.2	3.7
Transport	795.9	724.8	−71.1	−8.9
State	681.7	614.8	−66.9	−9.8
Private	114.2	110.0	−4.2	−3.7
Previously private	51.1	74.1	23.0	45.0
Co-operatives etc	63.1	35.9	−27.2	−43.1
Socialised	744.8	650.7	−94.7	−12.6
Previously private	51.1	74.1	23.0	45.0
Non-material sectors	3,208.0	3,092.7	−115.3	−3.6
State	2,623.7	2,560.9	−62.8	−2.4
Private	584.3	531.8	−52.5	−9.0
Previously private	180.7	163.4	−17.3	−9.6
Co-operatives etc	403.6	368.4	−35.2	−8.7
Socialised	3,027.3	2,929.3	−98.0	−3.2
Previously private	180.7	163.4	−17.3	−9.6

Notes:

[a] Employment is number of working people, including self-employed farmers

[b] 'State/Private' – post-1991 ownership classification system: this system actually divides activity into 'public' and 'private' sectors, but the public sector and the state sector are nearly identical in coverage. The 'private' sector includes the 'previously private' sector, co-operatives and a small residual category

[c] 'Socialised/Previously private' – pre-1991 ownership classification system: the 'previously private' sector was referred to as the 'private' or 'non-socialised' sector under this system. The 'socialised' sector includes the state sector, co-operatives and a small residual category

Source: MRS91: 276–7

units in co-operatives were quite small (retail shops, workshops). Some co-operatives were quite large, but these were usually conglomerates of small units (eg the retail trade co-operatives). The small size of most organisations in retail trade probably also explains the large degree of labour shedding by state-owned enterprises in this sector.

This is very good news in the sense that the proliferation of new private retail shops is a boon – the quality of the new shops is much better than the co-operatives they have replaced, as casual inspection by a visitor will reveal. On the other hand, the 'reserve' of small-scale assets is limited in size and will probably be exhausted in the course of a few years. The redeployment of assets in the central parts of the state-owned sector, involving as it does enterprises employing hundreds or thousands of workers, will take much longer and involve much more disruption of economic activity as enterprises are shut down and workers laid off. This was already clear in industry in 1990, a sector in which enterprises and establishments are much larger than in retail trade. There, state-owned enterprises shed almost half a million workers, and the previously private sector increased employment by less than 80,000.

Before closing this section I shall discuss several issues relating to the changes in the ownership system of the economy that result from growth privatisation.

First, the mass commercialisation and privatisation programme for large state-owned enterprises will probably have a limited effect on their economic performance. The NWMFs will face a tremendous task in establishing their role as 'active investors': it will likely take a lot of time and effort to get them into a position where they are able to promote major changes in management techniques in a significant number of enterprises. The largest impact that commercialisation and privatisation will have (certainly in the short- to medium-run) is on employment levels and industrial relations. The abolition of workers' councils may well accelerate the process of labour shedding already taking place in these enterprises. It may well also lead to a higher incidence of industrial action in formerly state-owned enterprises. It is worth mentioning here that labour unrest could be a larger problem for a commercialised but still state-owned firm than for either a traditionally organised state-owned firm with a powerful workers' council, or a privatised firm. When a firm ceases to be worker-controlled, disagreements between labour and management, and hence industrial action by workers, become more likely. This is true for the privatised firm too, but experience in other countries suggests that the state sector is more susceptible to strikes than the private sector.

It is for these reasons that economic growth in Poland, certainly in the short to medium run (five to fifteen years), will probably result largely from the growth of the indigenous private sector. This will take place both through the establishment and growth of new private firms, and through the absorption by these firms of the previously socialised sector and its assets. We expect the indigenous private sector firms to operate more efficiently and produce higher quality output than corresponding socialised firms, privatised or not. The importance of the absorption of previously socialised assets we have already seen in the form of the phenomenal growth of private retail trade via the transformation of the co-operative sector, the acquisition of its assets by the private sector, and the resulting large improvements in the quality of goods and service. Other statistical evidence from 1990 and 1991 tends to support the thesis that growth privatisation has, indeed, already started in earnest.

One thing likely to hold up the process is the state of the banking sector. Although the number of private banks has been growing, the state-owned (but soon to be privatised) banks still dominate the market for credit. Unlike the enterprise sector (which had some exposure to Western markets), the banking sector has very little experience of operating in a market environment, and the capacity of these banks to allocate credit sensibly is perhaps questionable. Furthermore 20–40 per cent of the loan portfolios of these banks are irrecoverable by some estimates. Another cause for worry is the large amount of outstanding inter-enterprise credit. The problems of the banking sector should not be exaggerated, though. The inflation of 1989 wiped out much of the debts of the enterprise sector, and so the stock of bad debt (as well as good debt) is not as large as it might have been. The still monopolistic structure of the banking system has meant that Polish banks often enjoy a high profit rate (the difference between the interest paid on deposits and the interest charged on loans is high). And the level of inter-enterprise credit, which has been fairly stable since mid-1990, is probably at least in part a natural market reaction to the economic environment in Poland. First, it is common in market economies for large firms to delay payments to their smaller suppliers in times of recession. Second, high levels of inter-enterprise credit are typical of developing countries, and reflect mainly the failure of the banking system to allocate credit efficiently (see *Warsaw Voice* 15 December 1991: B2).

We therefore have some cause for optimism on a medium- to long-term time horizon. The major short- to medium-term problem in this structural adjustment process is of course unemployment. Labour shedding by the socialised sector started with the Big Bang of January 1990 and has been proceeding at a very fast rate since. Unemployment has increased steadily, and had already passed 2 million by October 1991. Reported vacancies, after growing for the first ten months of 1990, have stabilised at a level of about 50,000 nationally. As of October 1991 there were about fifty registered unemployed for each reported vacancy. It is too early to say at what level the unemployment rate will stabilise, but 25 per cent of the non-agricultural labour force seems very possible. Unemployment benefit exists, but individuals cannot receive it for more than one year (Gora and Lehmann 1991). High unemployment levels and the social hardship they entail are difficult even for mature democracies to cope with; an emerging democracy such as Poland will be put under even greater stress.

Conclusion

Poland at the end of 1991 stands at a crossroads. The recession is deep, unemployment continues to grow, and inflation is still not yet firmly under control. Public support for anti-inflation policies is wavering at a time when the need to regain control of the budget deficit requires further austerity measures. Large-scale privatisation is making only slow progress, and nearly all of the state sector enterprises inherited from the communist regime remain state-owned. The elections of October 1991 produced a severely fragmented parliament. Whether or not it will be possible to form strong governments with the support necessary to enact the tough economic policies the situation calls for remains to be seen.

Yet the previous two years have seen a tremendous amount of progress along the transition path, much of it probably irreversible. There has been a properly functioning price system since January 1990; the shortage economy is a thing of the past. Exports have grown substantially, foreign trade has been successfully reoriented towards the West, and the zloty is moderately convertible. Considerable progress has been made in small-scale privatisation, and the growth of the indigenous private sector continues. Already one-third to one-half of the economy (depending on the measure used) is in private hands. And of course macro stability has returned, though whether this can be successfully maintained is still not yet clear.

Two sorts of medium- to long-term outcomes are possible. On the one hand, the Polish economy could move smoothly into the West European model. If macro-stability can be maintained over the next several years, and the economy remains relatively de-politicised (regardless of how fast or far the mass privatisation programme progresses), then Poland should be ready to join the European mainstream, and the European Community in particular, by the end of the 1990s or so. If, on the other hand, macro-stability is lost and the economy is re-politicised – with frequent episodes of industrial action in successful pursuit of inflationary wage claims, powerful economic interest groups (large firms, farmers) obtaining special subsidies from a weak government, and so on – then Poland's return to Europe will take a possibly lengthy 'Latin American' detour. So far (1989–91) Poland has managed to stay on the direct road to Europe. With some luck, it will arrive, having taken no detours, in time to greet the new millennium.

Acknowledgements

I should like to thank Saul Estrin, Qimiao Fan, Alan Gelb, Stanislaw Gomulka, Marek Gora, Hartmut Lehmann and Jan Rutkowski for helpful discussions during the writing of this chapter. I am particularly grateful to the editor of this volume, David Dyker, for his patience and guidance in seeing this work through to its completion. Portions of the chapter draw on Schaffer (1991) and Fan and Schaffer (1991). Financial support was provided by the Leverhulme Trust. The Centre for Economic Performance is funded by the Economic and Social Research Council. The usual disclaimer applies.

Notes

1   According to World Bank definitions, the infant mortality rate in the high-income countries in 1989 was 9 per 1,000 live births, and in the upper–middle income countries 50 per 1,000 live births; in Poland it was 16 per 1,000 live births (World Bank 1991: 259).

2   The nominal wage deflated by the official price index.

3   Employment is annual average, output in current prices. It is worth noting that the increase in the private sector share of output is partly due to changes in relative prices; in 1984 prices the private sector accounted for just 4.8 per cent of output in 1989 (*RS* various years; Statystyka Polski, *Rzeczpospolita* 2 February 1991).

4   Administered pricing extends only to energy, state sector rents, post and telecommunications, state rail and road transport, and alcohol (Gomulka 1991: 17).

5   On the basis of the consumer price index. The high February figure is an artefact of the mid-month to mid-month calculation of inflation rates, and most of the 'February' increase actually took place in the second half of January; end-January to end-February 1990 inflation was about 5 per cent.

6   There has been some controversy over the reliability of the official estimate of the fall in

GDP in 1990. The figure (12 per cent) probably overstates the drop (principally because of under-reporting of private sector activity), but not by a lot: see Schaffer (1991).

7   It is nevertheless puzzling as to why the enterprise sector responded this way in January, when real interest rates were still very negative. Enterprises, used in the past to lower interest rates on turnover credit, were apparently deterred from increasing their bank borrowing purely by the sudden increase in the *nominal* interest rate.

8   There were long queues to purchase shares, prompting the electronic daily *Donosy* to report that capitalism had arrived in socialist style.

9   An investment trust is a close-ended fund. A unit trust, by contrast, is an open-ended fund, meaning that when a new investor buys into the unit trust, the unit trust managers undertake to buy additional shares corresponding to the new capital brought in by the new investor.

10 That said, it is perhaps worth noting that investment trusts (and unit trusts) play a relatively minor role as financial intermediaries in the West; pension funds and insurance companies are much more important: see Schaffer (1990c).

Statistical sources

The bulk of the data originates in various publications of the Polish Central Statistical Office, GUS (*Główny Urząd Statystyczny*). Data collected and published by the World Bank and the CIA are also used.

BS   *Biuletyn Statysticzny* (Statistical Bulletin)
HES   CIA, *Handbook of Economic Statistics*
MRS   *Mały Rocznik Statystyczny* (Small Statistical Yearbook)
Polska   *Polska 1918–1988* (Warsaw 1989)
RS   *Rocznik Statystyczny* (Statistical Yearbook)
RSHW   *Rocznik Statystyczny Handlu Wewnętrznego* (Internal Trade Statistical Yearbook)
RSHZ   *Rocznik Statystyczny Handlu Zagranicznego* (Foreign Trade Statistical Yearbook)
RSPraca   *Rocznik Statystyczny Praca* (Labour Statistical Yearbook)
RSPrz   *Rocznik Statystyczny Przemysłu* (Industry Statistical Yearbook)
SP   *Statystyka Polski* (Statistics of Poland)

References

Central Intelligence Agency (1990) Eastern Europe: long road ahead to economic well-being. Paper presented to the Subcommittee on Technology and National Security, Joint Economic Committee, US Congress, May

Corrochano G, Barbone L (1991) Poland: recent developments in the private sector. Mimeo, World Bank, 21 October

Dabrowski J, Federowicz M, Levitas A (1991) Report on Polish state enterprises in 1990. Research Centre for Marketization and Property Reform, Gdansk, February

Dyker D A (1991) *Restructuring the Soviet Economy*. Routledge

Fan Q, Schaffer M E (1991) Enterprise reforms in Chinese and Polish state-owned industries. *Economic Systems* **15**(2): 211–42

Gomulka S (1970) Extensions of 'the golden rule of research' of Phelps. *Review of Economic Studies* **37**(1): 73–93

Gomulka S (1986) *Growth, Innovation and Reform in Eastern Europe*. Wheatsheaf

Gomulka S (1990) Reform and budgetary policies in Poland 1989–90. *European Economy* **43**: 127–37

Gomulka S (1991a) The causes of recession following stabilization. *Comparative Economic Systems* **33**(2): 71–89

Gomulka S (1991b) Polish economic reform: principles, policies and outcomes. *Centre for Economic Performance Discussion Paper* no. 51, London School of Economics, October, and forthcoming in the *Cambridge Journal of Economics*

Gomulka S, Rostowski J (1984) The reformed Polish economic system 1982–83. *Soviet Studies* **36**(3): 386–405. Also in Gomulka (1986)

Gora M, Lehmann H (1991) Flow and stock analysis of Polish unemployment: January 1990 – June 1991. *Centre for Economic Performance*. Discussion Paper no. 52, London School of Economics, October

Government of Poland (1989) Memorandum on the economic reform program in Poland and the role of foreign financial assistance. Mimeo, 23 September

Jorgensen E A, Gelb A, Singh, I J (1990) The behaviour of Polish firms after the 'Big Bang': findings from a field trip. Paper presented at the OECD conference *The Transition to a Market Economy in Central and Eastern Europe* Paris, 28–30 November

Kasperkiewicz W (1985) Autonomy of enterprises. In Krajewski and Smusz (1985)

Kornai J (1991) *The Road to a Free Economy: Shifting from a Socialist System: The Example of Hungary*. W.W. Norton, New York

Krajewski S, Krajewska, A (1990) The fitness of Polish enterprises on the march to the market economy. Mimeo, University of Lodz

Krajewski S, Smusz M (eds) (1985) *Functioning of Industrial Enterprises in Conditions of Economic Reform*. Mimeo, Institute of Political Economy, University of Lodz

Kwasniewski J (1985) Workers' self-management. In Krajewski and Smusz (1985)

Nelson R R, Phelps E S (1966) Investment in humans, technological diffusion, and economic growth. *American Economic Review Papers and Proceedings* **56**(2): 69–75

Nuti D M (1981) Industrial enterprises in Poland 1973–80. In Jeffries I (ed) *The Industrial Enterprise in Eastern Europe*. Praeger, New York

Schaffer M E (1990a) How Polish enterprises are subsidised. Mimeo, London School of Economics, January

Schaffer M E (1990b) State-owned enterprises in Poland: taxation, subsidisation, and competition policies. *European Economy* **43**: 183–201

Schaffer M E (1990c) On the use of pension funds in the privatisation of Polish state-owned enterprises. *Centre for Economic Performance*. Working Paper no. 127, London School of Economics, August (revised October)

Schaffer M E (1991) A note on the Polish state-owned enterprise sector in 1990. *Centre for Economic Performance*. Discussion Paper no. 36, London School of Economics, August, and forthcoming, *Comparative Economic Systems*

World Bank (1987) *Poland: Reform, Adjustment and Growth*. Washington, DC

World Bank (1990) *Poland: Economic Management for a New Era*. Washington, DC

World Bank (1991) *World Development Report 1991*. Oxford University Press

Zielinski J G (1973) *Economic Reforms in Polish Industry*. Oxford University Press

CHAPTER 11

Yugoslavia

DAVID A DYKER

Introduction

By the time this book is published Yugoslavia will have ceased to exist. At mid-1991 Slovenia, the most northerly and most prosperous of the constituent republics of the Yugoslav Federation, seemed already set for independence, after the failure of a brief, though destructive, attempt by the Yugoslav army to head off secession by force in June–July 1991. By the end of July of the same year armed clashes between Serbian and Croatian nationalist groups were threatening to escalate into full-scale civil conflict.

The threat turned to reality when the Yugoslav army started openly to support the Serbian irregular military groups. The result was a full-scale war, fought mainly in the Serbian minority areas of Croatia, which dominated the second half of 1991 in Yugoslavia to the exclusion of all else. At January 1992 the economy was in complete disarray, with key hard-currency earners like the tourist industry simply closed down for the time being. But hostilities were beginning to die down, partly due to economic exhaustion. Slovenia and Croatia had already started to issue their own currency. The EC was preparing to recognise the independence of any Yugoslav republic seeking such recognition, and it was clear that Slovenia, Croatia and Bosnia and Hercegovina would, indeed, make application to that effect.

There are, then, few positive reasons for studying the Yugoslav economy. But there are any number of negative ones. Yugoslavia stands out, along with Hungary, as a key witness to the proposition that market socialism, however successful it may be at resolving some of the X-efficiency problems of centralised socialism, does not lead anywhere, at least in the conditions in which it developed in Europe. Yugoslavia is also the outstanding example of how the great forces of change which began to sweep the continent at the end of the 1980s and beginning of the 1990s can be as disintegrative in some parts of it as they are integrative in others. More generally, Yugoslavia presents a classic instance of how local political factors can distort patterns of economic activity beyond recognition, *even in the context of a kind of market economy*.

We must begin with a brief outline of Yugoslavia's stormy history. The Kingdom of the Serbs, Croats and Slovenes was created in the aftermath of the First World War,

Map 11.1

through the unification of the independent kingdoms of Serbia and Montenegro (Orthodox in religion and for most of the post-medieval period part of the Turkish Empire, or at least within its sphere of influence) and the Slav-populated parts of the old Habsburg Empire – principally Croatia, traditionally Roman Catholic, though speaking a language almost identical to that of the Serbs, and Slovenia, also Roman Catholic and speaking a Slav language quite distinct from Serbo-Croat. Yugoslavia (the name was not officially adopted till 1929) was forged under the leadership of the Serbian Karadjordjević royal house, and from the very beginning the political ascendancy of the Serbs caused extreme friction with the other nationalities, particularly the Slovenes and Croats, who perceived themselves, with some justification, as being economically more advanced than the Serbs. It was the circumstances of the formation of Yugoslavia that created a number of peculiarities in the Yugoslav political structure which have survived to the present day. In particular, the army, the police and the civil service were all dominated by Serbs, and Serbian administrators in the old Habsburg regions did much damage to the cause of Yugoslav unity in the early 1920s with their insensitive and overbearing manner.

Behind these specific peculiarities lay a fundamental problem of political attitudes. For many Serbians, the new state of Yugoslavia was simply Serbia writ large. The political ambitions of Slovenes, by contrast, have never gone beyond the boundaries of their own ethnic region. For Croats, especially the more nationalistic ones, Bosnia, a region of mixed Serbian, Croatian and Serbo-Croat-speaking Muslim population, represented something of an *irredentum*. But there was no Croatian hegemonism to parallel Serbian hegemonism. This is not to say that the Serbs deserve all, or even the greater part, of the blame for the inter-ethnic strife that has bedevilled Yugoslavia throughout its existence. It is simply to point out that Yugoslavia meant very different things to different South Slav nationalities, and that this was bound to cause trouble.

Inter-ethnic political stalemate prevented Yugoslavia's fledgling parliamentary democracy of the 1920s from developing, and in 1929 a royal dictatorship was declared. Trouble between Serbs and Croats continued, now compounded by the great economic distress caused to a predominantly peasant country by the downward trend in world food prices from 1926. Such was the degree of rural overpopulation in pre-war Yugoslavia that the peasants could make ends meet on their tiny plots (most of them under 5 hectares) only when prices were buoyant. It was inevitable, therefore, that the 1930s should witness a serious build-up of peasant debt. In 1939 the royal government finally granted the Croats a degree of autonomy, while a number of partial moratoria on peasant debts were introduced in the course of the 1930s. But neither set of measures was really effective, and the Yugoslavia that was brutally destroyed by German attack in 1941 had not solved any of its essential problems.

As in France, the stress of collapse and occupation precipitated a crisis in Yugoslav society which in this case produced new extremes of nationalism, with the Croatian puppet-fascist Ustashe government launching genocidal attacks on Serbs and Muslims in areas of mixed population, in Croatia itself and in Bosnia. The Serbian Chetniks, nominally in resistance to the German and Italian occupiers, replied in kind against the Ustashe, at the same time engaging in open conflict with the communist-led Partisans. It was the Partisans, under the leadership of Josip Broz Tito, a Croat of mixed Croatian and Slovene descent, who came to dominate the heroic and costly fight against the Germans, with the Chetniks, it seems, more interested in settling scores with the Ustashe and the communists than in fighting the Nazis. But the communists were as determined as anyone that they alone should reap the fruits of victory when the occupiers were finally expelled. They ultimately gained the ascendancy for three main reasons: because they were tough and brutal, because they really took on the Germans, to the great admiration of the Western allies, and because they alone, of all the political organisations operating in occupied Yugoslavia, had credibility as a pan-Yugoslav organisation.

As soon as the war was over, the Yugoslav communists set about building a classic Stalinist dictatorship, complete with central planning. They did so not because the Russians forced them; on the contrary, the Red Army had played only a fleeting role in the liberation of Yugoslavia, and there were, after 1944, no Soviet troops in Yugoslavia such as might have been used to convince local politicians and populations of the virtues of Soviet-style socialism on the pattern followed throughout most of the rest of Eastern Europe. Rather the Yugoslav communist leaders saw themselves as disciples of Stalin, faithful but free. It was only superficially surprising when, in mid-1948, Stalin broke with Tito, and excommunicated Yugoslavia from the socialist 'commonwealth', to the extent of a total trade ban. For Stalin wanted puppets, not disciples, and he was deeply suspicious of any leader in Eastern Europe who did not owe his position totally to the Soviet dictator himself.

Market socialism – the first phase

It was the split with Stalin that forced the communist leadership in Yugoslavia into a fundamental reappraisal of the whole basis of socialism. By 1950 the reappraisal was beginning to take concrete shape, in the form of a series of propositions, the common thread of which was the principle of decentralisation. By 1952–3 legislation was in place to provide the institutional foundation of the first experiment in market socialism. The main features of the new system, as it had gelled by the mid-1950s, were as follows.

1 The apparatus of central planning was abolished, and the market re-established as the nexus of economic activity.
2 As a corollary, the Stalinist 'leading role' of the Communist Party was abolished, and with it even the name 'Communist Party'. The new 'League of Communists' would still, however, be the only legal political organisation in the country.
3 With the apparatus men gone, but the capitalists most certainly not invited back, sovereignty within the enterprise should pass to a *workers' council*, elected by the entire work-force of the given enterprise. These councils would have the power to decide on all strategic matters affecting development of the enterprise, including rates of plough-back, principles of wage policy, and so on. Day-to-day management would, however, continue to be the responsibility of professional management, while the League of Communists would seek to mould and direct the process of self-management.

Table 11.1   Growth rates of national income[a] 1948–90

1948–52	2.3	1971–4	6.8
1953–6	7.5	1975–9	5.9
1957–61	10.6	1980–3	0.7
1962–5	7.1	1984–8	0.5
1966–70	5.7	1989	0.8
		1990	−7.6

Note: [a] Net National Product minus 'unproductive' services

Source: Official Yugoslav statistics

4   The false federalism of Stalinism was replaced by a more genuine form of federalism, conceding significant autonomy to both republican and local (commune) levels, though again under the guidance of the League of Communists.
5   The capacity of the state to form and implement economic policy was maintained through the medium of
   ● a high degree of direct government control over investment funds
   ● a high degree of direct government control over foreign trade
   ● a more or less conventional array of fiscal and monetary instruments.
6   Collectivisation was abandoned, and private agriculture accepted as the dominant mode in the countryside, but with a new, highly egalitarian land reform and a 10-hectare upper limit on land holdings.

This limited version of market socialism proved highly successful in terms of fostering economic growth in the period to 1965, as Table 11.1 shows. Indeed Yugoslav growth in the period 1953–65 ranks – along with the early Soviet growth record and the 'economic miracles' of West Germany and Japan – among the outstanding growth efforts of the post-war period. It is interesting, too, to note that the similarities with the Soviet experience do not stop at aggregate growth trends. The *sources* of Yugoslav growth in the period 1953–65 were also strikingly similar to those of Soviet growth over the comparable period. As in the Soviet Union, massive transfer of labour from an overpopulated countryside into the towns marked post-war growth in Yugoslavia as Lewisian extensive growth *par excellence*. Over the period 1953–61 the total population dependent on agriculture fell by more than 1.1 million, while the agricultural work-force dropped in numbers by 670,000. That critical period of eight years also witnessed a near-doubling of the industrial work-force from 513,000 to 993,000, with substantial increases also in related activities like construction (Dyker 1990: 43–5).

   The similarities did not stop there. The ratio of gross fixed investment to Gross Social Product (GNP minus 'unproductive' services) averaged 29 per cent 1953–64 for Yugoslavia (Gnjatović 1985: 48). But whereas in the Soviet case the burden of the sharp increase in the investment ratio had been borne by the Soviet population itself, in Yugoslavia domestic accumulation received a big supplement from abroad. As Table 11.2 shows, the period 1953–65 was marked, with a couple of exceptions, by consistently large deficits on current account. These deficits cannot be argued to have been strictly unintentional, even though they were not planned as such. Rather they reflected an ongoing US commitment to support Yugoslav independence *vis-à-vis* the Soviet Union, specifically through economic aid programmes of various kinds. Over the period 1953–64 capital imports into Yugoslavia amounted to 25.4 per cent of gross fixed investment (Gnjatović 1985: 48). It was this that enabled the Yugoslav communists to implement what in many ways was an archetypal Stalinist industrialisation drive, complete with priority on heavy industry, without the political rigours and terrors of full Stalinism. US support for the balance of payments also allowed Yugoslavia, a country poor in energy sources, to pursue a policy of extensive utilisation of *imported* energy materials, where Stalin in the Soviet Union had sought extensive assimilation of *domestic* energy resources.

But the actual *pattern* of extensive development in Yugoslavia was different in some key details from the corresponding Soviet pattern. Most strikingly, the record on capital productivity seems to be distinctly better, with capital productivity showing an upward trend 1952–9 (if we can believe the official statistics: see Sirc 1979: 56), and then levelling off in the early 1960s. In the Soviet Union, of course, the trend in capital productivity was downwards right from the start. So market socialism combined with a high degree of state control over investment seems to have been a rather effective way of ensuring that an extensive investment drive aimed at mobilising a new labour force did not damage capital productivity too much.

Extensive development is, however, a transitory phenomenon at best, as the Soviets have learned to their great cost. Rapid industrialisation in the period 1953–65 tended to exacerbate regional disparities within Yugoslavia, and in the impoverished, mainly Albanian-populated region of Kosovo, for instance, massive reserves of under-employed rural labour persisted to the 1990s. But in the most advanced regions of (particularly) Slovenia and Croatia, labour shortage was beginning to constrain economic growth by the 1960s. More dramatically, the US Congress voted in 1961 to discontinue aid to Yugoslavia. By 1964 Yugoslavia was in the midst of the first of its post-war debt-service crises. The pressure on Yugoslavia to make a swift transition to an intensive growth pattern was therefore immediate and intense.

The reforms of the 1960s

The circumstantial changes of the early 1960s formed the background to a series of fundamental systemic reforms promulgated in the period 1961–5. These reforms addressed, most obviously, the need to do something about the balance of payments, while at the same time improving the level of efficiency of Yugoslavia's involvement in the international division of labour. The strategy here was to abolish the old system of foreign trade planning – clumsy and ineffectual and little different from the classical Soviet system – and begin the transition to a Western-style system, based on a realistic exchange rate and a conventional array of import duties. Export subsidies and direct controls on imports were scheduled for abolition, and this commitment paved the way for Yugoslavia's accession to the GATT in 1962.

The other main area affected by the reforms of 1961–5 was investment planning and finance. While the essentially state capitalist formulation of the investment system of

Table 11.2   The balance of payments 1953–90 ($ millions)

Year	Trade balance	Current account
1953	−245	−244
1954	−121	−113
1955	−205	−187
1956	−167	−123
1957	−272	−249
1958	−236	−183
1959	−217	−169
1960	−269	−218
1961	−347	−287
1962	−199	−11
1963	−278	−144
1964	−435	−273
1965	−200	−15
1966	−353	−113
1967	−455	−157
1968	−533	−175
1969	−660	−143
1970	−1,195	−452
1971	−1,438	−357
1972	−996	419
1973	−1,658	485
1974	−3,715	−1,183
1975	−3,625	−1,003
1976	−2,489	165
1977	−4,380	−1,529
1978	−4.317	−1,256
1979	−7,225	−3,661
1980	−6,086	−2,291
1981	−4,828	−750
1982	−3,446	−473
1983	−1,798	300
1984	−1,080	956
1985	−1,712	403
1986	−1,930	805
1987	−981	1,067
1988	−307	2,210
1989	−1,439	1,000
1990	−4,700	−2,400[a]

Note: [a] Estimated

Source: Gnjatović 1985; official Yugoslav statistics; WEFA; author's estimates

the early period of market socialism seemed to have worked comparatively well, it had done so in easy conditions of abundant cheap labour and massive subsidisation from abroad. The pressures of the 1960s required a more sensitive investment mechanism, one that would ensure that each individual investment project passed the test of profitability. Once again a market-led approach was adopted, with the big state investment funds largely wound up or transformed into autonomous banking institutions, and the burden of enterprise taxation greatly reduced so that enterprises might in principle be able to finance a much bigger proportion of their investment requirements themselves. The banking system as a whole was fundamentally reformed on a Western-style model, with the National Bank of Yugoslavia now operating as a conventional central bank, looking after the money supply and the rate of interest, and a battery of commercial banks lending to enterprises, short-term and long-term, on (theoretically) normal business principles.

A liberalisation *manqué*

But the notion that productivity and export performance could be improved simply by shifting the boundary between the state and market elements within market socialism proved to be a mistaken one. Nationality conflicts and tensions had been simply suppressed in the early post-war period in Yugoslavia. During the 1950s they were kept under control through a combination of constitutional concessions, which gave republican governments some decision-making power and some control over tax revenue, and a degree of political discipline imposed by police as well as party. The dismantling of much of the 1950s apparatus of state capitalism allowed tensions to resurface which within a few years were threatening the very existence of Yugoslavia.

The trouble with liberalising foreign trade and investment finance was that it opened up a whole series of issues focusing on the problem of *ownership*, a category which the directed self-management of the 1950s had largely ignored. And because Yugoslavia is Yugoslavia, the ownership problem came on to the agenda as an ethnic/tribal issue, rather than a personal one.

It was in Croatia that events took their most dramatic turn. Against a background of renascent cultural nationalism, Croatian politics came, through the late 1960s and early 1970s, to be totally dominated by the question of what had happened to the state capital of the 1950s state capitalist system. The typical Croatian line of argument ran as follows: the old state investment funds and import-export organisations, now operating on commercial principles but still with their head offices in Belgrade, the federal capital and the capital of Serbia, are using the capital inherited from the previous system, and the privileged position they still enjoy, to exploit the producers of Yugoslavia, and more specifically of Croatia. To add insult to injury, they are doing so on the basis of state capital to which Croatia originally made a more than proportionate contribution, because it was wealthier than Serbia and most of the rest of Yugoslavia. What is more, much of this hijacked state capital is now being used as a basis for dubious and essentially exploitative financial involvements in the Croatian tourist industry (the Adriatic coast is mainly in Croatia), one of the mainstays of the beleaguered Yugoslav balance of payments.

It is not necessary for us to try to make a precise assessment of the justice of these Croatian claims. Certainly, there can be no doubt that by the early 1970s Croatia was in the grip of a nationalistic emotionalism which made careful calculation neither easy nor particularly relevant. On the other hand, there are enough individual case studies of relationships among banks, import-export houses and enterprises to suggest that there was a degree of truth in the exploitation argument (Dyker 1990: 76–7). Indeed the issue was really much wider than the specifically tribal squabble might have suggested. The *general* systemic problem that emerged from the reforms of the early 1960s focused on the relation between enterprises and banks. The theory behind those reforms was that the control over investible funds previously exercised predominantly by the state should be decentralised in equal proportions to enterprises and banks. In practice, partly it must be said because of the imprudence of managements and workers' councils, financial power soon come to be overwhelmingly concentrated in the banks. By the late 1960s the bulk of enterprise net income was going on debt service, and the early 1970s witnessed a further worsening of the financial situation of industry (Dyker 1990: 67). So at one level the political crisis of the early 1970s was a 'class' crisis – a crisis of relations between producers and 'finance capital'. But because the new, 'autonomous' banks were largely set up on a regional basis, and were, indeed, rapidly interpenetrated by the 'new' nationalist politics, the national issue and the general systemic issue tended increasingly to become fused into one.

In 1971 President Tito finally acted to put an end to the ferment in Croatia, and the period 1971–2 was marked by a political purge in the best Bolshevik traditions. The Croatian Communist Party leadership was subjected to a systematic clean-out, but other republican leaderships were not spared, least of all the Serbian. By the end of 1972 the dictatorship of the League of Communists was once again firmly in place.

But the reaffirmed one-party system took a bizarre, uniquely Yugoslav form. The new constitution of 1974 codified a movement which had been going on throughout the early 1970s towards the transformation of Yugoslavia into something intermediate between a federation and a confederation – still a federation in the sense that the republics were not sovereign, but tending to confederation in that now, on a much wider range of issues, the central government would be able to exercise power only as delegated by the republics. In this way, Tito thought to allow some scope for expression of national sentiments. At the same time, he looked to the newly purged League of Communists leaderships at republican level to provide the cement that would ensure that Yugoslavia's national interest continued to dominate the process of political articulation.

The 1974 constitution also codified an effective retreat from market socialism. The leadership's response to the tensions and imbalances of the system as it had developed after the reforms of 1961–5 was to seek to replace the market, for strategic decision-making purposes, by a quasi-market based on planning agreements, aimed at ensuring that the pattern of investment decision-taking did not generate unbearable national tensions and an unacceptable distribution of income. This shift towards 'associationism' was an indigenous Yugoslav development, but it did closely parallel trends in British Labour Party thinking at the time.

In terms of the perennial Yugoslav problem of trying to half-neutralise, half-harness regional-national sentiment, the constitution of 1974 had a good deal to commend it. But from an economic point of view it was a disaster. The wager on the League of Communists as a guardian of pan-Yugoslav interests turned out to be an ill-starred one, with regional party elites taking an increasingly regional-autarkic line through the

1970s, and the one-party state of Tito turning more and more into a bickering collection of eight (six republics plus two autonomous regions) one-party mini-states, able to come to collective agreement only on the basis of lowest-common-denominator unanimity, if at all. In specific economic-policy terms, this had three major negative consequences.

1   Far from providing a basis for French-style *concertation*, the associationism of the 1974 constitution simply provided the vehicle for a process of extreme fragmentation of Yugoslav economic space.
2   Quasi-federalism produced a critical erosion of the power of the National Bank of Yugoslavia to control the money supply. Regional political elites were increasingly able to exploit the legitimate rights of republican national banks to make 'selective primary emissions' of money for specified purposes as a 'licence to print money'.
3   Quasi-federalism destroyed central control over the balance of payments. Republics and republican banks gained the right to borrow abroad, without having to take over stewardship of the hard-currency reserves or ultimate responsibility for debt service. As a result republics tended increasingly to perceive their interest in *maximising* the balance of payments deficit.

The crisis looms

It was with an apparatus such as this that Yugoslavia had to navigate the increasingly treacherous waters of the international economy in the period after the First Oil Shock of 1974. As a non-oil producer, Yugoslavia was hard hit by the immediate impact of the 300 per cent increase in oil prices, and a promising positive trend in the current account was cut short, with a reversal to deficit from 1974 (see Table 11.2). Much more insidious, however, was the tendency for the level of deficit to grow alarmingly from 1977. This reflected the secondary impact of the Oil Shock. With the private transnational banking system awash with petrodollars, international credit to countries and regimes deemed to be stable was cheap and readily accessible. It was simply too easy for the various actors in the quasi-pluralistic system which developed in Yugoslavia after 1974 to cover up for their policy weaknesses and mistakes by borrowing abroad, mainly from unregulated, private sources. In 1968 Yugoslavia's total foreign borrowing for the year was 73 per cent from public sources, 27 per cent from private. By 1982 it was 80 per cent private, 20 per cent public. By the latter year 65 per cent of Yugoslavia's total debt was unguaranteed (Gnjatović 1985: 86 and 95).

With this structure of debt, Yugoslavia was particularly vulnerable to international financial trends after 1979. Partly as a result of the monetarist stabilisation policies being followed in the majority of Western countries in the wake of the Oil Shocks, partly because a world-wide trend to public-sector deficit financing was now changing the balance of supply and demand for loanable funds, interest rates more than doubled between 1979 and 1980. By the latter year Yugoslavia was paying 17.6 per cent on guaranteed private-sector loans (World Bank, *World Debt Tables*). On non-guaranteed loans it must have been paying significantly more.

This forms the immediate background to the emergence, in late 1982, of a serious problem of debt service. With the total debt now in the region of $20 billion and the ratio of debt service to total hard-currency inflow well over 30 per cent, and amidst considerable confusion as the central Yugoslav authorities tried to discover just how bad the debt situation generated by the quasi-confederal system really was, a request for rescheduling was conveyed to Yugoslavia's creditors.

Rescheduling and stagnation

It was not particularly difficult for Yugoslavia to obtain agreement on an easing of debt amortisation commitments, and a major rescheduling package was announced in April 1983 which provided a total of more than $6 billion of roll-over and new money. Numerous further minor reschedulings were requested and granted through the mid-1980s. But these reflected specific elements of lumpiness in patterns of amortisation, rather than weaknesses in the balance of payments as such. In fact Yugoslavia was much more successful in terms of short-term balance of payments adjustment than either Hungary or Poland, which were labouring under similar debt-service problems at the time (see Hare, Chapter 9, and Schaffer, Chapter 10, in this volume, on Hungary and Poland). As Table 11.2 shows, the Yugoslav current account was in surplus from 1984, and remained in surplus until 1990.

But this degree of external financial stabilisation was bought at a high price. Reference back to Table 11.1 will confirm that economic growth effectively stopped in Yugoslavia in 1982. Worse, little progress was made with restructuring, either in the systemic or the industrial sense. Table 11.3 shows trends in inflation from 1979. The relentless acceleration into hyperinflation as the decade proceeded revealed a total incapacity on the part of the *political* constellation to address the weaknesses in the associationist system which had become so painfully apparent in the run-up to the Debt Crisis. Indeed as the 1980s went on, selective emissions of primary money came to dominate money supply trends more and more, as local political elites sought to use their monetary prerogatives to shield their constituents from the impact of recession and retrenchment. The current account was brought into balance primarily through cutbacks in imports, which fell by 7 per cent in real terms between 1981 and 1989 (*Statistički Godišnjak 1985*: 312; *Statistički Godišnjak 1990*: 313–14). Over the same period total exports grew by just 18 per cent in real terms. Among the main elements within the current account, foreign tourist earnings continued to grow rapidly, though this owed little to any strategic thinking on the part of the authorities. The pattern of visible exports indicated no breakthroughs in terms of new manufacturing export lines, though the late 1980s did witness a minor sally (not, alas, to be maintained) into the US market by the Yugo car (Dyker 1990: 137–9). As the decade wore on, the gulf between Yugoslavia and the East Asian NICs, which increasingly seemed the model for medium-developed, small countries to follow, just grew wider and wider.

Table 11.3 The retail price index (annual percentage change)

1979	1980	1981	1982	1983	1984	1985	1986	1987	1988	1989	1990
22	30	46	30	39	57	76	88	119	199	1,256	122

Source: Official Yugoslav statistics

The end of Titoism

We must digress here from strictly economic matters to sketch in a series of crucially important political developments over the period 1987–9 which form the essential background to the momentous events, on both economic and political planes, of 1990–1.

Tito died in 1980. He bequeathed to his successors a political system already declining into ineffectuality and corruption. The removal of the 'one true Yugoslav' deprived the country at the same time of the only individual capable of imposing any kind of discipline or cohesion on the petty regional oligarchies which now dominated everyday politics. Loss of confidence in government, loss of faith in the ideals of socialism, were in that context perhaps inevitable. The trend was, however, greatly reinforced by the sense of hopelessness which increasingly pervaded private lives in the mid-1980s, as living standards fell (real income per worker fell by 30 per cent 1979–88 – *Statistički Godišnjak 1990*: 151), and economic trends seemed to offer at best threadbare survival for the foreseeable future. The result was a major crisis of confidence in the federal government in 1987 (a public opinion survey in that year found that 79 per cent of the population believed that Yugoslavia's economic problems might never be solved – Grizelj 1987), as the Yugoslav population, deprived of a future, retreated further and further into the past, that is into traditional ethnic loyalties.

In 1988 Yugoslav politics was turned upside down by the arrival on centre stage of Slobodan Milošević. Ex-banker Milošević was able, in 1988, to take control of the Serbian League of Communists on a platform of settling scores with the Albanians of Kosovo. Kosovo, by far the poorest region of Yugoslavia with a level of national income per head of just 24 per cent of the Yugoslav average in 1988 (*Statistički Godišnjak 1990*: 405), is the ancient heartland of Serbia. During the eighteenth and nineteenth centuries, however, it was heavily colonised by Albanians, and is now some 85 per cent Albanian in population. Under the 1974 constitution it was conceded the status of an autonomous province within Serbia, which gave it very nearly as much effective independence as a fully fledged republic, and allowed its political structures, including League of Communists structures, to be largely taken over by Kosovo Albanians. Through the 1980s public resentment against the Kosovo Albanians among the population of Serbia proper grew, as stories of intimidation of Serbian and Montenegrin Kosovars circulated with increasing frequency. While it is very difficult to find reliable confirmation of any of these stories, their effect was to convince the majority of Serbs that there was an Albanian plot to push the Serbian minority out of Kosovo, prior to declaring independence, possibly even union with Albania.

In the course of 1989 Milošević was able, through a succession of massive rallies more reminiscent of Nazi Germany than of Titoist Yugoslavia, to mobilise overwhelming support for a campaign to deprive Kosovo of its autonomous status. This was done quickly and efficiently, and by the end of 1989 Kosovo was effectively under direct rule from Belgrade. But Milošević's victory had political repercussions throughout Yugoslavia, and formed a major input into the extreme centrifugal tendencies which started to develop in 1990.

Kosovo was not the only part of Serbia to enjoy autonomous province status. Vojvodina in the north, historically part of Hungary and still with a large Hungarian minority, is a relatively prosperous part of the country, with no history of serious ethnic tensions, and a tendency to identify with the 'Western' policy orientation of the republics of Slovenia and Croatia. Now Milošević had no quarrel as such with the (Serbian-dominated) leadership of Vojvodina. But if Kosovo was to be deprived of its autonomy, Vojvodina would have to share the same fate. The result was an acrimonious struggle between Milošević and the Vojvodina leadership, which Milošević of course won. But in so doing he did colossal damage to the fragile integument of Yugoslav unity. The leaderships of Slovenia and Croatia, still communist at this point but still harbouring the suspicions of Belgrade's motives which in the early 1970s had nearly boiled over, in the Croatian case, into insurrection, saw in the fate of Vojvodina a possible hint of what might be in store for them.

Slobodan Milošević's charismatic populism breathed new life into the communist cause in Serbia. Milošević's political genius lay in his ability to rally the increasingly powerful ethnic-sectarian sentiments of the Serbian population at large behind the very regional-oligarchical political structures which had seemed so threatened by the crisis of public confidence in the political system in 1987. But in creating that identification he created a second, more insidious one. To the peoples of the north and west of Yugoslavia, communism was now irrevocably tainted with a Greater-Serbian hegemonism strongly reminiscent of the pre-war variety. More than anything else, that may have served to kill communism in Slovenia and Croatia. On the economic side, too, Milošević's new political formula did tend to turn the weaknesses of the old political order into something positively destructive. As we saw, the associationist system had been exceedingly vulnerable to regional-autarkical tendencies, with much consequent loss of economies of scale and effective locational linkage. When in 1989 the government of Slovenia, responding to considerable public sympathy in the northern republic for the Albanians of Kosovo, vetoed Milošević's plans to stage a series of mass (Serbian) demonstrations within Slovenia itself, Milošević's response was to call for a Serbian boycott of all Slovenian goods. A year later Milošević, now President of Serbia, went so far as imposing a system of 'import' deposits amounting to tariffs on goods from Slovenia and Croatia. Thus the unity of the Yugoslav market, always under threat, was dealt a series of mortal blows by the political developments of 1989–90.

After the wave of democratic revolutions elsewhere in Eastern Europe in late 1989, events began to move swiftly in Yugoslavia. In April 1990 the first democratic elections in Yugoslav post-war history were held – for the republican parliaments of Slovenia and Croatia. In both cases the opposition won sweeping victories, with the League of Communists being all but annihilated as a serious political force. In both cases new governments came into office pledged to assert national sovereignty, implicitly national independence. In Croatia, the laurels of victory went to the Croatian Democratic Union (HDZ), a strongly nationalist configuration under the leadership of ex-general and ex-communist Franjo Tudjman. Tudjman was subsequently elected President of Croatia. Milošević was slow to take up the democratic challenge, but finally, in December 1990, Serbia too went to the polls, and delivered a landslide victory to the League of Communists, now renamed the Socialist Party of Serbia.

Ante Marković and the Marković Plan

In December 1988 the then prime minister of Yugoslavia, Branko Mikulić, finally yielded to the widespread loss of confidence in the federal government and resigned. He was succeeded by Ante Marković, an experienced but relatively unknown Croatian technocrat. Through 1989, with Milošević dominating the political scene at national as well as republican level, Marković kept a low profile. But in December 1989, with the rate of inflation now approaching 2,500 per cent, he announced a package of economic stabilisation measures, to be implemented from 1 January 1990. The main elements in the package were as follows.

1 A new dinar was created, on the basis of an exchange rate of 10,000 old dinars to 1 new.
2 It was initially pegged to a parity of 7 dinars to the deutschmark. The plan was to go over on to a floating exchange rate regime from 30 June 1990.
3 The new currency was placed on a regime of internal convertibility, ie Yugoslav citizens would be allowed to convert unlimited amounts of dinars into hard currency for current transaction purposes. Foreigners would be allowed to convert dinars into hard currency within limits. A foreign exchange market was to be created to trade in dinars and hard currencies. Capital transactions would remain subject to direct controls.
4 The import regime would be liberalised, though foreign exchange quotas for broad categories of imports (eg consumer goods) would be retained.
5 A process of deregulation and privatisation was to be set in motion which would give the private sector some 35 per cent of the Yugoslav economy by 1995, with the socialised sector retaining a reduced, but still substantial share of the economy. Agencies for Restructuring and Development, modelled on the German Treuhand-anstalt, were to be set up at republican level. These would be charged with the implementation of the privatisation plans and restructuring programmes within the socialised sector which would change the organisational profile of the economy.
6 Joint venture regulations were liberalised, and it became possible, for the first time, for foreigners to own 100 per cent of Yugoslav companies. Repatriation of profits was in principle guaranteed.
7 The golden rule of macroeconomic policy should be to 'shadow the deutschmark'. Clearly the parity of 7 new dinars to the deutschmark would remain tenable only if the value of the dinar held at least as stable as that of the German currency –

otherwise, against a background of liberalisation of import controls – the balance of trade would start to run into critical disequilibrium. Thus the primary goal of the internal convertibility package was the conquest of domestic hyperinflation. By implication, the re-establishment of firm control on the part of the National Bank of Yugoslavia over the money supply was to be a key instrument in the achievement of that goal.

The package was clearly modelled closely on the Sachs package adopted in 1989 in Poland. It laid primary emphasis on the external sector in terms of *instruments*, but directed that instrumentality towards the establishment of domestic macroeconomic balance, as a first condition of effective restructuring. The initial choice of a fixed-exchange-rate regime was primarily dictated by these considerations. As in the Polish case, one of the main goals of the 'shock therapy' was to break the hyper-inflationary psychosis, to combat the trend towards internal goods-inconvertibility – in a word to re-establish confidence in the domestic currency. The strategy of switching fairly quickly to a floating exchange rate system was, no doubt, based on an appraisal of the dangers, in terms of medium-term sustainability, of a fixed-parity regime. In the Yugoslav case in particular, the existence of a substantial stock of 'hot money', in the form of the accumulated remittances of Yugoslavs working abroad, worth an average of around $1.5 billion annually to the balance of payments throughout the 1980s, left Marković's fixed-exchange rate system vulnerable to speculative movements, just as the old Bretton Woods system had been.

Table 11.4   The monthly rate of inflation (retail price index) 1990

January	42	July	2.3
February	13.4	August	1.7
March	5.0	September	7.2
April	3.0	October	8.2
May	0.6	November	3.4
June	−0.6	December	2.7

Source: Official Yugoslav statistics

As Tables 11.4 and 11.5 show, Marković was remarkably successful in terms of short-term stabilisation. The monthly rate of inflation was down to an astounding −0.6 per cent by June, and the gamble on fixed-exchange-rate internal convertibility paid handsome dividends in terms of a large-scale flow of foreign exchange, previously held in foreign banks or under the mattress, into the Yugoslav banking system. (*Gastarbeiter* remittances totalled $1.5 billion for the first six months of 1990 alone.) This helped to cushion the balance of payments from the inevitable impact of internal convertibility in terms of increased imports. In the event, a sharp increase in the level of foreign exchange reserves from under $7 billion at the end of 1989 to nearly $10 billion by mid-1990 was recorded. There seemed to be every indication that the problem of macroeconomic instability had finally been cracked.

But while the first six months were a triumph for Ante Marković, the second

Table 11.5 Inflows and outflows of foreign exchange *vis-à-vis* the Yugoslav banking system, 1990 ($ million)

Month	Inflows	Outflows	Net
January	679.0	1.0	678.0
February	338.4	18.7	319.7
March	353.9	7.3	346.6
April	250.9	13.5	237.4
May	191.7	70.0	121.7
June	144.9	56.2	88.7
July	208.8	76.0	132.8
August	59.2	169.0	−109.8
September	1.0	581.5	−580.5
October	1.7	697.0	−695.3
November[a]	—	270	−270
December[a]	—	270	−270

Note: [a] Estimated

Source: Official Yugoslav statistics; author's estimates

brought nothing but disappointments. The trouble began with a slight slippage in control over the money supply in June, which accommodated an increase in nominal wages by 11.9 per cent in June by comparison with May. (This permitted the working population to claw back just a proportion of the loss in real incomes they suffered in the early months of the implementation of the stabilisation package.) The wage hike worked its way through to the retail price index in July, and though the recorded increase in that index was only 2.3 per cent (the cost-of-living index rose fully 4.9 per cent, due to one-off increases in the prices of municipal services), this was enough to damage the newly established confidence in the dinar, and create expectations of a devaluation. And as Table 11.5 demonstrates, that in turn quickly showed up, first in a slowing down in the rate of foreign exchange inflow into the domestic banking system, then in a reversal of that flow. When the monthly rate of inflation kicked again in September, that outflow turned into a torrent. By the end of the year Yugoslav was facing the first current account deficit since 1982, and hard-currency reserves had been depleted to $6.7 billion.

These developments provided striking confirmation of the proposition that it may be difficult to sustain fixed-parity internal convertibility packages beyond the short term. The new dinar proved to be extremely vulnerable to speculative pressure, and a relatively minor slippage of monetary control was soon dramatically amplified in terms of impact on the balance of payments. Transition to a floating dinar from mid-1990 would, arguably, have allowed the Yugoslav currency to float down to a realistic rate, taking into account the substantial residual inflation that had taken place in the early months of the year after the seven-to-one parity had been fixed, thus avoiding a cumulative speculative run on the dinar. The really striking thing about mid-1990 developments was, then, that the federal prime minister chose *not* to do what he had originally said be would do, chose not to take the most obvious step towards a dynamic stabilisation of the international status of the dinar. Why did Marković decide to stick with the fixed-parity regime, and indeed with the seven-to-one rate of exchange with the deutschmark? (The dinar was eventually devalued to a parity of nine to one in December 1990, and then to thirteen to one in April 1991. But the devaluations were too little too late, and the fixed-parity regime was retained right up until the effective collapse of the system under the pressure of the political crisis of mid-1991.) Why did he, in effect, attempt to institutionalise the unsustainable?

The explanation seems to be essentially twofold. First, Marković quite rightly gauged the original seven-to-one parity to be of great psychological importance in Yugoslavia, given the recent history of hyperinflation. Second, he was worried about the cost-inflationary impact of the increases in import prices which devaluation would bring about. Yet that only poses a further question. If monetary policy was under such a tight rein, why worry about cost-inflationary pressures?

The answer is that the new-look Yugoslav monetary policy of the first half of 1990 to a great extent flattered to deceive. It is certainly true that the budgetary situation was brought under control, largely through increases in taxation. It is certainly true that the National Bank of Yugoslavia was able to reimpose some discipline on the republic-level national banks in relation to selective primary emissions, through the establishment of a rule that prerogatives in relation to selective emissions could be exercised only with the prior approval of the Board of Governors of the National Bank of Yugoslavia. It is certainly true that on this basis the National Bank was now able to exercise much tighter control over the aggregate credit policies of the commercial banks.

The trouble was that, rather than eliminating the credit flow dynamics which had made universal soft budget constraints possible, these reforms merely succeeded in shifting their locus. Whereas in the associationist period it had been the relationship between National Bank(s) and commercial banks that had been critical in this respect, it was now that between commercial banks and enterprises. Constrained by a much tighter money supply discipline from the National Bank, the commercial banks continued to support enterprises in financial difficulty, mainly through the tactic of capitalising interest payments as they became due.

It is this that explains the reappearance of severe wage-inflationary trends in June 1991, and in turn the extreme, perhaps excessive, fear of import-led inflation which gripped the federal government in mid-1991. But the implications of such a systematic circumvention of the hard budget constraints policy of the government went far beyond that.

It is clear from the downward trend in national income in 1990 (see Table 11.1) that enterprises did, indeed, react to the Marković Stabilisation Plan with cuts in output. But continued support from the commercial banks allowed them do this across the board, rather than selectively, so that little real progress was made with restructuring as such. In addition, aggregate employment levels in the socialised sector were largely maintained, falling by just 6.2 per cent (406,700) between January 1990 and January 1991. (The failure of the Marković package to initiate any real restructuring dynamic is underlined by the fact that employment in the private sector increased by 10 per cent – just 100,000 – over the same period.)

This inevitably compounded and reinforced the problem of insolvency in Yugoslav industry. At the end of 1990 total unpaid bills were valued at nearly Din 400 billion. Behind this lay a rapidly escalating problem of loss-making. In 1990 total losses in the

Yugoslav economy amounted to Din 79,698 million (some $7 billion – 12–15 per cent of GNP), 197 per cent *more* than in 1989. If uncovered carry-over losses from previous years are taken into account, the figure rises to around Din 100 billion ($9 billion). Total net losses, after cancelling-out of elements of double-counting, added up to Din 67 billion. The business sector in every single republic made a net aggregate loss, and losses were fairly evenly distributed, with Serbia making relatively slightly heavier losses, and Croatia, Slovenia and Macedonia slightly lighter. Data on revaluation of stocks, work-in-progress and reserves suggest inflationary massaging of these magnitudes (revaluation of reserves, for instance, has often in the past been used as a way of covering payment of interest on loans). The official figure is, therefore, likely to represent an under-estimate of the true figure for total net losses, possibly by as much as 50 per cent (Dumezić 1991a). By the end of April 1991 a total of 7,704 enterprises and other organisations, employing a total of 1.6 million people (nearly 15 per cent of the work-force), were technically insolvent. Of those about 5,800, employing just under 1.2 million, should, according to existing regulations, already have been in receivership (Dumezić 1991b).

More insidiously still, the accommodating policies of the commercial banks inevitably sowed the seeds of a solvency crisis in the banking sector itself. At the beginning of 1990 bad debts in the sector were estimated at three times the value of capital, and 57.8 per cent of total deposits (Grličkov 1990). Through 1990 the situation worsened steadily, and the new Agency for Restructuring the Banking Sector appeared helpless. By May 1991 the Mortgage Bank of Ljubljana and Bankos were already in receivership, and Jugobanka Titova Mitrovica, two Bosnian banks, and the entire banking sector of Montenegro, the smallest republic, seemed likely to follow suit (Grličkov 1991b) . At the time of the outbreak of civil war in mid-1991, state financial assistance to the banking sector was still going through on an essentially linear basis, and little progress had been made on the critical issue of ownership of the banks. Most of them were, in accordance with associationist principles, still effectively owned by their own worst debtors, an absolute barrier to effective restructuring.

The last days of the Marković Plan

Amidst all its mounting difficulties, the Marković programme was still in business at October 1990, with the threat of a new hyperinflation just being held off, and valuable new legislation, on (*inter alia*) privatisation, going through the federal parliament. At that point there was still some chance that real restructuring would get going before the fragile macroeconomic balance of the Stabilisation Plan was shattered.

Perhaps the critical death-blow to the plan was struck by President Slobodan Milošević of Serbia. At the end of November 1990 Milošević prevailed upon the national bank of Serbia to rediscount 18 billion dinars ($1.7 billion) worth of bank loans, thus implicitly creating new, 'high-powered' money to the tune of some 10 per cent of the total Yugoslav stock of money at that time. This enabled the Serbian government to pay salaries and pensions to millions of state employees, retirees, invalids and others for the first time for months, just a few days before Serbia's first democratic election since the Second World War. The operation was in direct contravention of the new monetary regime under which republican national banks were allowed to rediscount loans only with the express approval of the Board of Governors of the National Bank of Yugoslavia. But it was only too clearly in the tradition of a pre-1990 Yugoslav system which had effectively given regional leaderships the right to issue currency.

A few months later the 'Great Bank Robbery' ploy was used by the government of Montenegro to compensate for funds (for pensions, covering of hard-currency obligations, support for exports, etc) which Montenegro should have received from the federal budget, but had not. Meanwhile a number of commercial banks, mainly in Slovenia and Croatia, were reported to have been using hard currency borrowed from the National Bank – purportedly to meet external payments commitments – to expand domestic credit in a way dangerously reminiscent of the practices of the late 1970s (Grličkov 1991a).

These renewed pressures on the money supply did, of course, reflect in part the growing problem of insolvency in the commercial banking network. They also reflected renewed pressure coming from the budgetary dimension. By the beginning of 1991 it was clear that the fiscal rectitude reported for 1990 was in part fictitious. Much of the increased taxation assessed for 1991 was not in fact collected (this is again reminiscent of an old Yugoslav habit of counting financial assets as invoiced, rather than as paid up), while some republics were already beginning to withhold tax revenue, particularly in relation to defence expenditure. As a result, the 1990 fiscal year had to be extended to the end of March 1991. The budgetary situation became progressively worse through the first half of 1991, as republican authorities showed an increased predisposition to hijack revenues, particularly customs revenues. By mid-June 1991 the federal government had already had to borrow Din 21.5 billion from the National Bank to cover the gap between budgetary revenues and expenditures. This Din 21.5 billion had been raised through primary emission, that is through a direct increase in the money supply (Emisija . . . 1991). Thus the classic, associationist pattern of treating the National Bank, less as the government's banker than as the government's paymaster, had been well and truly re-established. By May 1991 the monthly inflation rate had reached the dangerously high level of 10.9 per cent, 281 per cent on an annualised basis.

Can we draw generalised lessons from the failure of the Marković internal convertibility package in Yugoslavia? Certainly Yugoslavia's unique political problems did make a very major contribution to that failure. Not only did they continually sap the authority of the federal government, on which the successful implementation of any stabilisation package was crucially dependent, but also they tended to bring back many of the systemic bad habits which had made the associationist model so vulnerable to the malady of soft budget constraints. Ante Marković can certainly be criticised for seeking to ignore the challenge of ethnic sectarianism which was all around him. His attempt to rally support for his policies through the launch of his own, new political party, the League of Reform Forces, was a miserable failure. With the benefit of hindsight, we can conclude that it reflected a certain lack of political insight and realism. It is not clear, however, that he would have achieved much more in the end of the day, even if he had followed a more subtle political line. Everything that happened in the course of

1991 has confirmed that none of the regional-national leaders had any real interest in forming a grand coalition to save Yugoslavia and its economy.

Marković can also be indicted for making technical errors. His attempt to maintain the seven-to-one parity with the deutschmark long after it had ceased to be appropriate was a major reason for the sharp deterioration in the balance of payments situation in 1990. His worries about cost-inflationary pressures were justified, but the policy line he adopted thereon was not. Most fundamental of all, Marković made the mistake of thinking that macroeconomic stabilisation, the reconstitution of sound money, would by itself be enough to set up a powerful dynamic towards *microeconomic* restructuring in Yugoslavia. In making this mistake, however, the Yugoslav prime minister was in distinguished company (as Schaffer, Chapter 10 in this volume, on Poland confirms).

Prospects for Yugoslavia's successor states

It was clear by August 1991 that Yugoslavia was not going to survive in its Titoist/post-Titoist form. What exactly might take its place remained an open question. A battery of independent successor states, possibly (but probably not) linked together in a loose Yugoslav confederation, seemed the most civilised option. A renascent Greater Serbia, whether under its own name or that of Yugoslavia, plus three or four independent rump states on the periphery, seemed more likely. What are the chances of successor states doing significantly better than the old Yugoslavia in facing up to the deep-seated structural problems which have bedevilled the economy of the region since the early 1960s?

We begin by stating the obvious – economic *circumstances* will be significantly *worse* for almost any putative successor state. The Yugoslav foreign debt, which is set to grow dramatically through 1991–2, will have to be taken over and/or shared out, giving the worse possible start to a new Slovenia, Croatia, Serbia or whatever. Trade between the different Yugoslav regions, which has suffered through the years first on account of associationist autarky and then through Milošević's intransigence, will almost certainly suffer much more. The picture for individual putative successor states is, on the whole, gloomier than even these general considerations suggest.

Serbia suffered particularly badly during 1990 in terms of real personal incomes, mainly due to the collapse of traditional 'eastern-oriented' Serbian markets in the CMEA area (Yugoslavia had participated in the CMEA bilateral clearing system prior to its abolition at the beginning of 1991) and the Middle East, particularly in Iraq. It would suffer worse under independence, whether of the Greater or Lesser kind, because the weakness of its balance of payments would be cruelly exposed by the loss of Slovenian manufacturing strength and the Croatian tourist industry. (We assume that Slovenia would remain outside even the Greatest of Serbias, and that if Serbia managed to gain control of part of the Adriatic coast this would in itself do great damage to the tourist industry by turning Dalmatia into an embattled frontier zone.) Serbia would not be able to survive without further massive drops in living standards unless large-scale foreign economic aid were forthcoming. EC economic sanctions against an expansionist Greater Serbia would ensure that such aid would not be forthcoming, and that Serbia's *entrée* to the West European market would be barred.

Prospects are not so very much rosier for other possible successor states. Slovenia, with its ethnic compactness and relatively strong manufacturing base, is perhaps better placed than any. But the Slovenian manufacturing base is strong only by East European standards, and the problem of insolvency is currently only marginally less serious in that republic than in, say, Serbia. Early accession to the EC would be unlikely. With a very small domestic market (population less than 2 million) Slovenia has to trade intensively with its neighbours if it is to survive. There can be no strong supposition that it would find it easy to do so, either westwards, eastwards or southwards.

For Croatia, prospects are greatly complicated by the presence of Serbian enclaves within the republic. Though the Serbian-majority areas are of little economic importance in themselves, Serbian nationalists seemed at mid-1991 intent on consolidating their control over broad areas of Croatia, including parts in which there is no Serbian majority. There is a real possibility, then, that an independent Croatia might be left in control of little more than half the area of the present republic of Croatia, with the partition of Dalmatia killing the Adriatic tourist industry for Croatia, as for Serbia. The rate of insolvency in Croatian industry is about the national average, and with employment less buoyant than in Slovenia the implications of forced-draft restructuring in difficult circumstances are, to say the least, disturbing.

Of the other republics, Montenegro, one of the weakest of the regional economies, would, in the event of a break-up, likely go with Serbia, to weigh down the already battered economy of that republic even more. Bosnia's specifically economic prospects seem of secondary importance, since this ethnically mixed area might well be partitioned between Croatia and Serbia, leaving the biggest single group, the Serbo-Croat-speaking Muslims, an embittered minority on both sides of the new border. Macedonia in the south, poor and land-locked, would face a bleak economic future as an independent state, but might in any case be absorbed by a Greater Serbia.

So much for the 'objective' factors. What about systemic structuring as such? The old Yugoslavia was clearly hopelessly compromised by the inherent weaknesses of Titoism and associationism. Could successor states be counted on to provide new broom impetus to systemic restructuring?

The first thing that must be said in this connection is that new broom credentials of Slobodan Milošević's Serbia are dubious. Milošević's radicalism is almost purely of the ethnic-sectarian variety, and for all his experience as a banker Milošević has injected virtually no new ideas into the economic policy debate. On the contrary (as we saw on pp. 295–6) he has tended, when in trouble, to revert to the classic communist/associationist trick of fudging rather than solving economic problems – by using the printing press. The fact is that Milošević, as a populist, cannot afford to countenance any development that might bring with it the threat of mass unemployment. That effectively excludes any serious approach to restructuring. There are people in the Serbian opposition with more realistic and constructive ideas, but at time of writing their chances of gaining power seemed slim.

President Franjo Tudjman of Croatia is also a populist. It would be politically no easier for Tudjman than for Milošević to embrace wholeheartedly policies which would inevitably throw hundreds of thousands out of work, at least temporarily. But the history of economic policy in Croatia since the election of the HDZ (*Hrvatska*

Demokratsaka Zajednica – Croatian Democratic Union) government has shown another side to the economics of South Slav populism. While proclaiming a commitment to the principle of privatisation, the Tudjman government has in practice done much more in the direction of *nationalisation*. Public utilities and major elements in the energy complex like the big oil company INA have already been brought into Croatian public ownership. Under the rubric of so-called 'holding companies' a number of big engineering enterprises, including Rade Končar and Djuro Djaković, have been effectively put under state management. The same arrangement is now being proposed for the shipyards. That these developments are more than simply improvisations in difficult conditions is confirmed by a perusal of the draft Croatian law on privatisation. It talks about the need to 'safeguard the assets of the nation', and posits that the final decision on all key aspects of privatisation – who to sell to, at what price and under what conditions – is in every case to be made by the republican Agency for Restructuring and Development Fund. The Croatian state would become, on 30 June 1992, the default owner of all socialised enterprises that had not by that time been sold off (Kalodjera 1991).

In seeking to privatise through initial statification, its critics say, the draft law runs the risk of turning Croatia into a command economy for the next twenty years. Amendments to the draft legislation, based on the assessments of professional economists, have to a degree shifted the centre of gravity of the proposals away from the Agency and the Fund towards the workers of the given enterprises. Nevertheless the spirit of the draft legislation is clearly statist and autarkist – it is difficult, for instance, to imagine it providing a basis for any kind of satisfactory regime for foreign investment.

The approach to privatisation embodied in the Serbian draft law on privatisation is remarkably similar to the Croatian. The republican Agency for Restructuring and Development Fund would play major executive roles in the process. The former would have the right to veto all proposed privatisations, and this right would apply retroactively to privatisations implemented before passage of the law; 20 per cent of all share issues would go automatically to the Development Fund, as would all unsold shares (Bogdanović and Lakićević 1991).

The key elements in this bizarre populist approach to privatisation are not difficult to disentangle. There are definite residual traces of the establishment attitudes of the era of 'real socialism'. Beyond that, there is a kind of economic tribalism which perceives ownership, not as a basis for enterprise by individuals and companies, but as a basis for the survival and consolidation of the nation. The important thing, therefore, is that INA, for example, should be secured as part of the Croatian patrimony, just as, for Serbian nationalists, it is so crucial to secure Krajina (the main Serbian minority area within Croatia) as part of the Greater Serbian patrimony. These are not new ideas. If readers glance back at the earlier account of the Croatian crisis of the late 1960s and early 1970s they will discover an uncanny resemblance in the way that ownership issues were perceived. Nor should we be surprised to find them so dominant in a part of the world where tribes are still seeking to become nation-states. But economic tribalism is totally incompatible with an internationally integrated market economy. As long as it continues to dominate the thinking of the leaderships of the Yugoslav region, the economic prospects for that region, at best uncertain, are bleak indeed.

References

Bogdanović S, Lakićević M (1991) Država odumire jacajući. *Ekonomska Politika* 15 April 1991: 10–11

Dumezić T (1991a) Gubici poništavaju novac. *Ekonomska Politika* 15 April 1991: 26–8

Dumezić T (1991b) Posle kolapsa. *Ekonomska Politika* 3 June 1991: 12–13

Dyker D A (1990) *Yugoslavia: Socialism, Development and Debt*. Routledge

Emisija i budžet (1991) *Ekonomska Politika* 24 June 1991: 5

Gnjatović D (1985) *Uloga Inostranih Sredstava u Privrednom Razvoju Jugoslavije*. Ekonomski Institut, Belgrade

Grizelj J (1987) Koliko ste zadovoljni radom SIV-a. *NIN* 17 June 1987: 10

Grličkov V (1990) Kako pokriti gubitke. *Ekonomska Politika* 17 December 1990: 9–10

Grličkov V (1991a) Upadi u platni sistem. *Ekonomska Politika* 14 January 1991: 11

Grličkov V (1991b) Sudar koncepcija. *Ekonomska Politika* 13 May 1991: 10–12

Kalodjera D (1991) Nedopustiva avantura. *Ekonomska Politika* 15 April 1991: 12–13

Sirc L (1979) *The Yugoslav Economy under Self-Management*. Macmillan

Statistički Godišnjak 1985 (1985) Savezni zavod za statistiku. Belgrade

Statistički Godišnjak 1990 (1990) Savezni zavod za statistiku. Belgrade

CHAPTER 12

Soviet Union

DAVID A DYKER

Introduction

In many ways the Soviet Union serves as a counter-example to almost every principle of economic organisation that emerges from a general consideration of European economic development. For 'market' read 'centralised command planning', for 'open economy' read 'Leninist monopoly of foreign trade' (see Alan Smith, Chapter 6 in *The European Economy*, on integration in Eastern Europe), for 'multilateralism' read 'bilateralism', for 'international division of labour' read 'autarky'. Nor is there any need to labour the point that the counter-example has come unstuck, that it is precisely because of the wilful neglect of market principles, internally and externally, over a period of more than half a century, that the USSR now faces an economic crisis of colossal proportions. But we must begin in this chapter by analysing classical Soviet central planning on its merits, and this for two reasons. First, for better or worse, Soviet-style central planning was the dominant economic paradigm in the eastern half of Europe throughout the post-war period to 1989. Second, the system was highly successful in the Soviet Union itself – over an extended period – in terms of the limited priorities it set itself: principally the pursuit of maximum growth in national income, based in turn on all-out emphasis on the development of heavy industry. Over the critical period of the first two five-year plans, 1929–37, Soviet national income grew, according to official claims, at an average annual rate of 16.4 per cent. Western recalculations bring this figure down to a range of 5–11 per cent, depending on the index number formula used. Table 12.1 shows the rapidity with which the Soviet economy recovered from the devastation of Second World War – again Western recalculations bring the figures down somewhat, but not to such an extent as to call into question the proposition that the Soviet economy grew at an annual rate of 5 per cent plus over a period of, in all, fifty years. Table 12.1 tells another story – the story of the dramatic slow-down in Soviet economic growth rates from the early 1970s onwards. But before going on to the details of that story, let us set the scene by seeking to analyse how – and at what cost – Soviet central planning was able to deliver so impressively on growth over an extended period of time.

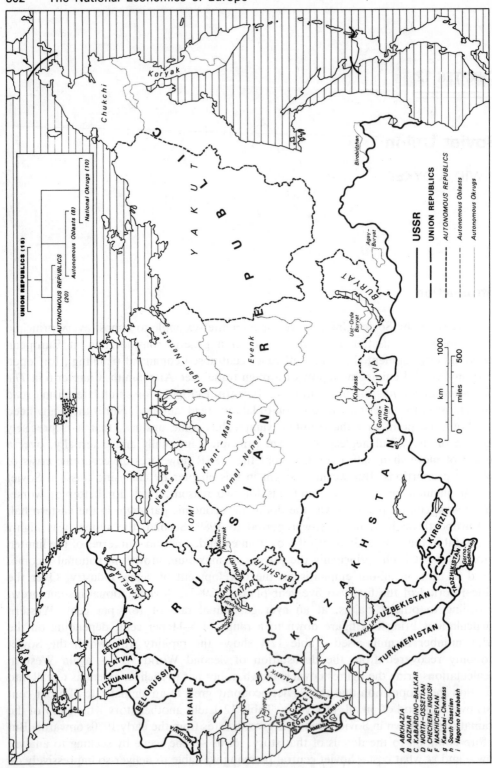

Map 12.1

Table 12.1 Soviet economic growth 1951–90

Period	Average annual percentage change in Net Material Product [a]	Average annual percentage change in GNP [b]
1951–5	11.4	5.5
1956–60	9.2	5.9
1961–5	6.6	5.1
1966–70	7.7	5.2
1971–5	5.7	3.7
1976–80	4.2	2.7
1981–5	3.5	1.9
1986–90	1.8	0.3 [c]

Notes:
[a] National Income, Marxist definition, excluding 'unproductive' services; official Soviet figures, calculated in constant prices
[b] CIA estimates, calculated in constant prices
[c] Author's estimates

Source: Dyker 1991: 42 and 172

Soviet planning for growth

It is not difficult to pin-point the major *source* of Soviet economic growth. Like a number of West European countries, and nearly all the smaller East European countries, the USSR was able to count, up until the 1960s, on an abundant supply of cheap labour from an over-populated countryside. The harsh imposition in the early 1930s of an unpopular system of collectivisation, which totally destroyed the traditional peasant household, certainly facilitated the transfer process – between 1928 and 1932 total urban/industrial employment increased from 11.4 million to 22.8 million, an overshoot against plan of 7 million – but it is probably fair to say that *any* explicit policy of growthmanship, energetically pursued, would have produced broadly similar results.

Central planning did, however, display a number of specific strengths in the context of the campaign to mobilise these reserves for rapid growth.

1 The vertical/hierarchical, quasi-military system of plan implementation facilitated the breaking-down of central growth priorities into explicit, quantitative targets at intermediate (industrial ministry) and enterprise level.
2 These quantitative targets provided clear signals to executives as to the directions that resource mobilisation should take, without taxing their very limited business training with the intricacies of optimisation.
3 By the same token they served as simple and sturdy vehicles for the psychological mobilisation of a 'new' working class which could see, in their own piece-work regimes, a microcosm of the great task of socialist construction, as embodied in the five-year plans. (It must be added that, in the Stalin period, fear of arrest was a significant supplementary spring of psychological motivation.)
4 Output planning also provided the basis for the tactics of 'taut' planning, whereby

key plan targets would be set at a deliberately over-ambitious level, in order to impose extra pressure on planners and producers alike to 'seek out reserves'. (Note that these tactics can work only where the number of ultimate priorities is relatively limited, so that there are always non-priority sectors from which resources can be diverted to ensure fulfilment of taut plans in priority sectors.)

5 Central control made it possible for the Soviet authorities to raise the savings–investment ratio to a level which would have been inconceivable if that ratio had been left to find its 'natural' level. Between 1928 and 1937 the Soviet savings–investment ratio doubled – from 13 per cent to 26 per cent (Gregory and Stuart 1990: 121) – leaving it substantially higher, in what was still a relatively poor country, than the corresponding ratio in either the UK or the USA today.

So far, then, we have outlined a 'model' of early Soviet growth which seems to correspond fairly closely to the familiar Lewis Model of growth, so central to standard Western development economics. The difference is that where the original Lewis Model leaves it to the indigenous entrepreneurial class to exploit the scope which exists in almost every developing economy for massive transfer of labour from country to town, in the Bolshevik variant of the model it is the vanguard of the proletariat, the Communist Party in its 'leading role', which performs this task. The Lewis Model interpretation of the early phase of Soviet economic development draws support from a comparison of output and productivity trends. In his recalculations of Soviet growth trends for the period 1928–40, Abram Bergson (1978) finds that when late-year price weights (which tend to produce lower rates of growth than early-year price weights) are used, growth of Net National Product (NNP) works out at an annual average of 4.2 per cent, while labour productivity growth shows up at a rate of growth of just 0.5 per cent. When early-year price weights are used, both figures work out much higher – 9.3 per cent for NNP and 5.4 per cent for labour productivity (Bergson 1978: 122). But the gap is the same, and the interpretation simple enough. Early Soviet growth was, *par excellence*, a process of *extensive development*, based on rapid increases in the level of absorption of resources, rather than in the efficiency with which those resources were utilised.

But here we must add a new and specifically Soviet element into the story. For while surplus rural labour is almost universal in the developing world, abundance of industrial raw materials is not. And indeed a number of the countries of the Middle East which do have, in particular, oil in great abundance, are very short of the resource mostly widely distributed among Third World countries – people. The Soviet Union during the Stalin period, in contrast, was perhaps unique in the world in having a rich and comprehensive endowment, both in energy materials and minerals, to complement its labour resources. The strength of central planning lay as much in its capacity to mobilise these resources, as to mobilise labour reserves. The grand projects of the early five-year plans were largely directed at developing existing and accessing new deposits of coal, oil, iron and non-ferrous ores, and so on. It was these projects which enabled the Soviet Union to go for very rapid industrial growth without fear of running into balance of payments constraints, and it is difficult to conceive of the implementation of such an array of projects outside the context of a system which gave the centre the prerogative to set the projects in motion, and to command the resources to implement them.

The slow-down

A glance back at Table 12.1 will suffice to remind the reader of just how dramatic the falling-away in the quantitative performance of the Soviet economy has been. (Adding in the qualitative dimension, including environmental degradation, would produce an even starker picture.) And indeed a quick review of the previous section will confirm that almost every 'strength' of centralised, command planning is a two-edged sword. Taut planning is fine when the number of priorities is limited. But once priorities start to escalate, as they inevitably did when Stalin's successors began to seek improvement in living standards after the dictator's death in 1953, taut planning at best produces structural sclerosis, at worst total chaos. It is certainly an advantage, from a growth point of view, to be able to push savings–investment ratios beyond their 'natural' level – as long as the resources thus mobilised are not simply frittered away on ill-conceived projects that just tie up resources, leaving the long-suffering population a loser in both the short and long terms. Most fundamentally, the virtues of the gross output planning indicator were only virtues as long as physical quantity was a reasonable proxy for end-usefulness (as with coal, steel, electricity), and as long as cost-efficiency considerations and details of resource allocation could be ignored with some impunity. As priority shifted towards consumer goods and technologically more complex and heterogeneous producer goods, the inherent weaknesses of the gross output indicator on the user side rapidly began to impinge at a critical level. The unravelling of the cost-efficiency side of the problem is so central to our whole story as to merit a new paragraph.

We noted earlier that the rate of absorption of 'new' labour in the course of implementation of the first five-year plan was way in excess of the planned level. This reflected a fundamental feature of the actual pattern of Soviet industrialisation which was, indeed, at odds with the dominant line of strategic thinking associated with the start of the industrialisation campaign. While Stalin, following Preobrazhensky, had sought to place primary emphasis on large-scale, capital-intensive industrial projects, operating at or near the world technological frontier, the pattern which actually gelled was a much more mixed one. Grand projects there certainly were, as we have already seen, some indeed so grand as to pass from the realm of rational exploitation of economies of scale to that of gigantomania. But the ancillary industrial developments of the 1930s and 1950s proceeded in a very different way. Encouraged by the planning regime to try to maximise short-term output results, but confronted with severe shortages in industrial supply, partly because of over-centralisation and extreme tautness, partly because the gross output regime created little incentive to produce 'fiddly' components, Soviet enterprise directors would seek to fill the gaps by accessing the most obviously abundant factor – labour. That factor would be used to staff 'dwarf-workshops' – low-tech, highly labour-intensive workshops, manufacturing, on a cottage-industry basis, the kinds of components that could not reliably be obtained from the official supply network. More generally, managers would simply follow a policy of systematic over-staffing – in order to have some kind of *masse de manoeuvre* at their disposal – 'just in case'.

Thus the Soviet economy developed a *sui generis* pattern of dual technology which played a key, if unplanned, role in the pattern of extensive development during the Stalin period. But as the scope for further transfer of labour out of the countryside inevitably narrowed, against a background of very heavy war losses of population, and as the birth-rate fell, partly because women had been strongly encouraged to join the full-time labour force as a function of the initial, mobilisatory campaign, so the labour supply situation became tighter and tighter. The Soviet labour force grew effectively by just 0.6 per cent per annum over the period 1956–60 (a two-hour reduction in the working week in 1956 exacerbated the underlying trend). In that context a planning system which positively encouraged systematic over-staffing was clearly set to become a major obstacle to further growth.

Fuel and power were never so abundantly available to enterprise management as labour. But there was nothing in the planning system to encourage economical use of energy resources, and some elements positively discouraged it – for example, the practice of planning the activity of railways and road haulage organisations in ton-kilometres, which gave them a direct incentive to waste fuel on unnecessary journeys. It was not surprising, then, that coefficients of energy utilisation to national income remained several times higher than comparable coefficients for Western countries. This must have imposed substantial costs on the Soviet economy and reduced growth rates, but it did not, during the period *c.* 1930–60, run it up against unbreakable bottlenecks such as might have brought growth to a complete halt.

By the early 1960s, however, the fuel situation was beginning to change fundamentally. As hydrocarbon reserves west of the Urals began to run out, the Soviet oil and gas industry had to begin to look to Siberia for future supplies. Commercial exploitation of gas in Western Siberia started in 1963, and of oil in 1964. In difficult natural conditions (the bulk of Siberian hydrocarbon reserves lie north of the permafrost line), with minimal local infrastructure, extraction was bound to be a relatively costly business. Isolated location entailed the construction of vast pipeline networks, which pushed costs of Siberian fuel to the user that much higher. Perhaps even more important, the long-run marginal cost curve for West Siberian hydrocarbons proved itself in the early 1970s to be a steeply rising one over critical output ranges, as fresh discoveries pushed the oil and gas industries ever further north and east (Dyker 1991: 36). Quite suddenly, then, the Soviet economy found itself in desperate need of a mechanism which would provide effective incentives to fuel- and energy-economy as well as higher labour productivity. The traditional system could provide only incentives for the precise opposite to that.

Table 12.2 provides aggregate statistical evidence to support this thesis. Rates of growth of labour productivity are generally moderate rather than high throughout the post-war period to 1975. (Note, however, that the period 1956–60 is a clear exception, with the average annual labour productivity increase above 5 per cent, accounting for the greater part of economic growth in that quinquennium.) But while the rate of growth of labour inputs is, at 2 per cent or under, consistently low relative to what it had been before the war (Bergson calculates a comparable figure of 3.7 per cent for the

Table 12.2 Average annual percentage rates of growth of GNP, factor inputs and factor productivity 1951–75

	1951–5	1956–60	1961–5	1966–70	1971–5
GNP[a]	6.0	5.8	5.0	5.5	3.8
Inputs					
Total[b]	4.5	3.9	4.1	3.9	4.1
Labour (man-hours)	1.9	0.6	1.6	2.0	1.9
Capital	9.0	9.8	8.7	7.5	7.9
Land	4.0	1.3	0.6	−0.3	0.9
Factor productivity					
Total	1.4	1.8	0.9	1.5	−0.2
Labour (man-hours)	4.6	5.1	3.4	3.4	1.8
Capital	−2.7	−3.6	−3.3	−1.9	−3.8
Land	1.9	4.4	4.4	5.8	2.9

Notes:
[a] These GNP estimates differ slightly from those presented in Table 12.1
[b] Inputs have been combined using a Cobb-Douglas (linear homogeneous) production function with weights of 60.2, 36.1 and 3.1 per cent for labour, capital and land respectively

Source: Greenslade 1976: 279

period 1928–40 – Bergson 1978: 122), and in relation to rates of growth of capital inputs, it shows no tendency to *fall* over the period 1950–75. (It was not until the early 1980s that the annual rate of growth of employment fell below 1 per cent.) If we want to understand the sharp falling-away of the rate of growth of GNP in the early 1970s, therefore, we have to focus, not so much on labour *input* trends, as on labour *productivity* trends. Just at the time when a reading of long-term factor availability trends was counselling a switch to productivity growth as the main source of growth in national income (the cherished transition from extensive to intensive growth), labour productivity trends turned sharply downwards. It was this, together with the secular poor performance in relation to capital productivity (echoes of Stalin's gigantomania), which conspired to produce that extraordinary result, a negative rate of growth for total productivity in the first half of the 1970s. As much as 0.5 percentage points of the drop in the rate of growth of total productivity 1971–75 could be attributable to diminishing returns in primary extraction. This still leaves a huge fall between late 1960s and early 1970s to be explained.

There could be no starker indication of deep systemic crisis than that negative rate of growth of total productivity. The really striking feature of the downward trend, however, is the fact that it set in more than ten years after the first attempts to reform the planning system had been made, and more than five years after the first comprehensive reform of the Soviet planning system, that of 1965.

Let us return for a moment to our analysis of the relationship between the planning system and the changing economic conditions facing the Soviet Union. To say that by the late 1950s the system developed by Stalin was becoming obsolete, and needed radical change, is no very extraordinary statement. In the West, after all, it is part of the routine of business and government life that institutional forms come and go as patterns of market structure, technology, and so on change. Nor was the Soviet leadership slow to perceive the need for reform, with the post-Stalin leadership, for instance, spotting the beginnings of a total productivity crisis as early as 1956. The extraordinary thing is that, even with a substantial political impetus towards reform, matters got rapidly worse rather than better. To try to make sense of this paradox, let us now look more closely at the early phase of Soviet planning reform.

Planning reform under Stalin's successors

In 1957 Khrushchev, by that time undisputed Soviet No. 1, though hardly a dictator in the Stalin style, began a series of reorganisations of the Soviet planning system. These seemed radical enough at first sight, extending, as they did, to the abolition of the system of industrial ministries which had dominated the process of plan fulfilment since the first five-year plan. But the regional economic councils (*sovnarkhozy*) which Khrushchev put in their place proved to be as bureaucratic, as hostile to considerations of cost efficiency, as the ministries had been – and to be highly vulnerable to the pressures of local nationalism into the bargain. In a word, the *sovnarkhoz* reform was a failure, and it was reversed by Khrushchev's successors in 1965. But by the early 1960s the Soviet government, egged on by a revitalised Soviet economics profession, had progressed from bureaucratic musical chairs to the (by the standards of the time) deeply radical notion that a cost-effective system could be constructed only on a parametric basis, through the interaction of a 'rational' price system and a success-indicator regime, at enterprise level, based on profit rather than gross output, with profit being used as a *source* as well as a criterion of bonus payments. As an implicit corollary of this, the market principle should supplant the command principle, not only in consumer goods markets, but also ultimately in the market for industrial goods also.

Khrushchev fell from power in 1964 before any of these ideas could be generally implemented. But his successors, Leonid Brezhnev (Party boss) and Aleksei Kosygin (prime minister, ie super-minister for industry) introduced in 1965 a comprehensive industrial planning reform which seemed to embody most of the principles which the debate of the early 1960s had adumbrated. The gross output success-indicator was indeed abolished, to be replaced by a combination of sales and profit, profit was to be used as a basis for new, autonomous incentive funds (with the classical system bonuses had been under the control of the ministries), and prices were to be reformed accordingly. Enterprises were to be given a degree of freedom to plan their own investment activity, and a general commitment to the development of 'wholesale trade' in producer goods was voiced.

There can be no doubt that the 1965 reform did have some positive impact on Soviet economic performance. There was some improvement in the quality of goods, and as Table 12.2 shows, the growth rate increased slightly 1966–70 compared to the previous five-year period. (This is the only blip on the smooth trend down to zero growth and below.) The recovery partly reflected a run of good harvests which may have been largely attributable to luck with the weather, but a closer perusal of Table 12.2 indicates a more systematic explanation. The rate of growth of labour productivity did not rise in the period 1966–70. But that of *capital* productivity did, and quite sharply – or rather the rate of decline in capital productivity that had been evident from the 1930s onwards was sharply reduced. There is substantial microeconomic evidence to suggest that this improvement was largely due to the impact of the introduction, in 1965, of a universal capital charge – prior to that capital had simply been a free good to enterprises. The capital charge forced enterprises to unload hoards of unused equipment which they had been holding on to – 'just in case' – thus engineering a significant improvement in the allocation of the capital stock.

Yet by the early 1970s the downward trend had set back in with a vengeance, to be further accentuated in the latter part of that decade. How, it may be asked, could a planning reform which had seemed to promise so much prove to be but the harbinger of economic stagnation and systemic stasis? It is clear enough that the specific impact of the capital charge on trends on capital productivity would be quickly exhausted. But why did the more general systemic changes not grip, why did the qualitative improvements reported for the first few years of the reform not develop into a sustained intensification of the whole economy?

The answer falls into two parts. First, the 1965 planning reform was imbued with the mistaken notion (the mistake, it should be stressed, was no monopoly of the Soviet government) that the categories of the market economy could somehow be superimposed upon the structure of traditional, Soviet-style planning – that profit would serve as a reliable guide to efficient resource allocation and a spur to effort and technological dynamism in a situation where the planning bureaucracy continued to fix all prices, to hand out modified output targets – in the form of sales targets – to enterprises *and* to impose supply and delivery contracts on those enterprises. The result, in practice, was a peculiarly Soviet version of what we recognise as the monopoly problem in market economies. With all the good intentions and limited successes of the price reforms of the late 1960s, it was, of course, beyond the capabilities of hard-pressed bureaucrats in charge of millions of prices to set them on any kind of consistent, rational basis. As Nikolai Shmelev was to say many years later, 'we do not really know which is in reality dearer – gold or bricks' (Shmelev 1989: 274). So the new price signals in many cases simply pulled in the wrong direction, inducing less, rather than more efficient allocation of resources. To make matters worse, the maintenance of the principle of central control over contracts ensured that the average industrial customer would still be a captive of his supplier – the more so that he still had a quasi-output target to fulfil. In that context, the simple way to increase profits was to cut costs by skimping on quality. The principle of profit-maximisation turned too easily into the practice of profiteering.

The other element in the story was political reaction. From 1968 (the year of the Prague Spring and the Soviet invasion of Czechoslovakia) onwards the realisation grew among the apparatus men of the Soviet Communist Party that real economic reform would inevitably mean the end of their status as elite of elites within the Soviet Union. They found it convenient to cite in their public arguments the problems of profiteering, increased second-economy activity, and so on, which the reforms had thrown up – but managed to ignore the ineluctable conclusion that the way to resolve these tensions was by moving forward to a full-blooded market economy. Their solution was to go backwards to 'real' socialist planning, and by 1972 the Kosygin planning reform had been substantially dismantled.

Then at the end of 1973 something happened which was to change the course of Soviet history, as of the history of the world. The fourfold increase in oil prices represented a huge windfall terms-of-trade gain for a country whose exports were dominated by energy materials. Brezhnev, by then very much the No. 1 as Kosygin's influence waned, seems to have decided at that point that the economic reform could be closed down altogether. The extra billions of dollars from oil exports could be used to buy foreign equipment and technology, and the Soviet economy modernised and dynamised in that way. With the pressure (it seemed to Brezhnev) lifted, there was no further need to flirt with the market mechanism.

Brezhnev's reaction to the First Oil Shock was probably the greatest mistake made by a Soviet leader since collectivisation. As we saw, much of the pressure for improved resource allocation procedures that built up in the 1960s came from the changing energy situation. The early 1970s witnessed further sharp rises in Soviet energy extraction costs (Dyker 1991: 36), and the signs were already there that aggregate Soviet oil output would start to contract at some point in the medium-term future. The fact that hydrocarbons were now receiving so much higher a valuation on international markets actually *strengthened* rather than weakened the argument in favour of radical reform such as would force producing units to be more economical with energy inputs. By chosing to force oil exports, while doing nothing to economise on oil utilisation at home, Brezhnev pushed his fuel industries up that sharply rising long-term marginal cost curve, so that by the late 1970s the rental element in Soviet hydrocarbon export revenues had fallen sharply, perhaps to zero, even after the second oil price hike of 1979.

But that was not the worst of the tale. The hard currency accruing to the Soviet Union as a result of this misallocation of resources was itself fearfully misallocated. There certainly was a tremendous kick in Soviet imports of technology-related goods (Soviet imports of machinery from West Germany, for instance, nearly doubled between 1974 and 1975 – *Vneshnyaya Torgovlya* . . . 1976: 188). But the wager on the import of foreign technology was to fail, as it was to fail even more spectacularly in Poland, because the failure to maintain the impetus of economic reform meant that the domestic Soviet economy was totally incapable of absorbing the new technology; under central planning, after all, the name of the game is to keep on fulfilling your plan, and the easiest way to do that is to continue to do what you have always done. Critical weaknesses in the construction–investment cycle also impinged here, with lead-times, always in the range of two to three times as long as in the West, actually lengthening in the Brezhnev period (Dyker 1983: 36). The Soviet Union missed out completely on the microelectronics revolution (gross output is a *peculiarly* unsuitable indicator for planning the production of semiconductors!), and by the early 1980s the technology gap between East and West had widened substantially, and was beginning to affect the Soviet Union's military credibility.

We must introduce one more element to complete the picture of productivity crisis in the late Brezhnev period. As we saw earlier, Stalin had sought to motivate people through a mixture of carrots and (sometimes terrible) sticks. The great dictator was also able to count on the very substantial degree of socialist idealism present among both managerial and line workers in the 1930s and 1940s. Khrushchev abandoned terror, laid a new stress on material incentives – but for everybody, including peasants, and sought to maintain the momentum of socialist commitment by proclaiming (the claim now seems ludicrous enough to us) that the Soviet Union would achieve 'full communism' (ie a state of plenty, with the state beginning to wither away) by 1980. Brezhnev tried to continue the policy of strengthening material incentives. At the same time he introduced a hitherto unheard-of degree of security of tenure for almost every member of the Soviet work-force - from central committee *apparatchik* to unskilled factory worker. By the late 1970s it seemed that everyone in the Soviet Union had a job for life, with gerontocracy dominating the highest counsels of the state, occasionally broken only by death itself, and a growing problem of labour discipline on the shop-floor, as workers – especially older, more highly skilled and highly paid workers – seemed increasingly inclined to test the patience of management on scores of absenteeism, drunkenness, pilfering, etc (Reznik 1980). At a more general level, a complex of social problems ranging from alcoholism to pollution-induced illness was reducing life expectancy at an alarming rate. Beyond the more technical reasons for productivity stasis, then, there stood a sociological drama which in turn reflected a looming crisis in the oligarchical, one-party system which had ruled the Soviet Union since the death of Stalin.

It is against this background that we must seek to understand the drop in the Soviet growth rate to a mere 1 or 2 per cent by 1979–80. This indeed, to use one of Gorbachev's favourite phrases, was *stagnation*.

The beginnings of *perestroika*

When Brezhnev died in November 1982 he was succeeded by former police chief Yury Andropov. Andropov wasted no time making public his fear that all was not well in the Soviet polity and economy. The policies with which he sought to address that fear were generally cautious to the point of conservatism. His labour discipline campaign, while attacking genuine enough problems, reflected also the limited perspectives of a professional martinet. His economic reforms, promulgated in mid-1983 and implemented from the beginning of 1984, were largely a re-run of the Kosygin reform of 1965, reflecting a welcome acceptance of the pressing need for real reform, but an inability to perceive that until the central problem of over-centralisation was attacked, nothing would move. At the same time Andropov showed intellectual incisiveness and imagination in his development of the notion of 'socialist self-management' (Andropov 1983), and an ability to spot and promote outstanding (comparatively) young apparatus men like Mikhail Gorbachev. Andropov's active General Secretaryship was cut short by serious illness in mid-1983, and he died in early 1984. He was succeeded by a terminally ill old Brezhnevite, Konstantin Chernenko. The most important thing about Andropov's last months, and the brief Chernenko interlude, is that the General Secretary of the day was frequently unable to be present at Politburo meetings because of indisposition. This permitted Gorbachev to build up an unassailable position as 'second secretary', and it came as no surprise when Gorbachev succeeded to the general secretaryship on Chernenko's death in March 1985.

Perestroika – the upswing

One of Gorbachev's first acts as General Secretary was to extend and deepen the economic planning reform initiated by Andropov. For the first time, reform started to go beyond the stage reached by the Kosygin legislation, in giving enterprise directors unprecedented rights, for instance, to work out their own investment plans and adjust their staffing levels to match – in other words make surplus workers redundant. From 1985, under the rubric of the 'Sumy experiment', *all* upgrading investment was transferred to the jurisdiction of the enterprise, while financial relations between enterprise and ministry/centre were for the first time to be ruled by what amounted to a profits tax, based – in principle – on stable assessments. (Hitherto, even under the Kosygin reform, the remainder of profits after all proper deductions had been made, including for enterprise investment funds, was payable back to the state budget in its entirety – ie the marginal rate of 'profits tax' was 100 per cent.) In agriculture, increasingly radical proposals based on the principle of a 'collective contract' between groups of peasants and collective/state farms finally took wing at the end of 1988 when Gorbachev publicly endorsed the development of long-term *lease-holding* (*arenda*) within agriculture, which opened up the possibility of something close to privatisation in this critically inefficient sector of the Soviet economy, short of the return of land to private ownership as such. In the same year legislation was passed which permitted, under the rubric of *co-operative enterprise*, a degree of scope for what was effectively private enterprise in a range of service and specialist production sub-sectors.

Radical change in production sectors inevitably generated pressure for change in finance and trade. The traditional *monobank* system, whereby the State Bank (Gosbank) combined the role of central, issuing bank with that of short-term credit bank for all domestic economic activity, with Stroibank (Investment Bank) and the Foreign Trade Bank financing, respectively, investment activity and the foreign trade monopoly, had been an essentially *passive* system. Its role was to monitor plan fulfilment and to seek to keep down costs, and indeed it enjoyed a degree of success in this role. But it had no *ex ante* role, no role in terms of the assessment of investment projects, of the creditworthiness of enterprises, and so on – because of course under the traditional system that was the monopoly of the planning authorities. By the late 1980s, however, Gosbank was being increasingly restricted to a classic central banking function, while the number of a new breed of independent Soviet commercial banks had by mid-1989 grown to 125 (Dyker 1991: 97–8). None of this yet amounted to a transition to a Western-style banking system based on a credit-creation mechanism, but the intention to pursue such a transition had been clearly stated.

Perhaps most strikingly of all, the foreign trade monopoly was abolished in 1986. As a result, the Ministry of Foreign Trade lost most of its directive powers. It was abolished altogether two years later and replaced by a new Ministry for External Economic Affairs with substantial prerogatives in terms of vetting organisations for direct participation in foreign trade and a remit to develop a long-term trade strategy for the Soviet Union, but no directive powers as such. By the end of 1988 all Soviet enterprises in principle enjoyed the right of direct access to international markets. Meanwhile legislation passed in 1987 had permitted, for the first time, foreign ownership of equity in the Soviet Union under the rubric of *joint enterprises*. Foreign equity participation in such enterprises was originally limited to 49 per cent, but was subsequently raised to 100 per cent, so that the joint venture rubric effectively developed into a basis for foreign capital to come in and set up subsidiaries in the Soviet Union. Taxation and profit repatriation provisions were not particularly favourable to would-be Western partners, but by 1990 almost 2,000 joint ventures had been agreed, the bulk of them with companies from Western countries.

As the new Soviet leader broke one taboo after another, the mood was optimistic. A new five-year plan for the period 1986–90 proclaimed the slogan of 'acceleration' (*uskorenie*), and set ambitious growth targets, with the emphasis on the modernisation of the technological heart of the Soviet economy – the machine-building industry. Sure enough, the plan fulfilment reports for 1986–8 proclaimed an average rate of growth of national income of over 3.5 per cent. At the beginning of 1989, then, the Soviet economy seemed to be on the brink of the kind of systemic break-through that leaderships had been seeking – some wholeheartedly, some halfheartedly – since the late 1950s.

Perestroika – the downswing

Yet by the early 1990s everything had turned sour. After falling back to 2.4 per cent in 1989, the offically reported growth rate of Soviet national income went negative to the extent of 4 per cent in 1990. It is likely to continue to fall at a rate of 10 per cent or more throughout 1991–2. Sharp falls in output in the temple of the 'cult of the gross' may not necessarily be a bad thing. But the downward trend in Soviet national income has been unaccompanied by any significant qualitative or structural improvements in the economic situation. On the contrary, the consumer supply situation has worsened, with food supply a particular problem, and much of the output which is still being recorded is of obsolescent goods, or heavy-industrial or defence-industry goods for which there is no obvious use under present circumstances. At the same time the quality of many public services has clearly fallen.

What went wrong? Before going on to list, with the benefit of hindsight, the string of mistakes and miscalculations which Gorbachev made in the mid–late 1980s, it is worth pausing to cross-refer to Chapter 9 in this volume on Hungary, where Paul Hare tells the fascinating story of the partial success but ultimate failure of Hungarian market socialism. By the late 1980s, after twenty years of the New Economic Model, the Hungarian government and people, never much fired by the ideals of Soviet-style socialism, were ready to accept that market socialism is but a transitional phase towards restoration of a full-blooded market economy, even capitalism. Mikhail Gorbachev came to the General Secretaryship of the Communist Party of the Soviet Union in 1985 as a man of impeccable party background, an *apparatchik* all his life, called now to be president of the oligarchs. He had no mandate to seek transition to a full-blooded market economy, and it is to his credit that after a few years at the top he was able to perceive that much more radical solutions were required than he had ever dreamt of. The fact remains that the symbiosis of plan and market, of centralisation and decentralisation, which was the officially proclaimed goal of first-stage *perestroika*, was a chimera. Even if its implementation had gone like clockwork, it would surely eventually have come to nought. But its implementation did not go like clockwork.

The most fundamental strategic error that Gorbachev made on the strictly economic side was accepting the advice of then senior economic adviser Abel Aganbegyan, a distinguished economist whose judgement Gorbachev cannot be blamed for trusting, to the effect that *perestroika* could be combined with *uskorenie*, that restructuring could go hand in hand with acceleration. Here, indeed, we gain an insight into just how unreconstructed the thinking of even the more reform-minded Soviet economists and administrators still was in the mid-1980s. The notion that the Soviet economy could be restructured, both systemically and in terms of production profile, just as a new drive for growth was unleashed, exactly paralleled the fallacy that planning in the traditional sense could somehow be combined with the market. It may seem difficult to understand how the Soviet leadership of the time was unable to perceive that the acceleration strategy was bound to reinforce precisely the weaknesses of the traditional system which had brought it to crisis, that the very idea of a new five-year plan which would seek to galvanise and modernise through the imposition of taut plans was simply a contradiction in terms. We should certainly bear in mind the Gorbachev was reacting, perhaps with a degree of panic, to a new realisation of just how bad a pass the Soviet economy had come to in the late Brezhnev era, just how deep the stagnation inherited from Brezhnev was. The reaction was, nevertheless, an inappropriate one. The fruits of that error are illustrated in Table 12.3. A plan which had set out to modernise the Soviet economy, to place a new priority on machine-building as the linchpin of technical progress, succeeded only, over its first two years at least, in extrapolating the investment trends of the past, with investments in fuel and energy continuing to rise inexorably, as the hydrocarbon industries were pushed further and further into diminishing returns, investment in machine building hardly changing at all in relative terms, and the shares of chemicals, a key high-tech sector, and the consumer industries, suffering a clear drop. (What evidence there is suggests that these trends continued through 1988 and 1989. By the latter year the five-year plan had been effectively abandoned, and the *uskorenie* policy with it.) It is not difficult to interpret the figures in Table 12.3. Pressure for growth on all sectors ensured that all sectors would continue to seek to pre-empt as large a volume of investment resources as possible, irrespective of how efficiently they were likely to use them. Pressure for growth on all sectors ensured that the chronic energy-inefficiency of the Soviet economy was not seriously addressed. Over the period 1986–9 the energy/national income coefficient is officially reported to have dropped by an annual average of 1.1 per cent (*NarKhoz* 1989: 320). Any reasonable allowance for elements of concealed inflation in the official national income series on which that calculation is based would yield a 'true' figure of zero or above. This in turn meant that the fuel/energy sectors themselves had to be treated as a special case – though even so investment strategy for those sectors continued to be seriously misconceived in that it was based on the maximisation of *gross* energy output, including the vast energy outlays of the Siberian fuel industry itself, rather than *net* energy output – the output actually available to the rest of the economy (Aksenov 1989).

Table 12.3 Structure of capital investment by sector of industry[a]

	1976–80	1981–5	1986–7
Production of the means of production (industrial and investment goods)	30.7	31.4	32.4
Production of the means of consumption (consumer goods)	4.3	4.3	4.1
By industrial complex			
Fuel and energy	10.5	12.9	14.4
Metallurgy	4.0	3.6	3.5
Machine-building	8.5	8.7	9.0
Chemicals and timber	5.2	4.1	3.6
Building materials	5.5	4.9	4.7

Note: [a] Percentage of total investment for the whole economy

Source: Loginov 1989: 24

Table 12.4 Soviet budget deficits (billion roubles)

	1984	1985	1986	1987	1988	1989	1990	1991[a]
Official Soviet figures	—	18.0	47.9	57.1	90.1	91.8	58.1[b]	200
CIA figures	11.0	17.0	49.8	64.4	68.8	—	—	—

Notes:
[a] Estimated
[b] There is some evidence that this figure represents an understatement

Sources: CIA 1988; *NarKhoz 1989*: 611; economic performance reports

A precious four years were lost, then, before the Soviet government finally came to accept that the old system of planning had to be totally abandoned, that a functional market-based system must be one in which the market is allowed to develop its own structural dynamism, form its own prices etc. But by then the sins of acceleration had compounded with the grim legacy of stagnation to produce a new crisis – this time of macroeconomic balance. Table 12.4 shows how the Soviet budget deficit has developed since 1984. The interpretation of the budget deficit is not a simple matter. If we think back to the institutionalised inefficiency of the late Brezhnev period and the structural sclerosis, which together meant that vast financial resources had to be committed to the shoring up of intrinsically loss-making operations, against the background of a defence budget that accounted for 10–15 per cent of national income and a wage policy that increasingly accommodated creeping wage inflation as the price of social peace, we may find it plausible enough to argue that budgetary disequilibrium was essentially a problem that Gorbachev inherited from the previous regime. Yet a glance at Table 12.4 will confirm that the deficit was only Rb 11 billion in 1984, climbing to Rb 17 billion in

1985. By 1986, Gorbachev's first full year in office, however, it had tripled to nearly Rb 50 billion. By 1989 it had reached almost Rb 100 billion. Why this explosion of macroeconomic imbalance under the most dynamic Soviet leader since Stalin?

Part of the explanation is certainly to be found in the fiscal impact of Gorbachev's ill-considered, though impeccably motivated, anti-alcohol drive. But that cost the budget at most some Rb 10 billion annually, which would explain only a small part of the escalation in the deficit between 1985 and 1986. More important, and the fault of neither Brezhnev nor Gorbachev, was the collapse in world oil prices from $35 per barrel in 1983 to $10–12 in 1985–6. This cost the Soviet budget about Rb 20 billion annually (Yur'ev 1989). Thus the big increase in the deficit 1985–6 can be accounted for by non-systemic, if not wholly non-Gorbachev factors.

That leaves unexplained, however, the fact that after 1986 the deficit continued to rise remorselessly. Here we must look at trends in the main elements within aggregate budgetary expenditure. The biggest single element of subsidy among those elements is for food and agriculture. In 1987 Gorbachev condemned the pattern of agricultural subsidisation that he had inherited from Brezhnev, and pledged himself to make sharp cuts in expenditures under this head (around Rb 60 billion in 1987). By 1989 food and agriculture subsidies had risen to Rb 90 billion, and they probably topped Rb 100 billion in 1990. This sums up the essence of the Soviet budgetary problem, and indeed shows that it is pointless to try to apportion blame between Brezhnev and Gorbachev. The roots of the hard-core deficit are certainly to be found in the 'period of stagnation'. But Gorbachev's failure to attack those roots – for example to follow up his general statements about the virtues of leaseholding with straightforward abolition of the monumentally inefficient collective and state farm system – meant that the underlying fiscal burden of the Brezhnev legacy simply grew and grew. It is also fair to say that Gorbachev's naive early attempts to neutralise that legacy tended to make things worse rather than better. This is most obviously the case with the anti-alcohol campaign. It is also true of the acceleration programme. State expenditures on the national economy, rather more than half of which go on investment with the rest being used to cover losses and subsidies, grew from Rb 209.1 billion in 1985 to Rb 226.3 billion in 1986 and Rb 242.8 billion in 1988 (NarKhoz 1989: 612). Total investment expenditures grew substantially faster 1986–8, but this partly reflected the switch in emphasis, under the early Gorbachev planning reforms, towards enterprise self-financing of investment (NarKhoz 1989: 529). It is clear, nevertheless, that budgetary support for investment grew significantly over the early perestroika period. These increases were a direct result of acceleration policies, with the number of new investment starts rising from 3,700 in 1986 to 4,500 in 1988. The total estimated value of 1988 starts was 50 per cent up on the corresponding figure for 1987 (O perestroike upravleniya . . . 1989). As we have already seen, this investment charge did nothing for Soviet economic performance. But it did impose an additional burden on the budget at the worst possible time.

By 1988–9 the Soviet budget deficit represented some 12 per cent of Soviet national income: this is certainly a very high figure. Yet comparably high corresponding figures can be found in the Western world, for example in Italy. As Pierella Paci shows (in Chapter 4 in this volume), the Italian budget deficit was in 1990 around 11 per cent of GNP. While this has, of course, created problems for the Italian economy, it has not presented an insurmountable barrier to sustained economic development. Why should it do so in the Soviet Union?

The simple answer is that in Italy, as Paci shows, there are financial institutions equal to the task of floating large volumes of government paper, and there are individuals and organisations (in this case mostly individuals) prepared to invest in that paper. In the Soviet case neither of those factors is present. There is no money market: indeed such an institution would have been considered incompatible with socialism. And even if there were one, the government would likely find it extremely difficult to persuade its citizens to hold paper denominated in roubles. For in the absence of a money market, and with severely limited scope for borrowing abroad (see pp. 322–3), the State Bank has had little choice but to cover budget deficits through direct increases in the money supply. This was the root cause of the accelerated build-up of repressed inflationary pressure in 1989 and 1990, as the money supply grew rapidly against a background of administratively fixed prices. It goes a long way towards explaining why queues, always a feature of the Soviet scene, became longer and longer through these years, until by the end of 1990 they had largely disappeared – because there was nothing left in the shops to queue for. It also helps to explain the sharp increase in second-economy activity, much of it centring on the new, quasi-private co-operatives. Beyond this, however, the oversupply of roubles produced an increasing problem of internal goods inconvertibility of the Soviet currency. The flight from the rouble was so marked that by mid-1991 it was difficult for foreigners to buy anything for roubles in Moscow. Soviet citizens *did* end up financing the budget deficits, in the sense that savings deposits grew rapidly over this period (from Rb 220.8 billion at the end of 1985 to Rb 380.7 billion at the end of 1990 – *NarKhoz 1989*: 92; Ekonomika SSSR . . . 1991a: 10), with 'under the mattress' savings probably increasing *pari passu*. But they did so largely involuntarily, and in a form which in itself represented a continuous threat to the solvency of the Soviet state, since all savings, whether in banks or not, could in principle be withdrawn at sight. Thus the peculiarities of the Soviet institutional set-up meant that the development of large-scale budget deficits *in itself* tended to pre-empt any rapid development of the kind of financial instruments which might have eased the burden of those deficits.

But the Soviet budget is more than just a problem of macroeconomic balance for the government. As we noted earlier, the passing of the early stage of naive *perestroika* saw a general acceptance by Soviet economists, administrators and politicians, even the more conservative ones, that transition to a market economy meant leaving the market to generate its own prices. Two or three years later less than dramatic progress had been made on this count. At mid-1991 55 per cent of total industrial output was still being sold at prices fixed by the state (Ekonomika SSSR . . . 1991b), while the bulk of foodstuffs being retailed through the state network remained under the same regime. Should we seek the explanation for this in terms of general conservatism? There is certainly a great fear of the possible effects of generalised price liberalisation among leaders and masses alike. The fact is, however, that there are solid grounds for such fears. With such a cumulative burden of repressed inflationary pressure, a general movement to market-clearing prices would almost certainly *ceteris paribus* lead rapidly to hyperinflation.

It is against this background that we witnessed, through 1990 and 1991, a series of attempts, some bizarre, some merely ineffectual, on the part of the Soviet authorities to cut the budget deficit and the repressed inflationary gap. In mid-1990 the then prime minister, Nikolai Ryzhkov, tried to push through big price increases, averaging around 100 per cent, for a number of basic food items. The justification for the move was clear enough: prices of items like bread and meat were ridiculously cheap, and in any case most Soviet citizens were unable to obtain supplies of them at those prices, certainly not without standing for long hours in queues. But the public outcry against the price increases, and the accelerated flight into goods that precipitated as shoppers tried to beat the increases, were enough to have the proposals shelved, and indeed to drive Mr Ryzhkov into retirement at the end of the year. His successor, Valentin Pavlov, who had as Minister of Finance presided over the escalation of the Soviet budget deficit, started off his premiership with an odd strategem. In January 1991 he withdrew all 50- and 100-rouble notes from circulation, with the proviso that holders of such bills would be fully compensated up to a maximum of Rb 1,000. This operation was supposed to have two aims: first, to undermine the black-marketeers and mafias which had certainly mushroomed since 1989, and second, to reduce the monetary overhang. It is difficult to take the first point seriously, since by early 1991 the Soviet second economy was operating largely in hard currency and goods considered to be as good as money. On the second point, one can say only that the withdrawal of high-denomination notes made only a trivial impact on the total stock of notes – reducing it by at most a few per cent. There is in any case little merit in chipping away at the accumulated monetary overhang resulting from past budgetary deficits if current deficits continue to feed that overhang. But Prime Minister Pavlov also had ideas on the current deficit.

At the beginning of April 1991 a series of price increases varying from 60 per cent to 300 per cent were imposed on a range of basic items – including the food items which had been the subject of Ryzhkov's attempted price reform of mid-1990, but covering also a number of non-food items like clothes. Pavlov did not meet the kind of massive public resistance to his measures that Ryzhkov had. In the meantime, perhaps, the Soviet population had grown resigned to the inevitability of price increases. Certainly, with the shelves universally bare by the end of 1990, the new prime minister did not have to worry about a further flight into goods. But in two critical respects Pavlov's price reform was as ineffectual as Ryzhkov's had been. First, it did nothing to improve *supply* of basic goods, since it changed only *retail* prices, without addressing the issue of how those changed retail prices could come through as production incentives for peasants, still imprisoned within the collective/state farm system, and light industrial enterprises which might in any case be tempted, in the context of monopoly advantage, to respond to price increases by *cutting* production. Predictably, the impact of the Pavlov price package on the streets of Moscow was to reduce the length of queues without putting substantially more goods on the shelves. Even more important, the price rises made no impact on the budget deficit at all. But one of the reasons for that, one that was, in all truth, beyond the control of the Soviet prime minister, was that a number of non-Russian republics were now refusing to hand over tax revenues to Moscow, in pursuance of their claims to independence. This brings us to another crucial aspect of the story of *perestroika* in disarray. To place that aspect in perspective, we must return to the critical years 1988–9.

At an early stage in the *perestroika* campaign Gorbachev realised that meaningful economic reform was infeasible within the strait-jacket of the system of one-party rule, which had, under Brezhnev, developed into an oppressive and corrupt oligarchy. So it was that Gorbachev swiftly proclaimed the slogan of *glasnost* – openness – as if to underline the nonsensicality of seeking to raise levels of personal motivation at work in the context of a political system which allowed no right of free individual activity, whether political or business, of trying to join the microelectronics revolution with a system in which photocopiers were treated as strategic goods, as dangerous to the regime as nuclear missiles. By the late 1980s *glasnost* was deepening into *demokratizatsiya*, with the first partially democratic elections in Soviet history taking place in 1989, and producing a Supreme Soviet of the Soviet Union which would actually debate and criticise government economic policies, and generate new political groupings independent of the Communist Party of the Soviet Union. In 1990 the one-party system was officially laid to rest.

But if Gorbachev expected democratisation to rally the Soviet masses behind *perestroika*, he was to be bitterly disappointed. Trouble came in three main forms. The year 1988 witnessed the the first major outbreak of inter-ethnic strife – involving in this case Muslim Azerbaizhanis and Christian Armenians in Transcaucasia. Inter-nationality tension there had, of course, always been in the Soviet Union, but under the old system it had been kept firmly under control by a mixture of political cajolery and (threatened or actual) coercion. Now that the Pandora's box had been opened, the scope for the emergence of ethnic sectarianism as a major political factor was menacingly large.

There was no explicitly economic dimension to the Armenian–Azerbaizhani dispute, and in that sense it did not represent a threat to the essence of *perestroika*. But worse (for Gorbachev) was to follow. The Baltic republics (Estonia, Latvia and Lithuania) had, after their forcible incorporation into the Soviet Union in 1940, developed into the most prosperous regions of the Soviet Union, and had been used as forcing-grounds for (comparatively) radical economic planning experiments during the Brezhnev period. Under Gorbachev, their leaders and populations initially welcomed the role of storm-troopers of *perestroika*, with the idea of republican *khozraschet* (independent financial accountability), first adumbrated by Gorbachev himself, being taken up with alacrity in this Soviet fragment of the Nordic world. But by 1989 the honeymoon was over, as Estonians, Latvians and Lithuanians increasingly began to pose the question: if independent financial accountability is such a good thing, why not complete national independence? In early 1990 Lithuania became the first Soviet republic formally to declare its independence, to be followed rapidly by the other two. Gorbachev's response was, first, to impose an economic blockade, and second, to use Soviet troops in sporadic attempts to intimidate the governments and peoples of the Baltic republics. At time of writing the three republics had still not achieved *de facto* independence, but were refusing to have anything whatsoever to do with Gorbachev's attempts to save *perestroika*.

Gorbachev's political difficulties did not stop at the nationalities issue. Throughout the first phase of *perestroika* Gorbachev had been able to count on wide support among the ranks of the intelligentsia, overjoyed at the unprecedented intellectual freedom they were now able to enjoy. From early 1990, just as the technical economic difficulties of *perestroika* were beginning to multiply, Gorbachev found himself increasingly outflanked by a new wave of radical political activists, taking full advantage of the democratisation of 1989–90 to criticise, even pillory the General Secretary, now named (but not elected) president of the Soviet Union.

The two themes of nationalism and radicalism came together with the election, on a fully democratic basis, of a new Supreme Soviet of the Russian Federation (RSFSR), the biggest of the Soviet republics, in May 1990. The new Soviet was dominated by a loose grouping under the name of *Democratic Russia* (*Demokraticheskaya Rossiya*), which brought together a wide range of political tendencies, ranging from liberal-radical to sub-fascist nationalist – but now *Russian* nationalist, united only by their opposition to the privileged position of the Communist Party. The election to the chairmanship of the RSFSR Supreme Soviet of Boris Yeltsin, a former communist and Politburo member who had fallen out badly with Gorbachev in 1987 and been sacked from the top elite, underlined the growing political problems Gorbachev now faced. Yeltsin, a member of no formal political party, epitomised the new compound of nationalist populism, economic liberalism and sheer anti-communism coming increasingly to dominate the dynamic of Soviet politics. To top it all, it was clear that Yeltsin bore a personal grudge against Gorbachev over his treatment in 1987, and that the Soviet president in turn had little affection for his erstwhile colleague. Boris Yeltsin's handsome majority in a one-man-one-vote election for the presidency of the Russian Federation in mid-1991 represented the highest point of the democratisation process at time of writing. It gave cold comfort to a *Soviet* president whose policy-making credentials looked increasingly beleaguered.

It is supremely ironic that Gorbachev, who could rightly be criticised for having concentrated too much on the Russian audience and having neglected the other 50 per cent of the Soviet population in the early stage of *perestroika*, found himself in the second stage increasingly deprived of an effective power base by a nationalist, anti-communist reaction among the dominant nation of the Union itself. Be that as it may, it was quite clear at mid-1991 that while the cause of reform lived on, Gorbachev's *perestroika* had failed. The Soviet president could not resist, however, the temptation to make one more attempt to square the circle.

The so-called 'Nine Plus One' agreement of April 1991 had brought together the governments of the nine Soviet republics still at that time committed in some degree to maintaining the Union (the Slav and Muslim republics) and the Soviet president in a programme designed to provide the framework for a new USSR. But the agreement left many economic issues unresolved. Of the things which the Nine Plus One were not able to agree upon, the most critical, perhaps, was taxation. Quite simply, without a watertight accord on the assessment and raising of taxation, the prospects for the Nine Plus One making a real impact on the budget deficit were absolutely minimal. On key systemic issues the 'Programme of Joint Measures of the Union and Republican Governments to Solve the Economic Crisis in Conditions in Transition to the Market' (Programma . . . 1991), which came out of the Nine Plus One agreement, was at best ambivalent. Market relations were proclaimed as paramount, but the state(s) retained the right to impose contracts on enterprises for specific deliveries under the rubric of 'state orders' (*gosudarstvennyi zakaz*), a euphemism invented in the early *perestroika* period for what remained effectively the old directive system. The Programme also prescribed 'unconditional implementation' of existing legislation on privatisation, lease-holding etc. in agriculture – but set aside just 5 million hectares of land, only 2 per cent of the total arable area of the Union, 'for the population'. It posited an 'optimal combination of free, regulated and fixed prices, with a gradual transition to world prices', without explaining the optimisation procedure to be used, or how, for instance, world prices were supposed to help in the setting of rents for apartments. The unity of Soviet economic space and the primacy of the rouble as a means of settlement were proclaimed, but at the same time barter deals between farms and consumer goods enterprises were encouraged.

Behind these apparently 'technical' problems lay unresolved and fundamental political problems, some general, some particular. At the general level, the programme was clearly a compromise document, which might have been good politics, but was certainly bad economics. With widely differing views on the appropriate pace of reform amongst the various leaders, the new 'inner cabinet' of the Soviet Union seemed to operate very much as its predecesssor, the Communist Party Politburo, had done – on the basis of lowest-common-denominator unanimity. At the more specific level, as Boris Yeltsin showed when he took the extraordinary (by the standards of the time) step in July 1991 of banning the operation of Communist Party cells within enterprises and public organisations in the Russian Federation, the CPSU was still the main quarry for many of the out-riders of the reform movement. Did they guess, one wonders, how soon they would be able to settle accounts once and for all?

A precarious, but still tempting future

The prospect facing the Soviet Union at time of writing was, then, one of deep uncertainty. The downside scenario was a bleak one indeed: continued political instability and constitutional deadlock would ensure that the problem of budget deficit was not effectively addressed, fragmentation of authority would mean a continued blockage on desperately needed systemic reform, particularly in relation to agriculture, the increasing degree of internal goods-inconvertibility of the rouble would mean a movement back to the crudest forms of barter as the only basis for inter-regional, and even inter-enterprise division of labour, with local political bosses happy enough to have an excuse for local empire-building. The West, public and private sector alike, would wish to have nothing to do with such a volatile mess.

There was also an upside scenario, which ran like this: it is perfectly feasible for post-socialist countries to remove large budget deficits very rapidly when the appropriate policies are followed, as witness the case of Poland. The West is anxious to build on the dramatic progress of recent years on arms reductions and general East–West confidence-building at the political level, and will require only evidence of significant progress (eg making the rouble partially convertible on the Polish/Yugoslav model, setting up a stock market) to give the Soviet Union the benefit of the doubt on the chances of achieving the final goal. On this basis the Soviet Union should be able to count on being permitted to 'join the club' of the world market economy, possibly even to the extent of membership of the IMF, and on substantial flows of funds, including private funds.

Table 12.5   The Soviet hard-currency external balance ($ billion)

	1983[a]	1984[a]	1985[a]	1986[a]	1987[a]	1988[a]	1989[a]	1990	1991
Balance of trade	1.3	2.2	−0.8	−3.9	0.4	−2.7	−6.5	−1.6	1.1
Balance of payments, current account	1.5	3.0	1.0	−1.0	1.5	−2.5	−7.5	−5.1	−1.8

Note: [a] Trade and settlements with Western industrialised countries only.

Sources: Official Soviet statistics, EIU, author's estimates; *Ekonomika i Zhizn*, No 6, 1992

These are, of course, limiting cases rather than likely paths to the future. Yet at present the 'central forecast' must favour the downside rather than the upside limiting case. The prospects are that the process of settling political scores, and, optimistically, moving towards a Western-style system of organised political pluralism, will take several years. Meanwhile the budgetary problem will remain unresolved, the pressure of inflation, repressed or otherwise, will grow, and the credibility of the rouble as a domestic currency will diminish further, if indeed that is possible. It goes without saying that in the context of such a marked degree of *goods* inconvertibility of the rouble, any idea of establishing *currency* convertibility, on however limited a basis (the Nine Plus One Programme envisaged 'internal convertibility' on the Polish model by 1 January 1992), or domestic financial markets with paper denominated in roubles (enabling legislation due to be passed by 1 November 1991), is pure fantasy.

Amidst talk of 'Grand Bargains' involving sums of up to $100 billion, of a whole range of projects, from tourism to military conversion, for which the Soviet Union would like to seek Western financial support, and a vintage Gorbachev performance at the July 1991 G-7 meeting in London to obtain a substantial commitment from the leading industrial countries of the West (short of hard cash) to support further reform, it is appropriate to pause to reflect on the kind of role that Western economic assistance might play in the critical years to come.

Table 12.5 presents trends in the Soviet balance of payments. It shows a fairly dramatic slide from an enviable strength in the current account to a contemporary situation which borders on the critical, with serious payments difficulties reported in 1990 and 1991 by a number of Western companies selling to the Soviet Union. The very real improvement reported for 1991 was achieved only through a cut in imports for hard currency of 13 per cent (*total* imports fell by 43 per cent), which is likely to be unsustainable in the medium-term future, given the dependence of the Soviet Union's modernisation prospects on foreign equipment and technology. In any case, with a large hump in Soviet debt repayment schedules in 1991 and 1992 to the tune of a total of $20 billion (EIU 1991: 22), the payments situation would remain critical even with a substantial surplus on current account. At time of writing, the great bulk of Soviet export earnings was going on debt service (Ekonomika SSSR . . . 1991b: 3).

Yet we must be wary of any argument that these figures somehow present an incontrovertible case for Western economic aid to the Soviet Union. It would, under normal circumstances, be a routine matter for the Soviet Union to re-finance all or part of the debt maturities falling due in 1991 and 1992. It is only because there have been difficulties with Soviet payments over the last year or so that the private international money markets have been reluctant to extend new long-term credit. And while the official Soviet explanation that payments difficulties have been largely a function of teething troubles with the new foreign trade system seems hardly credible, it is certainly the case that as late as 1990 total debt service was only hovering on the danger line of 25 per cent of hard-currency exports – even if gold exports, which run at $3 billion–4 billion per annum, are ignored. It is clear that in 1989 and 1990 the pressure of repressed inflation started to boil over into the external sector, with import demands of all sorts building up, and the share of machinery in total imports actually falling (Dyker 1991: 184). It seems proper, then, to treat the Soviet deficits of 1989 and 1990 as an essentially systemic problem – like nearly every other major Soviet economic problem. On that argument, short-term balance of payments support from the West would run the risk of reinforcing a traditional system of institutionalised soft budget constraints, rather than imposing pressure to develop a sturdy, cost-effective, market-based system. In any case, with gold reserves in the region of $10 billion–20 billion, the Soviet Union *need never have got into such payments difficulties in 1990–1*. It would, of course, be perfectly proper for the world financial community to help to repair the damage that has been done to international confidence in Soviet creditworthiness – at the same time putting pressure on the Soviet authorities to use their reserves of gold and diamonds more flexibly. A form of association with the IMF, perhaps backed up by a token financial facility, might be an appropriate way of doing that. But open-ended support for the Soviet balance of payments would likely do more harm than good.

Is there a more powerful argument for economic aid in terms of long-term investment requirements? There may, indeed, by a case for extending aid in terms of quite *specific* projects, the pay-offs from which affect not just the Soviet population, but the whole world. Major environmental retrieval operations would obviously come into this category. Looking at the Soviet investment scene in general, however, it is striking that the sharp cut-backs in investment reported in 1991 were largely a result of the failure of major investment clients to spend the roubles that had been allocated them. This in turn seems to have been primarily a function of the increasing disorganisation of a Soviet economy that is now neither planned nor market-driven, and in particular of breakdowns in the construction and construction materials industries – in other words once again of essentially systemic factors. There is no general argument that the Soviet Union is short of investible funds as such, and that conclusion is strengthened only if one takes a bullish view of military conversion plans. What the Soviet Union is certainly short of is specific elements of machinery and technology. Effective accessing of these is, however, often dependent on close relations with particular Western companies. So it is certainly important for the Soviet Union to be seen as an attractive location for private international investment. Once again the reasons that (at time of writing) this was emphatically not the case were of an overwhelmingly general systemic and political nature.

There is no escape, therefore, from the conclusion that contemporary Soviet economic problems are deeply domestic in nature. The issue of foreign assistance may, indeed, be something of a red herring, though it could well become more relevant as genuine systemic restructuring gathers pace. But that is simply to beg the essential question. At mid-1991 the Soviet Union had barely begun the real process of restructuring, so bravely proclaimed by Gorbachev some six years earlier.

January 1992 update

At the beginning of the year of the single market, most of the negative trends in the Soviet economic situation had intensified. The downward trend in total output accelerated through 1991 with output for the year down at least 15 per cent on the corresponding figure for 1990, and the budget deficit for the whole country escalated to Rb 204.7 billion for the twelve months of 1991 (*Ekonomika i Zhizn'* No 50 1991, p. 1). By the end of 1991 open inflation was running at around 150 per cent, with the money supply apparently out of control and the rouble reduced to virtual worthlessness. The average amount of cash in circulation increased from Rb 126.1 billion in 1990 to Rb 260.0 billion in 1991 (*Ekonomika i Zhizn'* No 51 1991, p. 5). But the pressure of repressed inflation also continued to grow, with savings bank deposits increasing by Rb 293 billion – 51.6 per cent – between 31 December 1990 and 1 October 1991 (*Ekonomika i Zhizn'* No 47 1991, p. 5).

The foreign payments situation worsened dramatically in the second half of 1991. While oil exports faltered, the liquidity situation, always likely to be critical, became impossible. According to some reports, Soviet gold reserves had fallen to just $3–4 billion by September 1991. These reports were certainly exaggerated, but they served as an effective signal to the West that something had to be done quickly. An agreement was reached in November with representatives of the G-7 on deferral of repayment of principal for one year on all Soviet official debt, following the Soviet Union's admission to associate membership of the IMF in October. A similar agreement covering private debt was then signed in December.

Behind these key economic trends lay a series of dramatic political developments. The abortive coup of August 1991, led, by among others, by Prime Minister Pavlov, precipitated the process of disintegration of the Soviet Union, and finally discredited the Communist Party of the Soviet Union, which was dissolved a few days after the end of the coup attempt. As well as providing a fitting end to Pavlov's undistinguished career, the coup proved to be a major milestone in the power struggle between Gorbachev and Yeltsin. It was the president of the Russian Federation who emerged as the hero of the hour in August, and he was more than ready to press home his political advantage in the public debates that followed the restoration of President Gorbachev.

But in the months succeeding the coup *manqué* Gorbachev once again demonstrated his extraordinary political adeptness, in managing to persuade the leaders of twelve of the Soviet republics (the full independence of Latvia, Lithuania and Estonia had by now been recognised) to initial an agreement on economic union which would maintain the integrity of Soviet economic space and guarantee free movement of goods throughout that space. But some republican leaderships, particularly the Ukrainian, remained unhappy about the details of the economic union treaty, particularly in relation to the crucial area of currency issue, and Gorbachev's attempts to reinforce the economic treaty with a parallel political union treaty, which would have created a reborn, confederal, Soviet Union, was met with widespread suspicion among the new republican establishments. Finally, at the end of December, the leaderships of the three Slav republics, Russia, the Ukraine and Byelorussia, torpedoed the whole idea by proclaiming their own Commonwealth of Independent States. Within a week or so eleven of the other twelve republics had expressed the intention of joining the CIS (Georgia, locked in civil war, was the exception), and President Gorbachev had resigned. The Soviet Union was dead.

With President Yeltsin now clearly the most powerful man in the former USSR, and with Russian Federation officials quickly moving in to take over the bulk of the old Soviet institutions and organisations, including the nuclear armed forces, Moscow was able to reassert to a degree its role as key source of economic policy formation. From 2 January 1992 the bulk of prices in Russia were liberalised, with controls being maintained over prices of just a few basic commodities. At the same time President Yeltsin announced an accelerated programme of privatisation, with privatisation of agriculture a top priority, backed up by cuts in subsidies to loss-making enterprises and defence spending.

The other republics greeted Yeltsin's package with considerable suspicion. There was little confidence that the Russian president, now in control of the issue of roubles, would show any more discipline on money supply than Pavlov had done, and republican leaderships were particularly worried that control over the printing press might allow Russia to plunder goods from other regions. It was, *inter alia*, worries like this that lay behind the decision of the Ukrainian government to start in January 1992 paying workers 25 per cent of their wages in special coupons which may eventually become the base for a new Ukrainian currency. Beyond that, the Yeltsin package, though more radical than anything that had gone before, seemed to share many of the weaknesses of the Gorbachev-Ryzhkov and Gorbachev-Pavlov packages. With the budget deficit now approaching 14 per cent of national income, the argument that price liberalisation must be preceded by a substantial degree of fiscal stabilisation has strengthened. But Yeltsin, like his predecessors, is disposed to change prices first and seek to cut the budget deficit second. As demonstrated in the main text, this will inevitably tend to produce hyperinflationary conditions – or else a reaction back to greater central control, possibly combined with a political reaction of an authoritarian cast. Again, the Russian president seems to have given but perfunctory consideration to the supply side of the question. Price rises which only produce hardship and inequality, without visibly improving supplies, are worse than useless, as Ryzhkov discovered to his cost. The elements of Yeltsin's package which do address the supply side – the privatisation plans, especially with regard to agriculture – seem to have been inserted at the last minute in response to criticisms from Russian economists and politicians couched in much the same terms as our own. It is salutary to bear in mind that Gorbachev first pronounced in favour of a form of land privatisation as early as 1988. By the time he resigned in December 1991 only a very small proportion of the Soviet land stock had been effectively privatised. Yeltsin will certainly be a good deal less inhibited than was Gorbachev when it comes to upsetting the vested interests of the collectivised system, which were pilloried in the Soviet press during the winter of 1991–2 for hoarding grain. It may still take the Russian president years rather than months to build the stable and effective system of family farms in Russia without which scarcity prices for foodstuffs simply cannot do their job.

References

Aksenov D (1989) Strategiya 'chistoi' energii. *Ekonomicheskaya Gazeta* **16**: 5

Andropov Yu (1983) Uchenie Karla Marksa i nekotorye voprosy sotsialisticheskogo stroitel'stva v SSSR. *Voprosy Ekonomiki* **3**

Bergson A (1978) *Productivity and the Social System – the USSR and the West*. Harvard University Press, Cambridge, Mass.

CIA (1988) *USSR: Sharply Higher Budget Deficits Threaten Perestroyka*. US GPO, Washington, DC

Dyker D A (1983) *The Process of Investment in the Soviet Union*. Cambridge University Press

Dyker D A (1991) *Restructuring the Soviet Economy*. Routledge

EIU (Economist Intelligence Unit) (1991) *Global Forecasting Service. Soviet Union*. **2**

Ekonomika SSSR (v 1990 godu) (1991a) *Ekonomika i Zhizn'* **5**: 9–13

Ekonomika SSSR (v I polugodii 1991 godu) (1991b) *Ekonomika i Zhizn'* **30**: special supplement

Greenslade R (1976) The real National Product of the USSR 1950–75. In Joint Economic Committee, US Congress, *Soviet Economy in a New Perspective*. US GPO, Washington, DC

Gregory P, Stuart R (1990) *Soviet Economic Structure and Performance* 4th edn. Harper and Row, New York

Loginov V (1989) Plany i realnost'. *Voprosy Ekonomiki* **4**

Narodnoe Khozyaistvo SSSR v 1989 godu (1990) Goskomstat SSSR, Moscow

O perestroike upravleniya investitsiyami i sovershenstvovanii khozyaistvennogo mekhanizma v stroitel'stve (1989) *Ekonomika Stroitel'stva* **10**

Programma sovmestnykh deistvii Kabineta Ministrov SSSR i pravitel'stv suverennykh respublik po vyvodu ekonomiki strany iz krizisa v usloviyakh perekhoda k rynku (1991) *Ekonomika i Zhizn'* **30**: special supplement

Reznik S D (1980) Trudovaya distsiplina. *Ekonomika Stroitel'stva* **3**

Shmelev N (1989) Economics and common sense. In Jones A, Moskoff W (eds) *Perestroika and the Economy*. Sharpe

Vneshnyaya Torgovlya SSSR v 1975 godu (1976) Statistika, Moscow

Yur'ev R (1989) Raskryvaem tainy byudzheta. *Pravitel'stvennyi Vestnik* **18**: 6

Index